Human Rights
in Commonwealth Africa

RHODA E. HOWARD

Human Rights in Commonwealth Africa

ROWMAN & LITTLEFIELD
Publishers

ROWMAN & LITTLEFIELD

Published in the United States of America in 1986
by Rowman & Littlefield, Publishers
(a division of Littlefield, Adams & Company)
81 Adams Drive, Totowa, New Jersey 07512.

Library of Congress Cataloging-in-Publication Data

Howard, Rhoda E., 1948-
  Human rights in Commonwealth Africa.

  Bibliography: p. 231
  Includes index.
  1. Civil rights—Africa. I. Title.
JC599.A36H68   1986   323.4'096   86-3860
ISBN 0-8476-7433-9
ISBN 0-8476-7434-7 (pbk.)

88 87 86
10 9 8 7 6 5 4 3 2 1

Printed in the United States of America

For Peter

Contents

Tables   ix

Acknowledgments   xi

1: The Human Rights Background   1

    The United Nations Definition of Human Rights   2
    The African Charter of Human and Peoples' Rights   4
    Human Rights under Colonial Rule   9
    The Argument in Brief   11
    Notes   14

2: Cultural Relativism, Social Change, and
    Human Rights   16

    An African Concept of Human Rights?   17
    Culture and Social Change   23
    Modernization and the Creation of the Individual   27
    Conclusion   33
    Notes   34

3: Social Structure, the State, and Human Rights   37

    Peripheral Capitalist Society   38
    The African Ruling Class   45
    Class, State, and Power   53
    Notes   57

4: Economic Rights   60

    The Substance of Economic Rights   61
    Causes of Underdevelopment   68
    The New International Economic Order   78
    Class, Development, and Rights   83
    Notes   85

5: State Formation and Communal Rights   90

    Ethnicity and "Tribalism"   91
    Citizens, Aliens, and Mass Expulsions   99
    Religious Tolerance and State Security   107
    Conclusion   112
    Notes   113

viii   CONTENTS

6: Political Rights   119
Freedom of Expression and Association   120
Trade Unions   128
Electoral Politics   133
The One-Party Model   140
Notes   144

7: Civil Rights and the Rule of Law   151
Preventive Detention   152
State Terrorism   159
Constitutionalism and the Rule of Law   164
Some Innovations in Legal Practice   172
Notes   177

8: Women's Rights   184
Political Rights of Women   186
Women and the Political Economy   188
Law and Custom: Women's Rights in the Personal Sphere   195
Female Genital Operations   202
Notes   206

9: Summary and Assessment   212
Summary   212
The Human Rights Debates   218
The Future   223
Notes   230

Bibliography   231
Index   241

⊕ Tables

Table 2.1. Indicators of Modernization   29
Table 4.1. Food Production and Consumption   62
Table 4.2. Health Indicators   64
Table 4.3. Population and Gross National Product   66
Table 4.4. Literacy and Education   69
Table 4.5. Economic Dependency   75

(†) Acknowledgments

During the preparation of this manuscript, I was very fortunate to have the assistance and encouragement of many fine scholars. While all errors, omissions and misinterpretations are my sole responsibility, what merit the work as a whole may contain is in large part a result of others' efforts. In particular I wish to thank my dear friend and colleague Jack Donnelly, who has read every word I have written over the past three years, including two complete drafts of this book. My intellectual and personal debt to him is unbounded.

Many other people have contributed much valuable time to reading drafts of various sections of this book or to assisting me with my research. I am especially grateful to James Ahiakpor, Douglas Anglin, James L. Brain, Roberta Ann Dunbar, Peter C. W. Gutkind, Bert B. Lockwood, Jr., Linda Freeman, and Gerald K. Helleiner. I also owe profound thanks to Edward Kannyo, Christopher Leo, Harriet Lyons, Allan McChesney, Robert Martin, Ifeanyi A. Menkiti, Barrington Moore, Jr., Craig Murphy, and Adamantia Pollis. I am indebted as well to Claire E. Robertson, James Scarritt, Roger Southall, Walter Tarnapolsky, John Vincent, Claude E. Welch, Jr., Audrey Wipper, and Laurie S. Wiseberg. For their comments on various presentations on the material in this volume which I have made over the years, I am grateful to Claude Ake, Christopher Brewin, Anthony Flew, Abdullahi Ahmed El Naiem, Nils Petter Gleditsch, Nigel Haworth, Frederick Johnstone, Jon Kraus, James Mittelman, Michael Piva, Jane Parpart, Timothy Shaw, Jane Sweeney, Peter Waterman, Warren Weinstein, Ronald Weitzer, and Don Wills. I am also indebted to my colleagues at the Development Studies Programme, University of Toronto, and in particular Christian Bay, Martin Klein, Michael Levin, Robert Matthews, Cathal Nolan, Cranford Pratt, Peter H. Russell, Richard Sandbrook, and Richard Stren, for their helpful criticism and personal encouragement over the years. At various times my colleagues and students at McMaster University, who include Omega Bula, Bruce Curtis, Mike Gismondi, Frank E. Jones, Graham Knight, JoAnn Krakauskas, Margaret Luxton, Evan Simpson, Vivienne Walters, James Zasha, and the late Roman Baumann, have read sections and drafts of the previous work which resulted in this book. I am also grateful to a number of Africans, both scholars and exiles, whose names it would be impolitic to publish here. If I have inadvertently omitted any other names, I apologize for the oversight.

Many people have helped me in locating the relatively obscure research material on which I rely for documentation. Laurie S. Wiseberg, the director of Human Rights Internet, very kindly allowed me the run of Internet's library in 1983. Amnesty International generously allowed me access to their data collection in London, and Amnesty International (Canada) was also very helpful. I am grateful to Friederike Knabe of Amnesty International, London, and to Sue Nichols, formerly of Amnesty International, Ottawa. My research was also greatly facilitated by the ever-courteous and intelligent assistance of the librarians at McMaster's Mills Library, especially David Cook, Barbara Freeze, and Anne Pottier. Peter I. Hajnal of the Robarts Library, Toronto, helped me to find many African government documents, as did Kate Thorne of the Carleton University Library, Ottawa. In the final stages of preparation of this manuscript, my students and research assistants David N. Brown and Jane Vock faithfully checked my sources. Over the years Mrs. Shirley McGill and Mrs. Cecile Spencer have carefully typed various pieces of this work.

Seed money for this research was provided by the McMaster University Arts Research Board, while the bulk of the research was funded by the Social Sciences and Humanities Research Council of Canada. I am grateful to both institutions for their confidence in my work and to the anonymous reviewers who evaluated three separate research proposals. For their assistance in the preparation and administration of my research grants, I am grateful to Emmi Morwald and Mary Robertson of McMaster University. I also thank the British Council for funding my attendance at a conference in the United Kingdom in 1982.

I am grateful to *Human Rights Quarterly* for permission to reprint part of my "Evaluating Human Rights in Africa: Some Problems of Implicit Comparisons" in Chapter 1 of this volume, to the State University of New York Press for permission to reprint, in a revised form, my "Women's Rights in English-speaking Sub-Saharan Africa" as Chapter 8 of this volume, and to *Third World Quarterly* for permission to reprint an abridged version of my "Legitimacy and Class Rule in Commonwealth Africa: Constitutionalism and the Rule of Law" in Chapter 7 of this volume.

I am grateful to Mrs. Linda Lattik, Mrs. Dorothy Henry, and Mrs. Shirley Turkstra and the staff of the McMaster Children's Centre, who relieved me of much of my household and childcare responsibility during the years I was researching and writing this book. My son, Patrick McCabe, whose lifespan roughly coincides with that of this project, has lightened my task by the joy he brings to every day of my life. My husband, Peter J. McCabe, has suffered through five years of dinner-table talk about human rights in Africa, a subject in which he had no prior interest. He is my most rigorous critic and my most beloved intellectual companion. Both as a scholar and as his wife, I am deeply grateful to him.

This book is about the many Africans whose integrity and fortitude, in the face of political repression and extreme poverty, can only be imagined by those of us who are fortunate enough to earn our livings as academics in the prosperous Western world. If, in my efforts to be scholarly, I have not shown my deep admiration for their courage, I beg their forgiveness.

Except for minor editorial changes, this manuscript was completed on July 19, 1985, and does not take account of any political events subsequent to that date.

R. E. H.

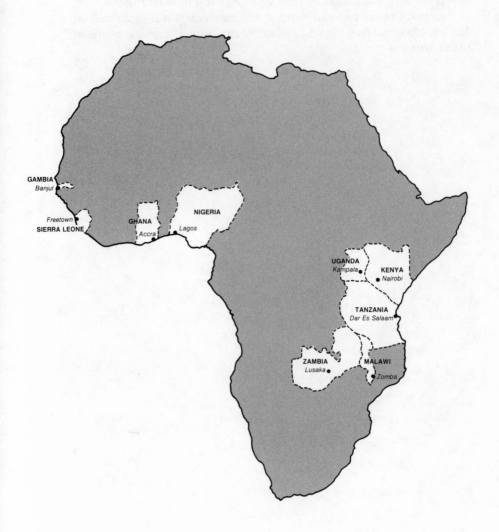

① The Human Rights Background

This book analyzes the human rights record of nine Commonwealth African countries: Gambia, Sierra Leone, Ghana, and Nigeria in West Africa; and Kenya, Malawi, Tanzania, Uganda and Zambia in East and Central Africa. All nine have been independent since the late 1950s or early 1960s; their dates of independence are respectively 1965, 1961, 1957, 1960; 1963, 1964, 1961, 1962, and 1964.

These nine countries, despite differences in state ideology and governmental structure, are sufficiently similar that they may be studied as a group. They have a common colonial heritage. The language of education and government in all the countries is still predominantly English. They share the same parliamentary myths, if not practice, as do other parts of the Commonwealth. The original nationalist elites of the colonies were educated in Britain or the United States, where in many cases they developed a commitment to the democratic ideals of the Western world; indeed, these philosophic ideals were used to justify the fight for independence. In addition, the British had made some pretense of setting up a judicial system in the colonies that reflected the basic principles of the rule of law. Thus Commonwealth Africa is a group of Third World nations which, at least in their ideals, resemble Western democracies.

Moreover, none of the nine countries has experienced any significant conflict between blacks and Arabs or between blacks and whites, with the exception of the conflicts between white settlers and land-poor Africans in Kenya in the 1950s. Aside from Kenya, the nine countries attained independence without violent nationalist struggles. Thus although there were nationalist elites engaged in political protest, there were no mass movements of urban or rural guerilla warfare. Commonwealth Africa became independent without having previously generated a strong sense of commitment among the populace to the nationalist elite or to the newly formed state.

Four Commonwealth African countries are excluded from this analysis. Lesotho, Botswana and Swaziland all exist within the orbit of South Africa, and in my view, their human rights performance cannot be separated from southern African regional politics. Zimbabwe is also excluded, as it was not independent at the time research was begun for this book.[1] References to Commonwealth Africa, therefore, should be taken to mean only the nine countries listed above.

The aim of this book is not to document either the successful realization of human rights or the extent of human rights abuses in Commonwealth

Africa. The material used herein is exemplary of major trends, but it is far from a complete record. Nor is this book intended to provide a picture of legal provisions for human rights in Commonwealth Africa. While the book refers to the most recent civilian constitutions of the nine countries, these constitutions are cited as a guide to ideology, not to legal practice. The intention is to analyze the social-structural factors that affect human rights, and thereby to contribute to more general debates about the possibility of protection of human rights in the underdeveloped world as a whole.

The United Nations Definition of Human Rights

The International Bill of Rights is used herein as a standard of reference for the presence or absence of human rights in Africa. The International Bill consists of four documents: the Universal Declaration of Human Rights (1948), the International Covenant on Economic, Social and Cultural Rights (1966), the International Covenant on Civil and Political Rights (1966), and the Optional Protocol to the last-named document.[2] My use of the International Bill as a standard does not necessarily mean that its list of rights is complete. But since the international discourse on human rights revolves around the International Bill, it is an appropriate starting point.

The fundamental document, from which the two 1966 covenants derive, is the Universal Declaration of Human Rights. This Declaration is a statement of principles and objectives. When it was formulated in 1948, extreme differences in interpretations of human rights were demonstrated by three competing political factions: the Soviet bloc, the Western European–North American allies, and the few Third World countries which were members of the United Nations at the time. Many Third World, including African, commentators have noted the relative absence of Third World participation when the Universal Declaration was formulated. This criticism, however, ignores the fact that by 1966, when the two covenants were passed, many Third World nations were members of the United Nations. On the other hand, United States pressure, in particular, caused economic, social, and cultural rights to be split off from civil and political rights in 1966, thus opening the way for the assumption of a hierarchy of the two different kinds of rights.[3]

Civil and political rights generally reflect the development of liberal society in Europe since the 18th century. Civil rights are essentially the legal rights of the individual, especially the individual's right to protection against the state. They include the right to life, liberty, and security of person (Article 3 of the Universal Declaration); the right not to be held in slavery or servitude (Article 4); the right not to be subject to torture or to cruel, inhuman, or degrading treatment or punishment (Article 5); the right to recognition as a person before the law (Article 6); the right to equality before the law (Article 7); the right to remedy for violation of rights (Article 8); the right not to be subject to arbitrary arrest, detention, or exile (Article 9); the right to a fair and public hearing by an independent and impartial tribunal (Article 10); the right to be presumed innocent until proven guilty, and a guarantee that one cannot be held guilty for an act not a crime at the time of commital (Article 11); and the right to protection from arbitrary attacks on privacy or reputation (Article 12).

These civil rights resemble the "basic right" of security posited by Henry Shue, insofar as they protect the individual against arbitrary and/or unjust arrest, imprisonment, and execution.[4] Political rights, on the other hand, are essentially rights to freedom of expression and to political participation, although a few others such as the right to asylum and the right to a nationality, are also included. The major political rights with which this book deals are the right to freedom of thought, conscience, and religion (Article 18); the right to freedom of opinion and expression (Article 19); the right to freedom of assembly and association (Article 20); and the rights to take part in one's government, to have equal access to the public service, and to vote in periodic and genuine elections with universal and equal suffrage (Article 21).

Both civil and political rights, according to the 1966 covenant, are to be implemented immediately (Article 3). By contrast, only the eventual implementation of economic, social, and cultural rights is envisaged (Article 2,1). But many Africans argue that despite their cost, economic, social, and cultural rights should take moral priority over civil and political rights.[5] Extremely poor people, it is assumed, find civil and political rights a luxury; until their bellies are full, they are more interested in economic rights.[6]

The economic, cultural, and social rights called for in the Universal Declaration are the following: the right to social security (Article 22 of the Universal Declaration); the right to work, to freely choose one's place of employment, and to have protection against unemployment; the right to "just and favourable remuneration ensuring . . . an existence worthy of human dignity," and the right to form and join trade unions (Article 23); the right to rest and leisure (Article 24); the right to an "adequate" standard of living, including security in the case of unemployment, sickness, disability, widowhood, and old age, and special care to mothers and children (Article 25); the right to free and compulsory education (Article 26); and the right to freely participate in the cultural life of the community (Article 27).

That economic, social, and cultural rights do not have the priority that some commentators feel they deserve is frequently attributed to an alleged "Western" bias in philosophical thought about rights. What is really meant is a Western *capitalist* bias, since socialist thinking, especially the Marxist variety, is also Western in origin.[7] There is some truth to this allegation of bias, since it was only with the victory of the Bolsheviks in the Soviet Union in 1917 that the world witnessed the first claim by a nation-state that it would ensure the economic and social (as opposed to the civil and political) equality of all its members. But even earlier than the Soviet revolution, philosophers in many capitalist states were advocating new forms of welfarism that also guaranteed, within a market economy, economic as well as civil/political rights. One must ask oneself, therefore, if the frequent assertion that capitalist or Western countries deny the concept of economic rights is merely a misreading of the political history of welfare capitalist states? Or is it instead a convenient rhetorical device for justifying self-serving denials of civil and political rights by African ruling classes?

For simplicity's sake (and because both the Organization of African Unity and a number of African constitutions refer to it) the Articles of the Universal Declaration of Human Rights have been used in this section. Throughout the rest of this book, however, the Articles will be referred to as they actually appear in the two 1966 covenants. Much of the book, moreover, will discuss articles of the 1981 African Charter of Human and Peoples' Rights that parallel articles of the two United Nations covenants. The next section, therefore, presents a brief introductory discussion of the African Charter.

The African Charter of Human and Peoples' Rights

In 1981 the Organization of African Unity (OAU) adopted the African Charter of Human and Peoples' Rights (sometimes also referred to as the Banjul Charter).[8] It is worth discussing this Charter in some detail, especially insofar as its provisions differ from those of the International Bill of Human Rights. The Charter represents the official ideological position on human rights now taken by governments in Africa.

Since the African Charter was passed by the OAU, it will be useful to examine the OAU's record on human rights as a whole as a means of predicting whether or not the African Charter will be anything more than a set of words, utilized to legitimize the African organization on the world stage, where some other regional organizations also have human rights charters.[9] Can we say that the OAU record as a whole indicates a real concern for the rights of individual African citizens?

The brief answer to this question is no. The Organization of African Unity has been criticized for being little more than an organization for the protection of rights of heads of state.[10] One of its chief functions appears to be to hold enormously expensive annual meetings, sometimes costing a considerable proportion of the host country's annual budget.[11] Indeed, one could argue that without the OAU, ordinary Africans' economic rights would be more thoroughly protected because more money could go to social services, rather than to OAU meetings.

One way to preserve the rights of heads of states is to preserve the states they head. The charter of the OAU clearly indicates its chief function, which is to guarantee the sovereignty and territorial integrity of all member states (Preamble; Article 2,1,c; and Article 3).[12] Such a guarantee also entails non-interference in the internal affairs of other states. A second guiding principle of the OAU is "absolute dedication to the total emancipation of the African territories which are still dependent" (Article 3, 6). While other principles are included in the charter, these are the two upon which political activity is most clearly based. The OAU's Liberation Committee was very actively involved in the guerilla struggles against the former Portuguese territories and the former Rhodesia (Zimbabwe) and is now involved in the guerilla struggles in Namibia and South Africa.

These two principal preoccupations of the OAU—preservation of national sovereignty and assistance to liberation movements—are clearly reflected in human rights–oriented activities of African states within the United Nations. Officially, the OAU is "persuaded that the Charter of the United Nations and the Universal Declaration of Human Rights . . . provide a solid foundation for peaceful and positive co-operation among states" (Preamble, OAU Charter). Within the United Nations, however, African countries have concentrated more on the rights to independence and on economic, social, and cultural rights than on civil and political rights. The only cases in which they have continuously insisted on investigating the latter rights have been with regard to forced labor in the former Portuguese colonies, and apartheid in South Africa.[13]

In fact, African conduct in U.N. human rights fora has been such as to elicit charges that African governments adhere to a "pernicious double standard."[14] Abuses of civil and political rights by independent black African nations are consistently ignored. During the late 1960s, for example, the OAU refused to consider violations of the right to life of Biafrans on the grounds that the civil war in Nigeria was an internal affair.[15] When the expulsion of Ugandan Asians was brought before the United Nations in 1972, Nigeria argued that it was "not a matter related to human rights,"[16] and despite the well-known facts of Idi Amin's atrocities, no United Nations forum criticized him until 1977.[17] The rights of black Africans inside the borders of independent African states appear to be of little real concern to the OAU.

The OAU's practice to date, then, does not augur well for the real implementation of the African charter of rights. Most African nations, including Commonwealth Africa, have little respect for the rule of law; most African rulers will not submit to legal judgments they perceive to be against their own interests. In dictatorial regimes such as Malawi, or in states ruled by militaries which have suspended civilian constitutions, it might well be risky for a citizen even to bring a matter of human rights to a regional human rights court. One can conclude that for the foreseeable future, the African Charter of Human and Peoples' Rights will have little or no practical impact, aside from its ideological and legitimating function of presenting a facade of concern for human rights to the international political community.

Nevertheless, the African Charter of Human and Peoples' Rights can be seen as a standard for human rights in Africa. It is an indigenously generated reference point for African human rights activists, who can point to an African, rather than an international or Western, document for support for their claims for more rights. As such, it may in the long run have an independent intellectual effect, helping politically active Africans to think in a new way about human rights. Insofar as the document exists and one can expect future reference to it, its specific provisions, especially those that differ from the International Bill of Rights, ought to be examined. These provisions will be discussed briefly now, while others will be referred to at appropriate points throughout the book.

Since the African Charter is officially one of human *and peoples'* rights, the question of what "peoples' " rights are needs to be determined. The African stress on peoples' or group rights is often defended by African intellectuals, who argue that such group rights protect the inherently communal, group-oriented African societies against the unbridled individualism they see as characteristic of Western capitalist society.[18] (This philosophical stance will be analyzed in Chapter 2.) Here, however, one should note that if the intent of peoples' rights is to protect the communal African society, then that is certainly not clear in the African Charter; what "peoples' rights" appears to refer to is the rights of sovereign states.

The relevant provisions are in Articles 20 and 21 of the charter. Article 20,1 states that "All peoples shall have the right to existence [and] the unquestionable and inalienable right to self-determination" and goes on to outline the rights of peoples currently under colonial rule. Article 21,1 states that "All peoples shall freely dispose of their wealth and natural resources." These two provisions echo the two most important provisions of the OAU Charter with regard to national sovereignty and territorial integrity. The right to self-determination clearly cannot be taken to apply to minority ethnic or national groups (peoples): their self-determination would violate the rule of territorial integrity. The right of sovereignty over national resources reaffirms U.N. declarations (discussed in Chapter 4) permitting governments the right to expropriate the private property of foreigners if it is in the national interest. That "peoples" is nowhere defined in the charter is no accident. Rather it is an attempt to use an ideology of African communalism to justify reaffirmation of national interests (or, as this book will argue, the interests of national ruling classes) by referring to weakly integrated nation-states as peoples.

The reference to peoples' rights is reinforced in chapter II of the African Charter, which discusses the duties of the individual. These duties are explicitly laid out as being to the family, the community, and the state. While the former two can be taken to be an affirmation of traditional or indigenous African values, the duty to the state is more problematic. Article 29,3 indicates that the individual has a duty "not to compromise the security of the State whose national or resident he is." In the African context, a very broad interpretation is normally given to the definition of national security. For example, during the last years of Jomo Kenyatta's rule in Kenya, even to discuss the aging president's possible death was a legal offence.[19] In all countries the individual has some duties, and certain of his rights can be removed if he fails to fulfill those duties. But to specify duties to an abstracted state, as opposed to other individuals whose rights must also be protected, is to set the state up as an entity above individual challenge. In fact, the state in Commonwealth Africa is composed of aspiring or existing members of the ruling class who use the privileges of office to accumulate wealth and power. In practice, duty to the state in Africa is, as Chapters 6 and 7 will demonstrate, duty to the ruling class.

A further aspect of the African Charter is its stress on the "right to development" (Preamble). Many Third World governments stress the right to development in order to counteract the bias alleged to exist in the International Bill of Rights toward civil and political, as opposed to economic, social, and cultural rights. The right to development is also stressed in order to buttress the case of the Third World in its demands for development assistance and economic concessions from the developed world. Article 15 of the African Charter, which states that "Every individual shall have the right to work under equitable and satisfactory conditions, and shall receive equal pay for equal work," is part of the same position. Article 15 does not specify whether its intent is that every individual have the absolute right to work, or whether if he does work the subsequent conditions will apply. If the former is intended, then work and development can be taken as the key to the African ideology of economic rights.

I do not necessarily quarrel with the idea that development ought to be a right or that work should be a right. But in the African context such stated rights should be taken as no more than rhetoric. Work simply cannot be guaranteed by any government in independent Africa, where official unemployment figures often run at 20 percent and unofficial figures may well be higher. More important, the stress on development is often used, in the African context, to justify the abrogation of civil and political rights (and women's rights) until such hypothetical time as a state of development has been attained. Development has become a convenient catchword to justify massive violations of individual rights with no tangible economic benefit in return. Ruling classes, in the name of development, entrench themselves in power and argue that political participation by individuals is intrinsically destabilizing, hence anti-development.

In principle, political participation is guaranteed by the African Charter. Article 13,1 states that "Every individual shall have the right to participate freely in the government of his country, either directly or through freely chosen representatives." In keeping with the provisions of the International Covenant on Civil and Political Rights (Article 21), the right of political participation does not specify multi-party elections. It does, however, imply that individuals must have the right freely to choose their representatives, presumably through some form of election. In one-party states, then, the key to political rights would be the freedom and fairness of the intra-party choice allowed to citizens. The allegedly consensual nature of pre-colonial African society is often used to justify either the elimination of formal elections, or the top-down control of single ruling parties. In this sense, the charter's failure to specify both an electoral process and some form of free competition among political personnel and programs conforms to the ideology of the African peoples or community, but at the same time eases the entrenchment of class rule.

This discussion of the African Charter of Human and Peoples' Rights has deliberately concentrated on those aspects of the charter that reflect an alleged respect for community, as against the rights of the seemingly alienated, asocial individual. (Other provisions of the charter to be discussed later are more orthodox in flavor and more closely resemble the provisions of the International Bill of Rights.) The argument of this book will be that individual rights must not be abrogated by way of specious ideology of the communal and inherently democratic nature of African society. As Chapter 2 will show, contemporary Commonwealth Africa is increasingly capitalist, individualistic, and stratified. The individual, male or female, needs rights of protection against the state. Human rights must be individual rights and must be universal, otherwise they do not protect real, concrete *people* against class-ruled "peoples."

Before further discussion, it is necessary to dispose of one shibboleth sometimes encountered among commentators on human rights in Africa. The above criticisms of Commonwealth African human rights practice should not be taken to imply that Africa was better off under colonial rule than it is now. Indeed, many of the state practices that violate human rights in contemporary Africa imitate British colonial procedure, as will be shown in the following section on the actual record of the British colonial rulers with regard to human rights in Africa.[20]

Human Rights under Colonial Rule

The opinion is sometimes expressed that Commonwealth Africa was better off, as far as human rights were concerned, under British rule than it is under indigenous African rule. This contention implicitly reflects a concern for political stability as the overriding priority of human rights.

It is true that, once Africa had been successfully conquered, British rule was relatively benign. The history of the conquest itself, however, reveals massive violations of the right to life and liberty.[21] The British were often quite ruthless in their suppression of resistance. For example, every person in the market of the village of Muruka (Kenya) was slaughtered to revenge the killing of one British soldier in 1902.[22] Recalcitrant chiefs were routinely exiled or detained. The Maxim gun was used in Africa as early as the 1890s against indigenous Ugandan and Tanzanian resistance.[23] That such brutality was not confined merely to the 19th-century imperialist phase is evidenced by the massive incarcerations of "Mau Mau" rebels in Kenya in the 1950s and by the confinement of Kenyan women and children to "protective" concentration camps.[24]

Civil and political rights as the contemporary world now defines them were certainly not practiced under colonial rule. Indeed, the British initially opposed U.N. passage of the Universal Declaration of Human Rights because they were afraid that the declaration would oblige them to implement those rights in their colonies.[25] The practice of preventive detention, now a favorite weapon of African governments, is a direct heritage of the colonial era.[26] Colonial Africa experienced no political participation to speak of. A few African members were allowed into the Legislative Councils of Ghana and Sierra Leone as early as the 1920s,[27] but all decisions of such councils could be overridden by the colonial executive and the colonial secretary. In other countries, admission of Africans into Legislative Councils was delayed until the 1940s or 1950s.[28] These African members were appointed, not elected (except for a few municipal seats); thus ordinary Africans had no political rights whatsoever. Nor was there any real independence of the judiciary. The local district commissioner was normally prosecutor, judge, and jury—in short, a patronizing "great white father." Only in the higher courts and the urban areas was separation of the judiciary and the other organs of government established.

In the economic field, the British practiced forced labor until well into the 1920s.[29] During World War I, West Africans forcibly recruited into the British Army's carrier corps died by the thousands from exhaustion, inadequate provisioning, and unhealthy living conditions.[30] Trade unions were not permitted until the 1920s, and when they did exist had very few rights. In Kenya, hundreds of thousands of Africans were expelled from their land to make way for white settlers, and African peasants were forbidden to grow profitable crops, such as coffee, in competition with the whites.[31] In general, the colonial state assumed no obligation for economic development until 1939, when the exigencies of wartime production forced more rational consideration of all British resources. Nor was there any notion that the British should ensure in their colonies even the limited range of social welfare provisions that existed at home.

In the cultural field, the British, perhaps unintentionally, undermined local pride and dignity by the introduction of Christian churches and mission-run schools, where members of a putative African elite learned to imitate whites in dress and manner and to denigrate their own cultural heritage. Cultural diffusion, in which Africans might have made their own choices about which aspects of Western mores they wished to adopt, was accompanied by cultural compulsion: the price of schooling was conversion to Christianity. Newly Westernized "youngmen" challenged the authority of their elders, while the traditional relations between the sexes were distorted by the imposition of Western patriarchal ideals. In defense of the British, it can be noted that "native" languages were not formally abolished, nor were indigenous religions disallowed, except when their provisions, such as infanticide of twins, were deemed contrary to "natural justice."[32] On the other hand, racial discrimination was commonplace. Indeed, Jomo Kenyatta, the late president of Kenya, could still rouse a cheer from the popular masses in the 1970s by explaining that the African elite now owned the best land, shops, and homes, formerly for whites only.[33]

This short description of human rights under British rule serves to illustrate that the colonial power was not concerned to grant to its subjects the rights held by citizens in the "mother country," even given the limited definition of human rights prevailing at the time. What the British did do during the colonial period was to eliminate all overt interethnic conflict; to abolish, where it existed, African domestic slavery; and to stop the expansion of African empires. Thus a great deal of political conflict that might have occurred in a noncolonized Africa was deflected, only to emerge, in sometimes more violent form, in the post-colonial period.

To compare human rights in contemporary Africa unfavorably with human rights in the colonial period, therefore, is to concentrate upon a very limited range of "rights"—namely peace, relative predictability, and "benign neglect" of indigenous ethnic groupings. In a country as wracked by internal tensions as Uganda has been since 1966, such elementary rights are valued indeed. The British did not murder individuals merely on the basis of their ethnicity, and once their conquest was assured, peace did reign within the narrow confines of paternalistic dictatorship. But were the British still in power today, the narrowness of the range of rights they allowed would be even more obvious than it was during the nationalist agitation of the 1950s and '60s. More is expected of independent African governments by way of human rights than was ever expected of the British; thus the former's attacks on those rights appear much worse than the latter's outright denial of them.

The Argument in Brief

In general, Commonwealth Africa does not figure among the worst violators of human rights in the Third World. This book focuses upon the nine countries strictly for analytic reasons.

Several major factors run through the analysis presented here. I argue that the difficulties of protecting human rights in Africa derive to a great extent from its underdeveloped economy, which sets severe limits both on the substantive economic rights that can be provided and on the possibilities of social changes that could facilitate greater civil and political rights. Since independence, Commonwealth Africa has been engaged in the process of state-building and many violations of communal rights have been a consequence of that process. But the evolution of individualism in Africa and of a class structure based on control not only of wealth, but also of the organs of the state, has also affected human rights. Regime consolidation and the use of the coercive organs of state power to deny both political and civil rights are major causes of human rights abuses. None of these factors is specific to Africa. Thus I reject the "cultural relativism" argument, which is frequently used to defend African human rights abuses by attempting to remove them from their social-structural context.

In the long run, the most enduring cause of human rights abuses, in Africa as elsewhere, is social stratification and the consolidation of political and economic power in the hands of a small ruling class. Although the class structure of Commonwealth Africa is not yet consolidated (see Chapter 3), it is the determining factor in analysis of human rights. Other human rights problems, especially "tribal" or communal conflicts and women's rights, must be analyzed in class terms. After national integration is completed and ethnic conflicts lose some of their saliency, class problems will predominate. The issue of sexual discrimination, which has a heavy ideological and cultural component, will remain, but how women are affected by it will depend on their class position.

This book, then, argues for a social-structural approach to human rights in Africa. The capacity to realize human rights, and the types of human rights abuses that occur, vary with social structure. The economic circumstances of a society exert a powerful influence on social structure. Commonwealth Africa is affected by three overwhelming economic circumstances: its colonial heritage of raw material extraction and labor exploitation, its extremely vulnerable position in the present world economy, and the domination of internal economies by the state and by parasitic ruling classes. The chief resource of black Africa is its raw materials. Commonwealth Africa is not an important or profitable market for goods produced elsewhere, nor is it even an important supplier of cheap industrial labor. This peripheral nature of the capitalist economy has resulted in a class structure in which there is a tremendous advantage in having access to the state and to the resources it controls. Consequently there is also a tremendous resistance to relinquishing political power or permitting any opposition to those in power.

Africa is not culturally unique. Africa's human rights performance can be discussed without taking into account any cultural uniqueness. Chapter 2 will dispute the myth that Africa is essentially communitarian, redistributive with regard to material wealth, and consensual in political matters by referring to the existence of social stratification and conflict in pre-colonial African society, and to the social structural changes that have occurred in the almost five centuries of contact with Europe. Nevertheless, I do not posit an absolute structural domination over culture. Cultural variations do indeed affect peoples' perceptions of human rights, and a "weak" culturally relativistic stance is a useful check against unabashed imposition of inappropriate human rights norms on a society.[34] (Such a weak relativistic stance will appear in Chapter 8's analysis of women's rights in the personal sphere.)

This book's adoption of a structural approach to the analysis of human rights should not be taken to mean that ideology has no relevance. While ideologies generally emerge from specific social structures, they can be transferred to other societies and can have an independent influence on social change. One cannot, for example, imagine that Tanzania's structural position in the world economy would have impelled her to take the socialist path she embarked upon in 1967 with the Arusha Declaration in the absence of Julius Nyerere and his well-articulated preference for socialism.[35] Nor should the structural approach be taken to mean that individual moral action has no place in human rights matters. If individuals can be independent actors in history, then they are also independent judges of the morality of their own actions; and this applies far more to well-fed, educated members of the African ruling class than to the ordinary peasant or poor urban dweller. Individuals are selfish; they normally act in a rational manner intended to achieve their own self-interest. The ruling classes in Africa, as elsewhere, manipulate human rights to their own ends. Despite this book's essentially structural approach, tempered by a modified cultural relativism, I maintain that it is people who make history, and members of the ruling classes who control people. Scientific analysis of such rulers' actions can explain their behavior, but should not be used as excuses for it.

This book, then, will present a social-structural analysis of human rights in Commonwealth Africa. Chapter 2 will discuss the myth of communal African society, and point out the roots of the noncommunal, socially stratified reality of the present day. Chapter 3 will explain the relationship between the peripheral economic structure of Commonwealth Africa, its class structure, and state violations of human rights. Chapter 4 will discuss economic rights; while acknowledging the independent effects of colonialism and peripheral capitalism on African poverty, it will also discuss the class-biased nature of economic policies. Chapter 5 will discuss violations of human rights of large communal groups and show how "tribalism," citizen-alien conflicts, and religious persecution in Commonwealth Africa can all be related to conflicts over allocation of scarce resources or, alternatively, to the ruling classes's desire to retain their power. Chapter 6 will discuss denials of political rights, especially freedom of the press and assembly, free trade union organization, and genuine political participation, perpetrated by African ruling classes to secure their power. Chapter 7 will discuss denials of civil liberties to political opponents, especially through Preventive Detention Acts, state terrorism, and the ideological and practical undermining of the rule of law. Finally, Chapter 8 will discuss women's rights, concentrating on how they are affected by an underdeveloped economy and by women's class positions. The conclusion will focus on the medium-term prospects for popular participation in the realization of both economic and civil/political rights, especially given the present existence, and possible continuation, of Africa's deep economic crisis.

An underlying argument running throughout this book will be the need for political participation as a basic human right. In his widely quoted *Basic Rights* (1980), Henry Shue argues that the two most fundamental rights are physical subsistence and personal security. I maintain that it is not possible to guarantee either security or subsistence rights without political rights. Civil and political rights cannot be left in abeyance until prior economic rights are guaranteed. In extremely poor and underdeveloped societies, it is naive to expect political/economic ruling classes to give up what wealth they are able to accrue for the benefit of their poorer countrymen. Moreover, many people value their freedoms of association, thought, and speech even at very low levels of economic development, as the many political prisoners and victims of political killings in Commonwealth Africa demonstrate.

From these essential premises, then, I derive my position on a number of debates currently being discussed among scholars and in international fora such as the United Nations General Assembly. First, I believe that human rights ought to be universal. They ought not to be contingent on the discharge of duties to the state, nor should they be conflated into an allegedly culturally unique view of "peoples' " rights; they must be universal among individuals. Second, with regard to the debate about where to lay the blame for non-realization of economic rights in Commonwealth Africa, while I accept the real structural effects of colonialism and of Africa's present weak position in the world economy, I believe that there are also internal class-generated causes of the denial of economic rights. Finally, with regard to debates about prioritizing different kinds of rights, I believe that human rights are interdependent and that neither civil/political rights nor women's rights can wait until economic rights have been achieved.

Notes

1. On Zimbabwe, see Ronald Weitzer, "Continuities in the Politics of State Security in Zimbabwe," in Michael Schatzberg, ed., *The Political Economy of Zimbabwe* (New York: Praeger, 1984), pp. 81–118; see also his dissertation "The Internal Security State: Political Change and Repression in Northern Ireland and Zimbabwe" (University of California at Berkeley, 1985).

2. These documents may be found in Walter Laqueur and Barry Rubin, eds., *The Human Rights Reader* (Scarborough, Ont.: New American Library, 1979).

3. Henry Shue, *Basic Rights: Subsistence, Affluence and U.S. Foreign Policy* (Princeton: Princeton University Press, 1980), p. 6.

4. Ibid.

5. E.g., Julius K. Nyerere, "Stability and Change in Africa" (an address to the University of Toronto, 1969), in Colin Legum, ed., *Africa Contemporary Record*, vol. 2 (London: Rex Collings, 1969–70), pp. C30–C31.

6. For my views on this debate, see Rhoda Howard, "The Full-Belly Thesis: Should Economic Rights Take Priority over Civil and Political Rights? Evidence from Sub-Saharan Africa," *Human Rights Quarterly* 5, no. 4 (November 1983): 467–90.

7. Thomas L. Hodgkin, "The Relevance of 'Western' Ideas for the New African States," in J. Roland Pennock, ed., *Self-Government in Modernizing Nations* (Englewood Cliffs, N.J.: Prentice-Hall, 1965), p. 51.

8. The African Charter is included as Appendix I in Claude E. Welch, Jr., and Robert I. Meltzer, eds., *Human Rights and Development in Africa* (Albany, N.Y.: State University of New York Press, 1984), pp. 317–29. For background to the establishment of the charter, see Edward Kannyo, "Human Rights in Africa: Problems and Prospects," working paper (New York: International League for Human Rights, May 1980).

9. Richard Gittleman, "The Banjul Charter on Human and Peoples' Rights: A Legal Analysis," in Welch and Meltzer, *Human Rights and Development in Africa*, pp. 152–76.

10. Olajide Aluko, "The Organisation of African Unity and Human Rights," *The Round Table* 283 (July 1981): 240.

11. David Lamb, *The Africans* (New York: Random House, 1983), pp. 98–99.

12. Charter of the Organization of African Unity, in Ian Brownlie, ed., *Basic Documents in International Law*, 2nd. ed. (Oxford: Clarendon Press, 1972), pp. 68–76.

13. Warren Weinstein, "Africa's Approach to Human Rights at the United Nations," *Issue: A Journal of Africanist Opinion* 6, no. 4 (Winter 1976): 16.

14. Ibid., p. 19.

15. Laurie S. Wiseberg, "Human Rights in Africa: Toward a Definition of the Problem of a Double Standard," *Issue: A Journal of Africanist Opinion* 6, no. 4 (Winter 1976): 4.

16. Weinstein, "Africa's Approach," p. 18.

17. International Commission of Jurists, *Uganda and Human Rights: Reports to the U.N. Commission on Human Rights* (Geneva: International Commission of Jurists, 1977), p. vii.

18. E.g., Asmarom Legesse, "Human Rights in African Political Culture," in Kenneth W. Thompson, ed., *The Moral Imperatives of Human Rights: A World Survey* (Washington, D.C.: University Press of America, 1980), pp. 123–36; and others cited in Chapter 2 of this book.

19. *Africa Contemporary Record*, vol. 9 (1976–77), p. B.218.

20. The following section is a slightly revised version of the author's "Evaluating Human Rights in Africa: Some Problems of Implicit Comparisons," *Human Rights Quarterly* 6, no. 2 (May 1984): 170–73.

21. Michael Crowder, ed., *West African Resistance: The Military Response to Colonial Occupation* (London: Hutchinson, 1971).

22. Ngugi wa Thiong'o, *Detained: A Writer's Prison Diary* (London: Heinemann, 1981), p. 35.

23. John Ellis, *The Social History of the Machine Gun* (New York: Random House, 1975), p. 88.

24. Ngugi, *Detained*, p. 49.

25. James Frederick Green, *The United Nations and Human Rights* (Washington, D.C.: The Brookings Institution, 1956), p. 56.

26. Ngugi, *Detained*, pp. 44–51.

27. See, for Ghana, A.K.P. Kludze, "Ghana [Constitutional History]," in Albert P. Blaustein and Gisbert H. Flanz, eds., *Constitutions of the Countries of the World* (Dobbs Ferry, N.Y.: Oceana Publications, 1984), p. 4; and for Sierra Leone, see W.S. Marcus Jones and G.F.A. Sawyerr, "Sierra Leone [Constitutional History]," (issued 1979), in Blaustein and Flanz, *Constitutions*, p. 3.

28. For details of each country, see Blaustein and Flanz, *Constitutions*.

29. On Ghana, see Roger G. Thomas, "Forced Labour in British West Africa: The Case of the Northern Territories of the Gold Coast, 1906–1927," *Journal of African History* 14, no. 1 (1973): 79–103.

30. David Killingray and James Matthews, "Beasts of Burden: British West African Carriers in the First World War," *Canadian Journal of African Studies* 13, nos. 1/2 (1979): 5–23.

31. E.A. Brett, *Colonialism and Underdevelopment in East Africa* (London: Heinemann, 1973), p. 208.

32. All-Africa Council of Churches, "Factors Responsible for the Violation of Human Rights in Africa," *Issue: A Journal of Africanist Opinion* 6, no. 4 (Winter 1976): 44.

33. "The President's Kenyatta Day Speech: Warning to Opponents," *Africa Contemporary Record*, vol. 5 (1972–73), p. C128 (reported on Radio Nairobi, October 20, 1972).

34. Cf. Jack Donnelly, "Cultural Relativism and Universal Human Rights," *Human Rights Quarterly* 6, no. 4 (1984): 400–419.

35. Julius K. Nyerere, "The Arusha Declaration," in Nyerere, *Ujamaa: Essays on Socialism* (London: Oxford University Press, 1968), pp. 13–37.

Cultural Relativism, Social Change, and Human Rights

Is there a specifically African concept of human rights, grounded in a unique African culture or society?[1] This chapter argues that African society has many aspects similar to advanced Western capitalist society. During five centuries of contact between Africa and the Western world, social changes have been introduced that increasingly undermine any social-structural or cultural uniqueness Africa might once have possessed. These aspects create human rights needs and ideals closer to the Western model than to the "traditional" models of privileges and obligations of indigenous Africa.

The philosophical position which I adopt in the present work is that human rights must be universal. Human rights are inherent in one's humanity. They are contingent neither upon fulfillment of one's obligations to society, upon membership in a particular group, nor upon the decision of the state to "grant" rights.[2] If a right exists, therefore, it must be available to all individuals. Rights, moreover, are entitlements, not merely privileges.[3] Any derogation or postponement of rights must therefore be thoroughly justified.

Rights are held by the individual against the state. The individual has the right to make claims on or against the state. Further, the individual as individual is the basic unit of human rights. The stress on "group" rights in the African Charter of Human and Peoples' Rights simply derogates from individual rights in favor of the "rights" of nation-states or, as this book argues, in favor of the "rights" of their ruling classes.

This philosophical position reflects my perception of the sociological reality of contemporary Commonwealth Africa. This chapter will demonstrate that the undifferentiated communitarian society (to which reference is often made to assert the cultural uniqueness of Africa) no longer exists; indeed, even in pre-colonial Africa there were state societies with rigid forms of social stratification.

It follows from my view of social change and social structure in Commonwealth Africa that I reject the extreme view of cultural relativity in which "Reverence for cultural values, rather than reverence for life, becomes the absolute virtue."[4] Cultural values and cultural practice are as legitimately subject to criticism from a human rights perspective as any structural aspect of a society. African "culture" may not be used as a defense of human rights abuses. The principle of cultural relativity as an excuse for violations of international human rights standards should be used sparingly, if at all. Jack Donnelly suggests that a distinction be made between radical human rights universalism and a weak cultural relativist approach. The latter approach would "serve as a check on potential excesses of universalism [and] allow only relatively rare and strictly limited local variations and exceptions."[5] Donnelly proposes a hierarchy of relativities: in the substance of rights, the interpretation of rights, and the form in which particular rights are implemented.[6] My own position is that I do not accept any relativity in the substance of rights. I do accept that implementation may vary and, further, the interpretation may vary in societies whose social norms (for instance, regarding marriage) do not accept particular rights. However, this derogation from the standard of absolute international human rights is acceptable only in the rare cases in which a weakened interpretation of a right does not support the entrenchment of a ruling class.

Thus while the principle of cultural relativity should not be raised to an absolute standard to excuse any and all deviations from international human rights standards, it may be used as a check on radical universalism in very carefully defined circumstances. These circumstances are rare in Commonwealth Africa, where changes in the direction of increased individual autonomy are occurring, partly because of severe structural dislocations and partly because of the introduction of new ideologies. Cultural stasis is unlikely, however indigenous culture may be. African cultures are changing to reflect the emergence of new social classes with differential access to property and power. Most assertions of cultural relativity in fact are an ideological tool to serve the interests of powerful emergent groups in Commonwealth African society.

An African Concept of Human Rights?

The argument that different societies can have different concepts of rights is based on an assumption that confuses human rights with human dignity. All societies have concepts of human dignity, but few accept the notion of human rights, in the sense that individuals have the right to make claims on or against the state.[7] Concepts of human dignity do indeed vary. They are embedded in cultural views of the nature of human beings, which in turn reflect the social organization of particular societies. In Africa, idealized versions of human dignity reflect idealized interpretations of precolonial social structure.

Those who argue for an African concept of human rights take as its key the alleged existence of a communitarian ideal in Africa. Within that ideal the group is more important than the individual, decisions are made by consensus rather than by competition, and economic surpluses are disposed of on a redistributive, rather than a profit-oriented, basis. A quote from President Kenneth Kaunda of Zambia, who calls himself an "African humanist," clearly identifies these three elements.

> The tribal community was a mutual society. It was organised to satisfy the basic human needs of all its members. . . . individualism was discouraged. . . . Human need was the supreme criterion of behaviour . . . social harmony was a vital necessity . . . Chiefs and tribal elders . . . adjudicated between conflicting parties . . . and took whatever action was necessary to strengthen the fabric of social life.[8]

President Julius Nyerere of Tanzania adopts a similar stance with his contention that "the idea of 'class' or 'caste' was non-existent in African society. The foundation, and the objective, of African socialism [communalism] is the extended family."[9]

Unfortunately, such harkening back to the "original," pre-colonial model of African communalism obscures the social changes that have taken place in Africa since the European incursion. In the process of social change Africans, like Westerners, have become more and more motivated by individual, not collective (whether family or societal), advancement. A detailed discussion of the three alleged value differences between African and Western society (noted above) will make this clear.

The first alleged value difference is that African society is communitarian, not individualistic, in orientation. The African is a human being by virtue of his or her fulfillment of prescribed social roles. Kaunda's stress on the mutuality of society and Nyerere's on society as an extended family are both understandable if one considers the traditional African concept of "personhood." The African philosopher Ifeanyi A. Menkiti asserts that there is no concept of person in traditional or folk society, independent of that person's fulfillment of the social obligations of his or her role. One grows into personhood through "the discharge of the various obligations defined by one's stations."[10] Such a concept of personhood is not a concept of human rights, however. There is no humanity in such traditional societies separate from fulfillment of one's obligations to and incorporation into the group; those who are not members of the group, such as slaves, strangers, or criminal outcasts, have no rights. Indeed, even those who are members of the group, but who fail to fulfil their obligations—for example barren women—may be considered less than fully human.

The so-called "African concept of human rights" is, therefore, actually a concept of human dignity. The individual feels respect and worthiness as a result of his or her fulfillment of the socially approved role. Any rights that might be held are dependent on one's status or contingent on one's behavior. Such a society may well provide the individual with a great deal of security and protection, and as such it "is undeniably morally defensible, is in many ways quite attractive, and can be said to protect basic human dignity."[11] One might even argue that people may well value such dignity more than their freedom to act as individuals. In relatively homogeneous, static, and small-scale societies this tendency is likely to be stronger than the tendency toward individualism. African thought, from this perspective, stresses the right of the individual to be part of the group, through the extended family and larger clan and tribal organizations. Kaunda asserts that "the tribal community was an *inclusive* society. . . .the extended family system constitutes a social security scheme which has the advantage of following the natural pattern of personal relationships rather than being the responsibility of an institution."[12]

In such societies even slaves have been held to have a recognized place and the dignity of fulfilling their prescribed roles. In an essay on African forms of domestic slavery, Miers and Kopytoff support such a familial view of African human "rights" by arguing that "In most African societies, 'freedom' lay not in a withdrawal into a meaningless and dangerous autonomy but in attachment to a kin group, to a patron, to power. . . . the antithesis of 'slavery' is not 'freedom' . . . but rather belonging."[13] The domestic slave's dignity was guaranteed by his incorporation as a junior member of his owner's lineage. On the other hand, that he was a junior member was always clear, and status differentiations between the descendants of freemen and of slaves are still made in contemporary Africa. Moreover, slaves were always threatened by the possibility of their being victims of mass ritual executions, as when Ashanti (Ghana) kings died. We can assume that group acceptance of slaves as inferior members of the society could not compensate for the threat to the most basic of human rights, the right to life.

In modern terms, a good example of the ambiguity of group acceptance based on conformity to societal custom can be found in an examination of the role of women. Two Ugandan women scholars reject the notion of human dignity in traditional African society as it applies to women. According to Grace Akello,

> The deepest human motive is to seek the respect of others, and women will conform to the basest of obligations defined for them to have access to some respect. . . . To gain a sense of achievement, [a woman] must exert herself to prove that she is capable of fulfilling the demands of traditional society on womanhood. To be proud of her own existence she must have the approval of her society; *she must be proud of her own subordination.*[14]

Similarly, Christine Obbo argues that African women are expected to bear the burden of "authenticity" (adherence to their traditional roles), while men are free to go their own new, individualistic ways in the changing national society. " 'Women must act as mediators between the past and the present, while men see themselves as mediators between the present and the future.' "[15]

The example of women's rights demonstrates that communitarian, rather than individualistic, modes of thinking are still much stronger in

Commonwealth Africa than in the fully capitalistic, ideologically liberal West. But the communitarian ideal is not a specifically African model in content; it is not culturally specific on a regional or racial basis. Rather, it represents typical agrarian, precapitalist social relations in non-state societies. It would be useful, for example, to compare such African societies with pre-industrial England. Undoubtedly, in the closed village societies of premodern Europe, one would also discover that people thought of themselves more as members of their own local groups than as individuals. Both premodern Europe and pre-colonial Africa were relatively undifferentiated societies. What some writers view as essentially different African and Western ways of thinking are actually differences between societal structures, on whatever continent they may be located.

The second allegedly unique characteristic of the African concept of human rights is its approach to politics. The communal model of human rights asserts that the African approach to decision-making is consensual by nature. For example, Wai states that

> The relationship between the chief and his people is based on a pattern of obligations: from the chief to the people and vice versa. . . . In the traditional setting Africans had the right to remove chiefs who acted arbitrarily or ruled dictatorially. . . . Discussion was open and those who dissented from the majority opinion were not punished.[16]

Thus a number of formal provisions in the International Covenant of Civil and Political Rights, particularly the right to genuine and periodic elections, are asserted to be redundant in African politics, on the grounds that all these freedoms are already inherent in the "traditional" African model.

This view of the consensual nature of African politics is exaggerated. Some writers tend to overgeneralize, as Mojekwu does in extending his analysis of his own (apparently Igbo) subunit of Nnewi to all of Africa.[17] It is true that local village decisions in non-state African societies such as the Igbo were made by consensus; elected chiefs and elders debated an issue until general agreement was reached, and errant officials who violated the general consensus could be deposed. But not all African societies were of this noncentralized village type, even before contact with the British. Some, like the Ashanti in Ghana, were a quasi-feudal bureaucracy in which appointed officials from the capital had power over local village chiefs. In northern Nigeria, a number of centralized Muslim states consolidated their power before British rule and retained it afterward.

Even noncentralized African societies differentiated among their members by status or rank. Women, aliens, and children were accorded different rights and privileges than adult native males. Males were graded according to age; in the modern period this has resulted in age-grade disputes between younger and older men over access to material resources and women. Slaves, especially those taken in war as opposed to those "pawned" in payment of debts, had lower status than freemen.[18] Finally, some societies, such as the Igbo in Nigeria and the Masai in East Africa, had castes of untouchables who could not intermarry with members of the larger society.[19]

As far as slaves were concerned, Miers and Kopytoff's benign view of them as having been integrated members of their owners' lineages is disputed by other scholars. Paul Lovejoy argues that African domestic slavery was a specifically economic (profit-making) institution.

> Slaves were property. . . . Slaves were outsiders by origin, who lacked kinship ties. . . . The relationship between slave and master was ultimately based on coercion. . . . Slaves were completely at the disposal of their masters: The labor power of slaves could be used however desired; even their sexuality and . . . their reproductive capacities were not theirs by right. . . . children who were born to slaves inherited slave status.[20]

Profit was made from selling slaves in the international slave trade, and from using them both in subsistence cultivation and in capitalist-oriented mining and cultivation for the world market. For example, among the Asante, slaves worked by the thousands in gold mines, where "the dangers of injury and death were considerable."[21] Among the Yoruba of Nigeria, slaves were used in the 19th century to produce palm oil for export.[22] Among the Nupe, also in Nigeria, slave villages produced both food to support the urban noble and military elite, and export goods that were traded to the British for firearms and to the northern Hausa for horses. Slaves from the villages were also sold in the international slave trade.[23] In Zanzibar, slaves were used on clove plantations where "physical punishment was at the heart of discipline."[24] That much of 19th-century African exploitation of slave labor took its form from relations with the international economy does not negate the fact that the idea of slavery, and of the inferiority of the slave, was already entrenched in pre-colonial African society.

The idealized view of a nonstratified, consensual pre-colonial African society is not shared by those contemporary politicians who have to unite large, heterogeneous new nation-states against the will of the leaders of formerly dominant African empires. In his 1970 "Common Man's Charter," then President of Uganda Milton Obote specifically rejected preservation of Buganda "feudalism," stating "we do not accept that feudalism . . . is a way of life which must not be disturbed because it has been in practice for centuries."[25] In his view, the highly advanced, centralized state system of pre-colonial Buganda was a threat to the new post-colonial state of Uganda, officered to a significant extent by individuals from northern non-state societies. To Obote, political consensus in Uganda was impossible as long as Buganda power remained untouched.

African intellectuals who accept the communitarian ideal of African "human rights" often espouse a noncompetitive "palaver" (talking out) form of government, in which consensus is reached after nonpartisan debate.[26] According to this view, the formal structure of parliaments and official oppositions set up by the British in independent Africa was eroded because it was antithetical to the much more intrinsically moral and consensual basis of African society. But the palaver system cannot work in large-scale state societies. Even in traditional societies, the weight of one's opinions as expressed in the palaver was dependent upon one's age, sex, and social status. Elder free males were normally the decision-makers.[27] Consensual politics (implying local and individual participation in the consensus) are not typical of large-scale indigenous African states; rather, they appear to have been one (but not the only) method of settling disputes in stateless societies only.[28] Nor can such consensual politics accomodate competing ethnic or class interests except at the long- (or even short-) run cost of increased state coercion. The one-party "palaver" state presumes the formation of a ruling class.

The existence of social classes in Africa belies the final argument for an African concept of human rights, namely that African societies are not profit-oriented; rather they distribute wealth on a need-determined, egalitarian basis. Legesse contends that "Most African cultures, whether they are formally egalitarian or hierarchical, have mechanisms of distributive justice. . . . Most African kings and chiefs were expected to use their wealth for the welfare of their subjects."[29] Here the anthropological past is confused with the sociological present. It is accurate to portray the pre-capitalist "tribal" way of life as one in which neither productive property nor surplus was privately held. Land was distributed to families for use on the basis of need. A certain proportion of the surplus was given to the chief, but his control over the surplus was as a steward on behalf of the group: he distributed food for ritual occasions or stored it against future poor harvests. Even in societies that were stratified not only by age and sex, but also into castes of nobles, freemen, and slaves, each individual was guaranteed adequate land for his or her own sustenance. While one may perhaps attribute this guarantee of livelihood to the African communal culture, economic factors were also influential. Adequate sustenance for all is a relatively costless allocation of resources in a society in which (as in much of Africa until recently) there is a surplus of land and a shortage of labor.

But the past distribution of land had an economic basis that is breaking down. The initial redistributive economy has now been affected by over five centuries of incorporation into the Western-dominated world capitalist economy. Faced with capitalist expansion, many Africans have responded with capitalist rationality. The evidence is overwhelming that social classes based on differential access to private property in tangibles such as land and industry, as well as in intangibles such as knowledge and public office, are emerging in contemporary Commonwealth Africa.

The redistributive ideal, like the ideal of the consensual political system

and the community-oriented individual, is based on inadequate understanding of pre-colonial African societies and on ignorance of the profound
structural changes that have taken place as a result of British colonialism
and Africa's incorporation into the capitalist world economy. In Chapters
3 and 4, evidence will be presented to show that contemporary Commonwealth Africa is now composed of different social classes based on highly
inequitable access to productive resources. The speed with which these
social classes have emerged indicates how readily culture can change in the
face of new opportunities for individualism and profit.

Culture and Social Change

The evidence that the communitarian, allegedly culturally relative ideal of
human rights is false is readily available. Why, then, are such historically
and sociologically inaccurate models of African "human rights" so
strongly propounded in international academic and political debate?

There is no specifically African concept of human rights. The argument
for such a concept is based on a philosophical confusion of human dignity
with human rights, and on an inadequate understanding of structural
organization and social changes in African society. Underlying this inadequate understanding, a number of assumptions regarding the meaning of
culture are used to buttress the reliance on the assertion of "cultural
relativity," in order to argue that the allegedly "Western" concept of
human rights cannot be applied to Africa.

The first implicit assumption underlying the communal model of
African human rights is that culture is a static entity. In sociological terms,
this is a functionalist perspective: it asserts that all aspects of customs,
norms, and values are functional to the persistence of the social system as a
whole, and extrapolates that therefore one aspect cannot be changed
without the whole edifice crumbling. But even though elements of culture
have a strong hold on people's individual psyches, cultures can and do
change. Cultural change can be an adaptation to structural change. It can
also result from individuals being exposed to and adopting new ideas.
Individuals are actors who can influence their own fate, even if their range
of choice is circumscribed by the prevalent social structure, culture, or
ideology. In so doing, both those who choose to adopt "new" ideals, such
as competitiveness, and those who choose to retain "old" ideals, such as
resource redistribution, may be doing so in their own interests. Culture,
like structure, is inherently dynamic, and it is responsive to conflict among
individuals or social groups.

A second implicit assumption underlying the communal model of
African human rights is that culture is a unitary whole; that is, people are
members of one culture or another, hence to attempt to judge African

human rights by the universal standards embodied in the main United Nations instruments is to impose one whole culture upon another whole culture.[30] But people are quite adept at being cultural accomodationists; they are able implicitly to choose which aspects of a "new" culture they wish to adopt and which aspects of the "old" they wish to retain. The religious syncretism of many African sects, which combine polygyny with Western Christian beliefs, is clear evidence of cultural accomodation. The process of urbanization provides evidence as well. Africans who urbanize do not suddenly adopt "modern" as opposed to "traditional" ways; rather, they create "urban villages" in the new cities, retaining ethnic links but adapting ethnic organizations to new social functions.

Thus, since culture is neither static nor unitary, one cannot preach a return to the quasi-mythical old ways; even if structures were suddenly to regress, new ideas would still persist in people's individual choices of how to live. It may well be that both the new ideals of individualism— competition and private profit—and new interpretations of old inequali- ties, such as that between slaveowner and slave or between young men and old men, have been introduced into Commonwealth Africa as a result of the ideological imperialism of the Christian missionary and the British educator. Nevertheless, these ideals have been adopted and retained independently by Africans, and nothing short of extreme ideological control can eliminate them from the African scene.

A third assumption underlying the cultural model of African human rights is that culture is unaffected by structure. But structure does affect culture; culture is adaptive. One can accept the principle that customs, values, and norms do indeed "glue" society together, and that they will endure, in the typical "cultural lag" syndrome, even when structures have changed, without assuming cultural stasis. To a significant extent cultures and values reflect forms of organization of the productive forces available to a society, and forms of social stratification. This does not mean that beliefs are completely determined by material forces. On the contrary, I argue throughout this book for the autonomy of the individual impelled by his or her own ideas in determining, within certain boundaries, his or her own fate. It does mean that since the overall economic and social structure of Commonwealth Africa no longer adheres, if it ever did, to the small- scale communal model, cultures, human rights ideals, and individual lives will have changed accordingly.

The final assumption is that culture is neutral. Yet very few social practices, whether cultural or otherwise, are entirely neutral in their impact. In considering any cultural practice it is useful to ask, who benefits from its retention? Do the "cultural policy-makers" have a personal interest in the custom?[31] Those who seek to preserve, as well as those who seek to change, customs may in fact be seeking their individual or group self-interest. Even in ethnic or national groups with coherent, shared customs and values, there can be, and in Africa usually is, social stratification. Those who speak for the group are usually those most capable of articulating the group's values to the outside world; but such spokesmen are likely to stress, in their articulation of "group" values, the particular values that are most to their own advantage.

In general, then, three useful principles emerge regarding the meaning of culture. First, people value customs even when they seem irrational to an outsider; the symbolic value is a real personal value. A second principle must also be recognized, however—namely that cultures can change endogenously. Urbanization, the search for profits, and the accumulation of power and privilege in Africa are not merely Western impositions; they are indigenously generated reactions to new economic opportunities and structures. Finally, conflicts occur within communities regarding the social or individual value of customs. Just as those who attempt to modify or change customs may have personal interests in so doing, so also do those who attempt to preserve them.

The above analysis suggests why, in the face of so much evidence to the contrary, some African intellectuals persist in presenting the communal model of social organization in Africa as if it were fact, and in maintaining that the group-oriented, consensual, and redistributive value system is the only value system in Africa and hence that it ought to be the basis of a uniquely African model of human rights. Ideological denials of economic and political inequalities assist members of the African ruling class to stay in power.

A more charitable explanation may be that African intellectuals are themselves victims of the intellectual imperialism they so vigorously decry. Blocked in their earlier attempts to Europeanize and join the dominant Western culture,[32] they have instead adopted the long-standing Western myth of the noble savage who exemplifies the virtues of generosity and self-sacrifice within his own community.[33] The noble savage is incapable of a selfish, profit-seeking act. But he is also incapable of the scientific and technological innovation that such selfishness allegedly impels, and that is the basis of Western economic, political, and cultural dominance in the contemporary world. The noble African is doomed to stagnation in his closed, isolated, subsistence-level village, while the mundane Westerner pursues individual wealth and collective economic prosperity in the modern city.

The Ghanaian philosopher J.E. Wiredu suggests that the search for "authenticity," whether in philosophy or in culture, may be an expression of the continued inferiority complex of black Africans. Reacting against their former acceptance of all things colonial, African nationalists now "need" to find their "authentic" culture. Wiredu is criticizing the contention that there is a unique African philosophy, but his remarks can apply just as easily to the contention that there is a unique African culture.

African nationalists in search of an African identity, Afro-Americans in search
of their African roots and Western foreigners in search of exotic diversion—all
demand an African philosophy [culture] that shall be fundamentally different
from Western philosophy. . . . Partly through the influence of Western
anthropology and partly through insufficient critical reflection on the
contemporary African situation, many very well placed Africans are apt to
identify African thought [culture] with *traditional* African thought. . . . these
Africans have been in the habit of calling loudly, even stridently, for the
cultivation of an African authenticity or personality.[34]

On the other hand, such a call for authenticity, in Wiredu's view, may
be "merely a political slogan."[35] Other authors agree. In a very early article
on African socialism, Kopytoff suggested that "profound social and
political reorganization is probably impossible without a body of mythology about the past and the desired future."[36] African communalism, then,
is a "social mythology" that, as interpreted in Kaunda's humanism or
Nyerere's socialism, provides a guiding tool for economic and political
reconstruction. The political function of the myth of African communalism is to provide an ideological mechanism for the social reorganization
necessitated by state-building.

But such a political function may serve a class as well as a national
purpose. The advocacy of a theory of African communalism by African
intellectuals may well be in their own self-interest. In general the defense
of "indigenous" customs by African intellectuals facilitates their "big-
man" domination over local groups who find their cherished values
threatened. The myth of the "palaver state," in which contentious issues
are "talked out" until a consensually agreed decision is reached, permits
the evolution of a one-party dictatorship and eventually of a ruling class.
The Nigerian political scientist Claude Ake maintains that African leaders
refer back to the "traditional" palaver form of government as a means of
blocking popular demands for participation in decision-making. The
leaders proclaim "the end of internal ideological conflict. . . . The African
tradition of unanimity has to be rehabilitated . . . as an argument against
dissent, interest articulation, and democratic participation."[37]

Similarly, the myth of the redistributive economy permits the corrupt
practice of nepotistic allocation of state resources to officials' kinsmen and
co-ethnics. Patron-client relationships based on the village model, in
which the better-off assume responsibility for the worse-off, substitute for
real structural change in the allocation of resources. All of these ideals
allow the new wealthy to justify their retention of power as long as they
allocate some of their (or the state's) property to those poorer than
themselves; the recipients then become their political supporters in a
round of clientilistic or ethnically based politics, which precludes political
organization across ethnic lines on a class basis. Keeping in mind, again,
that those who seek to retain, as well as those who seek to change, cultures

and custom may have a material interest in so doing, it is well to approach African intellectuals' proponence of the communal model of human rights with a judicious degree of skepticism.

Modernization and the Creation of the Individual

The obverse of the myth of communalism in Africa is the existence of a competitive, profit-oriented, individualistic society. In this section, I will argue that "traditional" African society has given way to just such a "modern" society.

The term "modernization" has justifiably fallen into some disrepute among theorists of underdevelopment in recent years. For too long, there was a false dichotomization of all societies into traditional and modern. While the traditional was often romanticized, the modern, quite often based on current American society, was held up as a model toward which all societies should strive. Furthermore, all traditional societies were assumed to share the same characteristics; no differentiation was made among them. Marxist theory, which differentiates among pre-capitalist societies through the use of mode of production analysis, was clearly an improvement over this tendency. Finally, the assumption was made that all modern societies would be the same. Yet cultural and structural differences abound—for example between Japan and the United States or between Britain and the Soviet Union.

I do not assume that Commonwealth Africa is traveling along an inevitable continuum, destined to become an exact replica of the industrialized Western world. Africa is underdeveloped, and its continued dependence for its economic progress on the world economy makes it doubtful that its economic path will exactly resemble that which occurred in Western Europe over the last several centuries. Even if such economic development were to occur, African culture would not become an exact copy of the Western. It is true that many "Westernized" features can be found in any urban, or even rural, African setting today, not only among the rich with their cars and personal electronic equipment but among the poor dancing to street recordings of black American and West Indian singers. On the other hand, certain specifically African cultural practices, such as polygyny, remain common. Moreover, both Islam and the Africanized Christian churches are powerful retainers of non-Western modes of thought. Modernization is neither a unidirectional, a continuous, nor an inevitable process.

Nevertheless, the term "modernization" is useful to describe certain social-psychological processes of individuation that have been occurring in Commonwealth Africa over the last hundred years, if not longer, and which strongly imply the need for individual human rights. By *social-*

psychological I mean processes of change that affect the psychologies of entire groups of people: their modes of personal behavior, their belief systems, and their individual "needs." A new "modern man" (and woman) has been emerging in Commonwealth Africa. Human nature is malleable, especially in situations of extreme social-structural change. Culture, similarly, is not static; rather, the sum total of all the individual changes in psyche results in new cultural organization as well.

Table 2.1 presents some standard indicators of modernization in Commonwealth Africa that have affected the process of individuation. Most important is the process of urbanization, which has detached many people from their primary kin/clan and village communities and has removed them to heterogeneous, multiethnic, and culturally novel environments. Four countries, Ghana, Nigeria, Sierra Leone, and Zambia, are now more than 20 percent urban. More important, urban growth rates are extremely high, well over population growth rates (see Table 4.3). Most of the urban growth is caused not by natural internal increase, but by rural-urban migration.

Both the "push" of the rural areas and the "pull" of urban areas cause such migration. The key factors involved, for both men and women, are "limited resources and personal satisfaction."[38] Life in the rural areas of Commonwealth Africa is becoming increasingly difficult as land scarcity increases and as peasants earn less for their cash crops (see Chapter 4). Urban areas, even when formal employment opportunities are few and housing, food and water have to be paid for in cash, offer many employment opportunities in the informal sector and far more facilities for education and medical care. Furthermore, many people find the cohesive, integrated rural life so extolled by some of the African intellectuals mentioned earlier in this chapter extremely repressive. The cities offer more personal freedom: the chance to attend the cinema, to listen to new music, to meet new people, and above all to escape the authority of family or village elders. Women flee rural areas to escape witchcraft accusations, the envy of jealous neighbors, or unhappy marriages.[39] Africans make personal decisions to live in cities for the same reasons that Westerners do: increased or more-varied economic opportunities combined with vastly increased occasions to exercise personal freedom in social matters.

The spread of national systems of education and the mass media also facilitates the creation of a national modern society. Adult literacy rates are often used merely as indicators of how many people in a society can read or write. But insofar as literacy programs and children's education are controlled by governments, literacy rates are indicators as well of the numbers of people who are modernized, in the sense that they encounter the new ideas that the authorities wish to promulgate. Tanzania, for example, appears to have made the most impressive strides in adult literacy among the nine Commonwealth countries, with 66 percent of the

Table 2.1 Indicators of Modernization

	Gambia	Ghana	Kenya	Malawi	Nigeria	Sierra Leone	Uganda	Tanzania	Zambia
1. Percent of population that is urban (1982)	n.d.	37.0	15.0	10.0	21.0	23.0	9.0	13.0	45.0
2. Average annual growth rate of urban population (1970–82) (percent)	5.0 (1970–80)	5.0	7.3	6.4	4.9	3.9	3.4	8.5	6.5
3. Adult literacy rate									
1960	6	27	20	n.d.	15	7	35	10	n.d.
1976	10	n.d.	45	25	n.d.	n.d.	n.d.	66	39
4. Number of daily newspapers (1979)	n.d.	5	3	2	15	1	1	2	2
5. Newspaper circulation per 1,000 people (estimate, 1979)	n.d.	n.d.	10	5	n.d.	n.d.	2	11	19
6. Number of fixed cinemas (35 mm and other films)	n.d.	7 (1979)	40 (1977)	n.d.	120 (1979)	n.d.	17 (1977)	34 (1981)	12 (1976)
7. Annual attendance at cinemas (millions)	n.d.	4.0	6.0	n.d.	3.5	n.d.	1.6	4.0	1.6
8. Radios per 1,000 inhabitants									
1965	115	71	n.d.	20	n.d.	11	n.d.	10	12
1981	120	166	33	46	73	98	22	28	24
9. TV sets per 1,000 inhabitants									
1965	n.d.	0.1	1.0	n.d.	0.6	0.5	0.7	n.d.	n.d.
1981	n.d.	6	4.0	n.d.	6.0	6.0	6.0	0.4	12

n.d. = no data.

Source: lines 1–3: The World Bank, Accelerated Development in Sub-Saharan Africa (Washington, D.C.: The World Bank, 1981), Tables 36 and 38; and idem, World Development Report (New York: Oxford University Press, 1984), Table 22.
Lines 4–9: UNESCO, Statistical Yearbook (Paris: United Nations Educational, Scientific and Cultural Organization, 1983), Tables 7:18, 8:3, 9:2, and 9:4.

adult population literate by 1976. Yet one outspoken critic of the Tanzanian regime suggests that the real purpose of education in Tanzania is political propaganda: "up to 75% of the school time is spent in the school farm, parading, slogan-singing, entertaining political leaders or receiving official guests. [Parents complain that] all [the children] know after . . . seven years of primary school is to sing Party slogans."[40]

But even if propaganda is the main function of schooling, the acquisition of literacy and numeracy cannot help but increase both the modern aspects of Africans' psychology and their potential to think critically about the society in which they live. Schools are indeed a socializing mechanism, but students are capable of turning received ideas to their own purposes, as Christian converts in colonial societies did in applying Christ's egalitarian doctrines to themselves. The literate person reads comic books, broadsheets, newspapers, and other printed sources. The literate person is thus individualized in the sense that he has not only the capacity to acquire a great deal of information, but a mode of expression of his individual thought.

Literates, then, are able to use the mass media. While the circulation of newspapers is still quite low, it does not completely reflect readership. Newspapers are passed about from one reader to the next, literates read them to illiterates, and they may end their days wrapped around produce in a marketplace, and then find a further reader in the purchaser of the groundnuts or other produce they protect.

Moreover, the numbers of radios and televisions in Commonwealth Africa are multiplying rapidly. In five countries, there are now fewer than 25 people per radio.[41] Even taking into account their uneven distribution among rich and poor, and between urban and rural areas, the possibility now exists that almost everyone in Africa has at least occasional access to a radio. Communal, not private, listening is the norm in rural areas. Most governments attempt to broadcast for a few minutes every day or week in each major language group; thus the national Nigerian news, broadcast in English, is briefly summarized every day in the minority Tiv language.[42] Even if one has never visited a city, then, one is still in touch with the national society, and one can still be affected by new ideas, modes of thought, and life.

Cinemas are also important socializing and individualizing mechanisms. Even the isolated peasant whose only experience with cinema has been an antimalarial film shown by a volunteer development agency has encountered a new view of the world and a new mode of expression. The urban dweller who sees imported Western films has had a much closer encounter with the world of materialism and individualism. Such a world is often attractive, conducive to the revolution of rising (material) expectations which so many Third World governments are now having difficulty fulfilling.

Urbanization, literacy, and the spread of the mass media are only a few of the indicators of how people are uprooted from or transcend their historical, small-scale village roots. Much more important are the new economic, political, and social relations briefly alluded to earlier in this chapter and described in detail in Chapters 3 to 8. The typical African of the late 20th century is no longer, if he or she ever was, the anthropologically unique inhabitant of a closed village society. The "peoples" whom the African Charter of Human and Peoples' Rights purports to protect are disintegrating. The concept of group rights fails to recognize that in modernizing, urbanizing Africa, people are less and less members of particular rural, ethnically homogeneous groups, and more and more individuals with a multiplicity of associational ties.[43]

Even the extended family, so lovingly extolled by many commentators as a symbol of the sense of community of traditional African societies,[44] breaks down in urban areas. The reason is quite simple: extended families make more economic sense in rural than in urban areas. In rural areas, especially where land is relatively plentiful, family members can cooperate in agricultural tasks (although their product is likely to be privately owned) and in child-rearing, food preparation, housing, and defense. In urban areas, where housing, food, fuel, and water have to be purchased in cash, extended families become very difficult to support, while their labor power is far less valuable. Kinship obligations are particularly onerous to the new privileged classes, those who have acquired modern educational and technical skills and with them "modern" tastes for material acquisition. Among Ghanaian businessmen, for example, the tendency is to give material support only to those kin who actually work in one's enterprise,[45] rather than to any kin who happen to be present. Among elite Lagos women, family size is declining as mothers juggle full-time modern jobs with child-rearing.[46]

In declining traditional Africa, social roles are undifferentiated. The villager who fulfills his role as husband is also fulfilling his role as farmer and as respected man in the community. But in urbanizing and modernizing Africa, role segmentation is increasingly the norm. What one does in one aspect of one's life does not necessarily reinforce what one does in another aspect. The roles of husband, economic man, and political man are differentiated; the good father who takes his sick child to the clinic is the poor employee who does not show up for work on time. A person's ascribed status, that is, the status he was born with, no longer completely defines his role. The son of a slave can become prime minister. Similarly one's biological sex and age are no longer complete definers of the role one plays in life; one's achievement in education, in occupation, and in competition for political rewards now has considerable bearing on one's life.

In a society in which achievement as well as ascription now define one's place in life, the breakdown of the traditional concept of dignity becomes apparent. If dignity is a sense of self-worth that comes from fulfilling one's prescribed role in life, from adhering to societal norms and expectations, how does one retain dignity when roles and norms change? The new values of achievement and competitiveness may well strike many Africans, as they strike many Europeans and North Americans, as repugnant. They are not values indigenous to all African societies; or where they are indigenous, they may well be subordinate to other values. According to Kirk-Greene, for example, the good man in Hausa society is the man who values truth, exhibits friendliness and generosity, and treats others (especially his inferiors) with courtesy and respect.[47] Nevertheless, inferiors do exist among the Hausa. The stated values of goodness should be taken as an indication of actual individual motives and practice no more than the stated Christian values of goodness in the Western world. The loss of dignity in the new Africa is also a loss of restrictive ascribed statuses, which many people find oppressive. Urbanization and new values may have been originally introduced to Commonwealth Africa by Western economic and ideological imperialism, but their retention in Africa today is as much a consequence of choice by African individuals as it is of any presumed cultural compulsion.

In contemporary Commonwealth Africa the individual's life, with its multiplicity of noncomplementary roles, is increasingly complex. So is the society he lives in: ethnically heterogeneous, stratified by class, characterized by a complex division of labor, and erosive of traditional status, age and sex rankings. In this situation, the individual begins to rely less on his primary group and far more on secondary groups, characterized not by affective or kin ties but by commonality of purpose. The individual is moving from community to association in his relations with the modern world. Thus he may be simultaneously a member of an ethnically homogeneous "hometown" group, an ethnically heterogeneous trade union, a Christian or Islamic denomination, a market association, a sports club, and a neighborhood or ratepayer's association. All of these associations are differentiated by function, and the individual member is easily able to separate them out in his own life.

The person who has moved psychologically from a homogeneous rural area to a heterogeneous urban area, from ascription to achievement, from primary to secondary groups, and from community to association, is a person who may or may not mourn the social rootedness he has lost. According to some social commentators, such an individual is characterized by a "homeless mind,"[48] a loss of sense of place. He is confronted by a routinized, bureaucratized, and impersonal society; his sense of self is at risk. But other commentators suggest that it is in just such an anonymous society, with its loosened social control, that the individual self is able to flourish. New kinds of communities, formed by choice rather than by accident of birth, arise in modern cities. Even in the most supposedly alienating urban environments, people form social networks, often based on modern characteristics such as education or profession.

Often these new social networks or associations constitute potential sources of opposition to governments that are attempting to become totalitarian, in the true sense of having total control over a society. Professional groups, such as lawyers and trade unions, are especially likely to become centers of articulate political unrest.[49] Indeed, it is precisely such voluntary groups, mediating between the isolated individual and the large centralizing state, that are crucial to the development of political democracy. Thus, when political leaders, like Kaunda of Zambia, reject such new associational ties as disintegrative of traditional communities,[50] one must query whether such rejection is not in fact expressive of the political ruling class's fear of the establishment not only of independent bases of power, but indeed of independent bases of thought.

In the final analysis, the newly created individual of Commonwealth Africa confronts the overwhelming power of the state. In the new national societies of Commonwealth Africa, traditional checks on the powers of chiefs in small-scale, homogeneous societies have long disintegrated. In contemporary Africa, the state and its occupants control all the different institutions of authority and economic distribution: law, government, police, defense, administration, education, and social welfare. In his confrontation with impersonal authority and with the overwhelming reality of class stratification, the individual finds himself and his life compartmentalized. In political relations, therefore, the individual has more than one interest and cannot easily rely on a community leader such as the rural village chief to express all his interests for him. For example, the individual who is denied a university position because of his ethnicity needs to be able to demand his rights as an individual, even while his ethnic group as a collectivity is agitating for a new university in its own geographical region. Similarly, the urban woman needs to be able to demand equal pay for her equal work, even if she is violating the roles her traditional leader would have her play.

The individual in contemporary Africa is, above all, an economic and political man or woman. The lost dignity of traditional society may be perceived by the individual to be personally very liberating; the lost repressiveness of traditional society may be perceived by the state and its ruling class to be very threatening. That the modern individual exists is unquestionable; and it is the modern individual who needs human rights.

Conclusion

The philosophical principle of human rights is as pertinent to Commonwealth Africa as elsewhere in the world. Its pertinence is a result of the fact that Commonwealth Africa is composed of state societies, socially stratified and increasingly individualized. While a weak cultural relativity is useful in correcting any tendency to impose particular forms of human rights on African cultures, such relativity must be confined only to rights that do not involve the citizen's claims on or against the state. Human rights in Africa must be analyzed in terms of the relationship of the individual to the state; the myth of the African communal society in which neither state nor individual existed must be exposed as such.

Human rights are the rights of individuals in opposition to the state. Insofar as the state is in its turn controlled by individuals, however, it is controlled, as I will show in Chapter 3, by a ruling class. Thus human rights are rights that members of the ruling class try to withhold from members of other classes. The principle of human rights is particularly important wherever there are socially stratified state societies.

Notes

1. For arguments propounding a uniquely African concept of human rights, see Asmaron Legesse, "Human Rights in African Political Culture," in Kenneth W. Thompson, ed., *The Moral Imperatives of Human Rights: A World Survey* (Washington, D.C.: University Press of America, 1980), pp. 123–38; Lakshman Marasinghe, "Traditional Conceptions of Human Rights in Africa," in Claude E. Welch, Jr., and Robert I. Meltzer, eds., *Human Rights and Development in Africa* (Albany: State University of New York Press, 1984), pp. 32–45; Chris C. Mojekwu, "International Human Rights: The African Perspective," in Jack L. Nelson and Vera M. Green, eds., *International Human Rights: Contemporary Issues* (Stanfordville, N.Y.: Human Rights Publishing Group, 1980), pp. 85–95; Adamantia Pollis and Peter Schwab, "Human Rights: A Western Concept with Limited Applicability," in Pollis and Schwab, eds., *Human Rights: Cultural and Ideological Perspectives* (New York: Praeger, 1979), pp. 1–18; and Dunstan M. Wai, "Human Rights in Sub-Saharan Africa," in ibid., pp. 115–44.

2. Jack Donnelly, "Human Rights and Human Dignity: An Analytic Critique of Non-Western Human Rights Conceptions," *American Political Science Review* 76, no. 2 (July 1982): 305.

3. Jack Donnelly, *The Concept of Human Rights* (London: Croom Helm, 1985), p. 3. See also A.J.M. Milne, "The Idea of Human Rights: A Critical Inquiry," in F.E. Dowrick, ed., *Human Rights: Problems, Perspectives and Texts* (Westmead, Farnborough, Hants.: Saxon House, 1979), p. 26.

4. David Bidney, "Cultural Relativism," *International Encyclopaedia of the Social Sciences*, vol. 3 (Macmillan, the Free Press, 1968), p. 545.

5. Jack Donnelly, "Cultural Relativism and Universal Human Rights," *Human Rights Quarterly* 6, no. 4 (1984): p. 401.

6. Ibid.

7. Rhoda E. Howard and Jack Donnelly, "Human Dignity, Human Rights and Political Regimes" forthcoming in *American Political Science Review*, September 1986.

8. Kenneth D. Kaunda, *A Humanist in Africa* (London: Longmans, 1966), pp. 24–25.

9. Julius K. Nyerere, *Ujamaa: Essays on Socialism* (London: Oxford University Press, 1968), p. 11.

10. Ifeanyi A. Menkiti, "Person and Community in African Traditional Thought," in Richard A. Wright, ed., *African Philosophy: An Introduction*, 2nd. ed. (Washington, D.C.: University Press of America, 1979), p. 162.

11. Donnelly, "Human Rights and Human Dignity," p. 312.

12. Kaunda, *A Humanist in Africa*, pp. 27–28. Italics in original.

13. Igor Kopytoff and Suzanne Miers, "African 'Slavery' as an Institution of Marginality," in Miers and Kopytoff, eds., *Slavery in Africa* (Madison: University of Wisconsin Press, 1977), p. 17.

14. Grace Akello, *Self Twice-Removed: Uganda Women* (London: Change International Reports, n.d. [1983]), p. 5. Italics in original.

15. Christine Obbo, *African Women: Their Struggle for Economic Independence* (London: Zed Press, 1980), p. 143.

16. Wai, "Human Rights in Sub-Saharan Africa," pp. 116–17.

17. Mojekwu, "International Human Rights," p. 94, fn.1.

18. T.O. Elias, *The Nature of African Customary Law* (Manchester: University of Manchester Press, 1956), p. 107.

19. Ibid., p. 108.

20. Paul E. Lovejoy, "Slavery in the Context of Ideology," in Lovejoy, ed., *The Ideology of Slavery in Africa* (Beverly Hills: Sage, 1981), p. 11.

21. A. Norman Klein, "The Two Asantes: Competing Interpretations of 'Slavery' in Akan-Asante Culture and Society," in Lovejoy, *Ideology*, pp. 152–53.

22. Babatunde Agiri, "Slavery in Yoruba Society in the Nineteenth Century," in Lovejoy, *Ideology*, p. 144.

23. Michael Mason, "Captive and Client Labor and the Economy of the Bida Emirate: 1857–1901," *Journal of African History* 14, no. 3 (1973): 457–58.

24. Frederick Cooper, "Islam and Cultural Hegemony: The Ideology of Slaveowners on the East African Coast," in Lovejoy, *Ideology*, p. 280.

25. Milton Obote, "The Common Man's Charter" (Entebbe: Uganda Government Printer, 1970), p. 7.

26. Eddison Jonas Mudadirwa Zvobgo, "The Abuse of Executive Prerogative: A Purposive Difference between Detention in Black Africa and Detention in White Racist Africa," *Issue: A Journal of Africanist Opinion* 6, no. 4 (Winter 1976): 38.

27. Robert G. Armstrong, "The Public Meeting as a Means of Participation in Political and Social Activities in Africa," in UNESCO, *Socio-Political Aspects of the Palaver in Some African Countries* (UNESCO: Paris, 1979), p. 15.

28. B. W. Karanja-Diejomaoh, "The Palaver in Kenya," in UNESCO, *Socio-Political Aspects*, p. 44.

29. Legesse, "Human Rights in African Political Culture," pp. 125–26.

30. This view is implied in ibid., p. 123.

31. Milton Singer, "The Concept of Culture," *International Encyclopaedia of the Social Sciences*, vol. 3 (Macmillan, the Free Press, 1968), p. 536.

32. Boris S. Erassov, "Concepts of 'Cultural Personality' in the Ideologies of the Third World," *Diogenes* 78 (Summer 1972): 130–31.

33. On this same point, see Igor Kopytoff, "Socialism and Traditional African Societies," in William H. Friedland and Carl G. Rosberg, eds., *African Socialism* (Stanford: Stanford University Press, 1964), p. 53.

34. J.E. Wiredu, "How Not to Compare African Thought with Western

Thought," in Richard A. Wright, ed., *African Philosophy: An Introduction*, 2nd. ed. (Washington, D.C.: University Press of America, 1979), pp. 135, 140. Emphasis in original.

35. Ibid., p. 135.

36. Kopytoff, "Socialism in Traditional African Societies," p. 55. See also Erassov, "Concepts of Cultural Personality," p. 127.

37. Claude Ake, "The Congruence of Political Economies and Ideologies in Africa," in Peter C.W. Gutkind and Immanuel Wallerstein, eds., *The Political Economy of Contemporary Africa* (Beverly Hills: Sage, 1976), p. 205–6.

38. Obbo, *African Women*, p. 70.

39. Ibid., p. 77.

40. Ludovic A. Ngatara, "Free Indoctrination in Tanzania" (Dar es Salaam: 1978), pp. 3–4. Unpublished; available through Human Rights Internet, Washington, D.C.

41. Calculated from Table 2.1, line 8.

42. James Zasha, personal communication.

43. John F. McCamant, "Social Sciences and Human Rights," *International Organization* 35, no. 3 (Summer 1981): 542.

44. Fasil Nahum, "African Contribution to Human Rights." Paper presented at the Seminar on Law and Human Rights in Development, Gaborone, Botswana, May 24–28, 1982.

45. Paul T. Kennedy, *Ghanaian Businessmen: From Artisan to Capitalist Entrepreneur in a Dependent Economy* (Munich and London: Weltforum Verlag, 1980), p. 113.

46. Wambui Wa Karanja, "Women and Work: A Study of Female and Male Attitudes in the Modern Sector of an African Metropolis (Lagos)," in Helen Ware, ed., *Women, Education and Modernization of the Family in West Africa* (Canberra: Australian National University Press, 1981), pp. 42–66.

47. Anthony H.M. Kirk-Greene, "Mutumin Kirkii: The Concept of the Good Man in Hausa." Third annual Hans Wolff Memorial Lecture, African Studies Program, Bloomington, Indiana, 1974.

48. Peter Berger, Brigitte Berger, and Hansfried Kellner, *The Homeless Mind: Modernization and Consciousness* (New York: Vintage Books, 1973).

49. See Chapters 7 and 6 of this volume, respectively.

50. Kenneth D. Kaunda, *Humanism in Zambia and a Guide to Its Implementation* (Lusaka: [Government Printer] 1967), p. 4.

3 Social Structure, the State, and Human Rights

A society's capacity to realize human rights is most strongly affected by its social structure. Social structure includes the modes of production, distribution, and consumption of material goods; social stratification and class relations; and the political realm, especially the control and powers of the state. Human rights abuses vary according to the type of social structure that exists.

The countries of Commonwealth Africa analyzed in this book are all state societies. However incompletely formed or integrated the still relatively new states are, they are the overwhelming political reality. States control the legal use of force, they defend borders and national integrity, they make economic policy, and they control the allocation of scarce welfare goods. The group that controls the state in Commonwealth Africa controls the many resources to which it has access. The key political battles are among groups competing for outright control of the state, while subsidiary battles are fought for access to the state. The state in Africa is the key not only to power and prestige, but to privilege, wealth and, in some cases, mere subsistence.

Thus it makes sense in Africa, as in the developed world, to define human rights as claims by the individual citizen on or against the state. One's rights can be violated by non-state actors; one can be tortured by common criminals; one's property can be stolen by common thieves. But these are incidental violations, normally prohibited by even the most repressive state, rather than systematic violations induced by state policy or by state practice. The more important violations of human rights are those for which the state is responsible.

The relationship between the citizen and the state, however, is actually a relationship between the citizen and those who control the state. The state does not behave in a neutral administrative fashion for the good of all; rather, the state reflects the interests of those social groups that make up and control it. In Commonwealth Africa, the state is some combination of the government, the ruling party, the civil service, and the military. The people who hold high office in all four of these institutions generally have group and personal reasons for using such office to further their private interests. Collectively they, and the interest groups they represent, are the ruling class.

To understand who comprise the ruling class in Africa, and also to be able to analyze possibilities for checks on the ruling class's use of power, one must first understand the underlying social structure. In Chapter 2, it was pointed out that independent Africa did not emerge from a romantic, egalitarian, and stateless condition, as many advocates of cultural relativism in human rights suggest. Rather, social stratification and the abuse of what we now call human rights was a common feature in most pre-colonial African societies. In Chapter 1, the main "human rights" features of British colonial rule were enumerated. Independent Africa inherited both the old social institutions of the pre-colonial era and the new social institutions of the colonial period. In the last 25 years, both sets of institutions have been modified by the ruling class in its own interests.

The exact nature of the African ruling class is a consequence of its economic basis. One of the chief difficulties in realizing human rights in Commonwealth Africa is its extreme poverty. Poverty both limits the resources that can be distributed and exaggerates the desire of the ruling class to control as many resources as possible. This chapter, therefore, will begin with a look at the basic economic and social structure of contemporary Commonwealth Africa. It will continue with an analysis of the nature of the ruling class and a discussion of the resources available to it. Finally, there will be an analysis of how and why the ruling class uses the state to abuse human rights. This discussion as a whole sets the analytical framework for Chapters 4 through 8, which describe in detail a variety of human rights abuses which serve to maintain the African ruling class.

Peripheral Capitalist Society

The economic structure of Commonwealth Africa can best be described as peripheral capitalism. Commonwealth Africa is integrated into the dominant world capitalist economy, but in a peripheral, rather than a central, location. Moreover, its own productive structure is incompletely capitalist. Precapitalist modes of production, especially peasant agriculture, continue to exist in Africa side by side with incipient capitalist production, and indeed to subsidize the capitalist sector.

Commonwealth Africa is peripheral to the wider world economy. It is dependent on the core capitalist countries for markets, capital, and a large proportion of its consumer goods. Yet this dependence is not reciprocal. The primary commodities that Commonwealth Africa exports to the West (e.g., cocoa, tea, coffee, tobacco, palm products, and minerals) are not crucial to the world economy and, increasingly, can be obtained elsewhere (for example, from Brazil for cocoa and coffee). Even Nigerian oil and Zambian copper, essential commodities for the industrial world, are subject to severe price fluctuations and to competition from other suppliers. Thus Commonwealth Africa is in a structurally weak position, dependent on world markets it cannot control to buy its few exports and to supply its multitude of import needs.

This structural position is the result of almost five centuries of incorporation into the world capitalist economy. From the 16th to the mid-19th century, West Africa was a chief source of slaves for the new plantation economies of the Americas. East Africa, more isolated from European influence, suffered from the Arab slave trade. In the mid- to late 19th century, both the European and the Arab slave trades were abolished and replaced by what was then known as "legitimate" commerce. This commerce was mostly in agricultural goods for the new mass markets of industrial Europe and America, although Zambia also became a major world supplier of copper. In East Africa, especially Kenya, white settlers began to colonize the better land in the early 20th century, displacing indigenous African producers who were then hired as laborers on the European farms. Since the beginning of the period of formal colonization in the late 19th century, the product composition of Commonwealth Africa's exports has changed little, even with attempts to diversify the various economies after independence.

After the inception of legitimate trade with Europe, a gradual transformation of the economic basis of the ordinary African's existence occurred. In the pre-colonial era, most ordinary Africans, whether freemen or slaves, had not been dependent on markets for most of their daily subsistence. While there were long-distance markets in rare goods such as salt, these were controlled by imperial officials and independent castes of merchants. The ordinary African had little to do with any market outside his or her own local area, where he or she might, for example, engage in a highly ritualized exchange of a woven cloth for a basket. The market place existed, but the market principle, whereby all commodities and indeed human labor power itself were assigned a monetary value, was not yet known. Most commodities necessary for human existence were produced and consumed by the family unit on land allocated to that unit by lineage or tribal authorities.

Legitimate trade gradually changed the pre-colonial subsistence cultivator into a peasant.[1] Peasants continue to produce some of their own subsistence needs, but they are heavily integrated into the world economy. They produce and sell, for cash, products the world economy demands, and they are in turn dependent on that economy for much of their own consumption. Originally, many African peasants "joined" the world economy on a voluntary basis; new opportunites to acquire material goods such as liquor, arms, cloth, and beads presented themselves,[2] and it was relatively costless to convert some land to produce whatever crops Europeans demanded. By the 20th century, however, most peasants, even the poorest, had become dependent on the world economy for a large part of their consumption needs—for example, kerosene, matches, sugar, salt, and cloth.

The new relations of Africans with the world market transformed economic relations at home as well. Once the profit motive was introduced, resources that had been distributed previously on a need basis began to command a price. Land, previously distributed on the basis of a family unit's ability to farm it, became increasingly valuable. Chiefs, who originally controlled land allocation by virtue of their ritual status, began to acquire an interest in keeping land for themselves in order to cultivate crops for the world market. Groups of migrants began to travel from their homes to "foreign" areas to rent or buy land for cash-cropping from the indigenous inhabitants. Labor also began to command a price, explicit in the case of the emerging market in migrants who traveled to prosperous cash-cropping areas to work for the indigenous land-owners, and implicit in the exploitation of the labor of "youngmen" and women by male household heads.

Peasants who were able to exploit larger areas of land for cash crops, who controlled more labor power, or who were otherwise able to acquire more resources began to be differentiated from those who were land-poor, had fewer relatives to work the land, or who simply had comparatively worse luck. The more prosperous peasants, including many chiefs, became middlemen in cash-crop exporting, merchants of consumer goods in the interior, or money-lenders. Thus an emerging "peasant bourgeoisie" began to dominate rural Africa. Male dominance over women was also consolidated as male household heads exploited women's labor power in their production for the world market, but kept the resultant cash income for themselves.

The social structure that emerged during the colonial period remains the basis of contemporary social stratification in Commonwealth Africa. The vast majority of the population is agrarian and peasant-based. Peasants are stratified by income level and by access to modern resources of economic progress, now including not only land and labor power, but also education, credit, and government agricultural aid programs. In analytical terms, what the peasants sell to the world market is not their actual productive capacity, but rather their "surplus" product. That is to say, they are not paid a wage on the basis of the cost of the resources they invest in producing the crop. Land is not yet fully capitalized in Commonwealth Africa, although it is increasingly scarce. As for labor power, the returns depend on the price paid for the crop either on the world market or by the state monopoly marketing board. Thus the peasant producer's products are vulnerable to world market vicissitudes, which he cannot control for economic reasons, or to arbitrary price changes set by bureaucrats running state purchasing corporations, which he cannot control for political reasons, or both.

This peasant mode of production is incompletely capitalist: it is not based upon a complete calculation of returns to the various factors of production. Insofar as peasants can still partially support themselves by production of subsistence crops, they will devote uneconomically large amounts of time (labor power) to relatively small marginal returns on the cash-crop market. Thus the existence of a subsistence sector subsidizes the production of cheap agricultural export commodities. Insofar as marketing of peasant-produced cash crops is controlled by state boards that often pay the original producers well below world market prices and retain the difference as a tax, African peasants thus also subsidize the urban population on whom that tax is most likely to be spent.

The large peasant sector subsidizes not only the world market in primary commodities, but also the incomplete industrial sector at home. Industrial activity in Commonwealth Africa consists of three distinct sectors. First is genuine industrial production for the world or home market. Very little of this type of production exists anywhere on the continent except in South Africa. In the modern world economy, profits depend on the existence of what Marx referred to as "relative," as opposed to "absolute," surplus value.[3] Surplus value, according to Marx, results when a worker produces more, in the course of a certain period of time, than is needed for his own continued existence. Absolute surplus value is generated by forcing the worker to toil for very long hours at very simple tasks with relatively uncomplicated machinery; such was the situation in early industrial England. In the 20th century, the extreme exploitation of the physical capacity of the worker has been replaced by the use of sophisticated machinery, so that in the course of a much shorter working day, the worker can produce much more value. This value, based upon a capital-intensive approach to production, is known as "relative" surplus value. But not only is the physical capital, in the extraction of relative surplus value, much more sophisticated; so also is the human capital, the worker himself. Contemporary workers in the Western economy are much healthier, much more educated, and much more disciplined to the time- and motion-specific needs of the industrial economy than either their 19th-century predecessors at home or their 20th-century counterparts in Africa.

Sub-Saharan African workers have not yet been necessary to the world economy as producers of industrial goods. So far, the industrial relocations of the new international division of labor have been to Southeast Asia and certain South American countries such as Brazil. Because Africans are not in world demand as industrial workers, there has been very little international investment in them as human capital, and thus they are still unsuited to sophisticated industrial production. Transnational corporations have little productive, as opposed to extractive, interest in Commonwealth Africa. The economic infrastructure in Commonwealth Africa is extremely limited, transport and communication are still very primitive, and administration is unreliable. In addition, since African laborers are not good producers of relative surplus value, for reasons beyond their own control, very little real industrial development has occured in Africa. Africa's share of world manufacturing in 1973 was a minuscule 0.6 percent.[4]

Thus industrial production in Africa consists mainly of a second type, extractive activities. The major type of extraction is mineral, and it is not coincidental that the most "Western" working class in Commonwealth Africa (with, as well, the most classically Marxist working-class consciousness) is composed of the copper miners in Zambia. Elsewhere mineral extraction employing African workers is limited, despite the diamond mines in Sierra Leone and gold mines in Ghana. Nigerian oil extraction is conducted almost entirely by transnational companies using highly sophisticated technology, which entails the employment of only a few, relatively highly paid Nigerian workers.[5]

Aside from such mineral extraction, industrial production in Commonwealth Africa is confined to a third type, low-level assembly operations. These assembly factories (for example, of automobiles in Nigeria) are often uneconomically protected by the state as "infant industries." Often such assembly operations are established not because they are profitable, but as a consequence of supposedly development-oriented policies. Transnational corporations, which frequently control or manage such industries, often have no choice but to establish them in exchange for government permission to continue with their more profitable extractive activities in Africa.

The small size of the industrial sector has important implications for class formation in Commonwealth Africa, and consequently for an analysis of human rights. In the Western world, there are two historical/theoretical models for the attainment of human rights. The liberal model, which focuses on civil and political rights as the means to establish democracy, is based upon the attainment of power by the bourgeoisie; that is, the class of industrial property owners who rose to power in 18th- and 19th-century Western Europe. The gradual extension of "bourgeois" rights to the rest of the citizenry allowed for further pressure on the state for welfare reforms in the 19th and 20th centuries. The socialist model, which focuses more on economic and social rights, is based upon the attainment of power by a party allegedly representing the proletariat; that is, the class of industrial workers whose exploitation by the bourgeoisie, it is contended, will inevitably rouse them to take power from the ruling capitalist class.

These two models of how class formation influences the eventual attainment of human rights are grossly oversimplified, yet the latter model, especially, has a powerful appeal in Commonwealth Africa. Many Marxist African intellectuals reduce the problem of human rights to a problem of economic equality, and they assume that the creation or entrenchment of an African proletariat will result in a revolution against the ruling classes, hence automatically in the acquisition of human rights. "Human rights," in this model, are analyzable only as the objective and inevitable consequences of a certain kind of revolution. This model also assumes that no human rights exist in "bourgeois" society. Yet a case can be made that in Commonwealth Africa, the development of a bourgeoisie that would possess economic resources independent of its ties to the state would substantially increase the opportunities for the attainment of human rights. Such a bourgeoisie would need to preserve its own capitalist interests against those of the state; for example, it might resent having to pay bribes or provide kickbacks for government contracts. When the bourgeoisie and the state come into conflict, the stage is set for demands for civil and political rights.

The underdevelopment of the capitalist sector in Commonwealth Africa must therefore be viewed as a serious structural obstacle to human rights, even if one does not accept the Marxist revolutionary view of rights. A small dependent bourgeoisie cannot fight for its own rights vis-à-vis the state, nor can it generate a large industrial sector, which, in its turn, would produce a class-conscious, autonomous proletariat. Yet the "bourgeois" model of human rights, based upon the historical experience of Western Europe and North America, presupposes that the bourgeoisie eventually generates its own opposition. An increasingly sophisticated, literate, and organized proletariat begins to demand the same civil and political rights as the bourgeoisie, as well as new rights of economic security and equality. The proletariat does not necessarily act in revolutionary fashion, but the threat of revolution, insurrection, or indeed only of interruptions in production is behind all its reformist demands. These threats frequently force the state to make concessions.

In Commonwealth Africa today the potential for realization of either the revolutionary or the reformist models of human rights is very limited. The largest social class is still the peasantry. Historically, the peasantry has been a quiescent social class. Peasants are too isolated, fragmented, and circumscribed by illiteracy and by the hardships of eking out their daily existence to be able to organize on a long-term basis for acquisition of human rights. Unless they are led by an efficient "vanguard" political party, as in China during the 1930s and '40s, their political action is limited to sporadic revolt against particularly oppressive masters. And both in capitalist countries and in those in which allegedly "proletarian" revolutions have succeeded, the peasantry tends to be exploited for its food- and raw material–producing capacity by the ruling class, regardless of whether the latter is a capitalist class or an official class representing the ruling party. Such is also the pattern in contemporary Commonwealth Africa, where the ruling classes consistently exploit the peasantry on behalf of the urban sector.

The urban population of Commonwealth Africa is subsidized by the continued existence of the peasant sector in two ways. First, as already discussed, much of the profit from peasant-produced cash-cropping is siphoned off through state marketing boards for eventual use by the ruling class that controls the government, ruling party, military, and civil service. Second, although the sex ratio in the cities is gradually becoming more balanced, many men still leave their wives and children at home on the land, where they are expected to support themselves through food crop production. Many people who migrate to African cities can do so only because when all else fails, they can return for limited periods of time, or permanently, to their rural base. Nevertheless, as land in the countryside is becoming increasingly commoditized and subject to sale to wealthier peasants or to urban residents, and to expropriation by the state in the name of "development" plans,[6] opportunities for the urban underemployed to return to the countryside are disappearing.

There is extreme underemployment of labor power in the burgeoning cities of Commonwealth Africa, where most employment exists outside the bounds of the stunted industrial sector. Many urban migrants become part of the "informal" productive sector. This sector consists of very small-scale craft production and services; in fact, a good designation for many people in this sector is "petty commodity producers,"[7] reflecting the fact that they create real value in the urban economy. One opportunity for male employment in the informal sector is traditional crafts, often organized by the remnants of pre-colonial guilds.[8] Men also make money in the interstices of the modern economy, taking casual employment in small-scale, indigenously owned industries or by providing nontraditional services; for example, as letter writers, bicycle repairers, and wandering "wayside fitters" for the broken-down automobiles ubiquitous on African highways.

Women, in the meantime, engage in retail trade and provide cooked food and sexual services for male bachelors or temporarily single migrants. Female labor power subsidizes the very low wages earned by industrially employed men in the urban areas. Very few African women are "housewives" in the sense that they employ themselves completely in domestic labor and child-rearing; more commonly they also engage in some sort of cash-earning activity. African families reproduce themselves by the combined earning power of both parents.

The economic structure of Commonwealth Africa, then, is peripherally capitalist for two reasons: it relies on the continuation of the peasant sector for its existence, and it engages in very little real industrial production, based on the generation of relative surplus value. Rather, it is a marginally capitalist economy. The chief resource of the nine countries under discussion is agricultural or mineral extraction, rather than industrial production or indeed even processing of agricultural/mineral products (such as Nigeria's oil). What little manufacturing does occur in the formal, modern sector is not geared toward self-sustaining internal development; few employment opportunities are created as a result of mining or assembly-type activities. The informal sector, which does provide employment for many Africans, is unfortunately not encouraged by government policies, which in both allegedly "capitalist"-oriented economies (such as Kenya and Nigeria) and allegedly "socialist" ones (such as Tanzania and Zambia) are dictated by the desire of the ruling class to control as much of the profit-making, or graft-producing, activities of the country as they can in their own interests.

The African Ruling Class

Human rights in Commonwealth Africa are dependent on a system in which the ruling class, as a collective body, manipulates the state in its own interests. Conflicts occur among different factions of the ruling class, but there is very little real political competition between it and any other social class. The non-ruling-class masses in Africa are generally excluded from the political process. Most governments are dominated by the military, by a one-party bureaucracy, or by a no-party dictatorship. Trade unions are generally banned or incorporated into the state structure, as are mass organizations of women or youth. Ethnically based organizations are tolerated as long as their activities are perceived to be cultural or dedicated to group self-help, but are frequently banned when they are perceived to have a political intent. Similarly, religious organizations are tolerated as long as nothing in their doctrine or practice challenges the authority of the state. There are few voluntary organizations dedicated to influencing the political process, in the lobbying manner typical of developed North American and Western European democracies. Thus politics in Commonwealth Africa is a competition among different factions of the ruling class for the biggest possible share of a very shallow bowl of stew.

This view of the ruling class is based upon an analysis of "class action [as] an interpretive conception."[9] That is to say, one must deduce the results of the ruling class's actions from their objective behavior. Subjectively, it is possible that individual members of the ruling class are motivated by the best of intentions. Objectively, however, their positions as members of the ruling class result in their taking actions that either explicitly or implicitly benefit themselves. A man might join the state bureaucracy, for example, to engage in better development planning, which he hopes will benefit the masses of peasants in his country. But he then becomes entitled to the benefits of state-subsidized housing, transport, and food; and, especially in a situation of economic crisis, such benefits begin to outweigh his rational perception of the inequities of state-subsidized resources for the already better-off. The subjective motivations of those who control the state cannot be ascertained. Even if, for example, one could interview a random sample of Commonwealth African leaders, it might not be in their interests to candidly reveal their motives. In any case, their motives and the objective consequences of their actions could contradict each other. What can be observed and analyzed are the actions taken, and policies generated by, the African ruling class and their consequences for the society as a whole.

In taking this position I do not wish to "objectivize" the actions of Commonwealth African rulers so completely as to absolve them of all capacity for rational action or moral responsibility. Chapter 2 argued that African peasants and workers, like their counterparts elsewhere, are rational human beings who manipulate all possible resources in order to survive in the manner of their own choosing. Exactly the same can be said of the African ruling class. While the motives of individuals are not easily, if at all, discovered by academic researchers, and while it is not the business of the social scientist to judge individual action, it is the business of both those who make, and those who are affected by, human rights policies to judge themselves. The individual is an actor in history, even if the history he makes is substantially affected by structural constraints. In this respect, members of the African ruling class are no less culpable or less susceptible to moral judgment than their ruling-class counterparts in Western democratic societies, or indeed anywhere else.

The different components of the African ruling class are easily identified. They are, first, those who occupy high office in the government, parastatal (government-owned) corporations, the ruling party (where it exists), the civil service, and the military. Depending on the level of economic development and the economic system of the country, the ruling class may also include independent members of the incipient bourgeoisie, as opposed to those whose economic wealth is predicated upon occupying state office. So-called "traditional" chiefs, who may control large ethnically based clienteles through their rights to allocate land and other resources, and whose sons or nephews will have privileged access to education and government employment, are also part of the ruling class.[10]

The ruling class has political power with no solid economic basis. A state system exists in Commonwealth Africa in which a multiplicity of organs of government and administration exist, all of which generate opportunities for employment, economic corruption and political power, even though they often do not actually govern or administer what they are supposed to. Hyden refers to a "state suspended in 'mid-air' over society," "in danger of becoming good for little except provision of boundless employment."[11] Although states are supposed to be sovereign over their own territory, national governments in Commonwealth Africa still have incomplete control over relatively inaccessible rural areas; the state's sovereignty is still questionable in such areas as the North-East provinces of Kenya. Transportation and communications systems are oriented to Europe, not to internal national consolidation. Militaries frequently occupy themselves more with plotting coups than with any real defense of the country. Parastatal corporations (state-owned industrial concerns managed by civil servants), ostensibly designed to control the economy, may occupy themselves primarily with making deals with foreign multinationals or with taking bribes from citizens attempting to circumvent regulations. In an administratively weak but organizationally overdeveloped institutional structure, opportunities for corruption are numerous.

Each member of the ruling class, through his control of office, is able to act for his own economic benefit, even when his own class membership is not solidly grounded in collective control of the economy, or indeed of the state apparatus itself. The ruling class, that is to say, is not yet fully consolidated in Commonwealth Africa. In Marxist terminology, it is neither a "class in itself" with overwhelming control of the economic resources of the society, nor a "class for itself"—a group of people acting consciously, consistently, and with positive results in its own interest. A major cause of the frequent shifts in government in Ghana, Nigeria, and Uganda is the lack of consolidation of the various ruling-class factions into one solid grouping. Consolidated class structures at least offer the advantage of minimal political stability and social order.

Collective control of the state by a consolidated ruling class appears to occur in Commonwealth Africa only where there is a single ruling party. In Tanzania, Zambia, and Kenya, strong political and economic benefits are connected with membership in the ruling party, and equally strong penalties are connected with non-membership. Particularly in Tanzania, where private enterprise is actively discouraged, party membership may be the only route to a comfortable life and to influence over, rather than vulnerability to, the various organs of the state. It is notable that so far, the countries which have varied between military rule and civilian rule in Commonwealth Africa have been Ghana, Nigeria, and Uganda, all of which have made more than one attempt at multiparty politics. Those which have so far escaped a successful military coup are those which have a strong single-party system, in which potential opponents of the regime can be either co-opted into the ruling party or rendered impotent through coercive means, such as preventive detention. Also in a single-party system, the party and the military can be united through such means as integrating party cadres (leaders) into the military structure, or giving military leaders high-ranking party and government positions. This lessens the chances of the military having its own motives for the takeover of state power, and of ruling-class factions persuading the military to intervene in politics on their behalf.

To summarize: insofar as a ruling class in Commonwealth Africa is in the process of becoming a genuine class in itself, it is doing so through control of the state, not through independent control of the economy. This generalization applies in broad terms even to Kenya and Nigeria, where an indigenous bourgeoisie has been developing since independence. To understand this phenomenon it is necessary to analyze the opportunities for political power and economic privilege available through both the strictly economic route and the control of office.

In the classical model of capitalist development (with the subsequent emergence of liberal democracy as a weapon of the new capitalist class against the privilege of the old aristocracy), capitalists emerged from the ground up, from the strata of rich peasants and master craftsmen, rather than being created as a class through manipulation of state monopolies of trade, commerce, and industry.[12] Historians of Europe disagree over exactly how the European, or more specifically the English, bourgeoisie emerged,[13] but it seems accurate to assume that at a certain point, the capitalist class found aristocratic control of the state and of trade a hindrance, and began to insist upon the liberal freedoms of speech, association, and suffrage as a means of gaining its own control over the state.[14] This process, by which absolutist royal control of the state was eroded, laid the groundwork for the institutionalization of civil and political human rights in Europe, although further conflicts between the bourgeoisie and the proletariat, and later between men and women, were necessary before those rights were extended to all adult citizens.

In contemporary Africa, the opportunities for the rise of an indigenous bourgeoisie from the ranks of rich peasants and craftsmen are limited. Many state policies over the past 20 years have been aimed against the incipient bourgeoisie that already exists. Not the least of these policies have been the various discriminatory measures aimed against ethnically differentiated petty bourgeoisies already in place, namely the Asians in East Africa and the Lebanese in West Africa. Similarly, prosperous women traders have suffered from the imposition of state monopolies on commodities they had previously retailed, from discriminatory credit and other assistance programs, and from the incorporation of new male-controlled technologies, such as the frozen-fish storage in Ghana that wiped out the businesses of women specializing in smoked fish.[15] "Aliens" and women, both of whom as groups possess substantial entrepreneurial skills in Africa, have been pushed out of business by state policy oriented to men and to racially identifiable Africans.

Perhaps more important, the evolution of an indigenous bourgeoisie has been blocked by centralizing state policies that wiped out small-scale peasant entrepreneurs in the countryside and small-scale businessmen in the informal urban economy. While some chiefs and rich peasants benefit from their contacts with officials of the state, others find themselves deprived of opportunities for agricultural investment, trade, and transport by policies that establish large-scale state farms and monopolies of trucking or marketing. In the cities, inappropriate licensing or "safety" regulations can eliminate small-scale production or services, such as beer bars, in favor of industries run by parastatals or of services provided, at much higher costs, by influential politicians.

Opportunities for the growth of an indigenous bourgeoisie are further limited by the existence of a "comprador" bourgeoisie: that sector of the bourgeoisie that depends for its wealth upon contact with foreigners. Such wealth can be derived directly through control of the state offices with which foreign-based transnationals must deal, or indirectly through the role of private intermediary between the state and the foreign firm. In the 1970s, one economist suggests, a new form of "pirate capitalism" emerged in Nigeria, in which "access to, and manipulation of, the government-spending process [became] the golden gateway to fortune."[16] Vast fortunes were made by acting as intermediaries for, or giving out contracts to, foreign oil or oil-related firms.[17] As the economy expanded, so also did opportunities for graft. For example, during the corruption trials that followed the December 31, 1983, military coup, one former state governor was convicted of taking a $3.7 million kickback from a $37.2 million contract with a French construction firm.[18] In June 1984, an attempted kidnapping in London of an exiled Nigerian, formerly a member of President Shagari's Cabinet, brought to public notice the fact that the man was accused of having stolen $1.7 billion.[19]

That the comprador bourgeoisie is dependent upon the relations between foreign-based transnationals and its home government for its existence should not be taken to mean that it is merely the creature of foreign-based transnationals. In the realm of individual motivation, members of the comprador class are capable of perceiving opportunities for gratifying their own self-interest, and acting upon them, even when such opportunities, e.g., for graft, are not originally offered by the transnational. In the realm of objective consequences, the comprador bourgeoisie may be able to transform the wealth it acquires into a more independent control of the local economy; that is, to transform itself, in the long run, into an indigenous bourgeoisie.[20] Any analysis that attempts to "blame" external economic forces for the existence of this class fails to locate the basis for social action in the rationality of individuals and self-conscious ruling classes.

The use of state funds or office for private purposes, which is the chief economic activity both of the comprador and the local parasitic bourgeoisies, is defined as corruption. One school of thought argues that corruption in Africa is not, in fact, an economically related phenomenon, but rather is rooted in traditional values.[21] According to this school, it is generally accepted that the role of the chief or, in the modern context, the "big man" is to distribute the resources over which he has control to his kin, co-ethnics, and clients. In African society, an individual is not considered corrupt as long as he distributes state resources in the approved manner, rather than keeping them all for himself.

It may well be that the "small" Africans who depend on their ruling-class patrons to distribute largesse to build local schools or clinics, or to find them jobs in the city, are not concerned by ruling-class usurpation of state resources. They may consider that their only access to state resources is through such a ruling-class patron, rather than through impersonal methods of redistribution. For example, President Moi of Kenya is said to distribute funds far in excess of his official earnings at *harambee* (self-help) rallies to build community resources,[22] apparently without public condemnation. But in practice, the acquisition and distribution of national revenues by members of the ruling class, acting in an uncoordinated fashion to patronize their own ethnic group or home area, is not an efficient method of development. Furthermore, much of the revenue appears not to be redistributed along allegedly traditional bases, but rather to end up in private hands and often to be exported for investment abroad.[23] Thus corruption is a serious economic, as well as political, problem in Commonwealth Africa.

Corruption, however, is not a cause of economic underdevelopment; rather it is a structurally induced consequence. In structurally weak and unvaried economies, there are few opportunities for local investors. This lack of opportunity is exacerbated in the more socialist-oriented countries, especially Tanzania and post-1980 Ghana, in which not only productive sectors of the economy, such as mining, but also distributive sectors, such as transport and trade, are nationalized. In the capitalist-oriented economies, such as Kenya and Nigeria, aspirant entepreneurs are still dependent upon the state for contracts, import licences, and access to scarce foreign exchange. Thus the chief resource of the putative capitalist class in Africa has become access to and control of the state.

Control of state office offers a number of economic resources. Corruption, the deliberate plundering of the state's resources or of the resources of those wishing to do business with the state, is merely one of them. Another resource is access to and influence over special government programs. Indigenization, the process by which foreign or "alien"-owned businesses are transferred to ethnic African businessmen, differentially benefits those with close contacts with the government. According to one study, indigenization policies in Zambia in the early 1970s "helped the 'new' Africans—lawyers, managers, civil servants and politicians—move into business," which, not suprisingly, was inefficiently run.[24] In the most famous case, the businesses of the Asians fleeing Amin's Uganda in 1972 were literally transferred to, and plundered by, Amin's military henchmen.

Land policies can also benefit those in or close to office. For example, if the state decides that certain lands are to be put up for sale for the establishment of agricultural businesses, the very state officials who made the decision can then acquire the land. In Ghana during the Acheampong regime, military officers and high-level bureaucracts acquired profitable rice-producing lands in the northern regions, thereby contributing to the 1977 famine in that area by depriving local peasants of subsistence land.[25] In Malawi, Life President Banda proudly parades his large estate holdings before his people as an example of what "Africans" can acquire.[26] In 1972 a number of top Zambian civil servants were revealed to have obtained large tracts of land though a credit scheme intended for local farmers.[27]

All these mechanisms contribute to the creation of a parasitic bourgeoisie, dependent for accumulation of wealth and investment resources on control of state policy and privileged access to the resources the state controls. Such privileged access occurs even in Tanzania, which has actively discouraged private enterprise and the creation of a private capitalist class since the proclamation of the socialist-oriented Arusha Declaration in 1967.[28] In Tanzania, a very strict Leadership Code prohibits high officials of the state, ruling party, and civil service (or their spouses) from engaging in private business, renting out homes, and other forms of accumulation.[29] Legislation facilitating expropriation of real estate and private commercial farms, the attempted creation of collective villages, and revocation of trade licences from Asian petty entrepreneurs have all combined to destroy an incipient bourgeois class.

The result in Tanzania, as in other socialist societies, is that membership in the key bodies controlling party, state, and civil service is even more important than in countries in which the private sector offers some independent basis for wealth acquisition. A "privilegocracy," what one Tanzanian critic refers to as a "bureaucratic bourgeoisie," is emerging.[30] Between 1966 and 1976 the Tanzanian civil service expanded by 13.3 percent per annum.[31] Jobs appear to be distributed by senior civil servants to their kin and co-ethnics as a form of patronage, and are especially valued because (in principle) the government is committed to providing housing for all civil servants.[32] For many Tanzanian party officials, the only alternative to office is a return to low-level peasant farming.[33]

Throughout Commonwealth Africa, an official position often brings with it as legal methods of payment a rent-free house, a car, and access to the better schools. In Zambia in the mid-1970s, top parastatal executives received, in addition to their salaries, "subsidised housing and furniture, an entertainment allowance, a free car with petrol provided, water, telephone and electricity bills paid, servants' wages, security guards . . . medical aid contributions [and] generous leave and pension arrangements."[34] Another real benefit of occupation of office is access to state-controlled food supplies, sold at below-market "control price" and distributed without the recipients' having to stand in line.

Where occupation of state office is, in and of itself, such an important economic resource, ruling-class formation or consolidation occurs not through the inheritance of wealth, but through the processes of nomination and succession.[35] Those outsiders who would enter the privileged inner sanctum of office must be nominated by those already in place. In one-party states, nomination is strictly controlled and limited to those with party membership. Office-holders also try to ensure that their children will be their successors, for example by sending them to the better schools or encouraging them to enter party youth organizations. These practices, already well documented in the Soviet bloc, can be expected to become the mechanism for class formation in those Commonwealth African countries where the only ruling class is office-holders, or even where the real capitalist class is dependent upon office-holders for contracts, import licences, and other economic privileges.

It should be noted that with respect to class formation, whether the members of the ruling class are civilian or military office-holders matters little. Despite the almost ritual announcements by military coup-makers that their intention is to clean up the corruption of previous regimes, and despite the actual corruption trials that occurred, for example, in Ghana after both Rawlings's coups (1979 and 1981) and in Nigeria in 1984, there is no evidence that the behavior of military rulers differs substantially from that of civilian rulers. The 1960s theory that the military was a unique institution, possessed of modernizing, development-oriented, non-nepotistic values, has not been borne out in Africa.[36] Rather, the military, like its civilian counterparts, is subject to intra-ruling-class "ethnic" conflict, as well as to conflicts between different age-cohorts of officers. Militaries in power are as vulnerable to opportunities for corruption as civilian authorities. Nor does the fact that some members of the military have acquired skills as engineers or architects while training in the developed world make them any more capable than civilians of drawing up effective development plans. In Commonwealth Africa, the record of military governments is mixed. Undoubtedly the worst military "government" experienced by any of the nine countries was the rule of Idi Amin; but evidence revealed in the mid-1980s that the second Obote regime had killed as many Ugandans as the Amin regime suggests that both governments' brutality is a symptom of deeper underlying tensions.[37] At the other extreme, the 1970–79 military regime in Nigeria was remarkably liberal with regard to civil and political rights, and remarkably successful with regard to economic rights; however, its success was undoubtedly a consequence of the oil-based economic expansion enjoyed by Nigeria during that period.

The principal difference between military and civilian members of the ruling class in Commonwealth Africa is that the former have direct access to weapons and can quickly intervene to take over governments when they see fit. In Africa, military interventions have normally occurred for one of three major reasons. Militaries will intervene when their interests as a corporate group are threatened: when they believe that they deserve more material benefits, such as pay and housing, as was the case in the Amin intervention in Uganda in 1971;[38] that their prestige is being undermined; or that they are faring less well professionally, for example in the acquisition of advanced weaponry, than their international reference group. Militaries will also intervene as the representatives of civilian ruling-class factions. Thus the first (Ironsi) coup in Nigeria in 1966 was perceived to represent the minority Igbo, while the second (Gowon) countercoup was perceived to represent the dominant Northerners. Finally, militaries will foment coups for stated reasons of principle. Frequently the principle involved is alleged disgust with the corruption of the preceding civilian regime. In addition, a relatively new phenomenon in Commonwealth Africa, evinced both in the second (1981) Rawlings coup in Ghana and in the failed air force coup in Kenya (1982), is a commitment to populistic socialism as a cure for corruption and capitalism practiced by civilian rulers.

Whatever the reasons for their intervention, militaries, as ruling-class factions, are subject to the same opportunities for corruption and profit as the civilians whom they replace. Both civilian and military rulers in Commonwealth Africa rely on the state for privilege, power, and wealth. Yet the state they rely on is incompletely formed, poorly integrated, and weak. The next section will discuss the fragility of the African state and how such fragility, combined with the importance of state institutions to the ruling class, inevitably results in severe denials of human rights.

Class, State, and Power

The previous section showed that in the underdeveloped peripheral economies of Commonwealth Africa, the most important economic resource is control of the state. Yet control of the state is also a political resource of the ruling classes in highly developed capitalist economies, where the protection of human rights, especially of civil and political rights, is well entrenched. Why, then, cannot Commonwealth African countries similarly entrench at least civil and political freedoms, if not economic rights, which would constitute a direct material cost to the ruling class?

The answer has two parts. First, as already discussed, the state is, in comparative terms, a much more important economic resource in Africa than in the Western world; indeed, in some countries it is the only significant economic resource. Second, the state in Commonwealth Africa is simultaneously highly repressive and extremely weak. The weakness of the state as an institution precludes the granting of civil and political rights that might undermine its own fragile existence and, more important, the opportunities for class consolidation of those who control it.

States in Africa are very weak because they are not yet, in a significant sense, nation-states. The formal definition of the state refers to its institutional capacity to safeguard its own existence. The state is above all a sovereign entity. It is sovereign insofar as it has definable borders that it is able to safeguard against external threat or internal attempts at secession. It is also sovereign insofar as it controls the legitimate use of force within its territory.

State sovereignty cannot, however, be based solely on the use of force. In the long run, sovereignty is based on international and internal acceptance of the legitimacy of territorially defined borders, and of the particular institutions and people which control the military and police. As discussed in Chapter 1, the prime objective of the Organization of African Unity is to safeguard both the formal and the substantive sovereignty of African countries. To date, no successful attempts have been made in Commonwealth Africa to challenge formal sovereignty; the most dangerous threat, that of the Biafran secessionists in Nigeria, was defeated after a protracted civil war. Yet the internal aspect of legitimacy in Commonwealth Africa is still very weak, as clearly demonstrated in the 1980s by the guerilla struggles of Buganda-based rebels—and others— against the Obote regime in Uganda.

Legitimacy implies citizens' acceptance of the state's right to give orders to them and to make decisions on their behalf. The state has not merely power, that is the capacity to make people do things they might prefer not to do; it also has authority, that is the right to make people do things they might prefer not to do. In a legitimate state the use of force is minimized, because most citizens accept that the state (or the personnel who comprise the state) is acting in their best interests, whether or not the facts bear it out. How the people are convinced of such legitimacy is an exercise not only in political practice, but also in political propaganda. The people must be made to feel that "the" state is their state.

The major internal reason for the lack of legitimacy in Commonwealth Africa is the lack of a sense of nationhood among African citizens. A nation consists of a group of people living in the same territory, who share a common culture, usually defined as some or all of common language, religion, ancestry, and customs. In Commonwealth Africa none of these bases of nationhood yet exist. Instead societies are divided among different ethnic groups and different religions, with many competing customary and legal structures. Nor have the national governments attempted to impose a minority or even a majority language or religion on all inhabitants as a unifying force.

The establishment of nationhood in Commonwealth Africa is occurring not through forced changes in religion or language, but through the creation of national institutions that gradually undermine primordial attachments, especially in multiethnic urban areas. Tanzania, for example, has created a unified legal system, and Nigeria in its 1979 constitution reduced the powers of Islamic (Shari'a) courts.[39] Normally, all radio and television communications are controlled by the government, which uses them both to socialize ordinary citizens into a sense of nationhood and to promulgate the particular views of the section of the ruling class in power. Schools provide another essential socializing mechanism, especially when young people all over the country compete to enter elite secondary boarding schools (of which the most extreme example is the imitation of Eton which Kamuzu Banda has established in Malawi) and universities.[40] When attempts are made at ethnic balancing of the civil service and the military, a further socializing mechanism exists.[41] In single-party states, the party with its various affiliated organizations, such as women's and youth groups, is undoubtedly the most important socializing institution. Such symbols of loyalty as the national flag and the party card differentiate political "insiders" from political "outsiders," and political deviants who refuse to accept such national symbols are ostracized as not worthy of real membership in the national community.

Aside from the mechanisms of national socialization directly under the control of the African state, a sense of nationhood that subsumes local ethnic affiliations is gradually emerging through the processes of urbanization and psychological modernization. Urban migrants form personal and organizational affiliations across ethnic lines. Multiethnic neighborhoods are becoming more common as African cities become more and more crowded. African Christian churches do not confine their recruitment campaigns to people of single ethnic groups. Educated and professional individuals form affiliations based on class membership and personal interests, as do trade unionists. All of these processes suggest that in the very long run, nationhood will be established in Commonwealth Africa to the same extent as it exists, for example, in multiethnic and religiously diverse Western countries such as Belgium or Canada, where ethnic hostilities and secessionist threats still exist but are contained.

In the short to medium run, however, the state in Commonwealth Africa is still weakened by its lack of legitimacy. The methods by which most rulers achieve power, either through military coups or through repressive entrenchment of a single-party apparatus, are not such as to elicit long-term support from the masses.

Such lack of legitimacy is further exacerbated by the state's institutional weakness. For example, militaries cannot always defend territorial integrity or internal political regimes. In 1981, a coup attempt in Gambia was defeated only with the active (and solicited) help of the Senegalese army. Despite highly repressive measures, Kenya has still been unable to stamp out secessionist Somali activities. Ghana had to close its borders completely in 1982–83 in an attempt to curb smuggling of cash crops out of the country and smuggling of arms into the Ashanti region.[42] Internally, state control over national populations in Commonwealth Africa is weakened by extremely inadequate transportation and communication links. Administration is overcentralized and often merely mythological in remote rural centers. At the same time, therefore, as ruling classes use the state for their own material welfare, they know that they are very vulnerable to attack from inside. Their repressive apparatuses, while often brutal, are far from totalitarian. They do not have total, extensive, and pervasive control over their existent or potential opposition, and they have few economic benefits, given the shallowness of the national bowls of stew, to distribute to those who may be waiting impatiently to replace them.

In such a context the most important political activity of the section of the ruling class in control of the state apparatus becomes regime consolidation. Whichever member, group, or faction of the ruling class controls the state tries to consolidate all possible means of power, including economic resources, coercion, and legitimacy, in its own hands. Power in Africa is much closer to a zero-sum matter than it is in the developed capitalist democracies of Europe and North America. The idea that different factions of the ruling class might compete and indeed even circulate in and out of office, according to commonly acknowledged rules of the game, as occurs during Western multiparty elections, is rightly perceived as a ridiculous political option in situations in which loss of office can mean complete loss of access to wealth, privilege, and influence. When African presidents state that they cannot tolerate opposition because oppositions in Africa are not "loyal" to the abstract entity of the nation-state, what they actually mean is that oppositions by definition cannot be loyal to the extant regime, because their purpose is to get control of the state's resources for themselves. Oppositions are not loyal to the particular regimes (or in the case of Malawi, individual) in place. Indeed, when they are genuinely loyal to the nation-state, they are an even greater threat to the ruling-class faction in control of the state because they are far less easily co-optable.

In the Commonwealth African context, therefore, in which the ruling class is incompletely grounded in real control of the economy, the means of compulsion are a genuine class resource.[43] One might even go so far as to agree with one eminent scholar that "class relations, at bottom, are determined by relations of power, not production."[44] Control of the state, then, means not simply access to resources, but control of power itself.

Class consolidation takes place through the dual process of acquisition of wealth and forceful protection of such acquisition through the state's monopoly of the legal use of force.

It is not surprising, therefore, that civil and political liberties in Commonwealth Africa are extremely precarious. Political oppositions and critics are assumed to be no more purely motivated than those who already control the state apparatus. Multiparty politics are assumed to be a facade for transfers of power from one self-serving faction of the ruling class to another. The rule of law cannot operate when the principal political aim of those who control the state is to ensure that such control remains as unfettered as possible. Preventive detention and state terrorism are used as punishments of, and warnings to, actual or potential opponents of the regime.

The following chapters of this book will analyze in detail the structurally caused difficulties of protecting human rights in poor, underdeveloped countries subject to the authority of weak state structures, which are in turn controlled by ruling classes highly dependent on the existence of the state for their own material well-being. The central role of social class, and its relationship to the state as analytical tools in explaining abuses of human rights, validates the claim made early in this chapter that human rights in state societies are a political matter, consisting essentially of claims on or against the state.

Notes

1. The following analysis of the development of the peasantry is based on Rhoda Howard, "Formation and Stratification of the Peasantry in Colonial Ghana," *Journal of Peasant Studies* 8, no. 1 (October 1980): 61–80.

2. Rhoda Howard, "Expatriate Business and the African Response in Ghana: 1886–1939" (Ph.D. dissertation, McGill University, 1976), p. 118.

3. Karl Marx, *Capital,* vol.I (New York: International Publishers, 1967), parts 3 and 4.

4. Richard A. Higgott, "Africa, the New International Division of Labour and the Corporate State." Paper presented at the 24th Annual Convention, International Studies Association, Mexico City, April 5–9, 1983, p. 10.

5. Julius O. Ihonvbere and Timothy M. Shaw, "Petroleum Proletariat: Nigerian Oil Workers in Contextual and Comparative Perspective." Paper presented at a conference on Third World Trade Unionism: Equity and Democratization in the Changing International Division of Labour (organizer, Roger Southall), Ottawa, Canada, October 25–27, 1984, p. 23.

6. David N. Brown, "The Transformation of Agrarian Structure: A Ghanaian Case Study" (Ph.D. dissertation, McMaster University, 1985).

7. Olivier LeBrun and Chris Gerry, "Petty Producers and Capitalism," *Review of African Political Economy* 3 (May–Oct. 1975): 20–32.

8. Richard Sandbrook, *The Politics of Basic Needs: Urban Aspects of Assaulting Poverty in Africa* (Toronto: University of Toronto Press, 1982), pp. 157–61.

9. Richard L. Sklar, "The Nature of Class Domination in Africa," *Journal of Modern African Studies* 17, no. 4 (1979): 548.

10. Irving Leonard Markovitz, *Power and Class in Africa* (Englewood Cliffs, N.J.: Prentice-Hall, 1977), pp. 153–58.

11. Goran Hyden, *No Shortcuts to Progress: African Development Management in Perspective* (Berkeley: University of California Press, 1983), pp. 7, xii.

12. Maurice Dobb, *Studies in the Development of Capitalism* (New York: International Publishers, 1963).

13. Rodney Hilton, ed., *The Transition from Feudalism to Capitalism* (London: New Left Books, 1976).

14. Barrington Moore, Jr., *Social Origins of Democracy and Dictatorship: Lord and Peasant in the Making of the Modern World* (Boston: Beacon Press, 1966), is the standard sociological reference on how bourgeois revolutions resulted in political democracy.

15. Claire C. Robertson, *Sharing the Same Bowl: A Socioeconomic History of Women and Class in Accra, Ghana* (Bloomington: Indiana University Press, 1984), pp. 80–92.

16. Sayre P. Schatz, "Pirate Capitalism and the Inert Economy of Nigeria," *Journal of Modern African Studies* 22, no. 1 (1984): 55.

17. Terisa Turner, "Multinational Corporations and the Instability of the Nigerian State," *Review of African Political Economy* 5 (Jan.–Apr. 1976): 63–79.

18. The *Globe and Mail*, June 1, 1984, p. 16.

19. "Exiled Nigerian Autocrat Amassed Fund of Ill-Will," *Globe and Mail*, July 7, 1984, p. 3.

20. Colin Leys, "Capital Accumulation, Class Formation and Dependency: The Significance of the Kenyan Case," in Ralph Miliband and J. Saville, eds., *The Socialist Register 1978* (London: The Merlin Press, 1978).

21. Ronald Wraith and Edgar Simpkins, "Nepotism and Bribery in West Africa," in Arnold J. Heidenheimer, ed., *Political Corruption: Readings in Comparative Analysis* (New York: Holt, Rinehart, & Winston, 1970), pp. 331–40.

22. *Africa Contemporary Record*, vol. 14 (1981–82), p. B194.

23. Schatz, "Pirate Capitalism," p. 47.

24. Andrew A. Beveridge, "Economic Independence, Indigenization, and the African Businessman: Some Effects of Zambia's Economic Reforms," *African Studies Review* 17, no. 3 (1974): 487.

25. Andrew Shepherd, "Agrarian Change in Northern Ghana; Public Investment, Capitalist Farming and Famine," in Judith Heyer, Pepe Roberts, and Gavin Williams, eds., *Rural Development in Tropical Africa* (London: Macmillan, 1981), pp. 168–92.

26. Government of Malawi, *His Excellency the Life President's Speeches, Malawi Congress Party Convention, Lilongwe, 3–12 September 1971* (Zomba: Government Printer, 1971).

27. Republic of Zambia, "Report of the Commission of Inquiry into the Allegations made by Mr. Justin Chimba and Mr. John Chisata" (Lusaka: Government Printers, May 1971), pp. 6–7.

28. Julius K. Nyerere, *Ujamaa: Essays on Socialism* (London: Oxford University Press, 1968), chap. 2.

29. Constitution of the United Republic of Tanzania, Article 78 (2), in Albert P. Blaustein and Gisbert H. Flanz, eds., *Constitutions of the Countries of the World* (Dobbs Ferry, N.Y.: Oceana Publications, 1971–   ).

30. I have taken the term *privilegocracy* from the novelist Nuruddin Farah, who in his *Sardines* (London: Heinemann, 1981) refers to the "privilegentsia." For reference to the "bureaucratic bourgeoisie," see Issa G. Shivji, *Class Struggles in Tanzania* (London: Heinemann, 1976), part 3.

31. Rwekaza Mukandala, "Trends in Civil Service Size and Income in Tanzania, 1967–1982," *Canadian Journal of African Studies* 17, no. 2 (1983): 254.

32. Ibid., p. 260.

33. Susanne D. Mueller, "The Historical Origins of Tanzania's Ruling Class," *Canadian Journal of African Studies* 15, no. 3 (1981): 491.

34. Republic of Zambia, "Report of the commission of inquiry into the salaries, salary structures and conditions of service of the Zambia public service and teaching services . . . etc., Volume I, The Public Services and the Parastatal Sector" (Lusaka, 1975), quoted in Morris Szeftel, "Political Graft and the Spoils System in Zambia—the State as a Resource in Itself," *Review of African Political Economy* 24 (May–Aug. 1982): 6.

35. Zygmunt Bauman, "Officialdom and Class: Bases of Inequality in Socialist Society," in Frank Parkin, ed., *The Social Analysis of Class Structure* (London: Tavistock, 1974), pp. 129–48.

36. Olatunde T. Odetola, *Military Regimes and Development: A Comparative Analysis in African Societies* (London: George Allen and Unwin, 1982).

37. See Chapters 5 and 7 of this volume.

38. Michael F. Lofchie, "The Political Origins of the Uganda Coup," *Journal of African Studies* 1, no. 4 (Winter 1974): 489–92.

39. Constitution of the Republic of Nigeria, "Chronology," p. 40 (issued April 1984), in Blaustein and Flanz, *Constitutions* .

40. "Malawi's Elite Academy: The Very Model of Eton," *New York Times*, July 4, 1983, p. 2

41. Cynthia H. Enloe, "Ethnicity, Bureaucracy and State-Building in Africa and Latin America," *Ethnic and Racial Studies* 1, no. 3 (July 1978): 336–51.

42. "Ghana Closes Borders Pending Economic Action," *Wall Street Journal*, September 23, 1982, p. 39 (E); and *Africa Contemporary Record*, vol.15 (1982–83), p. B447.

43. Sklar, "The Nature of Class Domination," p. 532.

44. Ibid., p. 537.

(4) Economic Rights

Sub-Saharan Africa is in economic crisis. In the 1960s, its Gross National Product grew at the rate of 1.3 percent per person per annum; in the 1970s, this had declined to 0.8 percent.[1] In the 1980s, ecological disaster, world recession, and the outcome of ill-informed internal development policies have converged to create an extremely severe economic crisis. Many countries are now experiencing negative per capita growth rates.

This chapter will concentrate on only three basic economic rights: physical subsistence (food), health care, and education. While economic rights include far more than these essential basics, the depth of the African economic crisis in the 1980s is such that to focus on these rights is legitimate; failure to realize them will render impossible other economic rights such as comprehensive social welfare plans. This chapter specifically addresses the debate about the cause of the decline in Africa's economic performance in the 1970s and 1980s. One side of the debate stresses internal factors, such as lack of opportunity for indigenous entrepreneurs, poor development planning, lack of human capital, and underpayment of peasant producers. The other side stresses external causes, namely Africa's colonial history and its present weak position in the international economy. A third, complementary approach addresses the personal and class interests of policy-makers. It acknowledges the impact of both internal and external factors while stressing the problems of attempting to implement economic development in class-ruled societies with repressive political structures, which do not allow political participation by those affected by development policy.

It is not my intention to try to resolve the debates around Africa's present economic crisis. The causes of the food crisis, in particular, are extremely complex and can only be touched upon here.[2] Commonwealth Africa's colonial heritage and weak bargaining position in the contemporary economy do provide real, perhaps insurmountable, constraints on development. On the other hand, internal economic policy, indigenously generated, has also been responsible for slowing down growth and innovation, especially insofar as economic policy has promoted the interests of parasitic state-centered ruling classes against the possible formation of a prosperous, and innovative, local bourgeoisie. More important, these class-biased policies have also deprived ordinary Africans of basic economic rights. Both absolute economic growth and equitable distribution of key resources, especially land, are needed in order to provide for basic economic rights in Commonwealth Africa. Egalitarianism without growth, as in Tanzania, cannot provide for economic rights in very poor countries. But neither can growth without fair distribution, as in Nigeria during the 1970s or Malawi.

The Substance of Economic Rights

Both African and international accords provide justification for a stress on economic rights. Basic subsistence rights have generally been taken to include adequate nutrition and a minimal level of health care. Education is also a key right, whether categorized as economic or civil/political, as it enhances the capacity of individuals both to earn a living, and to have an impact on economic and political policies that affect them.

In Africa, while education and health statistics show substantial improvement from 1960 to the present, basic food statistics show a different picture (see Table 4.1). In 1981, of the nine Commonwealth countries only in Sierra Leone did citizens enjoy 100 percent of their daily required caloric intake. Nigeria, which had the highest per capita income, $860 in 1982 (see Table 4.3), had a low caloric intake of only 91 percent of the daily requirement. Zambia, with the next highest per capita income of $640, provided only 93 percent of the required calories. Tanzania, despite its socialist and egalitarian rhetoric, provided only 83 percent of the required calories, only marginally higher than Uganda, whose figure of 80 percent undoubtedly reflects the economic effects of the continued civil war. While the absolute amount of food produced increased during the 1970s in all countries except Ghana, varying from a high of 3.1 percent per annum increase in Malawi to a low of 0.1 percent per annum in Gambia, the growth rate of food production per capita declined in all countries except Malawi and Zambia. The worst case was Ghana, with a negative growth rate per capita of 3.1 percent per annum; the best case after Zambia was Nigeria, with a negative rate of 0.8 percent per capita per annum. This figure is presented in different form in column 4 of Table 4.1, containing data on the average index of food production per capita. With 1969–71 as the base date, only Malawi was providing as much food per capita in 1977–79 as it had provided eight years earlier. It was predicted that for all of Africa, two to three times the 1983 level of food imports would be needed by 1990.[3]

Food is not equitably distributed. One of the perquisites of office in Commonwealth Africa is privileged access to food through government distribution schemes for state employees. As in any society, moreover, uneven income distribution means that the poor can buy less food than the rich. In Zambia in 1974/75, the average rural household had an income of about K29.20, or $45.55 per month.[4] In rural areas, 75 percent of cash and

Table 4.1 Food Production and Consumption

	Gambia	Ghana	Kenya	Malawi	Nigeria	Sierra Leone	Tanzania	Uganda	Zambia
1. Daily caloric supply as percentage of total requirement, 1981	97 (1977)	88	88	94	91	101	83	80	93
2. Average annual growth rate of volume of food production, 1969–71 to 1977–79	0.1	−0.1	2.9	3.1	1.7	1.4	1.9	1.7	3.0
3. Average annual growth rate of food production, per capita, 1969–71 to 1977–79	−2.9	−3.1	−0.5	0.3	−0.8	−1.1	−1.5	−1.3	0.0
4. Average index of food production per capita (1969–71 = 100), 1977–79	77	82	92	100	87	87	94	90	99

Source: The World Bank, *Accelerated Development in Sub-Saharan Africa* (Washington, D.C.: The World Bank, 1981), Tables 1 and 25; and idem, *World Development Report* (New York: Oxford University Press, 1984), Table 24.

kind income was spent on food alone (despite the myth of rural self-sufficiency); in the richer urban areas 47 percent of income went to food. The bottom 60 percent of Zambia's urban population controlled barely as much income, 26.6 percent of the total, as the top 4.7 percent of the population, with 26.7 percent of the income. In the rural areas, distribution was slightly less skewed; nevertheless, the bottom 61 percent controlled only 27.3 percent of income, while the top 5 percent controlled 23.6 percent.[5] A 1976 Kenyan survey indicated that the lowest 20 percent of the population earned only 2.6 percent of the national income, while the highest 20 percent had 60.4 percent, and the highest 10 percent held 45.8 percent of the national income.[6]

Declining food production combines with uneven income distribution to cause severe dietary deficiencies among the African poor. In the early 1980s, it was estimated that 26 percent of urban households in Zambia, and 79 percent of rural, did not earn enough to meet their basic needs. Increases in malnutrition were reflected in a decline in the height of Zambian children.[7] A 1977 Kenyan survey revealed that 2.5 percent of rural children aged one through four suffered from severe malnutrition, and fully a third of the children from moderate malnutrition.[8]

Moreover, the obverse of the land redistribution schemes that benefit wealthy individuals and state officials (discussed in Chapter 3) is that peasant cultivators are deprived of land. It is estimated that 22 percent of the people in Kenya are now landless, while absentee "telephone farmers" leave much of their large estate holdings idle.[9] When southern Ghanaian businessmen and state officials bought land in the north in the 1970s, subsistence cultivators lost their access to their livelihood, and a localized famine resulted.[10]

While the food production figures for Commonwealth Africa are distressing, health indicators present a decidedly more beneficial trend. Whether for reasons of genuine concern for the health of the populace as a whole, or merely as a means of political legitimation ("delivering the goods"), the commitment of all nine governments to improving the health of their citizens has had concrete, positive results (see Table 4.2). In addition, the eradication of some diseases, and international projects to increase the supply of clean water in Africa, have helped to lengthen life expectancy. Despite infant mortality rates which were still very high by contemporary Western standards in the 1970s, two principal indicators, life expectancy at birth and child death rates, show substantial improvement. In most countries the life expectancy at birth increased by about 10 years between 1960 and 1979, ranging from a 1-year increase in Sierra Leone to a 16-year increase in Kenya. The child death rate (the number of deaths per thousand children aged one to four) also decreased dramatically, in some cases by 50 to 60 percent. Infant mortality rates in Ghana, Kenya, and Tanzania are now reported to be less than 100 per thousand,

Table 4.2 Health Indicators

	Gambia	Ghana	Kenya	Malawi	Nigeria	Sierra Leone	Tanzania	Uganda	Zambia
1. Life expectancy at birth									
1960	37	40	41	37	39	37	42	44	40
1982	36	55	57	44	50	38	52	47	51
2. Infant mortality rate (birth through one year, per 1,000)									
1982	n.d.	86	77	137	109	190	98	120	105
3. Child death rate (age 1–4, per 1,000)									
1960	41	27	21	58	50	72	31	28	38
1982	34 (1979)	15	13	29	20	50	18	22	20
4. Percentage of population with access to safe water, 1975	n.d.	35	17	33	n.d.	n.d.	39	35	42
5. Population per physician									
1960	21,800	21,600	10,690	35,250	73,710	20,070	18,220	15,050	9,540
1980	13,171 (1977)	7,630	7,890	40,950	12,550	16,220	17,560	26,810	7,670
6. Population per nurse									
1960	n.d.	5,430	2,270	12,940	4,040	2,880	11,890	10,030	9,920
1980	3,930 (1977)	780	550	3,830	3,010	1,890	2,980	4,180	1,730

n.d. = no data.

Source: Line 4: The World Bank, Accelerated Development in Sub-Saharan Africa, Table 37.
All others: The World Bank, World Development Report 1984, Tables 23 and 24.

and only Sierra Leone reports a rate higher than 150 per thousand. (In the Western world, life expectancy is about 75 years, infant mortality about 12 per thousand, and child mortality below 1 per thousand.)[11]

Some crude indicators explain the increased life expectancy and reduced child mortality in Africa, despite declining food production per capita. Probably the most important is the percentage of the population with access to clean water. In 1975, the Economic Commission for Africa estimated that in the continent as a whole, only 10 percent of the population (7½ percent in the rural areas) had access to safe water.[12] Commonwealth African countries clearly do not represent the majority of Africa. Zambia, a heavily urbanized country, provided safe water for 42 percent of its citizens in 1975, while Kenya, also considered a relatively developed African country, provided safe water for only 17 percent. Unfortunately, figures are not available for Nigeria, which with a very conservatively estimated population of at least 91 million people (and probably well over 100 million) outnumbers all eight of the other countries put together.

Nigeria shows a dramatic decrease in the number of people per physician, another indicator of health levels, from 73,710 in 1960 to 12,550 in 1980. Gambia and Ghana also show dramatic declines in population per physician, while Kenya, Sierra Leone, Tanzania, and Zambia show smaller declines (see Table 4.2). In Uganda, the number of people per physician increased by two-thirds from 1960 to 1980; this anomalous situation was caused by educational breakdown and the exile and murder of professionals during and subsequent to the Amin period. Malawi's increase might also be caused by political repression and the self-exile of professionals. All the countries show substantial reductions in the number of people per nurse, who are perhaps more important than doctors. Nurses and paramedical personnel are responsible for running local clinics in rural and urban poor areas; for administering immunization; and for health education, nutritional education, and well-baby clinics. Yet one should keep in mind the severe imbalance in health delivery, both between rich and poor and between urban and rural areas. In Nigeria in 1979 there were seventeen times as many doctors and thirteen times as many nurses in the capital as in the rural areas; overall there were seven times as many doctors and five times as many nurses in the urban as in the rural areas.[13]

The improved health conditions since 1960 are undoubtedly a strong contributing factor to the population increase experienced by Commonwealth African countries (shown in Table 4.3). Population growth rates are very high, and have in fact increased in the 1970s over the 1960s. Populations in at least four African countries are expected to be three to four times as high in the year 2020 as they were in 1982. In the total period 1960 to 1982, the average annual growth rate in GNP per capita was

Table 4.3 Population and Gross National Product

	Gambia	Ghana	Kenya	Malawi	Nigeria	Sierra Leone	Tanzania	Uganda	Zambia
1. Total population (millions), 1982	0.7	12	18	7	91	3	20	14	6
2. Population density (per Km²), 1979	52	47	26	49	81	47	18	56	8
3. Average annual growth rate of population (%)									
1960–70	3.2	2.3	3.2	2.8	2.5	1.7	2.7	3.0	2.6
1970–82	3.0 (1970–79)	3.0	4.0	3.0	2.6	2.0	3.4	2.7	3.1
4. Projected population (in millions)									
in A.D. 2,000	1	24	40	12	169	5	36	25	11
in A.D. 2,020	n.d.	45	81	n.d.	341	n.d.	72	n.d.	n.d.
5. GNP average annual growth rate (percent per capita), 1960–82	2.5	–1.3	2.8	2.6	3.3	0.9	1.9	–1.1	0.1
6. GNP (gross national product) per capita (dollars), 1982	360	360	390	210	860	390	280	230	640

n.d. = no data.

Source: Line 2: United Nations, Demographic Yearbook (New York: The United Nations, 1979), Table 3.
All others: The World Bank, World Development Report 1984, Tables 1 and 19. Figures for Gambia from World Bank, Accelerated Development, 1981, also p. 112 for population projections 2,020.

positive in all the economies except Ghana, Uganda, and Zambia. But the growth in the 1970s was considerably lower than the growth in the 1960s.[14] Moreover, the World Bank predicted in 1981 that the most optimistic assessment for sub-Saharan Africa as a whole in the 1980s would be zero growth in per capita income, while the pessimistic prediction, for the poorest countries, was a (negative) rate of minus 1 percent per year.[15]

One approach to solving the problem of declining food production per capita and declining rates of growth in per capita income is to advocate a lower birth rate. At present the fertility rate in sub-Saharan Africa as a whole is six live births per mother.[16] Undoubtedly, the drastic population increase has put a severe strain on Africa's limited economic resources, and a reduction of the population growth rate, especially in countries such as Kenya, might lessen such a strain. But a simplistic policy of concentrating on population reduction would not succeed. Development is more a cause than a consequence of declining fertility. Population growth rates are known to decline with increased education, especially that of women. Growth rates also decline as infant mortality declines and parents can expect better survival possibilities for each child. As people move off the land into the cities, children become less valuable as workers and more costly if they go to school for extended periods of time. Finally, fertility declines with increases in social security, since parents need not have large numbers of children to provide for them when they are aged.

The principal economic problem for Commonwealth Africa in the next 40 or 50 years will be how to achieve not only adequate food production per capita for a rapidly expanding population, but also an absolute increase in the rate of growth. One major means to provide for both subsistence needs of the population as a whole and for absolute growth is through education. The World Bank stresses that human capital is still one of the scarcest resources of Commonwealth Africa.[17] Africa still lacks individuals with the expertise necessary in both the administrative and the investment sectors to improve the economy without relying on expensive expatriate "experts" with often irrelevant skills. This lack of highly educated individuals is, however, partly a consequence rather than a cause of underdevelopment. Many highly educated Africans are self-exiled: they prefer to reside in the Western world or to work for international agencies rather than experience the extreme poverty of their homeland. In Nigeria, for example, the wages of teachers and professors in many states have been in arrears for months or even years since the economic decline of the early 1980s. In addition, many African intellectuals are forced into exile for political reasons; or, if they do make informed criticisms of national development policies, they are thrown into jail.

As well as highly educated "experts," a reasonably educated citizenry as a whole can contribute to development. A minimal level of universal primary education can enhance the productivity of all members of the agricultural and industrial labor forces. In this connection, the substantial increases in the percentage of children enrolled in primary schools in all countries (except Uganda where, again, education has been severely disrupted since 1971) are very important (see Table 4.4). While the enrollment of girls lags behind that of boys, it is also growing, and in Kenya, Tanzania, and Zambia is approaching 100 percent of the relevant age group. Enrollments in secondary schools lag far behind enrollments in primary schools, however, and enrollments in university are minimal—in all countries except Nigeria and Zambia 1 percent or less of the relevant age group. Given the much higher costs of secondary and university over primary education, it is difficult to envisage a means by which African governments, with their limited budgets, could increase their investments in high-level human capital without limiting their investments in the basic education that is also necessary for profitable production. One early estimate suggested that the cost per student year at university was about 150 times greater than per pupil year in primary school.[18]

In general, then, it can be seen that from the early 1960s to the early 1980s, substantial improvements were made in Commonwealth Africa in health and education. These improvements may well be undermined by the end of the century if the general economic crisis of Africa is not reversed. For example, infant malnutrition as a result of declining caloric intake can cause permanent intellectual retardation, for which no amount of schooling will compensate. Education and health care in Commonwealth Africa in the 1980s are already suffering from limitations on funds to purchase school texts and basic medicines, to repair schools and hospitals. Dedicated middle-class teachers and health professionals are forced by the general economic crisis to spend more time looking for additional income than in attending to their jobs. Figures produced at the end of the 1980s may well show increases in infant and child mortality over the 1970s, and decreases in life expectancy and literacy levels. Thus amelioration of African underdevelopment is absolutely essential for the basic rights of ordinary citizens. Such amelioration, in its turn, is dependent on adequate understanding of the causes of underdevelopment.

Causes of Underdevelopment

All Commonwealth African governments aim, in principle, to provide for economic human rights. Above all they stress the right to development proclaimed in the 1981 African Charter of Human and Peoples' Rights.[19] Development is not defined merely as economic growth. The consensus of African opinion is represented by the articulated East African statements of economic philosophy, namely Kenya's 1965 statement on "African socialism," the various statements on "African humanism" by Kenneth

Table 4.4 Literacy and Education

	Gambia	Ghana	Kenya	Malawi	Nigeria	Sierra Leone	Tanzania	Uganda	Zambia
1. Adult literacy rate									
1960	6	27	20	n.d.	15	7	10	35	n.d.
1976	10	n.d.	45	25	n.d.	n.d.	66	n.d.	39
2. Number enrolled in primary school as percentage of age group:									
Total 1960	14	38	47	n.d.	36	23	25	49	42
1981	37 (1978)	69	109	62	98	39	102	54	96
Male 1960	n.d.	52	64	n.d.	46	30	33	65	51
1981	n.d.	77	114	73	94	45	107	62	102
Female 1960	n.d.	25	30	n.d.	27	15	18	32	34
1981	n.d.	60	101	51	70	30	98	46	90
3. Number enrolled in secondary school as percentage of age group									
1960	3	5	2	1	4	2	2	3	2
1981	12	36	19	4	16	12	3	5	16
4. Number enrolled in higher education as percentage of population aged 20–24									
1960	n.d.	(.)	(.)	n.d.	(.)	(.)	(.)	(.)	(.)
1981	n.d.	1	1	(.)	3	1	(.)	1	2

n.d. = no data.

(.) = less than half of 1 percent.

Source: Line 1: World Bank, *Accelerated Development*, Table 38.

Lines 2–4: World Bank, *World Development Report 1984*, Table 25.

Kaunda in Zambia, and the Arusha declaration and later statements on "ujamaa" socialism in Tanzania.[20] This consensus holds that development ought to include three complementary components: absolute economic growth, redistribution of wealth in a more egalitarian manner, and increased national autonomy or self-sufficiency.

To fulfill the aim of development, given the very low economic base from which independent African countries start, is a substantial task. The decrease in caloric intake per person in the 1970s and 1980s is merely an indicator, undoubtedly the most serious from the perspective of economic rights, of the inability of Commonwealth African governments to formulate and implement their own successful economic policy.

There are a number of explanations for the decrease in caloric intake per capita. One perspective, represented by the World Bank, focuses on possibly well-intentioned, but nevertheless inappropriate, internal policies as the main cause of the inability of a predominantly rural continent, which in the past had been self-supporting in food, to provide for itself. A major problem, according to the World Bank, is the underpayment of peasants both for food and export crops, which reduces their incentive to produce for both the national and the international markets.[21] These policies are exacerbated by the establishment of state marketing boards in basic food crops, nationalizations of food transport and retailing, and misguided attempts to collectivize food production. Tanzania and Ghana are examples.

Tanzania is now a net importer of maize, in which it was formerly self-sufficient. One reason for the deficiency in production is that, until recently, the government paid so little for maize through the state marketing monopoly that producers were encouraged to sell it on the black market instead.[22] Moreover, in pursuit of the socialist egalitarianism of ujamaa, in the early 1970s Nyerere's government expropriated the property of 35 large-scale African farmers, who produced about 30 percent of the country's marketed maize supply.[23] Their land was redistributed among small-scale peasant farmers who could not produce at the same high level as the former owners.[24] Most tragic, the "villagization" policy of 1973–75 resulted in a severe drop in maize production when hostile, suspicious peasants refused to plant in their new homesteads. This villagization policy was originally introduced in 1968 on a voluntary basis. When not enough people volunteered, however, 2 to 2.5 million were moved against their will. According to one commentator, "Force [was] liberally used . . . People have often been moved from their previous area of cultivation to new lands of unknown quality."[25] The drop in food production in the mid-1970s had devastating effects on the national economy. Massive amounts of foreign exchange had to be diverted from importation of other necessary items, such as industrial components, to food.[26] Some experts have debated whether the villagization policy, which coincided with a drought, was the main cause of the drop in agricultural production,[27] but it is known that experiments at collective production failed. Even among volunteer inhabitants of ujamaa villages, productivity was much higher on individual private, than on collective village, plots.[28]

In Ghana basic subsistence food production suffered severely in the 1970s. In the mid-1970s, the Acheampong government launched an "Operation Feed Yourself" program to try to return to agricultural self-sufficiency. Under this program, heavy agricultural machinery was imported, yet a shortage of cutlasses, the basic low-technology agricultural implement, was so severe that they were being distributed personally by regional commissioners. By 1978, 70 percent of farmers surveyed in the Ashanti region said that they did not grow enough food to feed their families.[29] All these failed policies had been instituted under a rhetorical commitment to provide for the basic economic rights of all Ghanaian citizens. One reason for the failure of "Operation Feed Yourself" was probably insufficient planning: the crusade for greater food self-sufficiency was launched only 34 days after the National Redemption Council, headed by Acheampong, took office.[30]

Not only production of food, but also its transport and distribution have been adversely affected by government planning. In Tanzania, for example, an overenthusiastic attempt to nationalize all village stores (frequently Asian-owned) in the late 1970s deprived many villages of their only source of supply.[31] In Ghana, state takeover of food transport and storage in the late 1970s resulted in the disintegration of these vital services,[32] while the destruction of large-scale "mammies' markets" in Accra, ostensibly because local (women) traders who hoarded goods were responsible for Ghana's rampant inflation, meant that the only sources of food were inefficient, ill-equipped government distribution or the black market.[33] Government distribution at below market prices in effect supplies subsidized food to civil servants, military men, and other government dependents, while leaving the masses of the people to search for food on the "parallel" black market.

The Tanzanian example has inspired much debate on the relative weights of internally and externally generated causes of underdevelopment. The Tanzanian government itself attributes its economic malaise almost entirely to climatic and external factors. Tanzania experienced drought in 1973–75 and drought followed by flooding in 1979–80. In addition, the extreme increase in the price of oil meant that, although Tanzania used less oil in 1980 than in 1972, she paid 50 percent of her foreign exchange for oil in the later year, as opposed to only 10 percent in the earlier. Moreover, the Tanzanian government points out, it had to cope with the falling price of coffee in the late 1970s after its rise earlier in the decade, and with the widening gap between world commodity and industrial prices. Finally, there were political factors: the $500 million war with Idi Amin in 1979, and the costs of the breakdown of the East African Community.[34] The Tanzanian government's view is supported by at least one authoritative source, which points out that Tanzania's economic performance in the 1970s was better than that of sub-Saharan Africa as a whole, but that it was severely hit by changes in the international economy after 1979.[35] On the other hand, one estimate suggests that Tanzania's internally generated agricultural losses from "regulating the market out of operation" were 250 percent higher than the increases in oil costs between 1973 and 1980.[36]

Whatever the causes of Tanzania's economic decline, it is clear that irrelevant or erroneous economic planning is only one component of the underproduction and skewed distribution of food. The World Bank overstresses this aspect and ignores others, perhaps partly for strategic reasons. Given that African governments cannot control the world economy, perhaps they ought to focus on what they *can* change, namely the role of the state in exacerbating an externally generated world recession by permitting erroneous at best, and pernicious at worst, internal "development" policies. Critics of the World Bank's analysis of Africa's economic problems do not quarrel with the specifics of its proposals, but rather with its unwillingness to focus attention on external as well as internal causes of the economic decline. As Helleiner puts it, "Where would Africa now be, relative to where it actually is, had the major current [economic] shocks not struck? Would the policies of the past look so 'inadequate,' or the present need for change look so great, had the world [economy] grown at 6% a year through the 1970s?"[37] The general economic crisis of the 1980s is also a consequence of the historic dependence of Commonwealth Africa as a whole on the world economy. Without elevating this factor into an "ideology of dependence," it is important to understand its effects on underdevelopment, and hence on the difficulties of providing basic economic rights.

No discussion of economic rights in Africa is complete without an understanding of the evolution of its low economic base. One is tempted to assume that Africa in 1960 was simply "poor": that it had, perhaps for climatic or cultural reasons, never developed an industrial base even remotely comparable to that of Western countries. One thesis suggests that the difficulty in Africa is that it never underwent an agricultural revolution that could provide a surplus sufficient to release human and other resources for sustained industrial development.[38] Similarly, Hyden's central argument is that the preservation of what he calls the "economy of affection," or kin-based peasant methods of production, has blocked any possible transition to capitalist growth in Africa.[39]

Another body of literature, however, suggests that the underdevelopment of Africa is not merely an original state; rather it is the result of four or five centuries of active underdevelopment of that continent by European imperialist powers and latterly, by a neo-colonial economic structure dominated by transnational corporations.[40] Had Africa not been originally integrated into the world economy on unfavorable terms, it is maintained, she might be more developed than she in fact is at present. It is important to consider critically this body of literature, as it has been quite influential on African and other Third World policy-makers in the last two decades. For example, the 1980 Lagos Plan of Action for economic reform contends that Africa's economic underdevelopment "has resulted from several centuries of colonial domination."[41] Indeed, an "ideology of development" has arisen that deflects responsibility for many of Africa's internal economic difficulties to its history of colonial economic exploitation and alleged present neo-colonial position.[42] For development dictatorships,[43] this ideology is a convenient means of ignoring the facts of extreme income inequalities, man-made famines, corruption, and other denials of basic economic rights caused by the self-serving policies instituted and implemented by those who control the state. There is a great deal of truth to the argument that Africa is so dependent on the world economy that it will not be able to overcome underdevelopment without international assistance. Yet this argument can be, and often is, distorted to ignore the internal dimensions of African underdevelopment, especially the class dimensions.

According to the dependency argument, when Britain withdrew from Africa the new African governments were faced with the task of trying to "catch up" with the Western economies as quickly as possible. Yet their position in the world economy had not changed with formal political independence. They still depended for their foreign exchange primarily on one to three export crops, for which prices fluctuated and, in some cases, appeared to be heading for a long-run decline. For example, in 1977 all of Gambia's exports were derived from palm tree cultivation. Seventy-four percent of Ghana's exports were cocoa, 9 percent aluminum, and 6 percent wood. Kenya, Malawi, and Tanzania had slightly diversified export packages, although Kenya and Tanzania were heavily dependent on coffee and Malawi on tobacco. Uganda was almost completely dependent on coffee, as was Zambia on copper. Nigeria derived 93 percent of its export earnings from oil by 1977.[44]

The phenomenon of heavy export dependence on one or two crops is known, somewhat inaccurately, as monoculturalism. Analysis of a country's exports does not constitute a total picture of its economy. Some countries, such as Canada, which are heavily dependent on the export of primary agricultural and mineral products, are nevertheless highly developed. But the problem of monoculturalism in Africa is particularly crucial because of Africa's intense need for foreign exchange, not only to import industrial equipment but also to build and maintain its infrastructure and, increasingly, to import the food it cannot supply itself. There is, according to the dependency thesis, a circularity of causation that is particularly poignant: as Africans deflect production from food crops to cash crops, so more food has to be imported.

One problem reflected by the heavy export dependence of African countries is the imbalance of terms of trade between agricultural and industrial products. Put simply, the dependency thesis states that for world trade as a whole, terms of trade have been changing adversely for the food- and mineral-producing nations; for example, the number of tractors to be obtained from a given quantity of cocoa or coffee or copper is declining. Row 2 of Table 4.5 looks at terms of trade for Commonwealth Africa. Much depends on the base year, in this case 1975. It can be seen that there is no clear pattern in net barter terms of trade during the 1970s. Gambia, heavily reliant on palm oil, and Malawi, heavily reliant on tobacco, have suffered declining terms of trade over the last 20 years. Nigeria's terms of trade improved tremendously when she began to export oil in the early 1970s, but Nigeria so overextended her government spending in the 1970s that she is now experiencing severe economic retrenchment as a result of the decline in the world oil price in the early 1980s. Zambia's terms of trade declined as a result of the drop in the world price of copper in the mid-1970s; between 1975 and 1979 the purchasing power of Zambia's exports was sometimes less than 50 percent of what it had been in 1974.[45] Kenya and Uganda profited (indeed, perhaps, Idi Amin was enabled to stay in power) because of the short-term increase in world coffee prices in the 1970s, but by the late 1970s the world price fell again.

In the 1980s, terms of trade for Africa as a whole are far worse than for the 1970s. Commodity prices have fallen dramatically since 1980, especially in coffee, cocoa, tea, palm oil and groundnuts (peanuts). The average price level of the 1980s is 15 to 20 percent below what it was in the 1960s and in the second half of the 1970s.[46] Between 1977 and 1981, Tanzania's terms of trade deteriorated by 50 percent, and its real material purchasing power declined by 18 percent.[47] These extremely adverse economic changes, which are completely out of the control of national African economies, lend credence to the dependency thesis.

Commodity prices are important in Commonwealth Africa because the commodity exports earn foreign exchange. Foreign exchange is needed to import not only basic industrial and infrastructural goods but, increasingly, consumer goods, including food. One result of the dependence of Africa on foreign exchange is the high charges for foreign debt and debt services, as shown in Table 4.5. In Kenya, Malawi, Nigeria, Sierra Leone, Uganda, and Zambia, debt servicing doubled, tripled, or quadrupled in the 1970s. Only for Nigeria, an oil exporter, did the cost of debt servicing drop significantly in the 1970s. But it increased again in the 1980s with the drastic decline in Nigeria's oil revenue.

The problem in Commonwealth African economies is not merely terms

Table 4.5 Economic Dependency

	Gambia	Ghana	Kenya	Malawi	Nigeria	Sierra Leone	Tanzania	Uganda	Zambia
1. Percentage share in total exports of three principal exports									
1961	95.7	84.5	34.2	93.8	45.6	19.6	49.2	69.8	93.9
1976–78 (average)	79.7	62.8	52.5	83.1	97.1	79.1	55.4	96.0	96.2
2. Net barter terms of trade (1975 = 100)									
1960	104	111	133	115	32	121	98	123	115
1970	109	121	119	99	32	136	103	130	227
1979	93	144	110	84	119	108	102	136	100
3. Debt service as percentage of exports of goods and services									
1970	n.d.	5.2	7.9	7.0	4.2	10.1	8.2	3.4	5.8
1982	n.d.	6.8	20.3	22.8	9.5	20.8	5.1	22.3	17.4
4. Net official development assistance as a percentage of GNP, 1979	23.8	3.8	6.0	12.0	(.)	6.1	12.4	1.0	7.6
5. Net official development assistance per capita, 1979 (dollars)	59.5	15.2	22.7	24.0	0.3	15.3	32.2	2.9	38.1
6. Net official development assistance as a percentage of gross domestic investment, 1979	162.3	33.7	29.9	39.4	0.1	44.0	66.9	10.9	39.7

(.) = less than half of 1 percent.
Source: World Bank, *Accelerated Development* (1981), Tables 13, 14, 17, 22; and idem, *World Development Report, 1984*, Table 16.

of trade, but also a lack of flexibility and variation. As already explained in Chapter 3, there is very little productive industry; a high percentage of the population is still employed in an agricultural sector that uses very low-level technology, and many urban dwellers are employed in the labor-intensive informal sector. The lack of variation and real investment opportunities in Commonwealth Africa is a more important reason for its economic underdevelopment than fluctuations in world commodity prices and the debt burden. Indeed, the debt burden would be alleviated if agricultural investments could increase productivity, and if there were more low-level, indigenous industrial development and less centralized state planning for large-scale and uneconomic industrial projects. Hyden suggests that even if the world economy were to emerge from the long-run recession of the 1970s and '80s, African governments would not know how to take advantage of the improved economic climate. "It would be wrong to assume . . . that the African economies will automatically benefit from a turn for the better in the world economy."[48]

One solution often suggested for African economic problems is an increase in foreign aid, and indeed the World Bank suggested in 1981 that aid to sub-Saharan Africa as a whole needed to be doubled in the 1980s.[49] Yet by 1982 aid to Africa was already declining.[50] Of the nine countries, Gambia is the most dependent on foreign aid, which constituted 23.8 percent of her total GNP in 1979. Tanzania received the equivalent of 12.4 percent of her GNP in foreign aid, while the percentage for the rest of the countries was lower. While 6 or 12 percent of the GNP might not seem to be a very high figure, were these countries to suffer a sudden cut-off of all aid, the drop in GNP would be severely felt. The dependence on aid is even more clearly evident when one considers aid as a percentage of gross domestic investment. Except for the anomalous cases of Nigeria and Uganda, aid constituted a third or more of most Commonwealth African countries' investment capacity in 1979, and two-thirds of Tanzania's. On the other hand, aid monies are not necessarily well spent. Many of the large investment projects initiated in the 1960s and '70s could not be sustained by African governments, so the World Bank had to recommend that aid donors consider covering recurrent expenditures in the 1980s, rather than initiating any new projects.[51]

Another aspect of Africa's economy often stressed by dependency theorists is the alleged dominance of transnational or multinational corporations in African economies. But in fact, as noted in Chapter 3, Africa is not a major area of investment for American or European transnational corporations: in 1971, direct investment in all of Africa was only about 5.5 percent of the world total,[52] and much of this was in South Africa. To repeat, the following reasons explain this lack of private capital investment: the African market is severely limited; African labor productivity is very low; political instability in a number of countries is high, thus discouraging potential investors; and economic policy fluctuates as governments make futile attempts to redress their overall economic decline. It is true that in small, weak African economies, even a few multinationals can appear to have a great deal of power. In Ghana, the Kaiser Aluminum Company and Reynolds Metals are accused of having a very profitable position, paying "notoriously low rates" for electric power, because of a 20-year contract made with the Nkrumah regime.[53] Companies such as the British Lonrho have acquired such widespread holdings in Kenya that they are alleged to constitute an independent source of power.[54] In West Africa, the conglomerate United Africa Company, deprived of its colonial monopoly over the purchase of cocoa and palm oil by the new government marketing boards, has acquired substantial holdings in import substitution and processing interests.[55] A few foreign banks, such as Standard Bank and Barclay's, have considerable say over the use of investment capital.

But on the whole, the problem in Africa is too little investment by transnational corporations, not too much. This can be asserted despite a number of criticisms commonly made of transnational corporations. They are accused of exporting their profits, rather than investing them in the countries in which they were first generated. Even when legal expatriation of profits is controlled by government regulation, transnationals can illegally export profits by transfer pricing (that is, undercharging their parent companies for products exported from Africa, and overpaying parent companies for imports from Europe or North America). Moreover, they are accused of importing inappropriate, capital-intensive technology, rather than using "appropriate" labor-intensive technology that would provide increased employment. For example, a 1970s study of multinational soap producers in Kenya showed that they provided less employment than local soapmakers; introduced new, expensive tastes for Western soaps; and drained scarce foreign exchange.[56] Finally, even when industries are nationalized, multinational corporations are hired on management contracts to provide expertise and access to the latest technology; but they do not, it is alleged, train African replacements, nor do they provide the contacts Africans would need to operate on their own as equals with foreign executives and businessmen.

These criticisms appear to assume that it is not the business of multinational corporations to make profits. Capitalist development, which is lacking in Africa, is predicated upon innovation and increases in productivity as a means to obtain profit. The problem in Commonwealth Africa is that much of the capacity for indigenous innovation has been blocked not by transnational corporations, but by a parasitic ruling class that controls the state. Illegal transfers of funds and other such abuses are perpetrated by local as well as by foreign businessmen. Monopolies on production can benefit the local members of government who grant them, as well as transnationals. For example, members of the ruling class in Kenya are alleged to have maneuvered a near monopoly of textiles for a joint state-transnational firm in 1975, causing the closure of locally owned textile firms.[57]

Overall, the role of transnational corporations is less important than indigenously generated economic policy in explaining underdevelopment. Despite their propensities to disobey local government regulations, what multinational corporations do or do not do in Commonwealth Africa is to a considerable extent the result of overall national development plans. Hyden argues that "African countries who have treated international capital as an ally . . . have been able to allow their national economies to expand and develop more than those who out of fear of its 'neo-colonial' threat have rejected such capital."[58] Whether collaboration with transnational corporations takes a parasitic form, with officials of the state demanding kick-backs and bribes, or a productive form is largely a matter for the indigenous ruling class, not external economic forces, to decide.

Thus the dependency thesis, despite both its contemporary empirical relevance and its ideological importance, does not provide a complete explanation of Africa's underdevelopment. It is true that Africa's historically weak position in the world economy hinders her ability to acquire foreign exchange, and that some of this weakness is explainable by colonial policies. But poor planning and state policies directed against productive peasants and against women and "alien" traders and producers are also responsible for Africa's present economic crisis. So are self-interested manipulations of national development policies by the ruling class. Later in this chapter, I will return to the relationship among class, development, and rights. Before doing so, however, it is necessary to discuss the impact that the dependency thesis, now transformed into an ideology of underdevelopment, has had upon the approach to economic human rights at the United Nations. The stress on international economic rights in that forum may in fact constitute a stumbling block to internal reform in Africa. In its international ideological guise, it can be a convenient cover for members of African ruling classes to pursue parasitic policies profitable for themselves, but detrimental to long-run productivity and equitable distribution of resources.

The New International Economic Order

The dependency thesis has had a major impact upon the way many Third World policy-makers think about the problems of underdevelopment.[59] Combined with the early stress in the Universal Declaration of Human Rights on economic, as well as social and political rights, it has resulted in a series of U.N. statements advocating a restructuring of the world economic system as a principal and priority step towards remedying human rights abuses. The new proclamations, in reaction to the alleged Western stress on civil and political rights, stress the interdependency of all types of rights;[60] in practice, however, civil and political rights take second place to economic rights.

The stress in official U.N. documents on a new international economic order (NIEO) starts with early attempts to protect the national sovereignty of independent states by asserting the priority of public (national) property over private (and often foreign) property. Article 17 of the Universal Declaration of 1948 states that "Everyone has the right to own property" and that "No one shall be arbitrarily deprived of his property." These clauses, however, are absent from both of the 1966 covenants—on Civil and Political, and on Economic, Social and Cultural Rights. Instead, Article 1 of both covenants contains a collectivist right to national economic sovereignty that "All peoples may, for their own ends, freely dispose of their national wealth and resources. . . . In no case may a people be deprived of its own means of subsistence." The notion that "peoples" (in practice nation-states) may not be deprived of their means of subsistence in the interests of outsiders' private property rests on the assumption that a nation-state with full control over its own economy will be able to provide better for the subsistence rights of each individual member of the polity than will a nation-state without such control.

This early U.N. redefinition of the right to property as a national right to collective subsistence was followed by a number of resolutions and documents advocating a reordering of the world economy in the direction of subsistence rights for the poorer countries. In 1974 there was a call for a New International Economic Order whose specific aim was to "correct inequalities and redress existing injustices, [and] to eliminate the widening gap between the developed and the developing countries."[61] This aim was to be accomplished by a series of changes in the way the world economy was organized. Commodity producer cartels were to be encouraged, while the development of synthetic substitutes for commodities was to be discouraged. Commodity prices were to be indexed so they rose and fell along with the prices of manufactured goods. In developed countries, tariffs discriminating against the products of underdeveloped countries were to be lowered. In addition, a reform of the international monetary system was called for, debts were to be forgiven or rescheduled, and increased aid was advocated.

In the new international economic order, it was envisaged, aid was to be given as a matter of right, not as a matter of charity or moral obligation. The 1974 Charter of Economic Rights and Duties of States, a companion to the NIEO document, stated that one fundamental principle of international economic relations should be the "remedying of injustices which have been brought about by force and which deprive a nation of the natural means necessary for its normal development."⁶² This principle was echoed in the 1980 Lagos Plan of Action, which stated that "Member states consider that they are owed a massive and appropriate contribution by the developed countries to the development of Africa."⁶³ The implication of this statement was that the redistribution of world resources, on a basis not necessarily profitable to the developed countries, ought to compensate for past injustices, including colonial authority imposed by force (as it had been in British-ruled Africa).

The principle that world economic relations should not be conducted entirely on the basis of profitability was also implicit in the new trend toward evolving codes of conduct for transnational corporations. The Economic Commission for Africa maintained that transnationals' economic planning "did not necessarily take into account the national objectives of the host countries, basic consumer needs or the imperatives of world wide equitable distribution of income."⁶⁴ The commission advocated that transnationals adhere to host-countries' development plans. It also argued that transnationals should refrain from interfering in host country politics, abstain from corrupt practices, and contribute to the host country's balance of payments. In general, the commission's recommendations were unrealistic insofar as they required the transnationals to put the development of the country (or the country's rulers' visions of development) over considerations of profit. They were also unrealistic in their assumption that all corruption was externally generated, rather than being a standard means by which indigenous occupiers of state office accumulated wealth.

The final stage in the attempt to implement economic rights in conformity with national development plans was the 1977 resolution, "Alternative approaches and ways and means within the United Nations system for improving the effective enjoyment of human rights and fundamental freedoms."⁶⁵ This resolution stated that equal attention ought to be given to civil/political and economic, social, and cultural rights, but then went on to say that in the U.N. system, priority with regard to human rights ought to be given to questions of sovereignty and to the realization of the new international economic order.⁶⁶ Thus, the importance of civil and political rights in permitting those affected by development plans to have a say in their formulation was ignored. So also was the possibility that national ruling classes would both abrogate civil and political rights in order to maintain themselves in power, and formulate "development" policies that would in fact increase their own wealth.

What, in fact, was new about this new series of statements regarding economic human rights? The strengthened statements regarding national economic sovereignty and the need to control the activities of Western-based transnational corporations provided a moral incentive, and a direction for further legislation, to control the activities of extremely large private corporations. It is ironic that the anti-transnational activities may have evolved just at the time when their influence was waning compared to the influence of private banks;[67] presumably, however, the principles regarding transnationals could be adjusted to apply to banks also. The new international economic order itself, however, was misnamed. Little is new about it other than the legitimacy accorded to cartels of primary commodity producers. What the NIEO advocates is essentially a series of marginal adjustments designed to assist the poorer countries to cope with world recession. Debt and tariff relief, increased aid, and a realignment of prices of commodity vs. industrial goods, even if implemented, would not result in a new structure of world trade. Nor would such measures lessen the dependence of African economies on the world economy as a whole. According to one commentator, even if all the NIEO principles were put into practice, it would be the more developed "Third World" countries which would benefit, at least in the short run. If all protective tariffs in the developed world were removed, sub-Saharan Africa would obtain only about 7 percent of the increase in Third World exports.[68]

Moreover, the proclamation that aid is a right based on past injustices, rather than a gift, is unfortunately merely a moral statement. From a philosophical point of view, those who advocate universal basic rights[69] might well agree that aid ought to be a right, whether or not past injustices toward Africa can be verified. The principle of aid as a right may have a long-term ideological impact, as more policy-makers in the developed world accept that their responsibilities to provide basic (economic) rights cannot be confined only to their own citizens. But it will have little immediate practical significance, especially in recessionary times and in the face of evidence that aid monies are frequently not well spent.

Even given that the NIEO is little more than a plea for a series of ameliorative measures designed to assist the poorer countries, is there any possibility that it could be implemented in the 20th century? One approach argues that the general expansion of trade that would result from a richer Third World with enhanced consumer power would, in the end, benefit the entire world economy. This is the view of the Brandt Commission on North-South relations, whose chairman argued that "All nations will benefit from a strengthened global economy . . . and an improved climate for growth and investment."[70] Certainly, there is substantial evidence that the developed (rich) world profits more from trade with itself than with its poorer partners. The problem lies in the assumption that an unprofitable (for the West) transfer of resources would actually result in increased economic production and consumption in the Third World. In the countries of Commonwealth Africa where planning is poor, such is not necessarily the case. The economy of Tanzania, one of the largest per capita aid recipients in the world, is in decidedly worse shape in the 1980s than it was in the 1960s.

Why, given that it is against their economic interests and would not necessarily increase world trade, would the developed countries then engage in the net transfer of resources that the NIEO advocates? What power does the underdeveloped world have, other than its rhetorical dominance in the United Nations, to enforce such a transfer? One approach advocated is, in essence, to use threats. For example, the Third World could point to its overwhelming demographic dominance (although it is certainly not historically the case that larger populations possess any military or economic superiority over smaller ones). Or the Third World could promise not to manufacture nuclear weapons, in return for resource redistribution.[71] Finally, it could resort to cartelization and to withholding key economic resources, a tactic already legitimized in the NIEO proclamation.

For the countries dealt with in this book, however, even the threat of economic cartelization is a weak one. OPEC (Organization of Petroleum Exporting Countries) is the model for the NIEO–inspired cartels of commodity producers. But in the early 1980s OPEC's influence declined as demand for oil dropped and new sources of supply were found in the West. Consequently Nigeria, a member of OPEC, now finds herself in serious financial difficulties, in the classic manner of the underdeveloped country dependent on one commodity export. The other Commonwealth countries must deal with even worse difficulties. Zambia produces a strategic commodity, copper, but in 1980 she produced only about 9 percent of the total world supply, which is in any case glutted.[72] Ghana, Kenya, Malawi, and Uganda produce the nonessential commodities cocoa, tea, coffee, and tobacco. Moreover, they are in competition with each other as well as with richer economies such as Brazil, which might well find it in its interests to push the African producers out of the market, rather than to cooperate with them in a cartel arrangement. Gambia is completely dependent on palm products, which can be supplanted by other products if they become too expensive. Sierra Leone produces little more than half of 1 percent of the world's supply of precious stones (diamonds).[73]

Other aspects of the NIEO pertinent to Commonwealth Africa would suffer similar difficulties. Regional integration is suggested as an economic option; but the East African Common Market, composed of Kenya, Tanzania, and Uganda, has already fallen apart. Political factors, such as the conflict between Tanzania and Amin's Uganda, were admittedly part of the reason for the Common Market's disintegration. But other reasons were the lack of diversity of the region's products and the fact that industry and administration tended to concentrate in Kenya, which possessed significant initial comparative advantages over the other two economies. On the whole, regional integration attempts, such as ECOWAS (Economic Commission of West African States), are plagued by the lack of economic diversity in Africa as well as by the historic and structural links of the various countries to their colonial mother countries.

All these difficulties indicate that the ideological attempt in the United Nations to restructure the world economy will founder in Commonwealth Africa on the problems posed by nondiversified, inflexible, and low-productivity economies. Furthermore, the NIEO approach completely ignores the responsibility of indigenous ruling classes in undermining African economies since independence. As one scholar puts it "the NIEO ideology helps strengthen the state and its functionaries [and helps] to deflect criticism from the government."[74] The national economic sovereignty established in principle by the United Nations is not being exercised on behalf of Commonwealth African "peoples"; it is being exercised on behalf of their rulers.

Class, Development, and Rights

The problem of underdevelopment in Commonwealth Africa has three aspects. One is the internal aspect: insufficient human capital, inadequate planning, poor infrastructure, unfortunate nationalizations, and the exploitation of the agricultural sector for the sake of industry. Another is the external aspect summarized above in the discussion of the dependency thesis. Finally, there is a human dimension often overlooked by analysts of both the "external" and the "internal" persuasion, the fact of social stratification. Third World rulers do not always represent their people; often, they represent only themselves.

Even if one disregards the issue of class formation and the role of the state as a basis for the acquisition of individual power and wealth, one cannot ignore the difficulty that Commonwealth African governments are dominated by a small group of people with little capacity to plan economic development. The information needed by the planners is simply not available, the transportation and communication facilities necessary to implement plans are breaking down, and there is a shortage of committed, reliable, rural-planning officers. Given that African economies are, as national entities, new and fragile, comprehensive economic policy-making requires flexibility, freedom of debate, and a real understanding of African complexities. Yet in Commonwealth Africa, economic policies are often made by executive fiat.

A number of commentators now suggest that the best route to economic development in Commonwealth Africa is to de-control the economy. If the choice is between an economy dominated by a parasitic ruling class that uses the state to accumulate wealth, which it then spends in a wasteful manner, and an indigenous bourgeoisie with the capacity to innovate and raise productivity, the latter is by far the better alternative.[75] Small-scale, local entrepreneurs are a good bet, in this view, for "appropriate" development. They are more likely to provide employment, more likely to use local resources in their production, and less likely to drain foreign exchange than state or foreign large-scale investors. Above all, they are more likely to produce inexpensive goods to satisfy the basic needs of ordinary African consumers.

Much evidence suggests that entrepreneurship is not a scarce commodity in Commonwealth Africa. The old view that peasants lacked initiative and that the communal ideal of redistribution of wealth prohibited the development of a profit-oriented productive class has been put to rest by many studies.[76] Both wealthier peasants in the rural areas and entrepreneurial urban migrants are capable of increasing production of food and providing necessary services. Given the lack of competent administrative and planning infrastructure, then, it would seem advisable to leave the local economy in Commonwealth Africa in local hands; that is, to allow more room for innovation to productive peasants and small-scale urban businessmen, as well as to women and "alien" entrepreneurs. This is not to suggest that no regulations should be placed on large-scale foreign investments or control of national resources, especially of minerals. Nor is it to ignore the problems of land alienation, possibly widening income distributions, and the unequal power of employers over employees in open-market economies. It is to suggest that moves to rectify Africa's position in the world division of labor must be made along with moves toward efficient use of human and material resources inside Africa, and with some guarantee that increased aid, debt relief, and (possibly) an actual net transfer of resources from the developed to the underdeveloped world would not be used by the governing classes merely for their own benefit.

Both the need for efficient use of resources and the need for distribution of aid and wealth to the African poor bring to our attention the need for public participation in the development process in Africa. The stress on the priority of economic rights over civil/political rights in the U.N. system ignores the importance of the latter for the former. The argument for giving priority to economic rights appears to be based on the assumption that in the Western world, civil and political rights were implemented only after "basic human needs" had been fulfilled. This assumption is erroneous. In 19th-century Europe, "political repression, by blocking out popular participation, enabled regimes to persist while ignoring the vital human needs of their population."[77] Only after the civil and political rights of suffrage, freedom of association (especially for trade unions), and freedom of the press and speech had been attained were economic rights enacted. Moreover, there is no justification for the assumption that contemporary development dictatorships are a strategically good choice of regime, from the point of view of providing for the economic rights of their citizens. A number of studies have shown that such regimes can sometimes generate economic growth, but they do not provide for development in the sense of combining growth with equitable distribution of basic economic goods.[78]

Development dictatorships in Commonwealth Africa will not provide for basic subsistence rights because they are dominated by ruling classes. Public participation in decision-making, therefore, is necessary to guard against abuses of economic power by the ruling class, such as were detailed in Chapter 3. Economic rights are a political matter. Peasants, workers, and the urban poor all require a political voice to protect their interests against the economic policies of the ruling class. While reference to the world economy can explain Commonwealth Africa's economic heritage and its present global constraints, and reference to internal inefficiencies can help to rectify mistakes in planning, only an approach to economic development that recognizes the class nature of African societies and the need for political participation from below will have any success in actually implementing economic rights.

To wait for economic development to occur in Africa before allowing for civil and political liberties is to invite the possibility that real development will never occur.[79] The economic resources presently available in Commonwealth Africa are extremely limited and are subject to capture by the ruling class. Ordinary people need rights of effective political participation, including freedoms of speech and the press, freedom of association, and the freedom to participate in government, to guarantee that their economic rights are respected. Without civil and political rights, the evidence suggests, economic growth may occur, but economic development will not.

But civil and political rights are not likely to be permitted in Commonwealth Africa. They are dangerous to regimes that are attempting to consolidate themselves in power. Newly formed, or forming, ruling groups control weakly integrated "nation"-states, in which "the political requirements of regime and personal survival take precedence over and can contradict the economic policies and practices needed to promote sustained economic expansion."[80] Because their own personal wealth is acquired though direct control of the state and its resources, the political imperative of power is a much stronger motive for the ruling classes of Commonwealth Africa than the imperative of economic development.

Notes

1. North-South Institute, "Briefing: Africa's Economic Crisis" (Ottawa: North-South Institute, February 1983), p. 1.
2. See Sara S. Berry, "The Food Crisis and Agrarian Change in Africa: A Review Essay," *African Studies Review* 27, no. 2 (July 1984): 59–112.

3. North-South Institute, "Africa's Economic Crisis," p. 2.

4. In 1975 one kwacha equalled $1.56 U.S. See *Readers' Digest 1976 Almanac and Yearbook* (New York: W.W. Norton, 1975), p. 476.

5. Republic of Zambia, "Household Budget Survey 1974/75: Preliminary Report" (Lusaka: Central Statistical Service, February 1980).

6. The World Bank, *World Development Report* (New York: Oxford University Press, 1984), table 28: "Income Distribution."

7. Rolph Van Der Hoeven, "Zambia's Economic Dependence and the Satisfaction of Basic Needs," *International Labour Review* 121, no. 2 (Mar.–Apr. 1982): 227–28.

8. Central Bureau of Statistics, Ministry of Finance and Planning, Government of Kenya, "The Rural Kenyan Nutrition Survey, Feb.–Mar. 1977," *Social Perspectives* (Nairobi) 2, no. 4 (September 1977): 6.

9. Anonymous, *In/Dependent Kenya* (London: Zed Press, 1982), pp. 53–55.

10. Andrew Shepherd, "Agrarian Change in Northern Ghana: Public Investment, Capitalist Farming and Famine," in Judith Heyer, Pepe Roberts, and Gavin Williams, eds., *Rural Development in Tropical Africa* (London: Macmillan, 1981), pp. 168–92.

11. The World Bank, *Poverty and Human Development* (New York: Oxford University Press, 1980), p. 79.

12. Economic Commission for Africa, "The Role of Women in African Development." Prepared for the World Conference of the International Women's Year, Mexico City, 1975. United Nations Document E/CONF.66/BP/8–81, Add.1, p. 23.

13. A. Mejia, H. Pizurki and E. Royston, *Physician and Nurse Migration: Analysis and Policy Implications* (Geneva: World Health Organization, 1979), p. 332 (chap. 14: "Nigeria").

14. North-South Institute, "Africa's Economic Crisis," p. 1.

15. The World Bank, *Accelerated Development in Sub-Saharan Africa* (Washington, D.C.: The World Bank, 1981), p. 4.

16. Ibid., p. 6.

17. Ibid., p. 9.

18. Margaret Peil, *Consensus and Conflict in African Societies* (London: Longman, 1977), p. 186.

19. African Charter of Human and Peoples' Rights, Preamble, par. 8, in Claude E. Welch, Jr., and Robert I. Meltzer, eds., *Human Rights and Development in Africa* (Albany: State University of New York Press, 1984).

20. These are, respectively, Republic of Kenya, *African Socialism and Its Application to Planning in Kenya* (G.P.K. 3938–5m-12/65); Kenneth D. Kaunda, "Humanism in Zambia and a Guide to Its Implementation" (Lusaka: Zambian Information Service, 1968); and Julius K. Nyerere, *Ujamaa: Essays on Socialism* (London: Oxford University Press, 1968), esp. chap. 2, "The Arusha Declaration."

21. The World Bank, *Accelerated Development*, chap. 5.

22. Carl K. Eicher, "Facing up to Africa's Food Crisis," *Foreign Affairs* 61, no. 1 (Fall 1982): 160.

23. *Africa Contemporary Record*, vol.4 (1971–72), p. B207.

24. Goran Hyden, *Beyond Ujamaa in Tanzania: Underdevelopment and an Uncaptured Peasantry* (Berkeley: University of California Press, 1980), p. 114.

25. P.L. Raikes,"Ujamaa and Rural Socialism," *Review of African Political Economy* 3 (May–Oct. 1975): 49–50.

26. Michael F. Lofchie, "Agrarian Crisis and Economic Liberalisation in Tanzania," *Journal of Modern African Studies* 16, no. 3 (1978): 452-75.

27. Hyden, *Beyond Ujamaa*, p. 146.

28. Ibid., p. 118.

29. Emmanuel Hansen, "Public Policy and the Food Question in Ghana," *Afrique et Developpement* 6, no. 3 (1981): 101.

30. Republic of Ghana, "Ghana Today 10: Operation Feed Yourself" (Accra: Ghana Information Services, n.d. [1975]), p. 4.

31. Hyden, *Beyond Ujamaa*, p. 132 ff.

32. Hansen, "Public Policy," p. 111.

33. Nii K. Bentsi-Enchill,"Destruction of Accra's Makola Market," *West Africa*, August 27, 1979, pp. 1539-41.

34. United Republic of Tanzania, "Tanzania: Who Is Dreaming? A Statement by the Government of the United Republic of Tanzania" (Dar es Salaam: Tanzanian Information Services, 1980).

35. "United Republic of Tanzania: The Year the Country Hit Rock-Bottom," *Africa Contemporary Record*, vol.14 (1981-82), p. B272.

36. Goran Hyden, *No Shortcuts to Progress: African Development Management in Perspective* (Berkeley: University of California Press, 1983), p. 200.

37. G.K. Helleiner, "Review of The World Bank, *Accelerated Development in Sub-Saharan Africa,*" *Journal of Development Economics* 13, nos. 1-2 (Aug.-Oct. 1983): 264. See also Charles Harvey, "The Economy of Sub-Saharan Africa: A Critique of the World Bank's Report," *Africa Contemporary Record*, vol.14 (1981-82), p. A114-19.

38. Arthur Lewis, *The Evolution of the International Economic Order* (Princeton: Princeton University Press, 1978), cited in Stanley Hoffmann, *Duties Beyond Borders: On the Limits and Possibilities of Ethical International Politics* (Syracuse: Syracuse University Press, 1981), p. 168.

39. Hyden, *No Shortcuts*.

40. For a broad overview of the thesis that Africa was actively underdeveloped, see Walter Rodney, *How Europe Underdeveloped Africa* (London: Bogle L'Ouverture Publications, 1972). See also Rhoda Howard, *Colonialism and Underdevelopment in Ghana* (London: Croom Helm, 1978).

41. Organization of African Unity, "The Lagos Plan of Action for the Economic Development of Africa: 1980-2000" (Geneva: International Institute for Labour Studies, 1981), p. 19.

42. Claude Ake, *A Political Economy of Africa* (Harlow, Essex: Longmans, 1981), p. 139.

43. Richard L. Sklar, "Democracy in Africa," *African Studies Review* 26, no. 3/4 (Sept.-Dec. 1983): 11. See also Rhoda E. Howard and Jack Donnelly, "Human Dignity, Human Rights and Political Regimes" (forthcoming in *American Political Science Review*, September 1986).

44. UNCTAD, *Handbook of International Trade and Development Statistics* (supplement) (New York: United Nations, 1980), table 4:3(d).

45. Van Der Hoeven, "Zambia's Economic Dependence," p. 224.

46. The World Bank, "Sub-Saharan Africa: Progress Report on Development Prospects and Programs" (Washington, D.C.: The World Bank, September 1983), pp. 3-4.

47. "Tanzania: The Year the Country Hit Rock-Bottom," p. B272.

48. Hyden, *No Shortcuts*, p. 3.

49. The World Bank, *Accelerated Development*, p. 123.

50. North-South Institute, "Africa's Economic Crisis," p. 5.

51. World Bank, *Accelerated Development*, p. 126.

52. Helge Hveem, "The Extent and Type of Direct Foreign Investment in Africa," in Carl Widstrand and Samir Amin, eds., *Multinational Firms in Africa* (Uppsala: Scandinavian Institute of African Studies, 1975), p. 65.

53. Kwesi Garbah, "Development and the 'Debt Trap,' " *West Africa*, April 30, 1984, p. 922.

54. The Editors, "The Multinationals in Africa," *Review of African Political Economy* 2 (Jan.–Apr. 1975): 7.

55. C.I.S. Anti-Report no. 11, "Unilever's World" (Nottingham: Russell Press, n.d.).

56. Steven Langdon, "Multinational Corporations, Taste Transfer and Underdevelopment: A Case Study from Kenya," *Review of African Political Economy* 2 (Jan.–Apr. 1975): 12–24.

57. Anonymous, *In/Dependent Kenya*, p. 102.

58. Hyden, *No Shortcuts*, p. 204.

59. Robert W. Cox, "Ideologies and the New International Economic Order: Reflections on Some Recent Literature," *International Organizations* 33, no. 2 (Spring 1979): 257–302.

60. General Assembly Resolution 32/130, "Alternative approaches and ways and means within the United Nations system for improving the effective enjoyment of human rights and fundamental freedoms," General Assembly, Thirty-Second Session, Resolution and Decisions (20 Sept–21 Dec. 1977) Supp. 45 (A/32/45), Preamble, par. 10. Hereafter referred to as Res. 32/130 (1977).

61. General Assembly, Res. 3201 (S-VI) (1 May 1974): "Declaration on the Establishment of a New International Economic Order," in United Nations, *Resolutions* (1972–74), vol. 14, pp. 527–29, preamble, par. 3. Hereafter referred to as res. 3201, NIEO.

62. "Charter of Economic Rights and Duties of States," General Assembly, *Official Records: Twenty-Ninth Session* (1974) Suppl. No. 31, res. 3281 (XXIX), article 1), i. Hereafter referred to as res. 3281, Charter.

63. Organization of African Unity, "Lagos Plan," p. 19, par. 55.

64. Economic Commission for Africa, "Code of Conduct for Transnational Corporations: (ECA African Regional Meeting's Report, Addis Ababa, 31 January–4 February 1977)," reprinted in *Africa Contemporary Record*, vol. 10 (1977–78), pp. C157–59.

65. Res. 32/130 (1977).

66. Ibid., article 1: a, e and f, p. 151.

67. Cox, "Ideologies," p. 288.

68. Hugh M. Arnold, "Africa and the New International Economic Order," *Third World Quarterly* 2, no. 2 (1980): 298.

69. Henry Shue, *Basic Rights: Subsistence, Affluence and U.S. Foreign Policy* (Princeton: Princeton University Press, 1980).

70. Report of the Independent Commission on International Development Issues, *North-South: A Program for Survival* (Cambridge: MIT Press, 1983), p. 23.

71. Cox, "Ideologies," p. 280.

72. UNCTAD, *Handbook of International Trade and Development Statistics* (New York: United Nations, 1983), table 4:4.

73. Ibid.

74. Craig Murphy, *The Emergence of the NIEO Ideology* (Boulder, Colo.: Westview Press, 1984), p. 173.

75. Hyden, *No Shortcuts*, p. 52.

76. See, e.g., Howard, *Colonialism and Underdevelopment in Ghana*, pp. 182–93; Polly Hill, "Some Characteristics of Indigenous West African Economic Enterprise," *Conference Proceedings*, Nigerian Institute of Social and Economic Research, (1962); Peter C. Garlick, *African Traders and Economic Development in Ghana* (Oxford; Clarendon Press, 1971); John Rees Harris, "Some Problems in Identifying the Roles of Entrepreneurship in Economic Development: The Nigerian Case," *Explorations in Economic History* 7, no. 3 (Spring 1970): 347–69.

77. Robert Justin Goldstein, "Political Repression and Political Development: The 'Human Rights' Issue in Nineteenth Century Europe," in Richard F. Tomasson, ed., *Comparative Social Research*, vol. 4 (Greenwich, Conn: Jai Press, 1981), p. 194.

78. See Sylvia Ann Hewlett, "Human Rights and Economic Realities: Trade-offs in Historical Perspective," *Political Science Quarterly* 94, no. 3 (Fall 1979): 472; Robert M. Marsh, "Does Democracy Hinder Economic Development in the Latecomer Developing Nations?" in Richard F. Tomasson, ed., *Comparative Social Research*, vol. 2 (Greenwich, Conn: Jai Press, 1979), p. 243; and Han F. Park, "Human Rights and Modernization: A Dialectical Relationship?," *Universal Human Rights* 2, no. 1 (Jan.–Mar. 1980): 91. See also Jack Donnelly, "Human Rights and Development: Complementary or Competing Concerns?," *World Politics* 36 (January 1984): 255–83.

79. I make this argument much more thoroughly in Rhoda Howard, "The Full-Belly Thesis: Should Economic Rights Take Priority over Civil and Political Rights? Evidence from Sub-Saharan Africa," *Human Rights Quarterly* 5, no. 4 (November 1983): 467–90.

80. Richard Sandbrook, "The Politics of Africa's Economic Stagnation." Paper presented at the South/South Conference, Montreal, Canada, May 15–17, 1985, p. 7.

⑤ State Formation and Communal Rights

The economic rights to subsistence discussed in Chapter 4 are a vital aspect of every person's needs. But people are not merely animal consumers reproducing themselves and their families; they are also social and cultural beings. Their dignity is rooted in their identification, through ethnicity, language, religion, and culture, with others. Individuals are members of communal groups based on such shared personal characteristics, and many of them value such communal membership. The preservation of community is thus an important aspect of the well-being of the individual, as the African Charter of Human and Peoples' Rights recognizes, at least in principle. Yet the rights of subnational communities are often violated by national governments. This is particularly the case when the state is new, fragile, and insecure.

One of the major tasks facing Commonwealth African countries is the creation not only of a viable state, but also of a real nation. A state is a geopolitical and administrative entity; it is legally defined by internationally accepted borders, and its existence is predicated upon adequate defense, a united system of communication and transportation, and a relatively efficient bureaucracy. In Africa, even these minimal preconditions for statehood are problematic. Although the borders of all nine Commonwealth states have been secure since independence, some secessionist and irredentist movements still exist. Communication and transportation systems are incomplete, often not even reaching remote rural areas, and bureaucracies are often inefficient, nepotistic, and corrupt.

Under such conditions of weak statehood, governments are also attempting to create a sense of nationhood among very diverse peoples. Such a sense of nationhood derives from a feeling that all citizens share certain personal characteristics: of ancestry, language, religion, or culture. People who feel themselves part of a nation will be loyal to, and intimately connected with, not only the legal entity of the state but also other citizens. It is this loyalty to the nation that can eventually overcome both schismatic tendencies among different ethnic or regional groups and nepotistic bureaucratic practices. The present weakness of Commonwealth African "nation"-states constitutes a major structural reason for African regimes' denials of both communal rights, such as ethnic solidarity and religious freedom, and civil/political rights, such as freedom of movement.

One of the key processes of nation-building is the subordination of local to national interests. In Africa, advocacy of local interests is frequently referred to as "tribalism." "Tribalism," however, is merely an expression of local or group interests, some of which are explicitly protected in both the International Bill of Rights and the African Charter of Rights. Especially important is Article 27 of the Civil and Political Covenant, guaranteeing to minorities the right "to enjoy their own culture, to profess and practice their own religion [and] to use their own language." Both the 1966 covenants also contain articles protecting the family.[1] These rights are the basis for the protection of the community against the centralized state. They are paralleled in the African Charter of Human and Peoples' Rights by Article 17, 2, guaranteeing each individual the freedom to take part in the cultural life of his community, by Article 17, 3, asserting that "the promotion and protection of morals and traditional values recognized by the community shall be the duty of the State," and by Article 28, preserving the family.

This chapter will investigate the conditions under which new African governments are likely to violate the rights of communal groups. A communal group is defined as any group based on the shared ethnicity, origin, religion, or language of its members. Violations of communal rights are violations of the rights of individuals specifically because of their membership in such groups. First we consider the actual reasons behind several well-known manifestations of ethnic or "tribal" conflict, then the expulsions of both non-African and African "aliens" from the new African states, and last, instances of conflict between certain religious minorities and the state.

Ethnicity and "Tribalism"

To many outside observers, the problem of tribalism appears to be endemic to Africa. Political events in Africa are frequently interpreted in tribal terms, whereas they would be interpreted in ethnic or class terms had they occurred elsewhere.[2] Yet European political events could also be interpreted as tribalism if no effort were made to differentiate small, simply organized, kin-based groups (genuine "tribes") from larger national groupings often with a highly developed state structure. The problem of "tribalism" in Africa is in fact not a problem of primordial communal sentiments that impede the unification of the nation-state, but rather a problem of incomplete structural integration.

In well-integrated nation-states, individuals have lateral ties of organizational membership, profession, educational status, class, etc., which complement or supersede their vertical ties of ethnic, religious, or linguistic membership. But in new nation-states, especially those containing largely illiterate or newly literate populations, there are fewer such lateral ties, and ethnic ties are more likely to predominate. Hence, "tribalism" appears to be an insurmountable problem of a unique African psyche, whereas in fact it is clearly modifiable by the establishment of new memberships in new groupings within the nation-state.

The problem for the new African states, therefore, is how to modify strong ethnic identifications in favor of more national ones while, at the same time, not trampling on the rights of ethnic groups enshrined in the various human rights documents. There are no rights of minorities, in opposition to the larger nation-state, in the African Charter of Human and Peoples' Rights; rather, the rights of "peoples" mentioned in Articles 19–24 are clearly meant to be the rights of national, not subnational, groups. Under Chapter II, "Duties," it is stated that "Every individual shall have the duty to respect and consider his fellow beings without discrimination, and to maintain relations aimed at promoting, safeguarding, and reinforcing mutual respect and tolerance" (Article 28), and further (Article 29, 7) that "The individual shall also have the duty . . . to preserve and strengthen positive African cultural values." Such clauses obliquely enjoin upon the citizenry the obligation to respect fellow-citizens of different ethnic origins, but nowhere do they guarantee the actual rights of minorities. This is not accidental. As discussed in Chapter 1, the chief objective of the Organization of African Unity is to preserve the territorial borders and the sovereign integrity of its member-states. This preoccupation clearly supersedes, in law, any rights of minority groups. In any case, the United Nations itself provides for minority rights only within the nation-state.[3] Thus there is no justification in international human rights law for ethnic secessionism.

But what have these proclamations on the rights of minorities and nation-states to do with the political problem of "tribalism" in Africa? To answer this question, it is necessary first to avoid the use of the term *tribalism,* and to recognize that there are political problems in Africa, as elsewhere, of competition between ethnic groups. Political problems of competition exist, also, between old, indigenous African states and the new, modern states of the post-colonial era. In all cases, these political competitions intersect with problems of regionalism and class; they are not merely ethnic or particularist in origin or enactment.

The pre-colonial histories of Africa and the method of integration of indigenous political groupings into the modern state structure affect regional and ethnic conflicts. In Ghana, the indigenous Ashanti state enjoyed a great deal of power in pre-colonial times; indeed, had its expansionism not been stopped by British conquest in the late 19th century, it might now control all of Ghana, as well as parts of surrounding countries. It is not surprising, then, that there is some resentment and fear of Ashanti among other Ghanaian ethnic groups. Before independence, the Ashanti-based National Liberation Movement was the chief opponent of Kwame Nkrumah's Convention People's Party. One of the NLM leaders, Kofi Busia, was the civilian prime minister in 1969–72 and was identified by many with Ashanti interests. Yet ethnic hostility in Ghana has so far been contained, partly because of cross-cutting political rivalries based on regionalism (especially the underdevelopment of the north) or on other ethnic competitions (especially, as will be seen below, alleged Ewe secessionism). Ethnic conflict has also been contained by concerted attempts, especially by Nkrumah and by the Rawlings military regime (1981–   ) to organize around populistically based "class" issues.

That the potential problem of Ashanti dominance in Ghana has not resulted in civil war is useful to keep in mind when discussing civil wars elsewhere, in order to remember that there is nothing inevitable about ethnically based bloodshed in Commonwealth Africa. The other country which also contains one very strong pre-colonial state is Uganda. Uganda is composed of the old feudal state of Buganda, surrounding small kingdoms such as the Ankole and Bunyoro, and a number of smaller minority ethnic groups, such as the Acholi, Langi, and other Nilotic groups in the north. Nineteenth-century Buganda was a very strong, hierarchically organized and expansionist state which plundered its neighbors.[4] During the pre-independence and early independence period, the Buganda-based Democratic Party was the chief opposition to Dr. Milton Obote's United Peoples' Convention. The first independence constitution enshrined the separate power of the Buganda kingdom, allowing it a separate parliament (Lukiiko) and giving its king, or Kabaka, a separate power-base.[5] Thus independent Uganda was originally not a unitary but a federal state, containing within it a separate, quasi-sovereign nation. Such an unusual constitutional arrangement was inherently unstable, and during the 1960s Obote, using increasingly repressive measures, tried to contain Buganda power. Eventually Buganda was physically conquered, the Kabaka fled, and Obote declared a one-party state.

The resentments occasioned by Obote's centralization of power hastened the coup by Idi Amin in 1971. During Amin's rule, the question of Bugandan separate status was merged into a general policy of state terrorism against all who could possibly oppose Amin. But after Obote's reassumption of power in late 1980, the Buganda question reemerged. While the Democratic Party was once again the legal opposition, Buganda-based guerilla groups constituted a serious threat to the Obote government. From 1980 to 1985, when Obote was overthrown, government troops perpetrated many brutal slaughters of guerilla and of civilian opponents of the regime.

Thus the main "tribal" question in Uganda is in fact better described as a national question: an indigenous, well-organized, and powerful African nation is fighting against its submergence in a new nation-state, composed of a number of ethnic groups. In some respects, the Nigerian civil war of 1967–70 was similar to the continuing struggle in Uganda, but there is one essential difference. The Nigerian conflict was the result not of pre-colonial political arrangements, but of new interethnic relations resulting from Britain's unification of previously separate geographical areas.

Nigeria is composed of about 250 different linguistic groups, but among these are three dominant ethnic groups with clearly identifiable regional bases: the Hausa-Fulani in the north, the Yoruba in the southwest, and the Igbo in the southeast. Prior to colonial times, the Hausa-Fulani developed as a predominantly Muslim people with large centralized nation-states; the Yoruba were organized as a number of city-states loosely tied by language and culture, although divided among Muslims and Christians; and the Igbo were a dispersed people, with no political organization larger than loose village alliances, who responded eagerly to the colonial opportunities of Christianization and education.[6] In 1914, these three groups were formally united. Unification resulted in free mobility within the new colony, and thus in contact among the three dominant ethnic groups. Especially important to subsequent events was the migration of several million Igbo to the north. Taking advantage of their education, Christianity, and relative westernization, they established themselves in trade, education, and the civil service, inciting the hostility of the relatively more isolated, non-westernized northerners.

The Nigeria which became independent in 1960 was, thus, an artificial geographic entity with few pre-colonial roots. The original multiparty political system was marred by corruption and by serious political rioting in the western and mid-western (Tiv) sections in 1964. In late 1965, rioting in the north resulted in the death of several hundred Igbo migrants. As a result, in January 1966 there was an Igbo-led military coup under General Ironsi, supplanted in its turn by another coup in July 1966, led by Yakubu Gowon, a Christian from the Northern Region. In late 1966, new riots against the Igbo began. In the event, somewhere between three and thirty thousand Igbo appear to have been murdered,[7] and a mass exodus of approximately two million back to their homeland in the Eastern Region began. The Igbo military leader, Emeka Ojukwu, began to preach secession; after negotiations between the federal government and Igbo leaders failed, the civil war began in 1967.

The Nigerian civil war received a great deal of attention in the Western media of the time and was perceived as an example of tribalism in Africa. It was widely anticipated that the federal forces, especially the Muslim Hausa, had genocidal intent. Shocking reports of starvation and of bombings of civilian targets, especially hospitals, emanated from the secessionist Igbo state of Biafra. Yet at the same time, the federal government offered to open a mercy land corridor for relief supplies, but the offer was turned down by Ojukwu, ostensibly for fear of infiltration by federal forces.[8] There is no official evidence that the federal government practiced or encouraged genocide. International observer teams from both the Organization of African Unity and the British Commonwealth specifically refuted charges of genocide during the war.[9]

That hundreds of thousands of Igbos died during the war itself is irrefutable. Some of the deaths would have occurred even in peacetime, however (given the high rates of infant mortality and malnutrition in Africa as a whole), or were attributable to the "normal" wartime conditions of a civilian population under seige. Others were occasioned by the sudden return of two million Igbo refugees to a very small geographical area, which grew even smaller as the secessionists were forced into an area of only about 70 by 100 miles. The death rate undoubtedly rose as the war was prolonged in the face of obvious eventual defeat. There were also clear instances of brutality, torture, and murder of innocent Biafrans by federal troops, as the Nigerian writer Wole Soyinka documents in his prison memoir *The Man Died.*[10] But similar brutalities were perpetrated by military and civilian Igbo upon minority ethnic groups within their own region. In fact, the original territory claimed as Biafra was populated by about seven million Igbo and five million others. In his memoir of life in a Biafran prison, the novelist and cultural commentator Elechi Amadi, an Okwerre, documents brutalities in all ways parallel to the federal abuse.[11]

The genocide that many Biafrans expected would accompany military defeat did not occur. This does not mean that they suffered no discrimination or economic hardship. Gowon's promises, to rehabilitate the Igbo areas, restore to individual Igbo the property they had abandoned in the north, and reintegrate them into national life,[12] were not entirely honored. Many Igbos attempting to return to their positions in government, parastatal organizations, and the military and police found that they had been supplanted. The property of the Igbo in the new Rivers State, made up predominantly of non-Igbos who had unwillingly been under Biafran rule, was declared abandoned. Igbos suffered discrimination when foreign assets were turned over to Nigerians under the indigenization rules. Finally, the two Igbo states, Imo and Anambra, carved out of the original East-Central state in 1976 when the total number of states was raised from twelve to nineteen, lost significant geological resources, including limestone and important oil-rich areas.[13] Nevertheless, the Igbo have not suffered the massive genocide and brutal slaughter that they and many of their Western sympathizers had expected when the war ended.

Just as the colonial creation of new nation-states not rooted in ethnic homogeneity was the original cause for the Nigerian civil war, so it also explains the origins of the secessionist/irrendentist movements of the Somali in northern Kenya. The North-Eastern Province of Kenya is heavily Somali in population. During the early years of independence, one of the most important tasks of the Nairobi regime was to secure the "loyalty" of the North-Eastern Province to the new central government. Unfortunately, the devices used to ensure this loyalty were highly repressive. Kenyan Somali leaders were routinely placed in preventive detention, where they remained well into the late 1970s.[14] The North-Eastern Province was closed to general access (along with other parts of Kenya) as a "scheduled" area (ostensibly closed to all outsiders, including members of parliament, as a means of protecting the nomadic inhabitants),[15] and news from it was very difficult to obtain. A number of reports, however, accused the Kenyans of mass slaughters of entire villages of Somali citizens and of setting up large "protected villages"—in effect concentration camps.[16] The government refused to acknowledge the ethnically based irredentist motives of the Somalis, making constant reference in official statements to the *shifta* (bandit) problem in the area. In the 1970s less attention was focused on the North-Eastern Province in Kenya, suggesting that perhaps the repressive measures of the state had succeeded in suppressing irrendentist tendencies among the Somali. In the early 1980s, however, the issue resurfaced. In February 1984, up to fourteen hundred people in Wajir district were murdered and more than four thousand members of one clan were arrested, many to be later tortured and executed.[17] The government still refers to nationalist Somalis as bandits, refusing to acknowledge the regional-ethnic basis of the conflict.[18]

One solution to the problem of Somali secessionism in Kenya, short of allowing them to join Somalia, would be to involve the Somalis actively, and to their own benefit, in the national life of Kenya; in effect, to create lateral ties through education, migration, commerce, etc., which would counterbalance their vertical ethnic loyalties. Such, indeed, seems to have occurred in the similar case of alleged Ewe secessionism in Ghana. The Ewe live in the eastern Volta region of Ghana, next to Togo, where many of their co-ethnics reside. Originally, all Ewe lived in one colonial area under the Germans, but when Germany was defeated in World War I they were divided between British and French mandates, and at independence were divided yet again between Ghana and Togo. The Ewe have periodically been regarded as a threat to the integrity of Ghana, even to the point of attempting to take over central state power in their own interests.[19] The 1972–78 Acheampong regime detained and convicted several alleged Ewe plotters.[20] The current military dictator, Jerry Rawlings, faces some hostility as the son of a Ewe mother and a white father; his closest advisor was one of the Ewe imprisoned by Acheampong. Yet at least one commentator argues that the Ewe "threat" has been manipulated by various governments as a scapegoat for other more serious problems, especially during the severe depression of the mid-1970s. He also argues that the Ewe are well integrated into national life, and that the majority of them desire not secession, but merely easier comunications and trade with their co-ethnics in Togo.[21]

There have been, in fact, only two large-scale instances in Commonwealth Africa of the stereotyped "tribalism" that Western commentators often attribute to African politics. In Uganda, ethnic and political conflicts continue to generate large-scale violence and brutality. In Nigeria, the 1979–83 civilian government continued to make efforts to defuse ethnic hostilities. President Shehu Shagari invited the secessionist leader Ojukwu to return to Nigeria, in 1982, so he could stand as a candidate of the ruling People's National Party in the 1983 general elections against the Igbo's long-time political leader, Nnmadi Azikewe. In Ghana, despite the potential for an ethnically based civil war, none has yet occurred.

The only other serious ethnic—in fact racial—conflict that has occurred in Commonwealth Africa was in Zanzibar, the formerly autonomous partner of mainland Tanzania in the United Republic. In mainland Tanzania, ethnic hostilities have little role in politics, since despite the large number (about 125) of ethnic groups, no single one has any real numerical dominance. When "ethnic" hostilities surface, they can be traced to political or economic causes, such as the anger of the Ismani land-owners over the expropriation of their land in the late 1960s.[22] Politics in Zanzibar, however, focus on antagonisms between ethnic Africans and ethnic Arabs. In the immediate pre-independence period this conflict crystallized in the rivalries between the mainly Arab Zanzibar Nationalist Party, and the mainly African Afro-Shirazi party. The Arabs of Zanzibar, the Zanzibar elite, were descended from slave-owners and controlled land, dispensed employment, and occupied administrative office. In 1963, the Zanzibar Nationalist Party won the pre-independence elections and took office. In 1964, in a violent coup by the Afro-Shirazi party, thousands of Arabs were killed.[23] Since that time, Zanzibar has been a repressive dictatorship in which political opponents have been routinely tortured and murdered.[24] Nyerere has unfortunately been unable to exercise much restraining influence on Zanzibari politics.

The Zanzibar situation, by its very anomalous nature, illustrates how much worse ethnic conflict in Commonwealth Africa could have been, had there been more configurations of rival (and economically differentiated) Arab and African populations, such as exist, for example, in the Sudan. In five of the nine countries studied in this book, there has been no serious ethnic conflict, although underlying ethnic hostilities have resulted in discrimination and corruption and have influenced politics, as they do in all multiethnic nation-states. In Sierra Leone, the hostility between Creoles (coastal descendants of freed slaves) and up-country peoples has been one of several factors influencing national politics and the eventual formation of a one-party state. Other factors have been the politics of chiefdoms, Temne-Mende hostilities, and north-south regionalism.[25] Creole-bush antagonisms have also influenced Gambian politics. In Malawi and Zambia, frequent complaints of ethnic favoritism are heard. In Malawi, these appear to have a real basis, as Kamuzu Banda apparently favors his own ethnic group, the Chewa. In Zambia, latent conflicts between the politically dominant Bemba and other ethnic groups cannot be analyzed in isolation from key economic conflicts, especially the role played by the powerful Copper Belt trade unions.

In Kenya, aside from the Somali conflict, there is an underlying tension between the Kikuyu ethnic group, from which Kenyatta originated, and the Luo group, from which Oginga Odinga, Kenyatta's chief political opponent and leader of the banned KPU, originates. But the rival ethnic groups have produced prominent members of both political parties. More important, much of Kenyan politics can be interpreted in terms of class. Odinga is explicitly socialistic in his statements, and during his influential years in opposition in the 1960s, called for the redistribution of land, thus challenging the property rights of rich Kikuyu landowners.[26] The Kenyan writer Ngugi wa Thiong'o spent a year in preventive detention for writing a play that dealt with the issue of land distribution,[27] despite the fact that he is himself a Kikuyu. The severe gap between rich and poor in Kenya generates obvious internal stratification among Kikuyu, about which many former fighters in the Land and Freedom Army ("Mau Mau") are particularly resentful.

What, then, is the relevance of the problem of particularistic loyalties, of an ethnic or national nature, to human rights in Commonwealth Africa? First, it is undoubtedly true that in some countries, a preoccupation with creating a sense of nationhood and mediating among competing ethnic groups has absorbed a large part of the states' resources, which might otherwise have been put to different, possibly more beneficial, use. In Nigeria and Uganda, civil war has meant violations of the most fundamental right of physical security. The weapon of preventive detention has been and is used in Uganda against Buganda, in Kenya against Somalis, in Ghana against Ewes. Moreover, the fear of the divisive issue of "tribalism" has become so strong that some countries have banned outright the very use of the word.[28] The centralizing needs of the state have, in this sense, deprived the citizenry of their right of free expression not only in promulgating local (ethnic or regional) demands, but also in discussing the very problem of ethnicity itself.

On the other hand, ethnic conflicts do not constitute the grave threat to human rights, in and of themselves, that Western commentators often assume they do. In general, the main threat to human rights occasioned by ethnicity has come from the state's reaction to ethnic demands, not from the ethnic factor itself. Unwillingness to redistribute resources from richer to poorer ethnic groups, or to attenuate regional disparities, is often behind the response of the state to ethnically based demands. If Hausa are less educated than Igbo, if up-country Sierra Leoneans are poorer than coastal Creoles, if Kikuyu leaders bought the best of the redistributed white lands after Kenyan independence, then these are primarily questions of resource distribution. Ethnicity can, as is apparently the Ewe case, be manipulated by the ruling regime to suit its particular interest. While ethnic or national loyalties can, as in Nigeria and Uganda, constitute a serious threat to the integrity of the new states of Africa, they can also be used as scapegoat issues to distract ordinary Africans from the real problems of economic underdevelopment and maldistribution of resources. The periodic expulsions of African and non-African "aliens" from several of the societies studied in this book illustrate clearly the economic causes, and politically based manipulations, of "ethnic" questions in Africa.

Citizens, Aliens, and Mass Expulsions

From a legal point of view, the question of the human rights of aliens and citizens is clearly covered by a number of provisions relating to civil liberties. From a sociological point of view, however, the rights of aliens in Commonwealth Africa are primarily an economic matter. Almost every expulsion of so-called "aliens" from a Commonwealth African country since independence can be traced to economic roots, sometimes supplemented by political factors when aliens are regarded as scapegoats around whose expulsions indigenous Africans can unite.

Under the Covenant of Civil and Political Rights, both citizens and non-citizens are protected against arbitrary action by the state. Article 12 states that "Everyone lawfully within the territory of a State shall . . . have the right to liberty of movement," that "Everyone shall be free to leave any country, including his own," and that "No one shall be arbitrarily deprived of the right to enter his own country." Article 13 further states that "An alien lawfully in the territory of a State Party . . . may be expelled therefrom only in pursuance of a decision reached in accordance with the law." The covenant does not explicitly prohibit mass expulsions,[29] but by implication, since every expelled alien lawfully in a country has the right of judicial review, this right extends to victims of mass as well as of individual expulsions.

The African Charter of Human and Peoples' Rights (Article 12) contains provisions similar to those of the United Nations covenant. It guarantees freedom of movement and the right to leave and to return to a country, and states that a "non-national legally admitted . . . may only be expelled from [a country] by virtue of a decision taken in accordance with the law." Furthermore, the charter guarantees the right of asylum and specifically prohibits, in section 12, 5, "the mass expulsion of non-nationals." Since the Banjul Charter did not come into existence until 1982, this last provision cannot be taken to be pertinent to the Ghanaian or

Ugandan expulsions of 1970 and 1972, respectively. But, in principle at least, it seems to constitute a moral prohibition of the Nigerian expulsions of one and a half to two million non-nationals in 1983 and of a further estimated seven hundred thousand in 1985, since mass expulsions are prohibited whether or not the non-nationals are legally in the country.

One of the primary difficulties in analyzing "alien" (non-citizen) rights in Commonwealth Africa is that, on the whole, rights to nationality are very weak. Under British rule, citizenship was not clearly defined. Borders were fluid and open, and the British encouraged mass migrations of individuals to supply both skilled and unskilled labor pools. For example, skilled Ghanaian artisans were in demand all over West Africa,[30] and unskilled miners were encouraged to migrate from Malawi to South Africa's gold mines and Zambia's copper mines. It did not matter to a British employer from what part of Africa a "native" worker originated. Moreover, the British introduced a three-tiered racial system of economic hierarchy. In settler areas, especially Kenya but also in parts of Tanzania and Zambia, the best land was reserved for whites. Whites engaged in retail trade and petty commerce to a limited extent, but far more significant was the participation of Asian-origin people in East Africa, and Lebanese-origin in West Africa. Immigration of these non-African racial groups from other parts of the empire was encouraged by the British.

Thus, independent African states have had to identify who is or is not a citizen, and then to provide priority for citizens in employment and in trade, professions, and government. This is not merely a nationalist goal; it is an essential economic goal. Rates of underemployment in Commonwealth Africa are extremely high. As the percentage of young people in the population increases and as rural land is increasingly consolidated in private hands, governments are faced with the specter of urban populist unrest generated by large numbers of unemployed "school-leavers" or "job-seekers." One way to deal with such people is to expel any who are not legally citizens of the country. In 1970 in Ghana, for example, an estimated two million of the total ten million of the population were not legally citizens.[31] In Nigeria, the 1983 figure for "illegal" aliens was also estimated at about two million.

The definition of citizenship in these countries is complex. Nevertheless, two characteristics of citizenship laws, as reflected in the most recent civilian constitutions of the nine countries (whether or not they are still in force), stand out. One is that, in a number of countries, including Nigeria, Uganda, and Zambia, birth within the borders of the national territory is not enough to guarantee citizenship; a parent or grandparent must either be a citizen (Uganda), an established resident (Zambia), or a member of an "indigenous community" (Nigeria).[32] In Zambia, moreover, only the father qualifies, not a mother or grandparent. Such a parent/grandparent condition disqualifies, for example, people of Ghanaian parentage born in

Nigeria. People of Asian, Lebanese, or European descent are also prevented by these clauses from acquiring citizenship, especially if such non-
Negroid people are not deemed to be members of any "indigenous
community." In Sierra Leone, requirements that citizens be of "negro
African" descent remove the right to citizenship from any of its Lebanese-
descent inhabitants, even if they, their parents and grandparents were
born in the country. As a result, they cannot acquire land in certain parts
of the country or engage in certain trades or businesses reserved for
citizens.[33]

Stringent qualifications are also put on the right to naturalization in
Commonwealth Africa. In Nigeria an individual can be naturalized only if
he is "acceptable to the local community in which he is to live permanently
and has been assimilated into the way of life of Nigerians in that part of the
Federation."[34] Given the long tradition in Africa in which "strangers"
from different ethnic groups remain in separate residential areas and are
defined as outsiders even after several generations of co-residence,[35] such a
clause could be invoked to exclude almost any applicant from citizenship.
It is not clear, moreover, whether naturalization confers full citizenship
rights. In Sierra Leone, the "anti-discrimination" clause in the constitution does not protect naturalized citizens.[36] In Ghana, Nigeria, and
Uganda, naturalized citizens may be deprived of their citizenship rights.[37]

Thus, aliens in Commonwealth Africa have few, if any, opportunities to
naturalize, even if they were born in their host country. They are victims
of the pervasive (but not unique) African distrust of "strangers": the
feeling that if those who share one's place of residence do not also share
one's ancestry and culture, they are not co-nationals. Finally, they are
victims of the economic underdevelopment of Africa. During the period of
expansion of African economies under colonialism, aliens, although strangers, were welcomed. In many instances, indigenous Africans preferred to
remain on their communally owned land and permit strangers to take up
wage-labor; indeed, in areas of land abundance, they also ceded land to
aliens. But as populations grew, as land became privatized, and as more
and more people sought urban jobs, hostility against strangers, especially
strangers of noticeable non-African descent, increased.

All these factors combined to result in a series of East African measures
that affected Asian-origin residents after independence. Asians were accused of not integrating with Africans and of harboring attitudes of racial
superiority. But the most important charge against them was their obvious
predominance in wholesale and retail trade, the professions, and the lower
ranks of the civil service. Under the initial post-independence constitutions in East and Central Africa (not those now in effect), ethnic Asians
born in Africa had the automatic right to citizenship, and all other Asians
had a two-year period in which to apply.[38] Despite these provisions, only
about 61 percent of Kenya's one hundred five thousand Asians, and 48

percent of Tanzania's fifty-two thousand, had citizenship by 1972.[39] Ethnic Africans often interpret such unwillingness to take citizenship as a sign of Asians' lack of commitment to Africa. But in Asian eyes, the alternative British citizenship was a protection against possibly capricious acts by African governments, such as that of Zanzibar, which in 1964 deprived some seven thousand Asians of the Zanzibari citizenship they had chosen in preference to British citizenship.[40]

In August 1972, the most publicized move against Asians in East Africa occurred: Idi Amin declared that all Asian residents of Uganda must leave the country within three months. Amin alleged that Asians were "sabatoging the economy and engaging in numerous acts of corruption . . . smuggling commodities . . . undercutting African traders [and] practicing price discrimination against Ugandan African traders."[41] It is quite conceivable that some Asians were committing some of these acts; undoubtedly, African businessmen were also engaged in various forms of corruption. But Amin's populist rhetoric aroused a deep-seated resentment against the more visible outsiders. Even those approximately fifteen thousand Asians who presented proof of citizenship to the authorities had it revoked.[42] Beatings, harassment, intimidation, and at least a few murders persuaded almost every Asian to leave.

But it was not only Amin's personal whim that was responsible for the expulsions. Amin was merely making good the threats that had already been made against Asians in Uganda by that country's previous president, Milton Obote.[43] Obote had become particularly angered against Asians in 1969 when one of two defendants in a sedition trial, Rajat Neogy, a citizen Asian, claimed and received British citizenship.[44] This incident apparently convinced Obote that Asians were not sincere in their professions of loyalty to Uganda. Nevertheless, after he regained power in 1980, Obote, realizing the economic importance of former Ugandan Asians, invited them to return, and some powerful families did so.[45] But in 1985, the Obote regime deprived an eminent Ugandan Asian scholar, Mahmood Mamdani, of citizenship after he made a speech suggesting that famine in Uganda was as much man-made as a result of climatic disaster.[46]

Amin's expulsions dramatized the conflict between ethnic Asians and ethnic Africans in other parts of East Africa. In Kenya there has been a consistent policy, starting with the Trade Licencing Act of 1967,[47] of excluding non-citizens from various trades and professions and from all but five specified General Trading (geographic) Areas. The legislation is specifically framed to exclude non-citizens, not ethnic Asians, and as such does not violate any human rights provisions, either internationally or in Africa. In practice, however, "Kenyanization" measures have meant "Africanization" measures.[48] The human rights implications of such government actions are not clear. If there is an historic discriminatory pattern against the African majority, then it is difficult to see how such structured inequality can be remedied without legislative measures to guarantee participation to those excluded. Many human rights specialists do not consider "positive" discrimination to rectify historic injustices as illegitimate. In the Kenyan instance, there appears to be no evidence of legislative discrimination against Asian citizens, although there is a popular hostility against the wealthier Asians, as evidenced in the looting of Asian-owned shops in Nairobi during the August 2, 1982, attempted coup.

In Tanzania, racial hostility against Asian citizens has not been encouraged by the government, and President Nyerere condemned (as did President Kaunda of Zambia) Amin's expulsion of Asian citizens.[49] But Asian citizens in Tanzania have undergone economic loss as a result of Nyerere's socialization policies. Both in Kenya and Tanzania, such government actions, in the former to encourage African capitalism, in the latter to encourage African collectivism, have resulted in high levels of voluntary Asian emigration. The total Asian population of East and Central Africa declined from about 360 thousand in 1961–62 to about 178 thousand in 1972, a drop of about 50 percent;[50] the figure has undoubtedly decreased even more since then. In effect, the "Asian problem" in East Africa has been solved by their removal.

The expulsions and voluntary migrations of East African Asians bring to our attention the responsibility of the United Kingdom in this human rights matter. At the time of independence, Britain used generous financial inducements to encourage white residents in East Africa to leave the new countries or to vacate their positions in favor of African citizens.[51] No such provisions were made for Asians, despite their requests for similar treatment.[52] When the emigrations and expulsions of Asians from East Africa began, Britain specifically reneged on the commitments it had given at the time of independence to those who retained British citizenship.[53] In 1968 a voucher system was set up under which only fifteen hundred Asian household heads a year from East Africa could enter Britain. By taking this action, Britain denied its obligations under Article 12, 4, of the Covenant on Civil and Political Liberties, namely that "no one shall be arbitrarily deprived of the right to enter his own country."

The question remains whether the expulsion or emigration of East African Asians has in fact resulted in any improvements in East African economies. In Uganda, the hasty expulsions simply resulted in arbitrary allocations of Asians' properties to soldiers and other Amin supporters, most without any business acumen. Once the Asians' stocks of goods ran out, the shops closed. In other East African areas, however, it appears that at least some Africans have benefited in the long term. "Most studies which have analysed the process of indigenisation of ownership and control of African economies have come to the conclusion that a national elite of politicians, civil servants and wealthy businessmen have benefited most from the economic transfers."[54] In other words, another opportunity has been created either for those already within the ruling class to consolidate their power through new economic resources, or for some Africans to take small steps into the petty bourgeoisie by replacing Asian traders.[55] But there is no evidence of long-term economic benefit for the African masses from such expulsions.

In Uganda, Amin expelled the Asians for reasons both of economic nationalism and of primordial racial solidarity. Similarly, Obote expelled ethnic Africans for both economic and political reasons. In the early 1980s, the second Obote government expelled a large group of rural people from southwest Uganda on the grounds that they were "alien" migrants from Rwanda. In fact, although ethnically Rwandan, they had begun their immigration into Uganda as migrant laborers in the 1920s and had lived in Uganda for decades.[56] Many were born in Uganda, although others were more recent refugees from the 1959–73 ethnic violence in Rwanda. In this case, the cause of the expulsion appeared to be the hostility of non-stranger "indigenous" Ugandans against successful Rwandan cattle farmers, exacerbated by the regime's unwillingness to countenance the presence of "aliens" who, if permitted to vote, would probably vote for the Buganda-based opposition Democratic Party.[57] In December 1983 it was reported that as many as 200 thousand, out of a population of 500 thousand ethnic Rwandans, had fled or been killed.[58]

In West Africa, there have been no large-scale expulsions of non-Africans, but several of Africans who were or are non-citizens. Expulsion of alien (non-citizen) Africans by West African states is a relatively common occurrence; there were early expulsions of Ghanaians from Nigeria and Sierra Leone, Nigerians from Cameroon in 1967, Nigerians from Ghana in 1965, and Voltaics (Upper Volta) from Ghana in 1961.[59] In 1970, Ghana decreed that aliens unlawfully in the country were to quit it within two weeks: some 100 thousand to 150 thousand people left. The vast majority of the expelled were non-citizen ethnic Africans; for example, Ghana-born children of Nigerians. The expulsion order also covered Lebanese-origin residents who engaged in small-scale trade, but it specifically exempted Lebanese and others whose businesses had a large annual turnover.[60] Thus while the expulsions made room for African petty traders, large-scale trade was not Africanized. Moreover, the borders were so permeable that many of the expelled returned almost immediately. No increased prosperity seems to have resulted from the expulsions.

In January 1983, Nigeria gave an estimated 1.5 to 2 million aliens, of whom it is estimated about 1 million were Ghanaian, two weeks to leave the country. Nigeria justified the expulsion on the grounds that aliens were responsible for a great deal of urban crime, that they were involved in persistent rioting by members of a Muslim sect in the north,[61] and that indigenous Nigerians needed the jobs they held. Aliens legally in the country and those whose employers could obtain papers for them were exempt, as were employees of the various governments.[62] Thus, the move fell differentially on the poor and uneducated, who, according to some commentators, actually held jobs that Nigerians were unwilling to fill. Again, reports of aliens trickling back to Nigeria started almost as soon as the expulsions were officially over, as did reports of economic dislocation.[63] In May 1985, a similar expulsion exercise, this time aimed at approximately 700 thousand people, of whom about 300 thousand were Ghanaian, took place.[64] It can be anticipated that many of these aliens will also return to Nigeria; in fact, that many are the same people who left in 1983.

The decision not to expel certain categories of workers, such as university professors, from Nigeria reflects the problem of the "brain drain" in Commonwealth Africa. Most governments invest large amounts in the training of high-level specialists, either at home or abroad. Yet, many African professionals leave their country of origin, either for more prosperous African countries, such as Nigeria, or for the West. The costs of training scarce high-level manpower have led some governments to consider various measures to restrict these individuals' freedom of movement. Yet Article 12, 2, of the Covenant on Civil and Political Rights states that "Everyone shall be free to leave any country, including his own." How then can African governments take any measures to stem the brain drain? One option is to invoke article 1, 2, of both the Civil/Political and the Social/Economic/Cultural Covenants, namely that "All people may, for their own ends, freely dispose of their natural wealth and resources" and to declare individuals in whom the state has invested considerable amounts a national resource. To do so, however, would be to declare people as things. Furthermore, it could easily result in a situation in which educated individuals attempting to leave their homelands for political reasons would be persecuted. Another option would be to impose a "brain drain tax" to be paid either directly by the individual or by the country which benefits from his immigration.[65] Presumably the tax would compensate the original country for the loss of its investment (although it would still have to wait some years for a trained replacement), while protecting the individual's right to leave his country. Nevertheless, individuals forced into exile for political reasons would still be economically penalized by such a provision.

A further aspect of freedom of movement to which the issue of expulsions is pertinent is the individual's freedom to move about and reside anywhere in his own country. In both Kenya and Tanzania, efforts have been made to expel citizens from urban to rural areas, where, ostensibly, they would be able to find land and support themselves.[66] In Kenya, the opposition KPU, when it was still active in the 1960s, strongly opposed such expulsions on the grounds that the contention that land was available for the taking in the rural areas was a myth.[67] The expulsions have been supplemented in Kenya by enforced bulldozings of city slums and by legislation that all citizens must carry identification cards at all times.[68]

Expulsions of aliens, legal discrimination in some constitutions against some racial categories of citizens or potential citizens, and the enforced movements of urban inhabitants to rural dwellings have all been justified in Commonwealth Africa on the grounds of economic necessity. The higher goal is alleged to be the collective economic sovereignty of the people. Yet that collective economic sovereignty has been attained at the expense of economic prosperity. The consolidation of a parasitic class dependent on state favors, such as the redistribution of "aliens' " property, when such a consolidation means a reduction in the supply of goods or the breakdown of distributional services, has a negative effect on the economic well-being of the masses of the poor. Expulsion, then, should perhaps be viewed as yet another mechanism by which an insecure African ruling class can consolidate its collective economic power.

Yet economic necessity is not the only reason alleged for expulsions of foreigners. Before the fact, the Nigerian scholar Osita Eze justified his country's expulsions on the grounds that large numbers of foreigners involved in crime or religious fanaticism constituted a threat to Nigeria's national security.[69] To evoke such bugaboos is to play upon the latent xenophobia and distrust of strangers that exists in Africa, as elsewhere. In this sense, expulsions have also served the cause of national integration. They have provided racially distinct scapegoats on whom can be placed the burden of a nation's economic ills, a rallying point for fervent feeling of nationalism and brotherhood, regardless of objective economic position. For many Africans, Idi Amin's abrupt expulsion of the Asians was a deeply symbolic act, both as revenge against an allegedly self-defined "superior" ethnic group and as a flouting of concerns for legitimacy in the eyes of the Western world.

Emotional fulfillment is not a substitute for economic progress, however. There is a limit to the numbers of foreigners to be expelled, or to the numbers of expulsions that can take place without straining the credulity of the popular masses. The legal problems of violations of individual aliens' civil and political rights will continue because of inadequate control of the highly permeable African borders,[70] and because even the wealthiest countries have neither the police forces nor the judicial staff necessary to conduct immigration/emigration hearings in a manner that conforms to international standards of legal practice. The more serious problem, however, is economic. Without real development, the only actions that Commonwealth African governments can envisage to protect their citizens' employment opportunities, to keep their educated personnel at home, and to cut down on rural migration to the cities, are bound to violate the provisions of both the United Nations covenants and the African Charter of Human and Peoples' Rights.

Religious Tolerance and State Security

While much is heard of the problems of ethnic conflict and racialism against non-blacks in Commonwealth Africa, very little is heard of religious intolerance or conflict. This is perhaps surprising. In independent modernizing Africa, political authority is often centralized in one charismatic leader, whose personalist rule invests him with quasi-mythical or religious authority.[71] In one-party states the ruling party becomes the focus of quasi-religious fervor, with militant youth groups enforcing loyalty. In such a situation it is reasonable to anticipate that all independent religions might be banned or strictly controlled, or that a state religion might be declared to supplement compulsory membership of the ruling party. This has not occurred in Commonwealth Africa, however, where instances of government persecutions of religious groups are relatively rare.

In Commonwealth Africa substantial Christian and Islamic communities live alongside each other as well as alongside those who still practice indigenous religions. Exact figures on religious affiliations in Africa are difficult to obtain. Estimates suggest that Gambia is 70 percent Muslim, Ghana 12 percent Muslim and 43 percent Christian, Sierra Leone 23 percent Muslim and 4 percent Christian, and Nigeria 47 percent Muslim and 34 percent Christian. In East Africa, Kenya is estimated to be only 6 percent Muslim and 25 percent Christian, Uganda 6 percent Muslim and 63 percent Christian, and Tanzania 24 percent Muslim and 20 percent Christian. Neither Malawi nor Zambia appears to have any significant Muslim population, although they are respectively estimated to be 33 and 45 percent Christian.[72]

One reason for the religious tolerance displayed in Africa may be that its traditional religions are polytheistic.[73] Foreign gods can easily be incorporated into local belief systems, and since different ethnic groups have always had different religious systems as well, there is nothing novel in the idea of a multiplicity of religions. Probably the most startling aspect of Africa's religious structure, to Western eyes, is the relatively peaceful coexistence of large numbers of Muslims and Christians. The Eurocentric expectation that two such groups cannot live together has resulted in a tendency to assume that when there is communal conflict in Africa, it must be of a religious nature. Thus an editorial in the *Journal of Church and State* on Uganda under Amin assumed that Idi Amin's Muslim beliefs were the central motivating force behind his slaughters, for example, of the predominantly Christian Langi and Acholi tribes.[74] It is true that

Amin eventually banned 27 small Christian sects,[75] but he did not do so until 1977, and he permitted the Anglican, Roman Catholic, and Ugandan Orthodox churches to function. While his sadistic murder of Anglican Archbishop Luwum in 1977 shocked the Christian world,[76] less attention was given to the murders of prominent Muslim leaders. "Being a Muslim did not necessarily guarantee anyone's safety . . . the majority of those killed were Christians simply because the majority of the people of Uganda were Christians."[77]

The civil war in Nigeria has also been popularly interpreted as a war between the Muslim north and the Christian south. Such an interpretation fails to take account of the fact that the federal camp in the war included the Yoruba-dominated western region, about evenly divided between Muslims and Christians. The complaints against Igbos emanating from the north, and the reasons for their massacres in 1966, had to do mainly with their perceived economic power. One underlying reason for Igbo predominance was indeed the fact that they had readily accepted Christianity and had benefited from learning English at mission schools, while the Muslim north was sealed off, at the request of Muslim Emirs and by official British policy, from Christian missions. But the Western world's unitary Christian intolerance of Islam as a religion has been wrongly ascribed to Christian Africans. Similarly, African Muslims do not routinely display hostility to African Christians. While religion did play some role in both the Ugandan and the Nigerian conflicts, it was not the primary motivating factor in either case.

Religious intolerance in Africa is displayed primarily when the security of the state is perceived to be threatened. There are only three major instances of such conflict between state and church in contemporary Commonwealth Africa.

One of the first internal problems confronted by the independent government of Zambia was how to control the Lumpa (Bemba for "above all others") sect. This sect started in 1953 when Alice Lenshina, a peasant woman, claimed to have died, confronted God, and been resurrected to life to teach His word.[78] Lenshina's teaching had two great appeals for uneducated Africans, especially women: first, she alleged that baptized Lumpa members would be immune from all witchcraft practiced against them; second, she preached against polygyny, adultery, and widow inheritance.

During the late colonial period, Zambian nationalists had no quarrel with the Lumpas. Indeed, they thought that the sect, with its provision of an African alternative to white-dominated Christianity and its hostility to colonial rulers, would assist the nationalist cause.[79] This changed in 1962 when Lenshina, returning to her Bemba home after an evangelical tour of the mining Copperbelt area, found that many of her supporters had defected. They had joined the United Church of Zambia and along with it the United National Independence Party, which became the ruling party upon independence. Apparently Lenshina reacted first by urging her followers to join the opposition African National Congress under Harry Nkumbula and, later, by outright prohibition of all political activities. Members were forbidden to vote, to join political parties, or to have party cards. The result was a series of extremely violent clashes between Lumpa and UNIP members (provoked by both sides) in 1963–64. Eventually the Lumpa were defeated by a full-scale attack on their villages, and 518 Lumpa members and 7 army and police members were officially reported killed.[80] Unofficial reports suggested that as many as 5,000 were killed.[81] Alice Lenshina was placed in preventive detention,[82] 4,000 Lumpa members were interned,[83] and some 20,000 others fled to Zaire, finally returning in 1972.[84]

Why did such bloody confrontations occur? According to official reports, the UNIP leadership, including Dr. Kaunda, did not encourage UNIP harassment of the Lumpas and indeed tried several times to mediate between local UNIP members and the church.[85] But since the anti-colonial patriotism of the decolonizing period had required that uneducated, isolated peasants imbibe a new loyalty to the nebulous entity of "Zambia," such emotions were most easily aroused by personalizing their loyalty to Dr. Kaunda and the party he organized, UNIP. Wearing party uniforms, carrying party cards, and organizing women's and youth brigades were all symbolic acts intended to bind the people to larger than local loyalties. When Lenshina challenged loyalty to UNIP, she challenged the state: the only religions not to be tolerated in an historically tolerant continent are those that directly ignore the overriding symbolic unity provided by the president and the ruling party. Whether or not the leadership of UNIP actually felt that Lenshina was a direct challenge to the state, rather than being merely the leader of one among many syncretic African Christian sects, was irrelevant. Ordinary UNIP members, newly trained to think of themselves as Zambians, were outraged by the deliberate flouting of symbols of Zambian-ness.

The Jehovah's Witness sect has also suffered various levels of discrimination and persecution in East and Central Africa, because of its members' refusals to take part in ritual affirmations of loyalty to the state. Jehovah's Witnesses "refuse military service, will not join political parties, do not vote, do not hold elected public office, and will not participate in patriotic exercises such as flag salute ceremonies."[86] In Zambia, where they constitute a potential political force as 1 percent of the population, they have not been banned,[87] but thousands of their children have been expelled from school, a dozen Witnesses were killed during clashes with UNIP during the 1969 elections, and official harassments of various kinds continued throughout the 1970s.[88] In Kenya, all foreign Jehovah's Witness missionaries were deported in 1973, but citizen Jehovah's Witnesses were then permitted to practice their religion, including their house-to-house evangelical activities.[89] In Tanzania they have been banned, as have a number of other sects, all accused of having "antidevelopmental" or "antinational" character. In 1974, 80 Jehovah's Witnesses were arrested in Dar es Salaam, and 46 held for worshipping illegally.[90]

In Malawi, Jehovah's Witnesses have been actively persecuted.[91] Beginning in 1967 and escalating in 1972, Witnesses were beaten, raped, and murdered (the estimates of death range from 50 to several hundred). They were excluded from public and private employment, "chased away" from their villages and expelled from schools, and their houses were burned down. Members of the Malawi Youth League were responsible for much of the physical violence and intimidation, which included torture and sexual mutilation.[92] Between 1972 and 1977, about 35,000 Malawi Witnesses moved about Central Africa, seeking refuge both in Zambia and in Mozambique (and being expelled from both countries) and eventually returning to Malawi. Since 1977, little has been heard regarding their situation in Malawi. Possibly, they have been peacefully reintegrated into Malawian society; possibly they are now too frightened to continue openly practicing their beliefs.

The persecution of Jehovah's Witnesses in Malawi was the direct result of government policy, personified in this instance in the constitutional Life President. At both the 1967 and the 1972 conventions of the Malawi Congress Party, generally regarded as a mere rubberstamp for Banda's policies, resolutions were passed prescribing persecution of the Witnesses in retaliation for their alleged disloyalty.[93] Their treatment is the extreme consequence of distrust by governments in newly independent Commonwealth Africa of religious groups who refuse to participate in rituals of loyalty and citizenship. They are a useful scapegoat on whom to deflect underlying political tensions. Indeed, as Wilson points out, the Witnesses serve an almost necessary function: their very refusal to participate in rituals of loyalty serves to reinforce the unity of the state.[94]

It is doubtful that the Jehovah's Witnesses in any way actually threaten the security of East or Central African states. They preach obedience to the laws of the land in all respects other than those that interfere, according to their theology, with their loyalty to God.[95] Indeed, they are now regarded in the Western world almost as model citizens. It ought to be kept in mind, however, that the legal measures taken against them in countries such as Tanzania and Kenya are no more severe than those taken against the Witnesses in Western countries, including the United States and Canada, until a series of court decisions finally guaranteed their rights in the 1940s and '50s. In those countries, too, they were regarded as traitors who would not fight for their land; children were expelled from schools for not saluting the flag; and Witnesses were physically harassed.[96] Witnesses were exterminated, along with Jews and Gypsies, in Nazi-ruled

Europe. The fear of an organized group that refuses to participate in ritual professions of loyalty is not unique to Africa, nor does a nation-state have to be as fragile as those in Commonwealth Africa to act on such fear in often-violent, oppressive ways.

There is only one clear-cut case in which local, if not national, security appears to have been genuinely threatened by religious activity in Commonwealth Africa, and that is in Nigeria in the 1980s. In December 1980, in October 1982, and again in early 1984, there were reports from northern Nigeria of large-scale fighting between an Islamic sect and the police and army. In the first incident, it was reported that at least 1,000 people had been killed, and that possibly the figure was thousands higher; in the second case, about 450 were believed killed.[97] At issue were the activities of a sect known as Yen Izala. This sect, which opposes both materialism and some traditional Islamic practices such as compulsory prayer hours and the facing of Mecca while at prayer, apparently has declared a "holy war" in which millions of dollars worth of property have been destroyed and many non-believers have been murdered.[98]

Islamic fundamentalism is apparently becoming a powerful force in Nigeria. According to one commentator, one reason for its spread has been that it has become a "useful ideology for a society undergoing considerable . . . dislocation. [It presents] Islam . . . as a blueprint of [a] socio-economic and political order that . . . would be able to provide the solutions to Nigeria's social, economic and political problems."[99] As such, Islamic fundamentalism has an attraction similar to the apocalyptic vision of the Jehovah's Witnesses or the simple rules for decent living provided by the Lumpa sect.[100] In all three religions, simplistic solutions to social problems are proposed, buttressed by a passionate faith in their applicability. For governments with little control over their own economies and very fragile political legitimacy, popular faith in a simple solution to social problems, combined with the belief that a religious hierarchy could run affairs better than the present political one, could well constitute a real political threat.

The concern in Nigeria regarding the Yen Izala sect is not because it threatens the central government, but because it reveals weaknesses in the government's control over its own borders and in its internal security system. The leader of Yen Izala, Alhaji Muhammadu Marwa (who died in the 1980 fighting), allegedly had reentered Nigeria from Cameroon after being deported in 1962. Many of his followers are allegedly aliens.[101] The Nigerian press has reacted to the Yen Izala violence by calling for stricter controls of aliens (foreshadowing the 1983 expulsions), better internal security service, and even internal informing by local inhabitants.[102] One northern legislator went so far as to advocate that all Nigerians carry compulsory identification cards.[103] The former civilian President Shagari was severely criticized for his "misplaced magnanimity" in releasing a thousand people convicted after the 1980 riot, shortly before the 1982 riot took place.[104] The Islamic conflicts have thus resulted in calls for greater restrictions on the fundamental human right of freedom of movement.

The above incidents suggest that freedom of religion is likely to occur only in a society in which religious passions are so temperate that violent confrontations among various religious groups, or between religious adherents and the state, do not occur. The issue in Africa is not, as in early modern Europe, state vs. church: African governments are not asserting themselves against the temporal authority of a centralized sacred power such as the Church of Rome. Rather, violent social change and personal upheaval have increased the likelihood that individuals will turn to new religions for all-encompassing guidance and reassurance, giving to such religions their complete loyalty, at precisely the same time as the new secular religion of the state is being created. Since the state is backed by coercive power, while religious groups are not, the state is bound to win in any such conflict.

Conclusion

In general, the myth of "tribalism" as the cause of political instability in Commonwealth Africa has been greatly exaggerated. Given the large numbers of different ethnic groups that exist, there is far more potential for ethnically generated conflict than has actually occurred. The solution to ethnic hostilities in Africa is twofold. One is to redistribute resources, including educational opportunities and all other accoutrements of modern life, on an equitable basis among regions and ethnic groups. The other is to encourage the type of individual mobility, both spacial and occupational, that will increase lateral ties among members of different ethnic groups at the expense of vertical ethnic ties. Yet this would still not solve the Ugandan civil war, whose intractability undoubtedly lies in the fact that the Buganda are not a less-privileged group to whom resources could be distributed, but an historically more-privileged group from whom resources, especially political power, have been removed.

No Commonwealth African government has attempted a wholesale eradication of ethnic loyalties in its territory. Persecutions appear to occur only when there is a real or perceived threat of secession, as in the Somali and Ewe cases. In general, national socialization occurs through education, state-controlled media, and the institution of the mass-membership single party. But people are not expected to give up their languages, religions, or ethnic affiliations in return for the resources that nationalist governments can distribute.

Under the colonial practice of indirect rule, little effort was made to create a national citizenry; insofar as independent regimes saw fit to change colonial practice, it was only to ensure no possible rupture of the new borders or challenge to the new central government. Relatively static, rural, homogeneous ethnic communities are more likely to buttress than to challenge national authority. As long as some of the goods of independence are delivered (mainly through ties of patronage and nepotism) and as long as their own way of life is not disturbed, such communities will live in peace with the external modern authority of the state. Conversely, the retention of communal authority structures is, from the central government's point of view, an efficient way to organize the country in the absence of an all-encompassing bureaucracy and of adequate systems of communication and transportation. Thus, central governments have neither the inclination nor the capacity, in Africa, to destroy the communal way of life. In the absence of a direct challenge to the state or to the regime, they will not act.

When a government does act against a perceived particularistic challenge to its authority, the underlying motive may be that not the state, but rather the regime or indeed the particular president is challenged. It is difficult to believe that the Jehovah's Witnesses in Malawi or elsewhere would have sufficient influence to induce masses of their compatriots to renounce all loyalty to the state; but by refusing to partake in symbolic gestures of loyalty to the ruling party, they threaten the individuals in power. Similarly, the Lumpa events were provoked more by UNIP threats against Lenshina and her followers than by any independent Lumpa thinking about the nature of the state. Finally, governments or presidents may manipulate a mythical threat of tribal schism to consolidate their regimes; such appears to explain the persistent Ghanaian focus on Ewe secessionism. Such scapegoating politics are even more effective when societal outsiders are the victims, which explains why mass expulsions of both African and non-African aliens are a favorite "solution" to economic inequality and unemployment.

In Commonwealth Africa, as everywhere else in the world, state-building can mean regime consolidation or indeed merely the consolidation of personalist rule. The next two chapters will consider the various means by which independent African regimes, under the guise of national unity, have abrogated political and civil rights, often for no reason other than their own power and preservation.

Notes

1. Article 23 in the International Covenant on Civil and Political Rights, and Article 10 in the Covenant on Economic, Social and Cultural Rights.

2. Archie Mafeje, "The Ideology of 'Tribalism,' " *Journal of Modern African Studies* 9, no. 2 (1971): 258.

3. Covenant on Civil and Political Rights, Article 27.

4. Lloyd A. Fallers, "Ideology and Culture in Uganda Nationalism," in Claude

E. Welch, Jr., ed., *Political Modernization: A Reader in Comparative Political Change* (Belmont, Calif.: Wadsworth, 1967), p. 338.

5. Albert P. Blaustein, "Uganda: Constitutional Chronology," p. 5, in Albert P. Blaustein and Gisbert H. Flanz, eds., *Constitutions of the Countries of the World* (Dobbs Ferry, N.Y.: Oceana Publications, 1971– , issued April 1983), p. 5.

6. I base my account of events preceding the Nigerian civil war largely on Marjery Perham, "Nigeria's Civil War," *Africa Contemporary Record*, vol. I (1968–69), pp. 1–12.

7. Ibid., p. 7.

8. Laurie S. Wiseberg, "Humanitarian Intervention: Lessons from the Nigerian Civil War," *Human Rights Journal* 7, no. 1 (1974): 78.

9. "No Genocide: Final Report of Observer Team to Nigeria from 1. Organization of African Unity 2. Britain, Canada, Poland, Sweden" (Apapa, Nigeria: Federal Ministry of Information, December 1968, document no. NNPG /279/68).

10. Wole Soyinka, *The Man Died* (New York: Harper & Row, 1972).

11. Elechi Amadi, *Sunset in Biafra: A Civil War Diary* (London: Heinemann, 1973).

12. Republic of Nigeria, "Ibos in a United Nigeria" (pamphlet, 1969).

13. Information on the treatment of Igbos after 1970 is taken from Arthur Agwuncha Nwankwo, "The Ojukwu Factor in Nigerian Politics," *West Africa*, October 11, 1982, pp. 2649–53.

14. In his *Detained: A Writer's Prison Diary* (Heinemann: London, 1981), Ngugi wa Thiong'o reports being imprisoned with several Somalis in 1978.

15. *East African Standard*, June 14, 1969, "Opposition Move to Open Closed Areas Defeated." On scheduled areas, see the Constitution of the Republic of Kenya, Chapter 5, 8, 1.

16. Amnesty International, *Annual Report* (June 1, 1966–May 31, 1967). See also *Peace News*, July 7, 1967, "Mass Killings of Somalis in Kenya."

17. Amnesty International Canada, *Bulletin*, July 1984, p. 13. See also *New York Times*, March 1, 1984, "Two Kenyan Officials Make Massacre Charges," p. A5.

18. See, e.g., "North-Eastern Province: Genocide Alleged," *Weekly Review* (Nairobi), April 13, 1984, p. 16.

19. I base my account of Ewe "secessionism" largely on David Brown, "Who Are the Tribalists? Social Pluralism and Political Ideology in Ghana," *African Affairs* 81, no. 322 (January 1982): 37–69.

20. Amnesty International, *Annual Report, 1979*, "The Death Penalty: Ghana," and other AI material on Ghana during the mid-'70s.

21. Brown, "Who Are the Tribalists?"

22. The *Guardian*, January 10, 1972, "Farmers Facing a Political Squeeze"; and the *Times*, January 14, 1972, "The Paradox of the Peasants: Judith Listowel Examines the Implications of Tanzania's First Political Murder." See also *Africa Contemporary Record*, vol. 4, (1971–72), p. B204.

23. Leo Kuper, *The Pity of It All* (London: Duckworth, 1977), pp. 145–70.

24. See periodic reports on Zanzibar by Amnesty International during the 1970s.

25. Christopher Allen, "Sierra Leone," in John Dunn, ed., *West African States: Failure and Promise* (Cambridge: Cambridge University Press, 1978), pp. 189–210.

26. Oginga Odinga, *Not Yet Uhuru: An Autobiography* (London: Heinemann, 1967), esp. pp. 260–63.

27. Ngugi, *Detained*.

28. In Republic of Zambia, "Report of the Commission of Inquiry into the Allegations Made by Mr. Justin Chimba and Mr. John Chisata" (Lusaka: Government Printer, May 1971), p. 2. One of the charges (dismissed) against Chimba and Chisata was that they had publicly discussed "tribalism." See also *Africa Contemporary Record*, vol. 4 (1971–72), p. B254.

29. Richard Plender, "The Ugandan Crisis and the Right of Expulsion under International Law," *The Review* (International Commission of Jurists) 9 (December 1972): 27.

30. Rhoda Howard, *Colonialism and Underdevelopment in Ghana* (London: Croom Helm, 1978), p. 204.

31. *Daily Telegraph*, November 26, 1969, "Threat to Ghana's 2m Aliens."

32. For Nigeria, see the Constitution of the Republic of Nigeria (1979), Chap. 3, 23, 1, a; for Uganda, Constitution of the Republic of Uganda (1967), Chap. 2, 4, 1, b; and for Zambia, Constitution of the Republic of Zambia (1974), Part 2, 7, 1; all in Blaustein and Flanz, *Constitutions*.

33. Donald George and Garvas Betts, "Citizenship and Civil Rights in Sierra Leone" (unpublished, 1980), pp. 10–11.

34. Nigeria, Constitution, Chapter 3, 25, d, in Blaustein and Flanz, *Constitutions*.

35. Margaret Peil, *Consensus and Conflict in African Societies* (London: Longman, 1977), pp. 117–20.

36. Constitution of the Republic of Sierra Leone (1978), Chapter 2, 17, 4, c, in Blaustein and Flanz, *Constitutions*.

37. Constitution of the Republic of Ghana (1979), Chapter 4, 17,3; Nigeria, Constitution, Chapter 3, 27; and Uganda, Constitution, Chapter 2, 5, 2. All in Blaustein and Flanz, *Constitutions*.

38. Yash Tandon and Arnold Raphael, *The New Position of East Africa's Asians: Problems of a Displaced Minority* (London: Minority Rights Group, June 1978), p. 11.

39. Ibid., p. 24.

40. Ibid., p. 12.

41. "Uganda Crisis II, Expulsion of Asians: Reasons Behind the Decision by the Government of the Republic of Uganda Requiring non-Ugandan Asians in Uganda to Leave Uganda; General Amin's Statements," *Africa Contemporary Record*, vol. 5 (1972–73), pp. C88–C89.

42. Tandon and Raphael, *The New Position of East Africa's Asians*, p. 15.

43. *World Broadcast*, April 22, 1970, "Obote and the Asians in Uganda."

44. *The People* (Uganda), December 7, 1968, "British Asians: Neogy Triggers Citizenship Issue"; and *Sunday Times* (London), January 5, 1969, "Human Rights Storm over the Fate of Mr. Neogy."

45. *Africa Contemporary Record*, vol. 14 (1981–82), pp. B311–12.

46. Letter from the Academic Staff Association, University of Dar es Salaam, to Dr. A. M. Obote, April 25, 1985; also transcript of speech by Mahmood Mamdani, "Disaster Prevention: Defining the Problem," to the Uganda Red Cross, March 19, 1985.

47. Maria S. Muller, "The National Policy of Kenyanisation of Trade: Its

Impact on a Town in Kenya," *Canadian Journal of African Studies* 15, no. 2 (1981): 297.

48. Ibid., p. 298.

49. "Uganda Crisis II," pp. C91–C93.

50. Tandon and Raphael, *The New Position of East Africa's Asians*, p. 24.

51. Gary Wasserman, *Politics of Decolonization: Kenya Europeans and the Land Issue 1960–65* (London: Cambridge University Press, 1976).

52. Yash P. Ghai, "Remarks," in Rosalyn Higgins, presider, "Expulsion and Expatriation in International Law: The Right to Leave, to Stay, and to Return," *Proceedings, American Society of International Law* 64 (1973): 125.

53. Tandon and Raphael, *The New Position of East Africa's Asians*, p. 14.

54. Muller, "The National Policy of Kenyanisation," p. 293.

55. Ibid., p. 301. On indigenization, see also Chapter 3.

56. Mamdani, "Disaster Prevention."

57. Jeff Crisp, "National Security, Human Rights and Population Displacements: Luwero District, Uganda, January-December 1983," *Review of African Political Economy* 27/28 (1983): 167.

58. *New York Times*, December 18, 1983, p. 5, "Attacks on Rwandans in Uganda Reported," and January 6, 1984, p. A5, "Tanzania Says 20,000 Flee Homes in Uganda."

59. Warren Weinstein, "Africa's Approach to Human Rights at the United Nations," *Issue: A Quarterly Journal of Africanist Opinion* 6, no. 4 (Winter 1976): 17.

60. Margaret Peil, "The Expulsion of West African Aliens," *Journal of Modern African Studies* 9, no. 2 (August 1971): 205–29.

61. See *West Africa*, January 31, 1983, "Nigeria's Deadline for Immigrants," pp. 245–46.

62. *West Africa*, February 14, 1983, "Exodus from Nigeria: The Reasons and the Outcry," p. 386.

63. *West Africa*, February 7, 1983, "Exodus from Nigeria: Limited and Temporary," pp. 307–9.

64. *New York Times*, May 5, 1985, "Expelled Foreigners Pouring Out of Nigeria," p. 1.

65. Jagdish N. Bhagwati and Martin Partington, eds., *Taxing the Brain Drain I: A Proposal* (Amsterdam: North-Holland Publishing Co., 1976).

66. See *Africa Contemporary Record*, vol. 3 (1970–71), p. B172, for Tanzania. On Kenya, see S.B.U. Gutto, "The Status of Women in Kenya: A Study of Paternalism, Inequality and Underprivilege," Discussion Paper no. 235, Institute for Development Studies, University of Nairobi (April 1976), p. 36.

67. *East African Standard*, March 17, 1969, "Vagrancy Act 'Turning Kenyans into Chattels,' " report of a speech by B.M. Kaggia, deputy-president of KPU.

68. *East African Standard*, April 7, 1967, "Squatters to Lose Homes in Mombasa"; January 26, 1970, "Big Demonstration Planned as More Shanties Come Down"; The *Nation* (Kenya), October 20, 1977, "All Kenyans to Get Identity Cards—Moi."

69. Osita Eze, "Ecowas and Freedom of Movement: What Prospects for Nigeria," *Nigerian Forum*, March 1981, p. 24.

70. Ibid., p. 27.

71. Robert H. Jackson and Carl G. Rosberg, *Personal Rule in Black Africa: Prince, Autocrat, Prophet, Tyrant* (Berkeley: University of California Press, 1982).

72. Figures are variously taken from Deadline Data on World Affairs (various dates), *Statesman's Yearbook* (1982–83), and *Europa Yearbook* (1983).

73. J.M. Assimeng, "Sectarian Allegiance and Political Authority: The Watch Tower Society in Zambia, 1907–1935," *Journal of Modern African Studies* 8, no. 1 (1970): 111.

74. Loyal N. Gould and James Leo Garrett, Jr., "Amin's Uganda: Troubled Land of Religious Persecution," *Journal of Church and State* 19 (1977): 434.

75. Ibid., p. 436.

76. M. Louise Pirouet, "Religion in Uganda under Amin," *Journal of Religion in Africa* 11, no. 1 (1980): 23.

77. Ibid., pp. 18–19.

78. The following account of the origin and growth of the Lumpa sect is based on Robert Rotberg, "The Lenshina Movement of Northern Rhodesia," *Rhodes–Livingstone Journal* (Lusaka: 1961), pp. 63–78; and Republic of Zambia, "Report of the Commission of Inquiry into the Former Lumpa Church" (Lusaka: Government Printer, 1965).

79. Rotberg, "The Lenshina Movement," pp. 75–76.

80. "Commission of Inquiry," p. 36.

81. *Daily Telegraph*, August 13, 1964, "Prophetess Lenshina Surrenders."

82. Mark R. Lipschutz & R. Kent Rasmussen., eds., *Dictionary of African Historical Biography* (London: Heinemann, 1978), p.120.

83. "Commission of Inquiry," pp. 15–16.

84. *Africa Contemporary Record*, vol. 2 (1969–70), p. B232; vol. 3 (1970–71), p. B213; and vol. 4 (1971–72), p. B269.

85. "Commission of Inquiry," p. 21.

86. M. James Penton, "Jehovah's Witnesses and the Secular State: A Historical Analysis of Doctrine," *Journal of Church and State* 21 (1979): 55.

87. Assimeng, "Sectarian Allegiance and Political Authority," p. 106. Tony Hodges, in *Jehovah's Witnesses in Central Africa* (London: Minority Rights Group Report no. 19, June 1976), p. 3, estimates that one of every 81 Zambians is a Witness.

88. Hodges, *Jehovah's Witnesses*, pp. 3–4. See also *Africa Contemporary Record*, vol. 2 (1969–70), p. B232.

89. Bryan R. Wilson, "Jehovah's Witnesses in Kenya," *Journal of Religion in Africa* 5, no. 2 (1973–74): 129.

90. David Westerlund, "Freedom of Religion under Socialist Rule in Tanzania, 1961–77," *Journal of Church and State* 24, no. 1 (Winter 1982): 95–97.

91. The following account of the persecution of Jehovah's Witnesses in Malawi is based on Hodges, *Jehovah's Witnesses*, and Amnesty International, *Malawi* (London: Amnesty International Briefing Paper no. 5, 1976).

92. Hodges, *Jehovah's Witnesses*, pp. 1–2.

93. Ibid., p. 3.

94. Wilson, "Jehovah's Witnesses in Kenya," p. 147.

95. Penton, "Jehovah's Witnesses and the Secular State," p. 69.

96. Ibid., pp. 61–67.

97. *New York Times*, January 12, 1981, p. A1, "At Least 1,000 People Are Killed as Nigeria Crushes Islamic Sect"; ibid., November 16, 1982, p. A2, "An Outburst of Cult Strife Tests Nigeria's Civil Rule."

98. *West Africa*, January 12, 1981, "After the Kano Rioting," p. 53.

99. Peter B. Clarke, "Ideology for Change?" *West Africa*, August 23, 1982, p. 2156.

100. "Commission of Inquiry," p. 17.

101. *West Africa*, January 12, 1981, p. 53.

102. *West Africa*, January 19, 1981, "What the Papers Said about Kano," p. 100.

103. *West Africa*, November 8, 1982, "More Religious Rioting in Nigeria," p. 2874.

104. Ibid., p. 2873.

⑥ Political Rights

In Chapter 3 I argued that an understanding of the class structure of contemporary Commonwealth Africa is crucial to any analysis of the presence or absence of human rights. I particularly concentrated on the benefits which the rising ruling classes could obtain from their control of state, party, military, and civil service. Given that such control is crucial, in an underdeveloped economy, to a person's wealth and material security, the incentives are high not to give up what marginal privileges one might have acquired. Therefore, political oppositions constitute a genuine threat to people in office in Africa.

In this chapter, the rights of freedom of the press and association, free trade unionism, and political participation will be considered. The 1966 Covenant on Civil and Political Rights guarantees the rights to freedom of thought (Article 18) and expression (Article 19), the rights to peaceful assembly (Article 21) and association (Article 22); and the right to take part in "the conduct of public affairs" (Article 25), including "genuine periodic elections" (Article 25b). The Covenant on Economic, Social and Cultural Rights spells out the rights of free trade unions (Article 8).The African Charter of Human and Peoples' Rights also guarantees the rights to freedom of conscience (Article 8) and expression (Article 9), to freedom of association (Article 10) and assembly (Article 11); and finally the "right to participate freely in the government of [the] country" (Article 13). There is, however, no mention of trade union rights in the African Charter.

The exercise of these rights of freedom of expression, association, trade unionism, and political participation is grounded in, and influences, real social issues. The economic right to development cannot be effectively implemented unless those affected by development policy have the chance to influence decisions and criticize results. The centralization of power into the hands of a ruling class cannot be challenged by ordinary peasants, workers, women, or ethnic minorities unless they have the right to freedom of expression and association and can present their views in an organized manner. Free trade unions are particularly important, both to obtain economic rights and to protect workers' civil and political rights. The right to some sort of participation in government, even if such participation does not imitate the Western model of multiparty competitive democracy, is also essential. Even in very poor countries, therefore, civil and political rights must be taken as seriously as communal and economic rights.

Freedom of Expression and Association

One of the most effective means by which citizens can participate in the affairs of their own government is through a free press, whose function it is not only to transmit information to the citizenry about government decisions and activities, but also to criticize such activities. A free competitive press encourages public debate and, insofar as specific constituencies in the population are identified with specific organs of the press, transmits to government the opinions of different groups. The degree of freedom permitted to the press is also a good indicator of the general degree of freedom of speech and conscience allowed in a country.

An ideally free press exists rarely, if ever. In the Western world, a chief limitation on the freedom of the press is its control by oligopolistic capitalist interests. In Africa, the problem of capitalist ownership is evident only in Kenya, where many criticize the continued foreign ownership of national dailies. The major limitations on press freedom in Commonwealth Africa come from actions of the government: censorship, harassment of individual editors and reporters, and state takeovers of organs of the press.

All the countries under discussion except Malawi and Tanzania have explicit guarantees of freedom of expression in their most recent civilian constitutions.[1] Whether or not these constitutions are presently in force, such guarantees can be taken as an expression of official civilian ideology. Most of these constitutions, however, also contain clauses permitting limitations on expression in the interests of defense, public safety, public order, public morality, and public health, clauses which can be interpreted widely in countries in which there is a very limited basis of public debate or competitive politics to buttress the freedom of the press. The 1979 Ghanaian Constitution explicitly states, no doubt as a reaction to the extremely repressive late Nkrumah period, that "there shall be no censorship in Ghana" (Article 28); it is the only constitution to have such an explicit statement. The Nigerian Constitution states that freedom of the press shall not apply to television or radio (Article 35, 2). The Sierra Leone Constitution allows freedom of expression except "for the purpose of . . . safeguarding the proper functioning of the recognized party" (Article 15, 2); while the Ugandan Constitution adds to the normal list of exceptions to freedom of expression controls necessary in the interests of running the national economy, and running essential services (Article 17, 2, a). Thus Sierra Leone explicitly prohibits freedom of political expression, while Uganda seemingly prohibits discussion of national economic policies or any matters concerning trade unions or labor disputes, insofar as they affect essential services. Malawi merely makes a token statement of acknowledgment of the Universal Declaration of Human Rights, while

Tanzania includes the right to freedom of expression in a list of "Foundations of the Constitutions" (Article A, iv).

Constitutional provisions are, in any case, a mere guide to statements of principle, to which adherence can be assumed only when the political culture engenders respect for the constitution, and when there are institutionalized means for forcing the government to respect it. In Commonwealth Africa, constitutions are not securely buttressed by these means. Moreover, constitutions have little meaning when states of emergency exist or when military governments rule by decree. Finally, within Africa, the already limited constitutional protections of freedom of expression have been constricted further through the use of various Press Bills. In Nigeria, for example, the civilian government of President Shagari attempted to introduce a Press Council Decree, which prescribed punishment for "journalists who are guilty of persistent violation of the code which says that their primary duty is to maintain the unity and stability of Nigeria."[2] In Sierra Leone, the government passed a bill in 1980 requiring prohibitively high registration fees for all newspapers, thus jeopardizing the independent student newspaper *The Tablet*, among others. The Minister of Information contended that the bill would improve the quality of journalism by removing small, irresponsible papers, arguing that "In a developing country such as Sierra Leone . . . the press should be an integral part of government, assisting in the dissemination of information on its policies."[3]

The constitutional and legislative controls of freedom of the press in Commonwealth Africa are not unique. Most of the controls were written into the original independence constitutions on British advice. Moreover, independent African governments inherited relatively unfree presses from colonial rule. In East Africa, there was very little African press prior to the 1950s. Newspapers represented either settler, mission, or government interests.[4] In West Africa, a much more prolific indigenous press emerged as early as the late 19th century. While the colonial governments did not attempt to stifle its emergence, they did adopt measures to control it when they found it too critical. Thus a Newspaper Registration Ordinance was passed in the Gold Coast in 1893 after the *Gold Coast People* accused British judges of being tipsy in court; and in 1934 the government passed an ordinance prohibiting the publication or possession of "seditious" material, defined as anything intended to "bring about a change in the sovereignty of the Gold Coast" or "bring into hatred or contempt or excite disaffection against the administration of justice in the Gold Coast."[5] In 1950 Kwame Nkrumah was charged with sedition under this Ordinance.

The idea that the African press should not be critical of the established government is thus a direct legacy of the colonial period. In the post-independence period, governments have become even more repressive of the press. All the television and radio stations are government-owned and are used directly as a means of socializing the citizenry toward "national integration." State control of the press also extends to the print media. Only Gambia, Kenya, and Nigeria (until 1984) can be said to have had a relatively free print press. In Kenya, however, the free press suffers from the liability of being partially foreign-owned (the *Daily Nation* is owned by the Agha Khan), although the highly respected *Weekly Review* is indigenously owned.[6] In Nigeria under civilian rule (1979–83), political competition in the press was implemented by a system in which many state governments owned, jointly or separately, newspapers, television, and radio stations. Since the various state governments were controlled by competing political parties, real political debate was possible. Moreover, private indigenously owned newspapers also circulated relatively widely.

Overall, Nigeria's record with regard to freedom of the press was surprisingly good, even under military rule, until the coup of December 31, 1983.[7] But in 1984 the new military regime published a "Public Officers (Protection against False Accusations) Act" (Decree 4) that gave the government the power to close down any public medium whose existence was deemed "detrimental" to the Federation of Nigeria. In addition, individual journalists could be charged with publishing false stories allegedly ridiculing, or bringing into disrepute, any public official. Journalists were to be tried before a court composed of one high-court judge and three military officers, without right of appeal. The onus was on the journalists to prove their innocence.[8] It is ironic that the new government appeared to be particularly concerned with accusations of corruption. The very military regime that took power allegedly to stop the corruption of its civilian predecessors resorted to legal measures that clearly violated both international human rights norms and previous Nigerian practice, to protect itself against similar charges.

In Malawi the press is completely controlled by the state. In Sierra Leone a small free press exists, but under threats of severe control and under the constitutional provision that the interests of the ruling party must not be affected. In Ghana the state owns the major daily newpapers, while smaller independent newspapers such as the Ashanti-based *Pioneer* come and go, depending on the regime. The prestigious, university-based *Legon Observer* has had an insecure career, its publication periodically banned and its editors imprisoned. In Zambia the state, which already controlled one of the country's two major newspapers, the *Zambia Daily Mail*, took over the other major paper, the *Times of Zambia*, in 1980, ostensibly because it was owned by the multinational corporation Lonrho.[9] The Zambian government also introduced a press bill in 1980 making it a punishable offence to write articles critical of the ruling party (UNIP) or of government.[10] In Tanzania all press is controlled through "refusal of official registration,"[11] ostensibly in conformity with Nyerere's policy of permitting criticism as long as it does not attack the fundamental objectives of ujamaa socialism. One Tanzanian critic argues that training of Tanzanian journalists in accordance with socialist aims means that news is reported only when the government wishes it to be made public.[12]

Because of the massive state ownership of the media in all countries except Gambia, Kenya, and Nigeria, there is little need for overt censorship. Editors of ostensibly independent, but state-owned, newspapers can be counted on to practice self-censorship. Employees of independent newspapers have to weigh their professional inclinations against possibilities of individual harassment or eventual state takeover. Harassment of editors and journalists is one means by which the press is controlled in Nigeria. In 1980, for example, mass purges of newspaper staff were reported.[13] In August 1981, six senior editors were arrested and three opposition dailies were raided.[14] Harassments and arrests, while relatively infrequent in Nigeria until the 1983 coup, serve as warnings of the limits the governments will tolerate, and they cannot help but have a censoring effect.

State control of the press is also buttressed by deportation of foreign journalists[15] and use of sedition laws. In 1969 the editor of the university-based paper *Transition* was tried, along with the author of a letter to him, for sedition against the government of Uganda. The actual content of the letter in question appeared to suggest that the Ugandan bench had not yet been Africanized, partly because eligible Ugandan judges were not of the "right" tribe; and furthermore that the Obote regime was happily retaining "outmoded" colonial laws designed to suppress freedom of expression. The judge acquitted the defendants on the grounds that the contents of the letter were not seditious and that, given the nature of *Transition*'s readership, the discussion would not have any harmful influence on ordinary Ugandans' views of the government.[16] The editor, Rajat Neogy, a British citizen, was released, but the letter-writer, Abu Mayanga, an M.P., was detained under the Preventive Detention Act.[17] Control of the Ugandan press under the Amin regime was effected by murder, torture, and exile. Under the post-1980 Obote regime as well, reports were frequent of imprisonment and deaths of prominent members of the press. Five opposition papers were banned in March 1981.[18]

The censorship which has been applied to the remnants of the free press in Africa extends also to foreign publications and to other modes of African expression, such as the newly developing popular theater. The best-known case of such censorship was the imprisonment of the Kenyan writer Ngugi wa Thiong'o in 1977. Ngugi's works, as long as they were written in English and were accessible only to a small audience, had not been censored in Kenya. But in 1977 he wrote a play in the Kikuyu language and had it performed by ordinary peasants in his own Kikuyu village. The play, which dealt with the question of land shortages, attracted such large audiences that it was soon banned, and Ngugi spent a year in preventive detention.[19] In Zambia, an award-winning play dealing with the social causes of Zambia's rising crime rate was withheld from an international festival in Canada, ostensibly for lack of funds. Questions were also raised about whether a play that dealt with urban Zambia and was not based on rural dance or folklore was "indigenous,"[20] thus demonstrating how the ideology of communalism can be used to block real discussion of contemporary African social problems. In Uganda, actors, producers, and playwrights took heroic risks during the Amin period. Shortly after the murder of Anglican Archbishop Luwum in 1977, the playwright and director Byron Kawadwa staged a play about the Catholic Baganda martyrs, burned to death in 1885 on the orders of the Kabaka (king). Kawadwa's mutilated body was found, along with those of five of his cast members, several days later.[21]

The press in Commonwealth Africa is the principal agency for monitoring government activities, especially in the absence of powerful, institutionalized lobbying groups. A second group with the capacity to criticize incumbent governments and to influence, indeed to mobilize, the public in Africa is students, academics, and professionals. With their international reference groups and the critical tendencies demanded by their studies, they are obviously interested in influencing government policy. Indeed, they are frequently interested in replacing the government altogether.

Adverse official reaction to the activities of students and professionals can be swift, and police action is routine when students actually demonstrate. When their actions are seen as a direct threat to the state, preventive detention occurs. In Zambia, for example, several (foreign and Zambian) academics and a number of students were detained following protests regarding Zambia's relations with South Africa and Angola in 1976.[22] In Ghana and Nigeria, occasional deaths have resulted from student clashes with police and military forces.[23] Student protests are as likely to be about university matters, such as food supplies in the dormitories, as about national policy. A frequent reaction to student unrest is to close the university and rusticate the students until they are willing to return to campus and sign undertakings of good behavior. Behind such government actions is the fear that students will expose national problems; for example, if students, an elite group, are improperly fed in dormitories, it is a sign of food shortages throughout the country. Before 1982, only under Idi Amin was wholesale slaughter of students reported, the worst case having been a mass murder that occurred on the Makerere University campus in 1977.[24] But in 1982, Kenya broke its relatively good human rights record by killing at least 50 students (35 were machine-gunned while sitting in a bus) after the August 2, 1982, coup attempt; several hundred more were imprisoned.[25]

Student protest in Africa is a serious political matter; students are one of the few articulate groups who can express grievances against government policies. They are also potential members of the ruling class; in a continent with scarce high-level manpower, the transition from university student to senior civil servant, or even government advisor, can be swift. Students have also been known to rally active worker support for their demonstrations, especially in Ghana in the late 1970s and '80s, and in Sierra Leone during the food riots of 1981.[26] In 1982, Nairobi University students were quick to respond to an appeal from the air force for support for its attempted coup.

One reason why African governments fear criticism from universities is that, in countries where ruling classes are very small, there are often village or kin ties between academics, businessmen, and potential coup-makers in the armed forces. African intellectuals are much closer to actual and potential centers of power than their Western counterparts. The professor from a disgruntled minority ethnic group may have a brother-in-law who is an army colonel. Thus, governments fear academic words and actions. The complete closure of the University of Nairobi after the 1982 coup incident, and the detention without trial of a number of professors,[27] is probably more a consequence of this type of class connection than a genuine fear by arap Moi's government of the Marxist theories emanating from the campus, theories which had gained backers as much as fifteen years previously but in a period in which there was no serious challenge to the central government.

African professionals also have a kind of secondary power, the power to unite as one coherent body to put economic pressure on the government. In 1977 the Ghana Professional Bodies' Association incited a general strike of all professionals, including doctors and engineers, which forced the military National Redemption Council to agree to a referendum on "Union Government" in 1978.[28] When the referendum proved to be a farce, the professional associations continued their pressure in face of direct threats on their lives by the head of state.[29]

It is tempting to come to the conclusion that these repressive actions are taken merely to protect the particular regime, or indeed the particular individual, in power. This conclusion is easy to reach in the case of Malawi, where the President-for-Life has an elaborate, almost ludicrous apparatus set up to censor all incoming books, where dissenting journalists have spent long periods of time in jail, and where foreign journalists and other commentators are routinely deported or denied entrance.[30] In Nigeria, arrests of seven senior staff from four newspapers followed publication of allegations in 1981 that President Shagari had tried to bribe opposition members to support some of his legislation, and that his party was planning to assassinate a political opponent.[31]

In addition to instances of personal interest on the part of heads of state, particular types of activities and writings seem to incite state controls on freedom of expression. National security and national development are frequently offered as explanations for such controls.

Commonwealth African governments appear to be particularly sensitive to criticisms of their foreign policies, perhaps because they are so heavily dependent upon foreign aid and so extremely vulnerable to outside attack. Land-locked Zambia, despite its abhorrence of white minority rule, relies heavily on trade with South Africa. Criticism of Zambian contacts with South Africa is construed not merely as an ideological matter, but as a possible detriment to Zambian transport routes. This type of fear was undoubtedly at the root of the crackdown on students and faculty at the University of Zambia in 1976. Similarly Malawi, which has pursued a policy of *rapprochement* with South Africa to facilitate trade and migrant mining, is extremely sensitive to criticism on this issue. In Kenya the government ordered the editor of the *Daily Nation* to cease serialization of a book on the Israeli raid on Uganda's Entebbe airport in 1976,[32] apparently because Kenya had been criticized for allegedly assisting the Israelis. In Tanzania the editor of the government-owned daily *The Standard* was dismissed in 1972 for "unacceptable criticism of a fellow African leader"; that is, for criticizing General Numeiri of Sudan's practice of executing rebels.[33]

Such incidents suggest that African leaders feel a need to demonstrate internal unity in their dealings with foreign governments. In the case of South Africa, the issue is emotionally charged, and criticism can easily be construed as an accusation that the regimes in place are neo-colonial collaborators. Since such criticism would undermine the nationalist ideology of anti-imperialism, it is not surprising that those in power find it a direct challenge to their authority.

Governments are also threatened, as discussed in Chapter 5, by schismatic and secessionist pressures. Thus censorship or state takeover is often used to squelch criticism by the ethnically based press. African leaders who criticize the media frequently stress the need for consensus and accuse intellectuals and journalists of "confusing" or misleading the people. For example, while opening a seminar for the press on August 1, 1972, President Kaunda of Zambia stated that his government would "no longer allow newsmen . . . to mislead the masses through misrepresentation or distortion of the facts."[34] Illiterates are alleged to be incapable of making critical judgments of press reports and thus to be particularly susceptible to misinformation. Frequently, military governments enact "rumors decrees" prohibiting the spreading of "false" information even by word of mouth. Such a decree was passed by the Acheampong regime in Ghana in 1974.[35]

Many government leaders appear to believe that their attempts to unite the nation and to develop the country are undermined by "irresponsible" criticism. Thus Kenya's then Minister of Finance, Mwai Kibaki, said in 1972 that "the role of the press ought to be one of trying to assist in building the nation."[36] Similarly, President Nyerere of Tanzania has clearly stated that the independence of the university ought to be subordinated to the national goal of development through socialism. "The aim of the University . . . must be to service the needs of a developing socialist Tanzania. This purpose must determine the subjects taught, [and] the content of the courses."[37]

Many African leaders, then, appear to believe that freedom of expression is an unaffordable luxury in newly developing, poor nations, where national unity in pursuit of the common purpose of development ought to be everyone's overriding concern. Many African and other Third World governments see such national purposes undermined not only by the indigenous press, but also by the foreign press and by foreign control of the international news media. Since 1970, UNESCO (United Nations Educational, Scientific, and Cultural Organization) has debated the possibility of creating a "new international information order" to parallel the new international economic order.[38] The idea is to break the monopoly of the few large, predominantly Western, international news agencies by providing national or regional agencies in the Third World. At the same time, Third World journalists would be less influenced by both the political biases and the content biases (toward "bad news" and unusual events) of the Western media.

Certainly these criticisms of the large Western news agencies contain a substantial degree of truth. There is a danger in suggestions of expelling the Western agencies from the Third World, however, in that it allows for even more censorship within Africa. Already Western journalists are frequently expelled from Commonwealth African countries and occasionally killed for reporting news the regimes in power would rather have suppressed.[39] Africans frequently listen to international wireless broadcasters for news they consider more reliable than that which they can obtain from their own national agencies.[40] In 1982 the Sierra Leone Broadcasting Company stopped relaying the BBC news service after the government expressed dissatisfaction with the BBC's reporting of industrial unrest in Sierra Leone.[41] In such a situation, the national news agencies may simply become a further means of censoring outside reports and of tailoring the news to suit the needs of the current regime. The ideology of anti-imperialism, in this as in many other guises, then serves as a useful mask of the interests of the ruling classes.[42]

On the other hand, a press cannot be said to be free of bias if it is controlled, as in the case of present-day Kenya and formerly in Zambia, by foreign owners. Such a press may criticize abuses of civil and political rights by African governments and, in Western liberal tradition, support the rule of law and the supremacy of the constitution. But a newspaper owned by foreign capitalists is not likely to invite debate over pro-capitalist economic policies, or to consider how land-holding might be restructured to ensure equitable distribution. If, as Chapter 4 argued, debate on economic policy is essential to the full implementation of economic human rights, then the left (in Kenya) as well as the right (in Tanzania or Zambia) must be allowed to have its say.

A press situation such as existed in Nigeria from 1979 to 1983, in which indigenously owned private newspapers competed against each other and against government papers, with only occasional harassment of journalists by the police, is probably the best one can hope for in contemporary Commonwealth Africa. If murder, torture, and long-term imprisonment of journalists, writers, academics, and students were abandoned in Malawi and Uganda, and if countries such as Sierra Leone, Zambia, and Tanzania allowed an independent press to operate, a much more effective check upon abuses of power by governments would result. The suspicion that suppression of freedom of expression is merely a means of enhancing regime or individual power would then be much less clearly based on fact.

Trade Unions

Trade unions are, in the words of one prominent commentator on Africa, "the typical and universal organization of the worker, the one that he cannot do without and through which he both discovers himself and imposes himself on society."[43] Certainly trade unions are one of the most important political organizations available for ordinary people to achieve their human rights. Through trade unions, both subsistence rights (to better wages, working conditions and welfare subsidies) and political rights (especially freedom of association, speech and assembly) are achieved. Actions initiated by trade unions on behalf of their own members frequently have favorable repercussions on non-unionized sectors of the working poor. Effective trade unions, however, need to be "free"; that is, not under government control, regardless of whether they exist in a capitalist or a socialist society.[44]

Conditions for trade unions are, in general, extremely unfavorable in Commonwealth Africa. The economy is underdeveloped and the industrial sector is small. Trade unions are relatively new; they were either prohibited outright or strictly controlled until very late in the colonial period. In the early independence period, before cooptative organizational measures were taken by the state, trade unions tended to be small and fragmented, and their leaders were easily corrupted. Leadership was, for many, "an entrepreneurial enterprise":[45] a means of obtaining marginally higher incomes, material wealth such as motorcycles, and a certain amount of prestige.

A federal commission investigating unions in Nigeria as late as 1977 reported that unions were riddled with personal rivalries, that union constitutions were flouted, that illegal elections were common, and that smaller unions were bribed to join union centrals; in short, internal union democracy was a sham.[46] This view of unions in Nigeria is substantiated by a case study conducted by Lubeck, who described the union he encountered as a "management-sanctioned extortion agency whereby supervisors forced workers . . . to pay initiation fees and monthly dues," and where officials used overseas training programs to further careerist ambitions to enter government, politics, or the employ of transnational corporations.[47]

Richard Sandbrook concluded from his review of the trade union literature that "in contemporary Africa, national union officials can more often be found stifling rank-and-file initiatives than articulating common grievances or co-ordinating industrial action."[48] Undoubtedly, this type of behavior is partly due to the weak internal organization of trade unions. Workers who are new to industrial employment and urban life, who may still consider themselves to be quasi-peasants or have aspirations to enter petty trade or commerce, and who may well be semiliterate, at best, are in a weak position to demand accountability from careerist trade union officials. But of more importance in explaining the behavior of trade union officials is the control of unions and cooptation of their leaders, increasingly practiced by the state in Africa.

Regardless of the alleged pro-capitalist or pro-socialist tendency of the regime, similar mechanisms are used to control trade unions. The task of the state in Commonwealth Africa is to transform trade unions that originally constituted competing bases of power[49] into neutralized, sycophantic bodies. The mechanisms the state uses to achieve these ends include the registration of all trade unions and the imposition of restrictive conditions upon them, the abolition of the right to strike, compulsory membership of all trade unions in state-sponsored federations, the cooptation of leadership through inducements of finance or office and, finally, when all else fails, coercive repression.[50]

In Nigeria and Kenya, the state has obtained a measure of control over trade unions without coopting them directly into a governing party. The purpose of the 1977 Tribunal of Inquiry into Trade Unions in Nigeria was to eliminate the small, feuding unions and unite them in one common, central union, thus consolidating the control already achieved by the periodic (but not entirely successful) banning of strikes, for example in 1968–69 during an official national emergency that lasted well into the 1970s.[51] In Kenya, the government has made a number of tripartite agreements with business and labor to ban strikes and freeze wages, at the same time effecting a 10 percent increase in employment.[52] The many small unions that existed in Kenya shortly after independence were brought together by the government into the Central Organization of Trade Unions; labor leaders acquiesced in this arrangement in return for union check-off privileges (that is, dues check-offs which ensure stable financing) for the new central.[53]

While the measures taken by the Nigerian and Kenyan governments might seem organizationally rational, especially given the internal problems demonstrated during their earlier union history, they allow the government to control which unions will be registered, and they also contain the threat that check-off privileges will be revoked if unions do not adhere to government wishes. Such control and threats do not, however, constitute the outright cooptation of unions, practiced especially in one-party states in Commonwealth Africa. In Malawi, unions are virtually nonexistent. They are affiliated to the ruling Malawi Congress Party, and no trade union activity is permitted without party approval.[54] One reason for the "economic miracle" of Malawi's high export-oriented growth is the fact that workers on the new capitalist plantations have no trade union protection.

The most complete integration of trade unions into the ruling party in Commonwealth Africa has taken place in Nkrumah's Ghana and post-Arusha Tanzania. The largest wage increases for unskilled labor in Ghana occurred when union-government ties were strongest.[55] In the 1950s, the Trades Union Congress and the ruling Convention People's Party made an alliance. In return for giving the TUC a £25,000 grant and the right to dues check-off, the government passed a bill which, among other highly restrictive measures, gave it the right to approve intra-union rules and procedures, to decide which unions could join the central TUC, and to control the right to strike.[56]

In Tanzania, a National Union of Tanganyika Workers was established in 1964. Trade unionists were no longer permitted to engage in political activity except through the ruling party. In return, they were constitutionally granted (Article 29, 1) the right to nominate a national trade union member to parliament, subject to vetting by the party. The purpose of the union was explicitly stated: to "foster loyalty [of workers] to TANU and government in mobilizing wage-earners for development."[57] The secretary-general of NUTA is directly appointed by the president and until 1982 was always also the minister of labor.[58] Originally, the union structure permitted workers' committees in the factories separate from the bureaucratic NUTA hierarchy, but these were abolished in 1976 and replaced by NUTA branches whose primary aim was to be "education in production" and political and military training.[59] One reason for the abolition of independent workers' committees was undoubtedly that some of them took seriously the socialist ideology of workers' control of factories, which had been officially pronounced in 1971. Workers at the

Mount Carmel rubber factory, for example, indulged in go-slows and strikes, with the result that they were fired, fingerprinted, and repatriated to the country, although they were later "rehabilitated" after a public outcry.[60]

How is it possible for governments so easily to coopt trade unions in Africa? It is notable, first, that one-party states, which are buttressed by general repressive measures such as preventive detention acts, are the most successful in such corporatist cooptation (although, as I will discuss below, the one-party government in Zambia has not been able to coopt the Mineworkers' Union). One-party states are generally quite cavalier about the rule of law, so trade unions are not able to appeal to the courts for protections they might have in principle. Union-shop and check-off privileges and promises of steady financing are powerful inducements[61] to union officials who, like officials in any type of organization, can easily become more interested in the continuation of the organization than in the achievement of its stated purposes. These inducements to official position are of course far more powerful in the extremely poor economies of Commonwealth Africa than in countries in which union officials are routinely well paid or have a variety of professional opportunities available in the event that they are removed from office.

The ideology of development is also a powerful weapon. Both nationalism and anti-imperialism are conveniently perverted to draw attention from class rule and to argue for a spurious "pulling together" by all ranks of society, which in fact benefits those in power more than others. The Tanzanian government, for example, argued when it created NUTA that it had to do so to stop unionized workers' wages from pulling far ahead of the incomes of the peasants. "NUTA's wages policy should be based primarily on the needs of the national economy. . . . NUTA officials should concern themselves less with the fear of exploitation and more with the sacrifice needed for Nation-building."[62] "Socialism" and "self-reliance" are, in the anti-capitalist rhetorical milieu of one-party states, strong rallying slogans against which one argues at one's peril, even if the objective consequences of such slogans are obviously in disaccord with their aims.

Repression of trade unions in the name of "sacrifice," or a general leveling of wages to that of peasants' incomes, has two detrimental human rights consequences. First, urban wage workers' spending power is not substantially higher than that of people working in the informal sector, or of peasants, given the higher costs of urban living, extended family obligations, remittances to home villages, etc.[63] In fact, Tanzania recently became one of the few countries in Africa in which peasants' real incomes now appear to be higher than those of urban wage workers.[64] In a country suffering from climatic disasters, insecure reliance on the world economy, and a history of poor economic policies and premature socialist centralization, workers who are denied union rights undoubtedly suffer more than they otherwise would.

But even more important than this undermining of workers' substantive rights (to material welfare) in Tanzania is the long-term undermining of those civil and political rights that are both preconditions for, and consequences of, successful long-term trade union struggle. The trade-offs the state offers to unionists in the form of more stable working conditions, closed-shop, and union check-off cannot substitute for the "fundamental human right of the workers to choose their leaders freely and to remove them from office when they forfeit their confidence."[65] Those in power do not voluntarily give up their power. The allegedly developmentalist model of trade unionism denies trade unionists the right to establish a principle that, in the long run, will benefit all those who are powerless; namely, the right to demand rights.

It is worth noting that not all trade union leaders are corruptible, nor do all bend to the government's will. The creation of NUTA in Tanzania was accompanied by the arrest and preventive detention of more than two hundred trade unionists; many were kept in prison for two years and blacklisted from all formal employment when they were released.[66] In Zambia, although the state has also created one union central and although the general labor policy consists of labor discipline, peaceful dispute resolution, and encouragement of increased productivity,[67] the government has not been able to bring the Mineworkers' Union under its control. The mineworkers are a large, concentrated labor force occupying a central location in the Zambian economy; copper mining in 1980 accounted for 91 percent of Zambia's export earnings. Because of its crucial location, the union has been able to maintain its independence of the ruling party and its responsiveness, through a branch system, to the rank and file. It is a policy of the union not to be involved in ruling party politics.[68] The Mineworkers' Union exists in one of the few developed capitalist (albeit extractive, rather than productive) sectors in Commonwealth Africa and still has considerable power, even since the world downturn in the price of copper in the mid-1970s. In 1981 President Kaunda detained a number of prominent union leaders because of a dispute over abolition of autonomous mining townships and the unionists' refusal to engage in party politics,[69] and more generally because of developing internal opposition and two aborted coups, but he was soon obliged to release and reinstate them.

Trade unionists, like members of the press, professionals, and academics, are groups of Africans with international human rights references, who are not completely cooptable. Even organizationally weak, internally corrupt unions are capable of fighting for workers' rights against the state.

But in the economic crisis of the 1970s and '80s, it is increasingly difficult for Commonwealth African governments to accede to the demands of trade unionists without reducing the amount of wealth available for appropriation by the ruling class. Thus one can predict that increased state repression will be applied in the foreseeable future to trade unions, as to all other oppositional bodies.

Electoral Politics

African leaders sometimes counter the criticism that freedom of expression is being suppressed in their countries by saying that free debate is still allowed within the structure of an internally democratic ruling party. They refer back to the myth of the indigenous consensual polity of pre-colonial Africa (see Chapter 2) to argue that the most appropriate forum for debate in contemporary Africa is within a single party that directs government policy, and which encompasses as members all who truly accept the basic ideals of how the society should be governed. The vast majority of the people, then, can become political insiders; the tiny number of dissenters is easily labeled subversive and is dealt with by various coercive means.

This section will focus on the evolution of the one-party state in Commonwealth Africa, with a view to discovering whether it does indeed provide a new model for democratic decision-making. The prototypical one-party state is Tanzania, along with its less successful imitator, Zambia. One-party states also exist in Sierra Leone (since 1977), Malawi, and Kenya (in practice since 1969, in law since 1982), and have periodically been tried in Ghana (under Nkrumah) and in Uganda (under Obote in the late 1960s).

It is important to remember, in considering one-party states in Africa, that the U.N. and African charters of rights nowhere suggest that political rights can be guaranteed only within a competitive, multiparty framework. The concern exhibited in both the U.N. covenant on Civil and Political Rights and the African Charter of Human and Peoples' Rights is for political participation, not political competition. Article 13 of the African Charter is less specific than the U.N. covenant regarding the form that elections should take. While it prescribes, along with the U.N. covenant, that every citizen should have the right to "participate freely" in government, "either directly or through freely chosen representatives," and also that every citizen should have the "right of equal access to the public service," it makes no mention of voting nor of "genuine periodic elections," whether in a one-party or a multiparty system. The omission must be presumed to have been deliberate and to leave open the possibility that representatives could be "freely chosen" by means other than elections on the basis of universal suffrage; for example, by elections or appointments within a ruling party.

In the nine countries under discussion in this book, there is no derogation from the principle of universal adult suffrage. In northern Nigeria, women were not permitted to vote under the Independence Constitution, presumably in accordance with the wishes of the traditional Islamic hierarchies; however, that disability was removed in the 1979 Constitution. But the biases in some constitutions against granting citizenship to people of non-African descent, as discussed in Chapter 5, means that some long-time residents of, or people born in, Commonwealth Africa are routinely denied political representation. There is similarly no legal discrimination against participation in the public service; however, where "Africanization" of the public service is interpreted in racial rather than in geographical terms, it also results in discrimination in practice against some citizens.

The major concern in discussing political rights in Commonwealth Africa is whether citizens have the genuine right to participate in the affairs of government. Such participation includes a genuine right to discuss and criticize government policies and, by implication, to change governments that citizens find unsatisfactory. While human rights covenants do not specify that such a right ought to include multiparty elections, it is nevertheless useful to consider briefly the fate of competitive electoral politics in Africa.

The multiparty competitive system was originally included in the independence constitutions of all former British African colonies. Even so, the only country in which the multiparty electoral system has functioned without a break since independence is Gambia. The perpetuation of the multiparty system in Gambia is probably due to the prestige of Gambia's leader, Sir Dawda Jawara, and to the suppression of any indigenous conflicts, such as that between the coastal Creoles and the upcountry "bush" people, in the face of the larger national problem of what the relations ought to be between Gambia and Senegal. The necessity for Senegal's intervention to defeat the attempted coup in 1981, instigated by revolutionaries with a quasi-socialist analysis of Gambia's current economic problems, reveals that even Gambia's system is very fragile.[70]

Multiparty electoral politics have given way completely to institutionalized, one-party states in Sierra Leone, Tanzania, Zambia, Malawi, and Kenya. In the other three Commonwealth countries, multiparty systems have been interspersed with attempts to consolidate one-party systems, and with military regimes. In Ghana, a one-party state under the rule of the Convention People's Party was formally accepted by 92.81 percent of registered voters in a 1965 referendum. That referendum, however, was conducted after a "massive propaganda and pressure campaign" by the

CPP, including threats, intimidation, ballot-rigging, and the elimination of all secrecy in voting.[71] There was no pretense of institutionalizing genuine popular participation within the new one-party state. After Nkrumah's overthrow in 1966, two multiparty elections were held. Dr. Busia, generally considered to be an economic conservative and a representative of the Ashanti elite, was elected in 1969 but overthrown by a military coup in 1972. In 1979 Dr. Hilla Limann, leader of the People's National Party, which many observers considered to be a reincarnation of the CPP,[72] was elected; in his turn he was overthrown by a military coup on December 31, 1981.

In Uganda similar events took place. After conquering the Kabaka of Buganda in 1966, Milton Obote began implementing a one-party state, formally proclaimed in 1969. In 1971, Obote was ousted by a military coup led by Idi Amin. Amin's overthrow in 1979 was followed by three interim governments. Obote returned to power in December 1980 after a multiparty election that was reported by a Commonwealth Observer Group to be, given the circumstances, fair on the whole. Although the observer team had "reservations" regarding the nomination process and unopposed elections in the West Nile part of the country, "In the remainder of the country, despite all deficiencies, the electoral process cohered and held together, even if some of its individual strands were frayed."[73]

Many independent observers dispute the Commonwealth Observer Group's views of the 1980 election. In particular, they cite the fact that for a 24-hour period after the elections, the Electoral Commission was deprived of its authority, with the implication that during these 24 hours, the votes were manipulated.[74] One observer alleges that "most of the ballots were correctly counted . . . But then the labels were switched," so that, for example, in the riding of Gulu West, the opposition Democratic Party candidate, who won the riding by 40,000 votes to 3,000, was announced to have lost by 3,000 to 40,000.[75] It is not surprising that parliamentary politics in the post-election period were largely a farce. Many opposition MPs were detained, tortured, or murdered, while opposition political parties turned to violent guerilla activities either to further their aims as a result of their allegedly rigged electoral losses, or in retaliation for the brutalities of the second Obote regime. On July 27, 1985, Obote was overthrown by a military coup.

For a multiparty system to operate effectively, there must be some agreement among all parties on the limits of competition, on a consensus of political values, and on an equitable division of political spoils. Such agreement does not appear to exist in Ghana or Uganda. In Uganda, especially, the idea of a unified federal state is not yet accepted; Buganda regional feeling still runs strong. In such circumstances, political stability appears to be impossible.

On the other hand, dictatorial one-party states with no provision for genuine internal criticism, which both Nkrumah and Obote attempted to create, are also not conducive to political stability. Not only do ordinary Africans feel excluded from such a top-down organization of politics but, and more important, factions of the ruling class in opposition to the particular clique in power have no institutionalized means to express their disagreements. It is, in other words, possible to institutionalize a "loyal" opposition in Africa only within a genuinely democratic ruling party, or at least a ruling party that allows for competitive access to the political spoils. Both ruling classes and masses interpret politics in Africa as a system of patron-client relations. The ordinary elector, as many commentators have pointed out, votes for the "big man" most likely to provide resources to him and his community.[76] Similarly, members of the political elite compete for office largely because of the perquisites it brings: material wealth for themselves and their families and the opportunity to dispense largesse to the communities they ostensibly represent. Political stability is possible, then, when the limited resources of the state are reasonably and equitably distributed among regions, ethnic groups, and competing factions of the ruling class. Patronage politics fail when only one group is patronized; the result is either a military coup or increased repression by the faction in power.

While many Commonwealth African countries have attempted to solve the problem of lack of political consensus by resorting to one-party systems, Nigeria recently attempted to impose a structural political consensus over real political dissension within the framework of a revised multiparty system. Nigeria's original multiparty system underwent a rapid decline from independence in 1960 to the military coup of 1966, because it was completely dominated by regional politics. The three major political parties, the Northern People's Convention, the National Party of Nigeria and the Cameroons, and the Action Group, had separate bases in the North, the East, and the West, respectively. These bases were clearly defined by the division of Nigeria into three regions. Each political party, in power in its own area, manipulated electoral rules to ensure its own predominance.[77]

During the period of military rule (1966–79), steps were taken to break up the three regions by redividing Nigeria first into twelve, then into nineteen states. Between 1975 and 1979 a new constitution was drafted. While the Independence Constitution had allowed considerable power to the states through exclusive or shared jurisdiction and by allotting them residual jurisdictions, the new constitution increased the exclusive jurisdiction of the federal government and allocated the residual jurisdiction away from the states to the center.[78] All political parties were to be national in composition, and complicated criteria of nationhood were included in the constitution. Membership of all parties had to be open to any Nigerian national, and the president had to receive at least 25 percent of the votes in two-thirds of the nineteen states to be elected.[79] As a result of these conditions, only five parties competed in the 1979 elections, out of an original nineteen which had been proposed. Six competed in 1983.

The second civilian experiment with multiparty competition in Nigeria ended with the December 31, 1983, military coup. Before the 1983 elections, some observers had predicted that civilian rule would last only if President Shagari was reelected; that is, that the dominant northern faction of the Nigerian ruling class would not tolerate a government formed by a party controlled by any other faction. Despite constitutional provisions for national representativeness, the parties competing in 1979 had very definable regional/ethnic bases. The winning party, the National Party of Nigeria, owed its success to its ability to make alliances with minority ethnic leaders in multiethnic states.[80]

The problem in Nigerian politics is that separate regional power groups manipulate ethnic sentiments to acquire political and economic resources. In the Nigerian system of patron-client politics, all patron groups must be accommodated; otherwise, even though the threat of regional schism was removed by the federal victory in the 1967–70 civil war, the possibility remains that regional elites will manipulate contacts within the military to foment coups d'état. In September 1983 the National Party of Nigeria won its second electoral victory in what was originally reported to be an election generally free of vote-rigging and violence, except in two states in the former Western Region.[81] Commentators argued that electoral mal-practices by the various parties probably canceled each other out, and thus that the reelection of Shagari, with a larger proportion of votes in the south than he had received in 1979, represented an emerging national consensus.

Yet despite the predicted new stability of the Nigerian polity, a military coup occurred on December 31, 1983. The coup was not caused by regional elite competition; the new military leader, Muhamadu Buhari, was also a northerner. The stated reasons for the coup were economic. As is usual in Commonwealth Africa, the military cited corruption as a major precipitating cause. But Buhari also cited his opposition to Shagari's announcement that the Nigerian economy, hard hit by the international oil glut, would have to undergo a period of austerity. Initially, there was popular support for the coup by ordinary people who naturally feared the consequences of austerity; but by mid-1984, as it became evident that the military regime was intending to implement similar economic policies, the popular support lessened. It is unlikely that Nigeria will return to civilian rule while the economic crisis in Africa lasts.

The failure of the second civilian government established through multiparty competitive elections in Nigeria indicates the seeming impossi-bility of such a model of government for present-day Commonwealth

Africa. Those countries which have so far avoided successful military coups are all one-party states, falling along a continuum from repressiveness to relative openness. The most repressive country in the group is Malawi. In essence, Malawi is a no-party state ruled by a paternalistic autocrat, H. Kamuzu Banda.[82] The Malawi Congress Party is little more than a vehicle for ritual expressions of gratitude and loyalty to Banda, while its Youth Wing operates as one of Banda's more coercive organs of state supremacy. In effect all officers of government are appointed directly by Banda. He enjoys

> the sole right to appoint members to the National Executive Committee of the MCP; . . . until 1978, he alone made the final selection of party candidates for Parliament; he has exclusive powers to discipline and dismiss MPs; he nominates the Speaker, as well as a number of 'Nominated Members' . . . and he appoints, rotates and dismisses cabinet ministers.[83]

In 1978, perhaps in response to strengthened threats from exiled opposition organizations, and also in response to bad publicity abroad in the face of the Carter administration's stress on human rights, Banda allowed the first general elections since independence, ostensibly with a choice of candidates from within the MCP.[84] In the previous three "elections" the president had chosen the candidates from within the MCP and there had been no voting.[85] Despite (or perhaps because of) manipulation of the elections by Banda, 31 former MPs lost their seats. The 1978 elections were repeated in June 1983.[86] No serious effort was made in either case to choose candidates through genuine popular participation. The Banda regime continues to be largely sustained by violence; for example, the leader of the Socialist League of Malawi, Dr. Ahaki Mpakati, was shot dead in Zimbabwe in March 1983.[87] Malawi is neither a model nor a candidate for the institution of a new form of popular democracy in Africa.

Similarly, the Sierra Leonean system cannot be considered a model of a new democratic form of one-party state. Since independence, the political battle-lines in Sierra Leone have been clearly drawn between the Sierra Leone People's Party and the African People's Congress. The SLPP controlled political power until 1967, when after allegedly rigged elections the military briefly took over and then handed power to the APC. In the face of sporadic political violence, the APC declared a one-party state in 1978.[88] As in Malawi, however, the Sierra Leonean one-party regime is not based upon broad consultation with or participation by the masses, although there have been recent moves toward greater participation.[89]

Elections have more meaning, and Parliament has in the past been more independent, in Kenya than in either Malawi or Sierra Leone. The Kenyan Constitution was amended to create a one-party state only in 1982, but Kenya had been a one-party state in practice since 1969. The major opposition party, the Kenya People's Union led by Oginga Odinga, has been effectively stifled by a variety of measures, including violence perpetrated by youth wingers of the ruling KANU (Kenya African National Union), denial of permission to hold election rallies, selective use of preventive detention against KPU leaders, vote-rigging, and denial of permission to opposition political candidates to enter the "scheduled areas."[90] Moreover, internally KANU is undemocratic, with no internal elections between 1966 and 1978.[91] Only Kenyans wealthy enough to buy life memberships in the party, at a cost of sh. 1,000, can be party officials.[92] In 1979, an attempt to declare only life members eligible for Parliament was revoked after it aroused a storm of controversy.[93]

Elections in Kenya have, therefore, essentially been opportunities for voters to express their dissatisfaction with the personnel of government. In the 1970 election, almost half the sitting members were defeated; in 1974, 4 ministers, 13 assistant ministers and 71 backbenchers were defeated; and in 1979, 72 incumbent MPs, including 7 ministers and 15 assistant ministers, were defeated.[94] The rate of voter participation declined significantly, however, after the opposition KPU was banned.[95] The opportunity to vote out specific KANU members of Parliament was supplemented in Kenya until the mid-1970s by the extraordinary freedom of backbench MPs to speak out and be critical in Parliament. The accepted boundary to criticism was that President Kenyatta himself, who was in many ways a symbol of nationhood mediating among competing ruling-class factions, could not be criticized.[96] In the mid-1970s, however, a number of the most outspoken MPs were arrested and detained, and one MP, J.M. Kariuki, was murdered.[97]

The relatively open Kenyan one-party system lasted after Kenyatta's death in 1978 only while his far less charismatic successor, Daniel arap Moi, could claim legitimacy through his "philosophy" of *nyayo*, meaning to follow in Kenyatta's footsteps. While the formal organization of Kenyan one-party politics ostensibly allows for intraparty competitive elections, Kenyan politics are in essence patron-client politics. Political office is the route to economic spoils for individual, family, ethnic group, and region. The stability of Kenyan politics under Kenyatta was rooted in his ability to mediate among competing ruling-class factions, both among ethnic groups (especially the Kikuyu and the Luo), and among differing Kikuyu factions.[98] Moi's ascendancy to the presidency was the result of the victory of one KANU faction over another, not of compromise between the two.[99] That he has less ability than Kenyatta to manipulate superstructural stability is evidenced by the 1982 air force coup attempt. What the ascendency of KANU has done is to ensure the power of a new ruling class, which encompasses non-Kikuyu as well as Kikuyu. The periodic elections are designed to give ordinary people a sense of participation, since they can vote out of office those MPs who do not visit their constituencies, or who do not distribute the spoils of political office in the approved patron-client manner.

KANU does not pretend to be a mass-based political party. One-party "democracy" in Kenya was not instituted after consultation with the masses. No provision is made for policy matters to be democratically and openly considered by all party members, with information and direction flowing from the base to the top. Tanzania and Zambia, on the other hand, both turned to a one-party structure ostensibly after broad consultation with the masses. What we must now consider, therefore, is whether the Zambian and Tanzanian models allow for genuine mass participation in government, or have the structural capacity to allow for such participation in the future.

The One-Party Model

One-party democracy was instituted in Tanzania in 1965. Zambia instituted one-party democracy in 1972, following the Tanzanian model in several key respects. In neither case was there any consultation with the masses as to whether or not the one-party state ought to be instituted; rather, the decision was made at the top. In Tanzania, the decision was ostensibly taken because there was no real competitive party system in place. Rather, it was claimed that the then TANU (Tanzania African National Union) enjoyed such broad popular support that multiparty elections had become a farce; everyone voted for the candidate TANU proposed. In such a situation, Nyerere maintained, it was preferable that competitive elections within TANU should take place, so that the people had a genuine chance to decide which candidate they preferred.[100] While it may be true that TANU enjoyed so much national support in the early 1960s as to render other political parties irrelevant, it is not clear why Nyerere chose to move to a system of one-party rule, rather than merely a system of primary elections within TANU. At least one of Nyerere's opponents, Charles Tumbo, who resigned from TANU in opposition both to the idea of a one-party state and to the 1962 Preventive Detention Act, was held in detention as of 1964.[101] Moreover, the commissioners appointed to investigate public views on the one-party state said outright that they did not want a new opposition to form.[102] It appears then, that Nyerere had and still has in mind a guided democracy,[103] in which certain fundamental principles, namely the one-party state and the socialist orientation, were not to be questioned, and in which no opposition was to be permitted. In his mandate to the Commission on the Establishment of a Democratic One-Party State, Nyerere said clearly, "It is not the task of the Commission to consider whether Tanganyika should be a One Party State. That decision has already been taken."[104]

When the National Commission on the Establishment of the One-Party Participatory Democracy was set up in Zambia in 1972, it too was instructed that its mandate did not include discussion of whether or not there ought to be a one-party system.[105] The commission toured the country, listening to views on such matters as the role of the judiciary and popular grievances against the ruling UNIP (United National Independence Party); it made a number of useful suggestions, some of which were rejected by President Kaunda. Kaunda could not claim, as Nyerere did, that a one-party state was inevitable in Zambia because of lack of opposition; rather, as one Zambian jurist put it, "the detention of opposition leaders and the banning of all parties other than UNIP must be seen as a kind of pre-emptive 'coup.' "[106] The one-party state was instituted in Zambia shortly after Kaunda's predominance was threatened by the decision of the Bemba leader, Simon Kapwepwe, to quit UNIP and form a new political party. Thus, although in both countries there was substantial consultation with the population about the form a one-party system should take, neither country countenanced any questioning of the leader's decision to move from a multiparty to a one-party electoral framework.

Keeping in mind, then, that in both Tanzania and Zambia the one-party state was imposed from above, the next question to be considered is whether such ruling parties are internally democratic. Structurally, UNIP and Tanzania's new unified ruling party, Chama Cha Mapinduzi (Party of the Revolution), are similar. (In 1977, TANU, the mainland Tanzanian ruling party, joined with the ruling Afro-Shirazi Party of Zanzibar to form CCM. Since the ASP is notoriously nondemocratic and indeed appears to have ruled largely by force, its one-party basis is not investigated here.) A number of features in the constitutions of both UNIP and CCM suggest top-down hierarchical control, rather than bottom-up democratic decision-making. First, both constitutions specify party supremacy; that is, the supremacy of the party over government.[107] It is the party's job to formulate policy and the government's merely to execute it. According to the Tanzanian One-Party Commission, this decision was taken because the people had difficulty differentiating TANU from the government.[108] In Zambia, presumably the decision was taken because UNIP's opponents did understand the difference and wished to separate government from party control by UNIP. The effect, in both cases, is that only party members have a chance to participate in political decision-making; non-members are excluded.

If, however, UNIP and CCM are genuine mass parties, encompassing anyone who is in basic agreement with party policy, then the problem of exclusion of non-members from political decision-making is less crucial. Kaunda stated, when the one-party state was instituted, that people were to be permitted to join UNIP in order to change its policies as long as they accepted the one-party state itself.[109] Article 18 of the UNIP Constitution, however, states that all members are subject to party discipline; in practice, this probably means curtailment of internal criticism.[110] Members of Tanzania's CCM must be prepared to "constantly . . . defend and implement the policies of the Party": before admission to the party they must be examined as to their suitability, and they can also be dismissed from the party. Moreover, they are obliged "to know that the Party is the supreme authority and that this supremacy springs from . . . its correct ideology."[111] Such constitutional rules suggest at least the possibility that the party could become the ideological organ of a ruling class. In practice, one Tanzanian argues, people are afraid to speak out at party meetings, and delegates "whisper that they are afraid of losing their job if they displease a more senior party member."[112]

As well as the loyalty of ordinary members to the party, the loyalty of MPs is required. In practice, such loyalty is easy to guarantee because only candidates from the ruling parties are allowed to stand for election; no independent candidature is permitted. The idea of independent candidates was explicitly rejected by the Tanzanian Commission on the one-party state, as its members felt that independents would form the nucleus of a new opposition.[113] In both Zambia and Tanzania, candidates for Parliament are nominated at the local level. All candidates, however, are vetted by the highest organ of the party before being allowed to stand; that is, by the National Executive Committee in Tanzania and the Central Committee in Zambia.[114] In 1982, in response to complaints from locally nominated candidates that they were not allowed to appeal the negative vetting decisions of the higher party organ,[115] the Zambian practice was changed to eliminate local-level primaries entirely. This decision appears merely to further the centralization of the party, rather than to address the problem of intraparty democracy. In the Tanzanian case, there is a further proviso that anyone who has been detained under the Preventive Detention Act for more than six months cannot stand for Parliament.[116] Thus, any serious intra-CCM challengers to the authority or policies of the ruling group can be detained, depriving them of their rights to stand for Parliament, without the chance to defend themselves or their views, either in the courts or in the party. Figures for the number of local candidates rejected by higher party committees are sparse, although sources suggest that in 1965, only 16 of 214 TANU candidates were rejected, while in 1969, over one-quarter of about 400 candidates were rejected.[117] One ought to keep in mind, however, that local-level committees would be unlikely to nominate candidates they thought might be rejected higher up.

The centralized nature of the party is further demonstrated by the fact that in both Tanzania and Zambia, only one candidate for president is allowed, and he is to be nominated by the National Executive Committee or Central Committee, not through a process of intraparty primaries or plebiscite. The Zambian Commission on a One-Party State had explicitly recommended that more than one presidential candidate be nominated, but this recommendation was rejected.[118] To his credit, Kaunda has resisted pressure from within UNIP to be created life president.[119] The large majorities received by both Kaunda and Nyerere in popular elections may reflect their real popularity among ordinary citizens, although according to one Tanzanian observer, "a 'no' vote at a single party election for the head of state must be exercised surreptitiously."[120]

Given the top-down nature of decision-making in both UNIP and the CCM, can it be said that Zambia and Tanzania fulfill the human rights provision that all citizens be allowed to "participate freely" (the African Charter's formulation) in politics, especially (in the UN formulation) through "genuine periodic elections"? The assessment by informed scholars appears to be that Tanzania approaches this ideal more closely than Zambia. UNIP appears to operate primarily as a system of local patronage, and membership in UNIP or any of its related organs is used as a means of upward social mobility. Among almost all constituencies in Zambia, UNIP appears to have declined in legitimacy since the institution of one-party rule.[121] Opposition continues to exist within Zambia, but in a factionalized form within UNIP. There is a great deal of public dislike of UNIP party militants. The 1972 Commission on One-Party Democracy reported many complaints that UNIP members demanded compulsory attendance at UNIP meetings.[122] It is common in Zambia to be stopped in public places and asked for one's UNIP card.[123] UNIP intimidations were a cause for complaint when Kaunda met with Zambian Christian leaders in 1982.[124]

In contrast to the Zambian situation, some informed commentators seem to think that the CCM leadership in Tanzania is making genuine efforts to decentralize and open up decision-making to the masses. The new CCM Constitution provides for elections of officials at every level from the "10–house cell" of party members to the district, region, and nation. While the party is still not as internally democratic as Nyerere's ideal, it is the direction of change, in this view, which is important.[125] On the other hand, some commentators have spoken about the "beer-bellied bureaucrats" who run both government and party, and have suggested that ordinary members are afraid to criticize members of the party hierarchy, whom they perceive as "domineering, extravagant and obstructive."[126] Genuine debate within the party is constrained by the fact that one may not question the goal of socialism;[127] this may explain in part why it was possible for peasants to be forced against their will into the new ujamaa villages in the mid-1970s. Genuine socialist organizations of peasants and workers, perceived as threatening state interests, have also been crushed in Tanzania. The Rwuma Development Association, a socialist village internally, not bureaucratically, organized, was disbanded in 1969.[128] No independent mass organizations are permitted outside the

CCM; women's groups, youth groups, and trade unions have all been incorporated into its structure.

Given these criticisms of CCM as presently constituted, can the Tanzanian goal of a genuinely democratic one-party state succeed? Nyerere's view of Tanzanian democracy appears to be that the people are still to be "guided" in their thinking. Similarly, in Kaunda's vision of Zambian "humanism," the government is to act as the "trustee" of the people;[129] normally, trustees act on behalf of minors or others incapable of looking after their own affairs. The increasingly hierachical nature of both UNIP and CCM suggests that there is no real internal democracy in either party. Rather, the party structures facilitate the creation of new ruling classes from among those who occupy high office.

This is not surprising. It is not in the objective interests of the marginally privileged, in countries as poor as Tanzania and Zambia, to undermine their own power. Rather, such people are more likely to wish to enhance their power, especially when the means to do so are available through a hierarchically organized "mass" party. A genuinely democratic one-party state is not possible in contemporary Commonwealth Africa. The more likely model is of a ruling party that is not internally democratic, but which simply incorporates all factions of an existent or emergent ruling class, and attempts to apportion the limited spoils of office in such a way that all politically relevant groups are bought off. When the goods cannot be delivered, even to the ruling class, then conflict is managed by the state by more coercive means. It is becoming more difficult to buy off all competing elite factions in contemporary Africa, given the economic crisis of the 1980s. Thus, even in those Commonwealth African states which do not have a history of deliberate tyrannical or authoritarian rule, preventive detention and other coercive measures are becoming the norm.

Notes

1. See constitutions of Gambia, Article 22; Ghana, Article 28; Kenya, Article 79; Nigeria, Article 36, 1; Sierra Leone, Article 15; Uganda, Article 17, 1; and Zambia, Article 22. All in Albert P. Blaustein and Gisbert H. Flanz, eds., *Constitutions of the Countries of the World* (Dobbs Ferry, N.Y.: Oceana Publications, 1971–   ).

2. "Nigeria's Press Council," *West Africa*, June 30, 1980, p. 1180.

3. "Brief Reports: Freetown Antics," *Index on Censorship* 9, no. 5 (October 1980): 52.

4. Ludovic A. Ngatara, "From Talking Drum to Talking Paper," *Index on Censorship* 7, no. 3 (1978): 29–32.

5. The foregoing information on West Africa is based on Sylvanus A. Ekwelie, "Ghana: Legal Control of the Nationalist Press, 1880–1950," *Transafrica Journal of History* (Nairobi) 5, no. 2 (1976): 148–60. Quotation from p. 154.

6. " 'Trust' Buys Stellascope," International Press Institute *Report* 30, no. 3 (June 1981): 3.

7. On the press in Nigeria, see "Assessing Nigeria's Newspapers," *West Africa*, July 21, 1980, pp. 1337–39; Graham Lambert, "The Mass Media in Nigeria: Freedom and Constraints of a Fractured Pluralism," *Index on Censorship* 10, no. 5 (1981): 34–36; and "Nigeria Spreads Out," International Press Institute *Report* 29, no. 8 (February 1981): 14.

8. Onyema Ugochukwu, "Nigeria: The Press on Trial," *West Africa*, May 7, 1984, pp. 968–69.

9. "Zambia Tightens Its Grip," International Press Institute *Report* 29, no. 5 (November 1980): 3. See also *Index on Censorship* 4, no. 4 (Winter 1975): 80.

10. International Press Institute *Report* 29, no. 5 (November 1980): 3.

11. "Brief Reports: Undesirable," *Index on Censorship* 7, no. 4 (July–August 1978): 58.

12. Ludovic A. Ngatara, "Objective Journalists Persecuted" (mimeo, n.d.). Obtainable through Human Rights Internet, Washington, D.C.

13. "Nigerian Editors Call for an End to Mass Staff Purges," International Press Institute *Report* 29, no. 3 (May–July 1980): 4.

14. *Index on Censorship* 10, no. 6 (December 1981): 109.

15. Reports of deportations of foreign journalists from Commonwealth Africa are frequently found both in *Index on Censorship* and the International Press Institute *Report*. They are too numerous to recount here.

16. Judgment by M. Saied, Chief Magistrate, Criminal Case no. 7995, Chief Magistrate's Court, Kampala, 1968, pp. 9, 14–15.

17. Amnesty International, *Annual Report*, 1968–69, p. 10.

18. *Index on Censorship* 10, no. 4 (August 1981): 48.

19. Ahmed Rajab, "Detained in Kenya," *Index on Censorship* 7, no. 3 (May–June 1978): 7–10. See also Ngugi wa Thiong'o, *Detained: A Writer's Prison Diary* (London: Heinemann, 1981).

20. Dickson Mwansa, "Zambian Political Theatre: How My Play *The Cell* Was Prevented from Being Seen Abroad," *Index on Censorship* 11, no. 2 (1982): 33–35.

21. Andrew Horn, "Uganda's Theatre—the Exiled and the Dead," *Index on Censorship* 8, no. 5 (Sept.–Oct. 1979): 13. See also Don Kabeka, "Uganda: No Censors Needed," *Index on Censorship* 8, no. 2 (April–May 1979): 18–21.

22. N.J. Small, "Zambia—Trouble on Campus," *Index on Censorship* 6, no. 6 (Nov.–Dec.1977): 9–14.

23. *Africa Contemporary Record*, vol. 7 (1974–75), p. B646 (Ghana); vol. 10 (1977–78), p. B646 (Ghana). See also (on Nigeria) *Index on Censorship* 7, no. 5 (Sept.–Oct. 1978): 68.

24. *Africa Contemporary Record*, vol. 9 (1976–77), p. B384.

25. James Reid, "Kenyan Academics, Students Victims of Government Purge," *CAUT* (Canadian Association of University Teachers) *Bulletin*, May 1983, pp. 11, 13.

26. *West Africa*, "Student-Police Tensions," May 21, 1979, pp. 879–80; ibid., "General Strike in Sierra Leone," August 24, 1981, p. 1913.

27. See Laurie Goodstein, "Trouble in Kenya," *Index on Censorship* 11, no. 4 (August 1982): 1, 49; and Reid, "Kenyan Academics."

28. Edward Kannyo, *Defending Civil and Political Rights in Africa: The Case of Ghana, 1976–1979* (New York: The Jacob Blaustein Institute for the Advancement of Human Rights, 1980).

29. Personal communication from a Ghanaian academic.

30. Harriet McIlwraith, "Dr. Banda's Banned Books," *Index on Censorship* 8, no. 6 (Nov.–Dec. 1979): 56–58; Victor Ndovi, "Censorship in Malawi," ibid., 8, no. 1 (Jan.–Feb. 1979): 22–25; and ibid., 2, no. 1 (Spring 1973) and Peter Edwards, "Press Purge in Malawi," ibid., 2, no. 4 (Winter 1973): 53–57. The author of this volume was denied entrance to Malawi and Kenya to pursue her research.

31. "Newspaper Arrests—Shagari Hits Back," International Press Institute *Report* 30, no. 2 (1981): 2.

32. *Index on Censorship* 6, no. 2 (Mar.–Apr. 1977): 67.

33. Ibid., 1, no. 1 (Spring 1972): 89.

34. Ibid., 1, no. 3/4 (Winter 1972): 127.

35. Ibid., 3, no. 1 (Spring 1974): iii.

36. Mwai Kibaki, "Kenya, the Press and Nation-Building," *Africa Contemporary Record*, vol.5 (1972–73), p. C180. Reproduced from *The African Journalist* 4 (June 1972).

37. "President Nyerere on the Role of the University," *Africa Contemporary Record*, vol. 3 (1970–71), p. C197.

38. For discussions of the UNESCO debate, see Leonard R. Sussman, "Freedom of the Press: A Personal Account of the Continuing Struggle," in Raymond D. Gastil et al., *Freedom in the World: Political Rights and Civil Liberties 1981* (Westport, Conn: Greenwood Press, 1981), pp. 57–78. See also Frank Barber, "UNESCO: Threat to Press Freedom," *Index on Censorship* 10, no. 1 (February 1981): 15–22; and Raphael Mergui, "UNESCO: The State and the Media," *Index on Censorship* 10, no. 1 (February 1981): 23–26.

39. See *Index on Censorship* 8, no. 4 (June–Aug. 1979): 69–70; and ibid., 9, no. 2 (April 1980): 75.

40. Ludovic A. Ngatara, "A Long Way to Go," *Index on Censorship* 10, no. 3 (June 1981): 51.

41. International Press Institute *Report* 31, no. 1 (Dec.–Jan. 1981–82): 18.

42. Ludovic A. Ngatara, "False Freedom of Expression in the Third World." Paper presented to the Annual Conference of the International Institute of Communications, Dubrovnik, Yugoslavia, September 10–15, 1978.

43. Peter Waterman, "Third World Workers: An Overview," Working paper no. 9 (McGill University: Centre for Developing-Area Studies, August 1975), p. 7.

44. Rhoda E. Howard, "Third World Trade Unions as Agencies of Human Rights: The Case of Commonwealth Africa," in Roger Southall, ed., *Trade Unions and the Industrialization of the Third World* (London: Zed Press, forthcoming 1986).

45. Jon Kraus, "African Trade Unions: Progress or Poverty?," *African Studies Review* 19, no. 3 (1976): 103.

46. Federal Republic of Nigeria, *Report of the Tribunal of Inquiry into the Activities of the Trade Unions* (Lagos: Federal Ministry of Information, 1977): 25. For a different view, see Nicholas Van Hear, "Recession, Retrenchment and Military Rule: Prospects for Nigerian Labour in the Later 1980s." Paper presented at a conference on Third World Trade Unionism, University of Ottawa, October 25–27, 1984.

47. Paul Lubeck, "Unions, Workers and Consciousness in Kano, Nigeria: A View from Below," in Richard Sandbrook and Robin Cohen, eds., *The Develop-*

ment of an African Working Class (Toronto: University of Toronto Press, 1975), p. 147.

48. Richard Sandbrook, *The Politics of Basic Needs* (Toronto: University of Toronto Press, 1982), p. 138.

49. Claude E. Welch, Jr.,"The Right of Association in Ghana and Tanzania," *Journal of Modern African Studies* 16, no. 4 (1978): 651.

50. Sandbrook, *Politics of Basic Needs*, p. 203.

51. Federal Republic of Nigeria, "Report . . . on the Activities of Trade Unions," p. 87.

52. Kraus, "African Trade Unions," p. 99. See also *Africa Contemporary Record*, vol. 11 (1978–79), p. B275.

53. Wogu Ananaba, *The Trade Union Movement in Africa* (London: C. Hurst & Co., 1979), p. 40.

54. Ibid., p. 52.

55. Kraus, "African Trade Unions," p. 102.

56. Ananaba, *The Trade Union Movement*, p. 10.

57. United Republic of Tanzania, "Report of the Presidential Commission on the National Union of Tanganyika Workers" (Dar es Salaam: Government Printer, 1967): 15.

58. Theo Mushi, "Tanzania: New role for labour union," *Weekly Review*, June 28, 1976.

59. Ibid.

60. Paschal Mihyo, "The Struggle for Workers' Control in Tanzania," *Review of African Political Economy* 4 (November 1975): 82–83.

61. Welch, "The Rights of Association," p. 651.

62. United Republic of Tanzania, Government Paper no. 2, "Proposals of the Tanzanian Government on the Recommendations of the Presidential Commission of Inquiry into the National Union of Tanganyika Workers" (Dar es Salaam: Government Printer, 1967), p. 14.

63. Sandbrook, *Politics of Basic Needs*, p. 130.

64. *Africa Contemporary Record*, vol. 15 (1982–83), p. B278.

65. Ananaba, *The Trade Union Movement*, p. 36.

66. Ibid., p. 35.

67. S. D. Sacika, "Trade Union Rights in a One-Party State," in International Commission of Jurists, *Human Rights in a One-Party State* (London: Search Press, 1978), p. 83; Robert Bates, *Unions, Parties and Political Development: A Study of Mine-Workers in Zambia* (New Haven: Yale University Press, 1971), cited in Kraus, "African Trade Unions," p. 98.

68. Nsolo N. Mijere, "Zambian Decentralization and Integration Policy: The Case of the Mineworkers' Union." Paper presented at a conference on Third World Trade Unionism, University of Ottawa, October 25–27, 1984, p. 18.

69. Ibid.

70. Arnold Hughes, "Why the Gambian Coup Failed," *West Africa*, October 26, 1981, pp. 2498–2502.

71. "Recent Developments in Ghana," International Commission of Jurists, *Bulletin* 24 (December 1965): 20.

72. "President Limann and Nkrumahism," *West Africa*, December 15, 1980, pp. 2533–35.

73. Commonwealth Observer Group, *Uganda Elections, December 1980: Report*

(London: Commonwealth Secretariat, 1980), Final Report, par. 147, reprinted in *Uganda Information Bulletin* 6 (January 1981): 13–15.

74. Mamadou Tall (pseudonym), "Notes on the Civil and Political Strife in Uganda," *Issue: A Journal of Africanist Opinion* 12, no. 1/2 (Spring/Summer 1982): 43.

75. Ned Munger, "Preface" to Yusef Lule, "Human Rights Violations in Uganda under Obote," *Munger Africana Library Notes* 67 (November 1982), n.p.

76. See, e.g., Fred M. Hayward, "Political Participation and Its Role in Development: Some Observations Drawn from the African Context," *Journal of Developing Areas* 7 (July 1973): 600–602; and Goran Hyden and Colin Leys, "Elections and Politics in Single-Party Systems: The Case of Kenya and Tanzania," *British Journal of Political Science* 2, no. 4 (1972): 389–420.

77. John A. A. Ayoade, "Electoral Laws and National Unity in Nigeria," *African Studies Review* 13, no. 2 (September 1980): 39–50.

78. C. S. Whitaker, Jr., "Second Beginnings: The New Political Framework," *Issue: A Journal of Africanist Opinion* 11, nos. 1/2 (Spring/Summer 1981): 9–10.

79. Constitution of the Republic of Nigeria (1979), articles 126, 1 (b), 202 (b) and 203, in Blaustein and Flanz, *Constitutions*.

80. Richard A. Joseph, "The Ethnic Trap: Notes on the Nigerian Campaign and Elections, 1978–79," *Issue: A Journal of Africanist Opinion* 11, nos. 1/2 (Spring/Summer 1981): 19.

81. *New York Times*, October 1, 1983, p. 3.

82. This characterization is from Robert H. Jackson and Carl G. Rosberg, *Personal Rule in Black Africa* (Berkeley: University of California Press, 1982), p. 159.

83. Ibid., p. 164.

84. *Africa Contemporary Record*, vol. 11 (1978–79), p. B302.

85. Ibid.

86. Alan Cowell, "Odd Man Out in Africa: Malawi Votes," *New York Times*, June 30, 1983, p. A3.

87. Amnesty International, *Bulletin* (Canada), June 1983.

88. W. S. Marcus Jones and G. F. A. Sawyerr, "Sierra Leone: Constitutional Chronology," in Blaustein and Flanz, *Constitutions*, p. 11.

89. Fred M. Hayward, Ahmed R. Dumbuya, and Jimmy Kandeh, "Changing Electoral Strategies in Sierra Leone." Paper presented at the African Studies Association, Boston, Mass., December 1983, pp. 29–31.

90. Hyden and Leys, "Elections and Politics in Single-Party Systems," p. 399; Henry Bienen, *Kenya: The Politics of Participation and Control* (Princeton: Princeton University Press, 1974), pp. 89–95; and *East African Standard*, "Opposition Move to Open Closed Areas Defeated," June 14, 1969.

91. Anonymous, *In/Dependent Kenya* (London: Zed Press, 1982), p. 93.

92. Ibid., p. 95.

93. *Weekly Review*, July 27, 1979, pp. 7–8.

94. *Africa Contemporary Record*, vol. 2 (1969–70), p. B127; ibid., vol. 7 (1974–75), p. B198; and Jackson and Rosberg, *Personal Rule in Black Africa*, p. 111.

95. Bienen, *Kenya*, p. 90.

96. Jackson and Rosberg, *Personal Rule in Black Africa*, pp. 103–4.

97. See Chapter 7 of this volume.

98. Jackson and Rosberg, *Personal Rule in Black Africa*, p. 103.

99. Ibid., p. 109.

100. United Republic of Tanzania, "Report of the Presidential Commission on the Establishment of a Democratic One-Party State" (Dar es Salaam: Government Printer, 1964), pp. 13–14. Hereafter cited as Tanzania, Commission on One-Party State.

101. "Tanzania: A One-Party State," International Commission of Jurists, *Bulletin* 23 (August 1965): 36–37.

102. Tanzania, Commission on One-Party State, p. 16.

103. See, e.g., the description of Nyerere's political style in Cranford Pratt, "Democracy and Socialism in Tanzania: A Reply to John Saul," *Canadian Journal of African Studies* 12, no. 3 (1978): 407–26.

104. Tanzania, Commission on One-Party State, p. 2.

105. Republic of Zambia, "Report of the National Commission on the Establishment of a One-Party Participatory Democracy in Zambia" (Lusaka: Government Printers, 1972), p. 67, Appendix 1. Hereafter cited as Zambia, Commission on One-Party Democracy.

106. Simbi V. Mubako, "Zambia's Single-Party Constitution—A Search for Unity and Development," *Zambia Law Journal* 5 (1973): 69.

107. Republic of Zambia, The Constitution of the United National Independence Party, article 45 (annexed to the Constitution of the Republic of Zambia by Article 4,1), in Blaustein and Flanz, *Constitutions;* and Tanzania, Constitution of Chama cha Mapinduzi (CCM), in *Africa Contemporary Record*, vol. 10 (1977–78), pp. C95–C110, article 1,1.

108. Tanzania, Commission on One-Party State, p. 16.

109. Comments by Kenneth D. Kaunda, included in International Commission of Jurists, *Human Rights in a One-Party State* (London: Search Press, 1978), pp. 125–26.

110. Constitution of UNIP, article 18.

111. Constitution of CCM, articles 8, 2; 12; 14b; 16. Quotation from article 2, 16, 1.

112. Pius M. Msekwa, "The Doctrine of the One-party State in Relation to Human Rights and the Rule of Law," in International Commission of Jurists, *Human Rights in a One-Party State*, p. 29.

113. Tanzania, Commission on One-Party State, p. 18.

114. Constitution of CCM, article 3, part V, par. 61, subsection 6, b; Kenneth D. Kaunda, "A Nation of Equals—the Kabwe Declaration." Addresses to the National Council of UNIP, Hindu Hall, Kabwe, December 1–3, 1972.

115. R. M. A. Chongwe, "An Address to the African Seminar on Human Rights and Development," May 24–29, 1982, Gaborane, Botswana, p. 6.

116. United Republic of Tanzania, *Constitution*, Article 26, 2, c, ii, in Blaustein and Flanz, *Constitutions*.

117. Hyden and Leys, "Elections and Politics in Single-Party Systems," p. 408; Bienen, *Kenya*, p. 92.

118. Zambia, Commission on One-Party Democracy, p. 11; Republic of Zambia, *Constitution*, Article 38, 3.

119. Kenneth D. Kaunda, closing address, included in "The Kabwe Declaration," p. 50.

120. Summary of Nathan M. Shamuyarira, "Individual and Group Rights in a One-Party State: Some Reflections on the Tanzanian Experience," in International Commission of Jurists, *Human Rights in a One-Party State*, p. 105.

121. James R. Scarritt, "The Decline of Political Legitimacy in Zambia: An

Explanation Based on Incomplete Data," *African Studies Review* 22, no. 2 (September 1979): 13–38.

122. Zambia, Commission on One-party Democracy, p. 48–49.

123. Scarritt, "The Decline of Political Legitimacy," p. 22.

124. Kashima Shayame, Philip Simuchoba, and James Spaita, "A Letter from the Leaders of the Church in Zambia to Their Members about the President's Seminar on Humanism and Development," May 11, 1982, par. 10, 5.

125. Cranford Pratt, "Tanzania's Transition to Socialism: Reflections of a Democratic Socialist," in Bismarck U. Mwansasu and Cranford Pratt, eds., *Towards Socialism in Tanzania* (Toronto: University of Toronto Press, 1981), pp. 193–236.

126. Summary of Workshop II Discussion, in International Commission of Jurists, *Human Rights in a One-party State*, p. 98.

127. Hyden and Leys, "Elections and Politics in Single-Party Systems," p. 413; Jackson and Rosberg, *Personal Rule in Black Africa*, p. 229.

128. Ralph Ibbott, "The Fall of Village Socialism," *Peace News*, July 8, 1970, p. 6; see also John Saul, "Tanzania's Transition to Socialism," *Canadian Journal of African Studies* 11, no. 2 (1977): 333.

129. Henry S. Meebelo, *Main Currents of Zambian Humanist Thought* (Lusaka: Oxford University Press, 1973), p. xiii.

⑦ Civil Rights and the Rule of Law

Civil rights are frequently considered to be analytically prior to political rights. This view stems from the fact that civil rights were some of the first rights ever to be enunciated in law. It also stems from the belief that basic rights ought to reflect basic needs, hence civil rights are more crucial, as they protect the individual's physical safety. In the 1966 International Covenant on Civil and Political Rights, civil rights are enumerated as the right to life; the right not to be tortured or taken into slavery; and the right to liberty and security of the person, including protections against arbitrary arrest and in favor of due process. The African Charter of Human and Peoples' Rights also protects respect for the life and integrity of the human person, it bans slavery and torture, and it protects rights to liberty and security of the person and explicitly refers to a prohibition of arbitrary arrest and detention.

Civil rights, then, preserve the physical person from abuse by the state. Yet civil rights are subject to widespread violation in practice. In Commonwealth Africa, violations of civil rights are a consequence of overt political decisions. The most widespread violation is so-called "preventive" detention, although state terrorism has also been a prevalent form of political intimidation in some countries. Since such violations occur as a result of political decisions, this chapter follows Chapter 6's discussion of political rights. Because this book focuses on class rule and the role of the state in Commonwealth Africa, non-politically motivated cases of civil rights abuses are not included. The literature on criminology in Africa indicates that ordinary African criminals (e.g., thieves) also suffer serious violations of their civil rights. These violations, however, are caused by lack of legal, judicial, and prison resources, and by inexperience in organization of a criminal justice system, rather than by direct political motivations. Similarly, this book does not discuss the use of capital punishment in criminal cases. Analysis of the practice, social meaning, and morality of criminal executions is outside its scope. I concern myself with "criminal" executions only when they are a mask for political repression.

This chapter begins, then, with a discussion of preventive detention and state terrorism in Commonwealth Africa. Preventive detention, despite the fact that it violates a number of international norms of civil rights, is legal in most of the countries I discuss. Therefore the second half of the chapter discusses the meaning of constitutionalism and the rule of law in Africa, and ends with a discussion of some recent innovations in legal practice.

Preventive Detention

The chief weapon used against political dissidents in Commonwealth Africa is "preventive" detention, a practice by which people are detained allegedly to prevent their committing anticipated crimes of violence, subversion, or treason. The individual is normally detained for an indefinite period, with no possibility of trial. Although he is formally entitled to be told the charges against him, these are usually couched in very general terms. He may have no right at all to appeal, or he may have the right to have his case sporadically reviewed by a nonjudicial tribunal with very limited powers. Conditions of detention are nowhere pleasant, and frequently are heavily punitive.

Preventive detention violates many basic rights. Article 9 of the Covenant on Civil and Political Rights expressly states that anyone arrested should be promptly informed of the reasons for his arrest and promptly brought to trial before a judicial authority entitled to decide on the lawfulness of such detention. Article 10, 1, states that "All persons deprived of their liberty shall be treated with humanity and with respect for the inherent dignity of the human person." Article 6 of the African Charter similarly prohibits arbitrary arrest and detention, while article 7, d, provides "the right to be tried within a reasonable time by an impartial court or tribunal." The use of preventive detention in Commonwealth Africa is a serious breach of human rights. It is a breach, moreover, that also has severe consequences for economic, social, and cultural rights, insofar as it prevents opposition to the persons and policies of entrenched governments, and cuts off possibilities for organized political participation.

Preventive detention is a direct carry-over from colonialism. Although political imprisonment was practiced throughout colonial rule, the actual British model for African Preventive Detention Acts was Regulation 18B, promulgated at the beginning of World War II. This regulation provided for the detention without appeal of people in Britain deemed to be "of hostile origin" (i.e., enemy aliens).[1] The new African governments, however, designed their constitutional provisions regarding preventive detention to cover internal, not alien, "enemies." Two processes occurred. The first was to include, in the earliest constitutions, provisions regarding states of emergency. The second was to write separate legislation (sometimes also incorporated into constitutions) regarding preventive detention. When constitutions are suspended under military rule, preventive detention decrees are frequently enacted. The general civilian pattern is either to rely on a separate preventive detention law, or periodically or continually to invoke states of emergency under which derogations from normal constitutional protections of civil liberties are permitted.

The legislation presently or formerly in force permitting preventive detention in the various countries of Commonwealth Africa has common characteristics. The general pattern is that at its most liberal, preventive detention legislation mandates that detainees will be informed of the reasons for their arrest within a reasonable time (usually five to fourteen days); that the public will be notified of their arrest within a reasonable time (two weeks or one month) in the government *Gazette;* that they will have the right either to a personal hearing before, or to make a submission in writing to, a review tribunal, initially within perhaps one month and thereafter every six months or a year; and that the tribunal will be able to make nonbinding recommendations regarding release or continued detention to the relevant authority (normally the president). Even these provisions, weak as they are, are very rarely adhered to in practice. Judicial review in the few *habeas corpus* cases that have come to trial is usually confined to instructing the government to adhere to the legal conditions of detention, rather than questioning the legality of detention itself.[2]

How has preventive detention been used? The nine countries under discussion fall into three distinct groups: those which routinely imprison large numbers of people (Malawi, Tanzania, Ghana, and Uganda); those which use the weapon fairly sparingly to contain political opposition (Sierra Leone, Zambia, and Kenya until 1982); and those which use the weapon rarely (Nigeria until 1984) or not at all (Gambia).

Since independence, Gambia, the least repressive country, has had a functioning multiparty political system. In 1980 six people were arrested and charged with being members of an unlawful society, MOJA (the Movement for Justice in Africa), but they were tried in court, not subjected to preventive detention.[3] In 1981 an attempted coup claimed 500 to 2000 victims. A state of emergency was declared and more than a thousand people were arrested. They were brought relatively speedily before the constitutionally created Review Tribunal and five Special Courts; although their conditions of imprisonment were severe, deliberate maltreatment and torture were not reported.[4] In early 1984, a number of people who had been sentenced to death for their participation in the attempted coup had their sentences commuted to life imprisonment.[5]

Nigeria has made relatively sparing use of preventive detention since the end of the civil war (during which it was used massively by both sides), despite the fact that Nigeria was legally under a state of emergency from 1966 to 1979. In 1979, when the military turned over power to a new civilian government, there were no known political prisoners in Nigeria.[6] From 1979 until the 1983 coup, Amnesty International reported no "prisoners of conscience" nor use of preventive detention.[7] Under the civilian regime Nigeria was not under a state of emergency and had, therefore, no basis in law for preventive detention. Moreover, despite harassments by government of critics, whether journalists, intellectuals, or politicians, political debate still remained open.

After the military coup of December 31, 1983, conditions in Nigeria became much harsher. One prominent Nigerian observer considered the new regime to be much more repressive than any previous one.[8] One of the first laws promulgated by the Buhari regime was a preventive detention act: Decree no. 2, the State Security (Detention of Persons) Decree. Dr. Tai Solarin, a prominent newspaper columnist, was detained under this decree from April 1984 until at least June 1985 after writing articles critical of the new government's policies.[9] The end of economic prosperity in Nigeria seems to have made it more difficult to buy off potential oppositions through corruption, graft, and political bargaining. Instead, the new military government, like others in Commonwealth Africa, resorted to outright coercion.

Similarly, the smaller countries of Commonwealth Africa resort to coercion when the faction of the ruling class in power fails to coopt potential opposition from other regional or ethnic centers. Such a pattern explains the gradual implementation of more and more repressive measures in Kenya. In 1966, when the socialist-oriented and Luo-led Kenya People's Union became a serious threat to the rule of Jomo Kenyatta, the government responded by introducing the Public Security Act, which gave the President authority to declare anyone a detainee.[10] The protective clauses contained in the act were largely cosmetic. Thus, for example, when Ngugi wa Thiong'o was detained, the charges against him were so general as to be meaningless. The statement given to him said merely that he had engaged "in activities and utterances which are dangerous to the good Government of Kenya and its institutions."[11] Ngugi's Review Tribunal (which had, in any case, merely advisory powers) was composed entirely of members of the civil service and was chaired by a foreigner presumably dependent on government toleration for his job.[12]

Until 1982 preventive detention was used sparingly in Kenya. Its two largest groups of victims were (a) alleged leaders of Somali secessionism in the northeast and (b) individual politicians, initially from outside KANU (the Kenya African National Union), but later from among outspoken backbenchers inside KANU, as well. From 1966 to 1982, only 79 detentions were reported in the Kenya *Gazette*.[13] These included, in the late 1970s, the MPs George Anyona, Martin Shikuku, and John-Marie Seroney, who had spoken out against corruption and the one-party state.[14]

After the attempted coup in 1982, the Kenyan use of preventive detention entered a new phase as hundreds of students and academics, and literally the entire Kenyan air force, were arrested and detained. While many were released, others were convicted or still await trial. Aside from the actual event of the coup, the regime has been suffering from factional in-fighting between arap Moi, who became president after the death of Kenyatta in 1978, and Charles Njonjo, the power behind the throne in Kenyatta's time. Since Njonjo's resignation in June 1983, allegedly as a result of corruption charges, and his subsequent trial for treason, arap Moi may now feel secure enough to release many of his detainees. Indeed, more than 8,000 prisoners were released in mid-1983.[15]

The Kenyan pattern of preventive detention is almost replicated in Sierra Leone. From 1968, when the military decided that the All People's Congress, not the Sierra Leone People's Party, was to rule the country, until 1978, when a one-party state was officially established, the APC used preventive detention to control political protest. Since 1977, sporadic political violence has occasioned more detentions. The legislative justification for these actions is the 1971 Public Emergency Regulation, which aside from providing for detention also provides for South-African style bannings.[16] The number of political prisoners in Sierra Leone varies. There were about 500 in 1976, before the one-party state was declared. After its declaration, all were released, but by 1981, because of trade union unrest and other alleged violence, the figure was up again to about 180.[17] A state of emergency is periodically, and constitutionally, renewed in the one-party Parliament to allow the regime to continue to use preventive detention as it sees fit.[18]

Like Sierra Leone, Zambia is also a country living under what one eminent African jurist referred to as a "perpetual state of emergency."[19] A state of emergency was first invoked in Zambia in 1964 to deal with the Lumpa insurrection.[20] In 1965, after the Rhodesian Unilateral Declaration of Independence, it was invoked to deal with the apprehended attack by white Rhodesian forces, and remained in force until at least 1982, despite Zimbabwe's independence in 1980.[21] Undoubtedly, Zambia has had real cause to institute a state of emergency. As a front-line state against Rhodesia, it was frequently attacked by foreign troops, and on one occasion even the capital was bombed.[22] Thus Zambia was, in effect, more or less at war. In the mid-1980s Zambia is at risk from South African attacks against black South African refugees living in her territory.

Other reasons given by Kaunda for the state of emergency suggest that he is also concerned with stifling any criticism of his rule. In his 1976 address to the nation invoking the state of emergency, Kaunda referred to "criminals . . . who . . . disrupt order, undermine public confidence in the Party and Government . . . saboteurs and subversive elements sowing seed of discord . . . [and] foreigners or Zambians . . . working . . . to infiltrate institutions responsible for the production and distribution of food, raw materials and services." Kaunda also referred to the infiltration of universities and the "invisible orchestration" of student groups.[23] Such a sweeping list of threats suggests that Kaunda had in mind the complete control of the country under the ruling United National Independence Party. Other events bear this out; his chief challenger, Simon Kapwepwe, who formed the UPP (United Progressive Party), was detained from February 1972 until December 31, 1973.[24] On the whole, preventive detention has been used sparingly in Zambia—against prominent political rivals and occasionally against trade union leaders. The latter, however, are sufficiently powerful that prolonged detention, as in 1981,[25] would result in cessation of copper production as their followers went on strike. Alleged coup attempts in 1980 and 1981 resulted in the detentions of several prominent individuals, seven of whom were sentenced to death for treason in January 1983.[26]

The behavior of governing regimes toward their political opponents in the countries discussed above is relatively mild. Political detainees seldom number more than one hundred, and deaths in detention are rare. By contrast, wholesale arrests have been common in Ghana, Malawi, Tanzania, and Uganda.

The first wholesale detention of political prisoners in Commonwealth Africa occurred in the early 1960s in Ghana. Ghana's messianic, pan-Africanist leader, Kwame Nkrumah, espoused a populist brand of socialism that allowed him to consolidate and centralize all political power. Only a few months after his accession to power, he passed the Preventive Detention Act, which permitted him to detain his political opponents for up to five years (later increased to ten) without even the minimum protections of notification of charges, publication of detention, or right of appeal to an advisory tribunal.[27] By October of 1961, the International Commission of Jurists estimated that 200 to 250 of Nkrumah's political opponents were in jail, but later investigations and memoirs by Nkrumah's victims spoke of 2,000 detained in one prison alone.[28] The detainees included political opponents of Nkrumah's Convention People's Party, such as the leadership of the Ashanti-based National Liberation Movement; dissidents from within Nkrumah's own party and entourage; and people who simply had had the misfortune to have stood in the way of the CPP youth, such as one father who refused to marry his daughter to a CPP member without the traditional payment of bridewealth.[29] The most prominent victim of Nkrumah's massive purges was the respected lawyer and nationalist leader Dr. J.B. Danquah, who died in detention on February 4, 1965.[30]

Since Nkrumah's overthrow, preventive detention has been used sporadically in Ghana, depending on the regime. Under General Acheampong (1972–78), perceived opponents, such as the perpetual Ewe "plotters," were detained, as also was J.B. Mensah, minister of finance in the civilian regime of Dr. Busia (1969–72), after he privately circulated a pamphlet calling for discussion of Acheampong's economic policies.[31] No political prisoners were executed, however, despite early legislation prescribing the death penalty for "subversion."[32] But during the brief military interregnum of Jerry Rawlings in 1979, six people, three of them former heads of state, were executed; the executions were discontinued after international protests.[33] Rawlings's second coup in late 1981 was followed by the wholesale detention of almost 500 political leaders in Ghana, including almost all MPs and cabinet ministers; most of these were reported released at the end of 1982.[34]

In Malawi, preventive detention is a consistent and vicious government policy, designed not only to quash all dissent, but also to prevent any internal challenge to the authority of the aging President Banda. The largest single bout of detentions apparently took place about 1973, when more than a thousand people were detained in very harsh prison conditions.[35] Since 1977, for reasons which are largely unexplained but which may have had to do with Banda's subjective perceptions of the challenge to his power (buttressed by the objective fact that his major opponents were by then either dead or in exile), many political prisoners have been released, but selective detentions still take place. In Malawi, preventive detention is used not, as in other countries, as a warning or as an inducement to join a ruling political party, but rather simply to eliminate all potential opposition.

A somewhat different picture emerges for Tanzania, where numbers of detained (at about a thousand) resembled Malawi's in the late 1970s. In 1962 Tanzania introduced a highly repressive Preventive Detention Act, which is still in effect. The act permits detention entirely at the president's discretion, prescribes no time limit on detention, orders no publication of names of those detained, and is subject to no review.[36] It is difficult to obtain accurate information on the use of preventive detention in Tanzania, since legislation there, unlike other Commonwealth African countries, requires no publication of detainees' names. Mainland political prisoners seem rare, although in the late 1960s a number of relatives of one of Nyerere's most prominent political opponents, Oscar Kambona, were detained in what appears to be a version of collective guilt.[37] The vast majority of Tanzanian political prisoners appear to be either prisoners on the island of Zanzibar or economic "saboteurs."

In 1972 more than a thousand people were detained after Zanzibar's dictator, Sheik Abeid Karume, was assassinated. After a political trial that did not follow due process, and in which it was evident that almost all confessions had been extracted by torture, 43 people were sentenced to death for treason. None, in the event, was executed, apparently because of pressure exerted by Nyerere at the time of consolidation of the mainland and island ruling parties into one central body; but several died in prison, some of torture.[38] Nyerere, after having earlier turned over Zanzibari exiles for trial only to hear that they were then executed, refused to turn over 18 exiles wanted for trial in 1972. He did, however, relieve the exiled Zanzibari communist Abdul Rahman Babu of his post in the mainland cabinet, and detained Babu for several years in very severe conditions.[39]

The other major group of political detainees in Tanzania appears to be those accused of economic crimes, such as hoarding or sabotage. One such detainee was James Magoti, an Amnesty International prisoner of conscience, who was detained in 1977 and held until 1979, when he was released following the death in detention of his brother, who had apparently been detained for no reason other than kinship.[40] Ordinary criminals are also often detained, rather than being sent for trial. It is difficult to understand why Nyerere has chosen to use "preventive" detention as punishment for nonpolitical crimes. One possible reason is that, in a socialist country bent on restructuring the entire economy, the wealthier strata are bound to present some degree of opposition to state economic policies. And since judicial manpower for proper trials may be lacking, preventive detention may be a means of conveying the seriousness of the government's economic intentions. In addition, ethnic Asian Tanzanians may be more subject to detention for economic sabotage than ethnic Africans, but this suspicion is difficult to verify in the absence of a legal requirement for public notification of detentions.[41]

The final country under discussion is Uganda. The practice of preventive detention in Uganda is relevant only when one considers the pre–1971 and 1980–85 periods of Obote's presidency. The rule of law broke down completely, and all pretense of judicial legitimacy disappeared under Amin's rule. As the conflict between Obote and the Kabaka of Buganda intensified during the 1960s, and the state moved toward one-party rule, the number of political prisoners increased. One estimate is that there were several hundred prisoners just prior to Amin's takeover in 1971, the number having increased dramatically after the first assassination attempt against Obote in 1969.[42] Prior to 1969, a circulation of prisoners appears to have been the norm. After Obote's return to power in 1980, political imprisonment was supplemented, or perhaps superseded, by outright abduction, torture, and murder. While one apologist for Obote claimed that his political prisoners were well treated in Kampala's main civilian prison, others documented the appalling conditions, torture, and arbitrary murders in the military prisons to which most accused opponents of Obote were taken.[43]

Preventive detention, then, is a common method of political coercion in almost all Commonwealth African countries, practiced by almost all regimes. But preventive detention is not the only weapon that political regimes in Commonwealth Africa use against their opponents. It is unique, however, in being a legal means of squelching political dissent. The other weapons used by African regimes, some regularly and some only sporadically, include state terrorism, institutionalized vigilantism, and torture.

State Terrorism

State terrorism can be defined as a system under which the state, through its organs of public security or through "private" (but officially backed) political agencies, uses physical brutality as a weapon not merely to punish those already in opposition, but also to forestall future opposition. In state terrorist regimes, political murder and torture are the norm. The victims include not only political dissidents, but also their relatives, friends, and even those with whom they have had only the most casual contact. Moreover, entire classes of people may be terrorized: Idi Amin at his height ordered the slaughter of entire villages (e.g., Obote's home village) and entire ethnic groups within the army and public service.[44] One Ugandan exile claims he also ordered the slaughter of all "intellectuals," defined as people wearing glasses.[45]

The Amin regime is the best-known case of state terrorism in Commonwealth Africa. But the post-Amin rule of Milton Obote also appears to have been buttressed by a heavy dose of state terrorism. Appalling tortures in military prisons have been amply documented not only by Obote's political opposition, but also by respected international organizations, especially Amnesty International.[46] In August 1984, U.S. officials cited estimates that 100,000 to 200,000 people had died in Uganda since Obote's return to power.[47] One of his political opponents, Yusef Lule, a prominent Baganda who was prime minister for a brief period after Amin was overthrown, went so far as to suggest that Obote's human rights record was worse than that of Amin.[48] Particularly severe massacres occurred in the West Nile region, inhabited by peoples tied by ethnicity and (allegedly) personal loyalty to Idi Amin, and in the Lowero Triangle area near Kampala, occupied by Baganda.[49] In the latter area, as many as 120,000 people were held in detention camps as long as two years in the early 1980s, as Obote's forces attempted to clear out Baganda-based guerilla opposition.[50]

To these charges of state terrorism the Obote regime replied that the main threat to peace and democracy in Uganda was the terror unleashed upon the population by the several extra-legal guerilla movements that had been active since the 1980 elections.[51] Since Amin's overthrow, three separate guerilla groups had been operating in Uganda: the United National Recovery Force, nominally loyal to Amin, in the West Nile area; the small Marxist-oriented National Resistance Army; and the Buganda-based Uganda Freedom Movement, the military wing of the opposition

Democratic Party.[52] One observer, however, suggests that many supporters of the Uganda Freedom Movement were motivated mainly by fear of Obote's own troops, not by any prior disloyalty to his government.[53] In any case, by 1985 much of this opposition had succumbed to the superior force of Obote's own army; yet the tortures, murders, and rapes perpetrated on a large scale in military prisons and alleged "organs of state security" continued.

During Obote's second regime, it was speculated that much of the terrorism occurred because Obote was actually not in control of his army. The torture and murder in military prisons may have taken place by the military's own initiative, especially because normal social controls on human brutality all but disappeared in Uganda during the Amin period. Obote, however, denied that tortures and murders took place on a systematic basis and resisted any suggestions that he was not in control of his armed forces.[54] The military coup of July 27, 1985, is clear evidence that Obote did not, in fact, have complete control over the military, but does not exonerate him from responsibility for the terrorism during the five years of his second regime. Yusef Lule refers to Obote's use of preventive detention and periodic massacres of opponents in the pre-Amin period, to argue that the post-1980 terrorism was direct government policy.[55]

The people of Uganda have been the tragic victims of massive state terrorism for the last fourteen years. By contrast, the weapons used by regimes in other countries, while still terrorist, are far less horrific. The Malawi government also relies heavily for its security on state terrorism. The average Malawian citizen knows that as long as he "lies low" no harm will be done to him; but political dissidents are severely repressed, and the supposedly mass-based Malawi Congress Party is firmly in Banda's hands. The main principle of government-citizen relations in Malawi is "unity, loyalty, obedience, discipline."[56] Kwame Nkrumah also relied to a significant extent on state terrorism during the latter part of his reign, but the terror was confined to known political opponents and their known associates. The masses of the population were integrated into the various organs of the Convention People's Party, and many genuinely felt that Nkrumah was a legitimate leader.

One weapon used by political dictators such as Banda and Nkrumah is party "youth wings," in Malawi the Malawi Youth Congress, in Ghana the Young Pioneers Movement. These young people act as vigilantes, observing, harassing, and publicly persecuting suspected dissidents, or merely those who are not believed to be religiously loyal to the leader. The torture, murders, and sexual mutilations of Malawian Jehovah's Witnesses in the 1970s were largely perpetrated by Malawi Youth Congress members, at Banda's personal instigation.[57] In a perverted way, these youth congresses perhaps reflect the age-grading of African societies into warrior groups of young men, and older married elders. Insofar as warfare is a culturally approved means of proving one's manhood, a good substitute for the ethnically differentiated enemy of pre-colonial times is the modern political dissident. Even in relatively peaceful Zambia, it was the UNIP Youth Wing who fought with the Lumpas in the mid-1960s.[58]

Youth movements are supplemented by political indoctrination of very young children and their incorporation into national quasi-military organizations. In 1962, a British bishop was expelled from Ghana after he criticized the indoctrination and intolerance practiced in the CPP Young Pioneers. In a public statement, he said

> At its worst . . . such a [children's political] movement engenders irreligion, intolerance and willingness to inform against parents and family. . . . no amount of good work in national service is able to counteract such evils if the basic principles of a movement are designed to forward a political theory or racial or nationalistic outlook."[59]

To politically indoctrinate children, whose notions of good and bad are very primitive, is to run the risk that they will become authoritarian adults, willing to use extreme measures against those whom they view as outside the realm of legitimate human respect.

State terrorism and youth vigilantism are supplemented in Commonwealth Africa by "judicial" (i.e., legal) murders, and in some cases by "accidental" murders of political opponents. In June 1983, for example, four Malawian cabinet ministers died in a traffic accident; the suspicion is that they were murdered because they were maneuvering for power after Banda's anticipated death.[60] Kenya has managed to keep political opposition within acceptable boundaries by the judicious use of political murder. In 1965, a prominent backbench MP, Pio Tinto, was murdered.[61] In 1969, the Luo cabinet minister and trade unionist Tom Mboya was killed,[62] apparently because his growing popularity posed a challenge to Kenyatta's personalist rule. In 1975, the populist politician J.M. Kariuki was murdered, seemingly on orders of the chief of the Criminal Investigation Department,[63] and possibly on the orders of a member of the president's own entourage.

An important weapon of state terrorism is torture. The threat of torture must be taken into account in any analysis of how political opposition is contained in Commonwealth Africa. The psychological torture of being in prison, in and of itself, is most severe, as the testimony of two former political prisoners indicates. After his release from a Ugandan jail in 1969, the former *Transition* editor Rajat Neogy wrote "the most frightening thing about detention is its arbitrariness and the suddenness. . . . Like death, you think it only happens to other people."[64] Likewise, Ngugi wa Thiong'o wrote of the day-to-day psychological torture of the prison routine: "Life in prison is . . . dull, mundane, monotonous, repetitious, tortuous in its intended animal rhythm of eating, defecating, sleeping. . . .

But it is the rhythm of animals waiting for slaughter . . . at a date not of their own fixing."[65]

In addition to psychological torture, physical torture of political prisoners is practiced in even the most lenient of Commonwealth African countries. The type of torture witnessed by one escaped victim of a military prison in Uganda (under Obote) is not normally encouraged by political leaders: deliberate amputation of limbs, disembowelments, gang-rapes, and long-term starvation[66] must be attributed in part to the long-term effects of brutalization on the very "soldiers" who commit these horrendous crimes. But in other countries, minor malefactions by prisoners are also punished by torture. In Ussher Fort in Accra, a common punishment was to spread-eagle prisoners in the sun for hours at a time.[67] Igbos imprisoned by federal forces in Nigeria during the civil war were chained to the walls and beaten, while non-Igbo prisoners in Biafra were whipped.[68]

What explains this use of torture? Torture, even the severest kind practiced in Uganda, is not unique to Africa nor attributable to a less "civilized" African culture, as the mass tortures perpetrated by highly refined Nazi officers during World War II constantly remind us. There does, however, seem to be an aspect of political culture in Africa attributable partly to the belief that one does not question the authority of political leaders (elders) except in a highly ritualized manner. For example, Kenya's Charles Njonjo said in Parliament that "every prisoner in Kenya must receive the cane regularly, to teach people that prison is not a luxury."[69] Another example is the state governor in Nigeria who ordered local elders to be given fifty strokes in his presence, as punishment for polite criticism contained in their welcoming address to him.[70]

The idea that torture is an unacceptable form of punishment, while deprivation of personal freedom is acceptable, is relatively new, even in European history. Until the 1800s, torture was a routine punishment for political or ordinary crimes in Europe. New ideals about the inviolability of the human body arose at the same time as the state acquired the physical and administrative resources to build prisons for criminals. But for many people, long-term deprivation of physical mobility and personal contacts seems much harsher than short-term physical punishment. Such physical punishment, combined in severe cases with exile (often as slaves), was the traditional means of dealing with recalcitrant criminals in pre-colonial Africa. Therefore, the use of violence in African prisons may possibly contain a cultural component, which is exacerbated by the lack of resources for training and supervision of prison warders. But this does not explain the extremely sadistic tortures and murders that the people of Uganda have suffered for the past fourteen years. The breakdown of moral inhibitions among those in authority in Uganda is not an African phenomenon, but one frequently found in societies (such as Northern Ireland) in which brutal civil war and ethnic hatred dominate all social relations.

There are, therefore, some reasons not directly attributable to the political interests of African ruling classes for the practice of torture. Nevertheless, the effect of torture is directly political; it incapacitates and demoralizes those already in prison, and serves as a warning to anyone contemplating political action.

The effect of preventive detention and state terrorism in the short term, then, is clearly to check political opposition to the ruling regime. Both are direct political weapons. Apologetic statements about the cultural value placed on consensus in traditional African societies cannot be taken as explanations for such practices, in the face of the obvious evidence that ruling classes in Africa entrench themselves in power for blatantly material reasons. Preventive detention and state terrorism are directed against known political opponents, their families, friends, and associates. As one Ghanaian lawyer puts it, "Preventive detention is no longer used in these countries to protect state security, but to grind down legitimate opposition to the existing political order."[71]

Yet while the intent of preventive detention and political terrorism is to stabilize existing political "orders" (rulers and ruling classes), the effect is often the opposite. Those who consistently imprison their opposition run the risk of being overthrown by violence themselves. When civilian opponents find all means of dissent blocked, they may turn to ethnic or personal contacts within the military for cooperation in the violent overthrow of the regime. Those who have already been brutalized in prison may, in turn, become even more brutal to their former persecutors, once they themselves have taken power. Or civilian political competition may be completely banned by a military that decides to take power to "clean up" politics in general.

Politically repressive governments are not yet buttressed in Commonwealth Africa as they are, for example, in Soviet bloc countries, by administrative and spying networks so all-pervasive and efficient as to ensure the long-term stability of entrenched ruling classes. Nor have they, as have some Latin American countries, received massive doses of "foreign aid" that can teach them the finer arts of political repression (although the 1982 military agreements between the United States and the arap Moi regime in Kenya could possibly include such types of foreign aid).[72] Thus, instability is the normal price for African authoritarian rule, which lacks the administrative and human capacity for outright totalitarianism.

In his assessment of the eventual overthrow of Nkrumah in Ghana, the former political prisoner Kwame Kesse-Adu, a journalist with the *Ashanti Pioneer* before his arrest, presented a succinct assessment of the contradictions of political repression.

> What did the P.D.A. [Preventive Detention Act] achieve? Its objective was to silence the entire nation. . . . It succeeded temporarily . . . but it forced opposition to go underground. [The] one-party state was a political time bomb

which would explode unexpectedly anywhere, particularly where a semblance of unity has been artificially created, and dissent was absent.[73]

Legitimacy of government cannot be enforced by political coercion. In Commonwealth Africa, states are not yet nations. National ruling classes, occupying offices in government, military, ruling party, and the civil service, have only fragile claims to the privileges, perquisites, and wealth they accrue. They abuse the principles of constitutionalism and the rule of law in order to fabricate a paper legitimacy that is undermined by the lack of any real principle of fairness or justice.

Constitutionalism and the Rule of Law

The preceding sections of this chapter have demonstrated how basic civil rights are violated with some frequency in a number of Commonwealth African countries. The means for violation of civil rights are often entrenched in legal Preventive Detention Acts. The courts appear to be relatively powerless against coercive centralized governments. What then do constitutionalism and the rule of law actually mean in Commonwealth Africa?[74]

The definition of constitutionalism used in this book is provided by an African scholar, who asserts that constitutionalism is "the art of providing a system of effective restraints on the exercise of governmental power."[75] Constitutionalism is not simply the provision of a written document, even one to which strict adherence is given. If the document does not provide for checks on government power, and if checks are not free to operate, then constitutionalism does not exist.

One effective means of restraining government power is the rule of law. When the rule of law exists, the judiciary is separated from the legislative and executive branches, is independent of government interference, and is entitled to review government actions; the government accepts the judgments of the courts. The rule of law is "not only strict adherence to legality, but the existence of a body of substantive and procedural law adequate 'to protect the individual from arbitrary government and to enable him to enjoy the dignity of man.' "[76] Even in underdeveloped countries the rule of law is necessary, although its specific form may not be identical to that of developed, Western democracies.

Despite a colonial heritage that included an alleged respect for British legal and constitutional principles, there is little real respect for such principles among the ruling classes of Commonwealth Africa. Rather, governments frequently change constitutions to suit the interests of those in power. Respect for due process is rendered farcical by the provisions of preventive detention acts. Judges and lawyers are harassed, imprisoned, and sometimes murdered. And the ordinary citizen is seemingly passive in the wake of these developments.

One possible reason for this passivity is that constitutionalism and the rule of law in Commonwealth Africa were originally imposed from above, hence they may still be seen as both foreign and colonial institutions. Moreover, they were imposed upon a population that was still, in many senses, traditional, and in which, to use Weberian terminology, authority was patrimonial, not rational-legal.[77] Under patrimonial authority, legitimacy is based on a system of sacred and inviolable norms. In the African context, the legitimate ruler is the chief who, with his elders, makes political and legal decisions in the village. Decisions are not made according to strict procedural rules, but follow local, time-honored beliefs regarding substantive ethics. Rules of evidence are unnecessary in a society in which it is believed that the telling of falsehoods will be punished by supernatural intervention.[78] There is a cultural disjuncture between traditional and modern views of judicial legitimacy.

But the Africa of today is also a class-ruled society of great disparities between rich and poor, in which constitutions, laws, and political office are used by the ruling class to ensure both wealth and continued power. Ruling classes exaggerate the perceived lack of popular legitimacy of constitutions and the rule of law, and use the supposed disjuncture between foreign practice and African culture as an excuse to abrogate these institutions in their own interests. The problem of illegitimacy of legal systems in Commonwealth Africa, therefore, is not merely the clash between indigenous patrimonial systems and colonial rational-legal systems; it is also one of considering how this clash is manipulated by African ruling classes to satisfy their own desires not to be checked by constitutions or judiciaries. To understand this manipulation one must look both at the system of law originally set up by the British, and at how both law and constitutionalism have changed in the post-colonial period.

Colonial law was originally imposed by force of conquest.[79] A dual legal system existed: "traditional" law was permitted to operate in those sectors which did not interest or affect British overrule, while British law obtained elsewhere. Guarantees of fundamental human rights were nonexistent in the colonial period. Preventive detention and exile were used by the British whenever they deemed necessary; even the most basic formal protections now included in most (but not all) African constitutions, such as periodic appearances by a detainee before a review tribunal, were unheard of. The post-independence constitutional changes providing for preventive detention and abrogating fundamental rights are direct inheritances of British rule.

In the colonial system, "traditional" authorities and courts were left to operate in principle without British interference, through the policy of allegedly indirect rule. But in fact there was a great deal of interference in "native" courts. It was justified by the repugnancy clause, which stated that traditional law repugnant to natural justice, morality, or good conscience would be abrogated by the British.[80] But no consistent philosophy explained the content of natural justice; rather, it was decided by British civil servants, acting in their judicial capacities, on an ad hoc basis. Another principle held that native law could not breach English substantive law, or conflict with any written colonial law already in force.

The British also interfered in the native court system by legislating as absolute those powers which traditional chiefs had previously held only with the consent of the people, as expressed through their elders. By removing traditional checks on the abuse of power by patrimonial authorities, while at the same time strengthening their powers by permitting them to impose prison sentences and fines, the British made the chiefly judges' positions extremely valuable. This, combined with the British habit of deposing chiefs who did not submit to their authority, resulted in the development of a new cadre of "traditional" chiefs highly dependent on the British for their existence. Nevertheless, they managed to adopt the cloak of patrimonial authority and to come to some accommodation with the common people.

The British practice of imposing foreign law and reinterpreting traditional law was not reversed upon independence; rather, it provided a precedent for the new centralizing, executive-based governments. Separation of powers was an important theme of the new constitutions, yet it had been unknown under colonialism. At the local level, district officers, often young and inexperienced, had acted as both administrators and judges; often, in court cases, as judge, prosecutor, and jury, seemingly without any inner soul-searching.[81] Executive direction of judicial decisions was the norm.

Thus the African politicians who came to power in the early 1960s were guided more by the colonial precedent of executive interference in the judiciary than they were by the formal provisions for judicial review in their constitutions. Throughout the former British colonies, central governments started to assert their control over local authorities. While some traditional authorities survived, perhaps the main reason for their limited independence was that the central government lacked the actual infrastructural capacity to take over village-level government and judicial institutions. Where such institutions were actively retained, as in Malawi, they were frequently manipulated by the central authority in its own interests.

In the modern sector, the British precedent already existed for control of political dissent, despite the formal protections offered by constitutions. After independence, sedition laws were strengthened.[82] Preventive detention laws were used against internal enemies. The need for strong central authority to unify ethnically disparate nation-states, buttressed by the colonial precedent of executive rule untrammelled by judicial review, was used to justify ignoring the formal constitutional provisions for the rule of law.

The argument is sometimes made that the usurpation of strong central authority by the new African rulers was eased by the fact that many ordinary Africans perceived the imposed system of British colonial law as illegitimate. Despite colonial interference in traditional courts, it is argued, the indigenous patrimonial judicial system remains intact enough, and responsive enough to local African norms, to be considered as much more legitimate than the outside authority. Yet while it is true that there are strong differences between the indigenous African system of justice and the imported British system to which African national governments are now expected to adhere, it is certainly not true that principles of justice and fairness are unknown in indigenous African cultures. Nor are ordinary Africans necessarily incapable of understanding those same principles when they are expressed in a more formal, though originally foreign, rational-legal system of law.

In the traditional African system of justice, it is argued, conflict resolution was mediatory and reconciliatory; the aim was to restore harmonious family, clan, or village relationships. Procedures were largely informal, and adjudicators were concerned with the substance of morality, not the formalities of law. It was more important to come to a decision perceived as fair by all parties than to follow certain rules. Usually the judges were personally acquainted with the people concerned, and it was relatively easy to ascertain the truth of what every party said.[83]

This model of traditional justice, however, is increasingly less relevant to contemporary Africa. Indeed, it presents an overidealized picture of justice even in pre-colonial Africa. Chapter 2 warned against accepting a picture of traditional African societies that takes into account neither elements of conflict and stratification nor the social changes that have occurred since Africa's incorporation into the wider world economy. While some Africans may still be more comfortable with local-level, personally known, and informal systems of justice, more and more Africans, as they migrate to the cities and interact in the modern economy, are coming to understand and to use the post-colonial rational-legal model.

At a Conference on Local Courts and Customary Law in Dar es Salaam in 1963, it was concluded that there were many advantages to the retention of the customary system. It was agreed that customary proceedings were both understood and accepted by ordinary people; that justice was accessible and cheap; that the courts responded to the usage of the area; and that laymen could participate.[84] Twenty-odd years later, the traditional system of justice is probably still legitimate and useful in relatively homogeneous, rural areas. In ethnically heterogeneous areas, however, whether in the cities or in rural areas to which "strangers" have migrated, problems arise as different individuals' personal (ethnic) laws conflict. Thus there is a great deal of justification for contemporary attempts to rationalize the legal system into one that is consistent on a territorial, not an ethnic, basis. But any such attempt will face the difficulty that in personnel, procedure, and substance, national law is still influenced by the colonial heritage.

In African traditional law, the executive and the judiciary are normally not separate. The chief frequently combines executive, judicial, military, and religious authority. Numerous commentators argue that the contemporary African head of state is still, for many citizens, a chief writ large. Separation of powers, then, is not fully institutionalized in contemporary Commonwealth Africa. Because the principle is still alien to many Africans, it is easy for centralizing African authorities to abrogate it in their own personal or class interests.

The legitimacy of judicial review in Africa is further undermined by the fact that, in many cases, the court personnel are not identified as local or as African. Immediately after independence, and to a lesser degree even in the 1980s, a large percentage of the higher court judges were of foreign origin and/or citizenship. Many had been appointed before independence and, under the security of tenure provisions of the independence constitutions, could not be removed.[85] In East Africa the judiciary was entirely white at independence; later, judges of West Indian and West African origin were appointed, and finally some East Africans.[86] Some of the East African judges, however, were ethnically Asian, and as such their loyalty to the new African states was questioned by many people, including the political leaders, even when they were citizens. In West Africa, more indigenous lawyers had been trained and appointed as higher court judges prior to independence. The reason why indigenous lawyers were trained in West, but not in East, Africa was quite simply that in East Africa (especially Kenya) the European settler class banned Africans from legal training until 1961 on the grounds that they would use their training to go into politics.[87]

Under such circumstances the resentment that both governments and citizens have occasionally shown toward the bench is, from one point of view, quite understandable. For example, in 1969 members of the Zambian Youth Service attacked and vandalized the High Court after a decision by a white judge, upheld by the white (but citizen) chief justice, acquitted two Portuguese soldiers accused of violating Zambian territory.[88] Foreign law administered by foreign judges would be resented in any country of the world; yet that is, in substance, what Commonwealth Africa inherited at independence. On the other hand, the very foreignness of the judiciary can serve a political purpose for the ruling class. It is much easier to ignore judicial decisions handed down by foreigners or by suspect (Asian) citizens than to ignore judicial decisions handed down by full-blooded Africans, firmly embedded in the society they judge. By keeping lawyers and judges as strangers, African rulers have a further strategy for legitimizing their own desires to ignore constitutions and laws.

The view the ruling classes take of the colonial inheritance of legal procedure may be tinged similarly with political motivations. It is true that due process, as used in British courts, was originally part of imposed law. The African president who complains that courts tend to release prisoners on technicalities and who then detains acquitted individuals under preventive detention laws may be reflecting a deep-seated conviction that the substance of morality is more important than formal adherence to procedural rules. On the other hand, preventive detention laws are the most convenient political weapon available to ruling classes in Commonwealth Africa. If they can be justified by the contention that international standards of due process are aspects of ideological imperialism, then opposition is much easier to curtail than it would be if all allegations of subversion, disloyalty, and treason had to be proven in the courts.

In summary, the cultural conflict between indigenous patrimonial systems of justice and imposed rational-legal models in Commonwealth Africa should not be reified into an absolute barrier to the implementation of constitutionalism and the rule of law. Africa has changed and is changing. In the new, heavily stratified political economy, individuals need new legal protections that were irrelevant in the long-ago communal society that is still sometimes taken as a model for contemporary legal practice. The real barrier to constitutionalism and the rule of law in the late 20th century is not cultural variations in perceptions of justice. Instead it is the existence of political regimes that denounce as illegitimate and colonial any structural impediments to their continued power.

Just as the British legal system was originally imposed on Commonwealth Africa from above, so also were the original independence constitutions. Frequently, constitutions following the model of multiparty politics and liberal protections of human rights were conditions for independence. But while the argument that the particular constitutions negotiated by the British and nationalist leaders at independence were inappropriate to African social conditions must be taken seriously, it certainly does not follow that the principle of constitutionalism is inappropriate to Africa. The dominant society to which all Africans now belong is a large, territorially based entity that is increasingly heterogeneous, stratified, and institutionally complex. It is governed by modernized, Westernized, and educated members of the ruling class, whose loyalties to the nation-state and dreams of development and social justice are tempered by their own personal and class interests in acquiring wealth, office, and power. Constitutions appropriate to present African polities, and judiciaries integrated into African culture and sensitive to African legal traditions, are what is needed, not complete abrogation of the principles of constitutionalism and the rule of law. Indeed, the constitutional exercises that accompany even the most blatantly illegitimate usurpations of power in most Commonwealth African countries illustrate that their leaders acknowledge the importance of constitutionalism. The difference between the new and the original constitutions is not so much in the appropriateness of the revised constitutions to African traditions and culture as it is in their appropriateness to the ruling party's or class's interest in preserving its own power.

A major difficulty in a number of independence constitutions was their creation of extraordinarily weak central governments, despite the need for nation-building and political stability. The British concern for compromise among the various political factions and regional/ethnic groups in Africa was bound to produce conflict as soon as independence was attained. In a number of countries, the first modification of the constitution was the abrogation of provisions for regional or federal power. In Ghana, the CPP–dominated Regional Assemblies met once, in 1958, to vote themselves out of power.[89] In Nigeria, where the regional elites were too powerful for the northern-dominated central government to abrogate constitutional provisions for federalism by executive fiat, civil war produced the desired change in practice. In Uganda, the original constitution provided considerable independence for the four kingdoms of Buganda, Ankole, Bunyoro and Toro, and within that, for a special status for Buganda. The arrangements whereby Obote was head of government while the Kabaka (king) of Buganda was head of state were abrogated by an internal coup and subsequent wholesale change of the constitution. Thus the intent of the negotiated independence constitutions—to provide for federal sharing of power to guarantee the rights of insecure minority or regional groups—was very quickly undermined.

Nation-building was not the only concern of the new African governments. National security also quickly became an issue. The problem of national security was indeed real, especially in East and Central Africa where some colonial regimes still existed in the 1960s and '70s. It was also alleged that political oppositions were clearly not loyal to the nation-state as a whole. A final ostensible reason for changes in constitutions was a concern with economic development, a concern allegedly inadequately reflected in the independence constitutions with their stress on civil and political liberties.

Regardless of the alleged inappropriateness of the original independence constitutions to African political or economic goals, it is clear that constitutional changes have also occurred for overtly political ends. Malawi's constitutional change making Kamuzu Banda Life President, or Nkrumah's rigged 1964 referendum in favor of a one-party state, cannot be justified by the necessity for national integration, national security, or economic development. Constitutional changes have been used to mask political manipulation through the conveniently legitimizing, but sterile, definition of "constitutionalism," as meaning simply "rule according to the constitution" rather than a system of law that provides for restraints on government action. Kenya, for example, changed its constitution in 1966 to state that members of Parliament who switched parties had to stand for reelection. That this change was made when members of KANU left to join the opposition, but not earlier when members of the opposition decided to join KANU, shows the political intent of the constitutional maneuver.[90] This action illustrates the need for a real constitutional process in which there are effective restraints on the exercise of government power. Unfortunately, such a need is unlikely to be fulfilled.

Given both some possible public perception of the judiciary, laws, and constitutions as illegitimate, and the overt political manipulations of constitutions in Commonwealth Africa since independence, it is not surprising that judicial review of constitutional changes and practice has been weak. Only in Nigeria has judicial review occurred in a relatively untrammelled manner. In 1979, the judiciary decided the outcome of the Nigerian elections by ruling that Shehu Shagari fulfilled the constitutional provisions for popular support in thirteen of Nigeria's nineteen states. (However, the government might have reacted adversely had the judges found against Shagari.) Elsewhere, judges have occasionally reviewed constitutional cases; for example, in Uganda a number of cases were referred to the courts in the 1960s, but in most of the more important ones the judges found for the government.[91] In Kenya, judges have been reluctant to be constitutionally innovative, perhaps because lawyers of non-African descent still dominated the Law Society and staffed the Attorney-General's office, at least up to the late 1970s, and non-African lawyers "are more amenable [than Africans] to pressure to conform to the wishes of the state."[92] In Tanzania judges are excluded from decision-making in major areas of public policy, which are reserved for Party control.[93]

Most lawyers in Commonwealth Africa have been trained in the British tradition. As late as 1980, Sierra Leone did not have its own law school and was obliged to train all its lawyers abroad.[94] A major distinguishing characteristic of the British tradition is that while lawyers respect and advocate judicial review and the rule of law, they do not take a legally "activist" position. British-trained lawyers and judges tend to defer to the legislature and executive in matters of legal substance. As a result, lawyers and judges work within the letter of the law. African lawyers have been involved in drawing up such restrictive legislation as the Protective Custody Decrees and Subversion Decrees of the Acheampong regime (1972–78) in Ghana.[95]

Even this formalistic approach to law has, however, resulted in some legal activism. In Ghana, the Bar Association brought a writ of *habeas corpus* on behalf of 451 political detainees against the military government in 1977; as a result, the judiciary ordered some detainees released.[96] Justice K. Abban risked his life in 1978 when he insisted on adhering to the letter of the law as supervisor of the "Union Government" referendum in Ghana; he refused to permit vote-counting at regional centers rather than at the actual polling stations, as required by law.[97] In Amin's Uganda, lawyers and judges suffered torture, abduction, and murder. While they have not usually suffered such severe penalties elsewhere, they have often been constrained. In both Zambia and Kenya the lawyers for persons who were on trial for treason or in detention have themselves been arrested.[98]

Considering the possible dangers not only to their freedoms, but also to their lives, as a result of legal activism, we should not be surprised that African lawyers and judges on the whole steer clear of a politically involved approach to the law. The blame for their punctilious approach to preventive detention acts, for example, lies not with them but with the ruling classes that extract such a heavy price from the bar for attempting to defend the rule of law. In fact, as will be shown in the next section, legal innovations that are supposedly being created to return Africa to its indigenous traditions of justice are designed more and more to circumvent constitutions, the rule of law, and the actual involvement of judges and lawyers.

Some Innovations in Legal Practice

The specious view that constitutionalism and the rule of law are irrelevant to, or inappropriate for, Africa has contributed to a number of innovations in the legal field in the last two decades. Those which merit discussion here are the creation of "traditional" courts in Malawi, the introduction of "People's Courts" under the second Rawlings regime (1981–) in Ghana, the creation of Special Tribunals in Nigeria in 1984, and experiments with local assessors and a Permanent Commission of Enquiry in Tanzania.

In Malawi, Life President Banda used his dictatorial powers in 1970 to pass the Local Courts (Amendment) Act. In theory this act, influenced by the criticism that the national system of law is alien in origin[99], gives back to the traditional courts, manned by chiefs, many of the functions that under British rule had been designated for the modern judicial sector. In practice, the major function of these courts is to allow quick and easy sentences to be passed against Banda's political opponents. The chiefs who sit in the courts are Banda's hand-picked men; indeed, he has made it quite clear that chiefs owe their positions to him and that those who are not loyal will be replaced.[100] These local courts have the power to pass death sentences, even though the judges have no legal training. There is no right of appeal, and no defense lawyers are permitted.[101] There is no presumption of innocence, and the accused does not even have the right to specification of the charges against him.[102] In June 1983, two long-time Banda opponents, Orton and Vera Chirwa, were condemned to death by a traditional court after having been kidnapped from Zambia. Only after international pressure were their sentences commuted to life imprisonment.[103]

In cases involving local Africans, it may be useful "to go back to rural and village morality"[104] to deal with crimes that are not political in nature, and which involve the state only as the protector of judicial independence. To use such reasoning to abrogate internationally accepted guarantees of due process completely, however, as in Malawi, is deliberately to pervert the theory of the communal nature of African society into a weapon for political repression. The state is not merely a body of individuals regulating the law and changing constitutions in the interests of national unity, national security, and national development plans. It is also a body of individuals pursuing their own personal or class ends.

Moreover, the general body of citizenry is stratified. Members of the more powerful classes have more access to the law than members of the powerless. Landlords and employers are more likely to have access both to lawyers and to judges than are tenants and employees. Moreover, laws unfavorable to the urban masses are more likely to be enforced than laws unfavorable to the wealthy. In a study of how the law in Kenya is manipulated by the ruling class, Gutto notes that vagrancy laws are enforced to deport the urban unemployed to their rural "homelands," while regulations specifying that employers must supply housing and transportation for their employees are routinely undercut by special ministerial exemptions. The neglect of law enforcement is particularly apparent in the areas of smuggling and corruption, from which the rich profit.[105]

Class-biased uses of the legal system in capitalist-oriented countries such as Kenya have provided the justification for radical experiments in legal systems elsewhere, especially in populist or socialist-oriented societies. The more carefully thought-out case has been that of independent Tanzania, whereas the more radical in technique, as well as in theory, has been the post-1981 Rawlings regime in Ghana. Concerning Tanzania, it could be argued that allegedly socialist reforms of the law are simply another mechanism for legitimating the party-bureaucratic ruling class. In Ghana, because of the newness of the regime and the instability of political relations after 1981, it is not clear that any social class, including that for which the legal reforms were intended, is benefiting from the new "people's courts."

In reaction to political abuse and flagrant violations of laws prohibiting various forms of corruption and smuggling, the "revolutionary" military regime under Jerry Rawlings has introduced new Public Tribunals (people's courts) in Ghana. These tribunals may pass the death sentence in cases of economic sabotage, smuggling, corruption, embezzlement, abuse of power, and subversion.[106] There is no right of appeal nor judicial review,[107] and even evidence of torture in the extraction of confessions seems to be ignored. It has been alleged that the courts are manned by laymen with no legal training, that trials often last for only a few minutes, and that sentences of forced labor are long and inconsistent.[108] There appears to be no presumption of innocence on the part of the accused.[109] However, the accused does appear to be allowed legal counsel.[110]

The creation of these courts originally seemed to be an attempt to control Ghana's floundering, highly inflationary economy in the absence of any real economic weapons available to the government. Economic policy in 1982 was dominated by a scapegoatist philosophy, in which corruption was taken as the cause, not as a symptom, of deep economic malaise. The summary justice meted out in people's courts was supplemented by impromptu floggings and beatings of those who appeared to be overcharging in the markets. Even such summary justice was not always impartial, however. Three members of the "Pre-Trial Investigation Team" that investigated economic crimes during the first Rawlings regime (June 4– October 1979) claimed that bribery and favoritism dominated the charges and hearings.[111] Allegations have been made that political factors influence the decision to send accused people to the Public Tribunals, where there is a higher chance of conviction, rather than to the ordinary courts.[112]

In late 1982 the Ghana Bar Association decided to boycott the people's courts because of their violations of the basic principles of the rule of law. The bar's boycott was also impelled by the brutal abduction and murder of three judges, K.A. Agyepong, (Mrs.) C. Koranteng-Addow, and F.P. Sarkodee, and a retired army major, in June 1982. Although Rawlings launched an investigation of the abductions, suspicion was widespread that they had been ordered by the government or a member of the government as a reaction against Sarkodee's quashing of a revolutionary court conviction during the first Rawlings's regime (Rawlings had staged a coup in 1979 and then handed over power to civilians), and Koranteng-Addow's and Agyepong's adverse ruling against workers petitioning against wrongful dismissal by a parastatal firm (the populist Rawlings regime is militantly pro-worker).[113] In the event, a Public Tribunal sentenced four men, including a former member of the Provisional National Defense Council (the government) to death in August 1983 for murder of the judges.[114] But it was also widely rumored in Ghana that Cptn. Kojo Tsikata, Rawlings's closest advisor, had ordered the killings.

Not all commentators believe that the Ghana Bar Association's decision to boycott the Public Tribunals is wise. One observer who visited Ghana, the British socialist lawyer Lord Gifford, found the tribunals fair and serious and commended the appointment of lay judges.[115] Two major problems are associated with the Public Tribunals. First is the legal problem that there is no right to appeal their decisions, and second is the substantive problem that their jurisdiction, especially regarding "economic sabotage," is very wide. For example, Public Tribunals can pass judgment on anyone found by a National Investigation Committee to have engaged in "any . . . acts or omission . . . detrimental to the economy of Ghana or to the welfare of the sovereign people of Ghana" and anyone who either sells or buys commodities above the (unrealistically low) control price.[116]

In 1984 the military government in Nigeria set up Military Tribunals that resembled, in their lack of protection of civil rights, Ghana's people's courts. The Buhari regime in Nigeria did not espouse a socialist philosophy. But despite the laws it enacted to protect itself against any charges of corruption from the press (see Chapter 6), it went on an almost evangelical campaign to "clean the society of the cankerworm of pervasive corruption,"[117] at least insofar as former officials and politicians were concerned. Undoubtedly many of those accused of corruption had profited from their control of office in the past; however, it appears that the real purpose of the courts was to use the accused as scapegoats for Nigeria's economic ills in the 1980s. A series of new laws was enacted, including the Recovery of Public Property (Special Military Tribunals) Decree. The death penalty could be imposed by these courts for arson, dealing in counterfeit currency, sabotage of oil pipelines or power cables, illegal dealing in petroleum products, and cocaine trafficking. Some of the new crimes were retroactive. People charged under these laws were tried by a tribunal consisting of one legally trained judge and three members of the military. Trials were held *in camera*, and the onus was on the accused to prove that he was innocent. Legal counsel was permitted, but as in Ghana, the Nigerian Bar Association declared a boycott of the new courts. There was no appeal from the judgment of the Special Tribunals, although sentences had to be confirmed by the Supreme Military Council.[118]

In both Ghana and Nigeria, the governments claimed that the new courts were set up to prevent the rich buying justice and escaping convictions through legal technicalities, as under the old British system. Is the solution to rigid legalistic formalism the establishment of people's courts without right of appeal, and is the solution to class-biased manipulation of law the dispensation of summary justice to those who are viewed to be society's enemies? In the new Ghanaian revolutionary view, class-based justice appears to be substituting for the rigorous discovery of evidence. It is difficult to maintain that this type of justice at least encourages economic development. While some of those "economic saboteurs" who are convicted may indeed have abused their office or engaged in corrupt activities, many others were merely carrying out business as best they could in a disintegrating economy.

The problems of the rule of law in Africa are threefold: (a) how to guarantee a means of responding to local, indigenous needs for justice in an understandable and accessible fashion, while at the same time (b) coping with the new needs of national, urban, and stratified societies for justice, and (c) especially guaranteeing the right of political dissent. Tanzania has made a serious attempt to remedy the first two of these problems, although her record on the third remains poor.

At the local level, Tanzania has instituted a system of magistrate's courts in which the magistrate is assisted by two assessors, who represent the community; even at the high-court level, the opinions of assessors are sought.[119] Thus although Tanzania has established a uniform system of law, abolishing specific customary or religious (Muslim) jurisdictions, at the same time she has preserved some of the accessibility and understandability of traditional courts. To cope with the problem of class manipulation of law, the Tanzanian approach is twofold. First, as discussed in Chapter 3, state policy aims at preventing the formation of a dominant capitalist class. Second, abuses of power or simply insensitive decision-making by members of the party, government, or civil service are subject in principle to review by the Permanent Commission of Enquiry.[120] This body can respond to enquiries initiated by the president or by individuals, or can initiate enquiries on its own. While it has no enforcement powers, it can negotiate agreements, and it reports gross violations of justice to the president, who is, however, himself immune from investigation.[121] As of 1978, the Permanent Commission of Enquiry had an office only in Dar es Salaam and was used mainly by urban residents.[122] It is doubtful that the low number of complaints it investigates reflects a relatively pure system of administrative justice in Tanzania;[123] rather one must assume that its ombudsman character is a very incomplete substitute (perhaps an economically unavoidable one) for a system of administrative courts.

The concern for economic development and control of corruption in Tanzania is buttressed by the heavy use of preventive detention orders against suspected economic criminals, as documented earlier in this chapter. Judicial review of political and economic imprisonments in Tanzania is prohibited by the exclusion of the Preventive Detention Act from any sort of control. The Tanzanian legal innovation, then, is also incomplete, although it addresses the problems of a particular type of class rule (based on wealth) more carefully than do the Ghanaian people's courts, and although it has tried seriously to reconcile patrimonial and rational-legal forms of authority at the local level, rather than merely setting up spurious traditional courts, as has Malawi. But in Tanzania, the final problem of allowing for political dissent has not been addressed. Instead, in Tanzania as in most other Commonwealth African countries, legal and constitutional manipulation is a standard means of safeguarding the particular regime in power against any challenge.

Constitutionalism and the rule of law are necessary, although not sufficient, guarantors of human rights in Africa. The examples of Malawi and Ghana show the dangers of populistic resurrections of "traditional" courts or new African versions of "socialist justice" that defy international standards of due process. The imaginative experiments of Tanzania in some areas of justice are undermined by the lack of any constitutional restraint on government actions against political opposition or indeed against accused economic criminals. Constitutional restraints on executive action are even more important in newly developing poor countries which suffer from incomplete political integration than they are in developed countries with long traditions of popular political participation and effective mediation between citizen and state by organized, independent political parties and pressure groups. The absence of the rule of law and an independent judiciary in Commonwealth Africa will continue to allow the ruling regimes to ride rough-shod over the rights of the masses.

The distinguished African jurist R. Hayfron-Benjamin recently suggested several innovations in the body of law that could help to guarantee real human rights. He suggests that in one-party states, the ruling political party should be declared a public institution rather than a private one, as political parties are in Britain and other multiparty states; this would open up its internal procedures and decisions to judicial review. Impeachment procedures could be validated in one-party states so the president could be removed from office even if the government itself could not. In military states, he suggests, the actions of soldiers should be considered representative of the government; thus the government would be legally liable when soldiers beat and looted ordinary citizens. Citizens, Hayfron-Benjamin suggests, should be allowed to seek civil remedies against breaches of their rights by representatives of the party, state, or government.[124]

It is unlikely that the kinds of legal protections that Hayfron-Benjamin envisages will be implemented in Commonwealth Africa. Establishment of the rule of law depends not on the political will of the ruling class, but on the political clout of those whose rights it abuses. The more political opposition is stifled, the less it is likely that political dissidents will be able to demand constitutional protections of their rights. In such a context, even lawyers who attempt to protect civil rights are perceived as political threats to the ruling regime. A vicious circle ensues: the more calls there are for civil rights, the less likely it is that civil rights will be protected. A weak, insecure, and factionalized ruling class, dependent for its wealth and power on control of the various offices of the state, cannot afford to subject itself to judicial overview and the rule of law.

Notes

1. "Ghana's Preventive Detention Act," International Commission of Jurists, *Journal* 3, no. 2 (Winter 1961): 71.
2. See, e.g., reports of such cases in Ghana in ibid. See also R.M.A. Chongwe, "Address to the African Seminar on Human Rights and Development" (Gaborone, Botswana, May 24–29, 1982), p. 4

3. Amnesty International, *Annual Report*: "Gambia," 1981.

4. Ibid., "Gambia," 1982.

5. Amnesty International, *Bulletin* (Canada), May 1984, p. 2.

6. James W. Skelton, Jr., "Standards of Procedural Due Process under International Law vs. Preventive Detention in Selected African States," *Houston Journal of International Law* 2, no. 2 (Spring 1980): 319.

7. Amnesty International, "Nigeria," *Annual Reports* 1980, 1981, 1982.

8. Personal communication, October 26, 1984.

9. Amnesty International, *Bulletin* (Canada), June 1985, p. 4

10. Kevin Conboy, "Detention without Trial in Kenya," *Georgia Journal of International and Comparative Law* 8, no. 2 (1978): 445. For the original Act, see "Kenya: The Public Security (Detained and Restricted Persons) Regulations 1966," United Nations, *Yearbook of Human Rights* (1966), pp. 226–28.

11. Ngugi wa Thiong'o, *Detained: A Writer's Prison Diary* (London: Heinemann, 1981), p. 204.

12. Ibid., pp. 147–48.

13. Kiraitu Murungi, "Legal Aspects of Detention without Trial in Kenya," (Nairobi, September 1982), p. 21. Unpublished; available through Human Rights Internet, Washington, D.C.

14. Amnesty International, "Kenya," *Annual Reports* 1975–76, 1976–77; and Amnesty International *Bulletin* (Canada), June 1976, June and September 1977, and elsewhere.

15. "Njonjo's Fall from Power Accelerates," *Weekly Review*, July 8, 1983; Amnesty International, *Bulletin* (Canada), July/August 1983, and *Weekly Review*, June 3, 1983, p. 3.

16. For the original legislation, see "Sierra Leone: The Public Emergency (No.2) Regulations, 1971," section 7, b, in United Nations, *Yearbook of Human Rights* (1971), pp. 209–12.

17. Amnesty International, "Sierra Leone," *Annual Reports* 1976–77, 1979, 1982.

18. Amnesty International, *Annual Report*, 1979.

19. According to T.O. Elias, an eminent African jurist, paraphrased in John K. Ebiasah, "Protecting the Human Rights of Political Detainees: The Contradictions and Paradoxes of the African Experience," *Howard Law Journal* 22, no. 3 (1979): 266.

20. Skelton, "Standards of Procedural Due Process," p. 320. On the Lumpa crisis, see Chapter 5 of this volume.

21. Chongwe, "Address to the African Seminar," p. 3.

22. *Africa Contemporary Record*, vol. 9 (1976–77), p. B415; vol. 11 (1978–79), p. B450.

23. Republic of Zambia, "Invocation of the Full Powers of the State of Emergency by H.E. the President Dr. K.D. Kaunda: Text of His Address to the Nation on ZBS Radio/TV" (January 28, 1976), pp. 3–5.

24. Amnesty International, "Zambia," *Annual Reports* 1971–72, p. 29; and 1972–73, p. 43. See also *Africa Contemporary Record*, vol. 5 (1972–73), p. B299.

25. Amnesty International, "Zambia," *Annual Report*, 1982.

26. There were alleged attempted coups in Zambia on October 20, 1980 (*Keesing's Contemporary Archives*, February 27, 1981, p. 30738) and in June 1981 (ibid., November 13, 1981, p. 31185). See also Amnesty International, Urgent Action circular no. AFR 63/02/83; January 21, 1983.

27. For the original legislation, see "Ghana: The Preventive Detention Act,

1958," in United Nations, *Yearbook of Human Rights* (1958), pp. 82–86. See also International Commission of Jurists, "Ghana's Preventive Detention Act."

28. International Commission of Jurists, ibid., p. 66; Kwame Kesse-Adu, *The Politics of Political Detention* (Accra-Tema: Ghana Publishing Corporation, 1971), Foreword.

29. Kesse-Adu, ibid., p. 30.

30. Republic of Ghana, *Dr. J.B. Danquah: Detention and Death in Nsawam Prison: Extracts from Evidence of Witnesses at the Commission of Enquiry into Ghana Prisons* (Accra-Tema: Ministry of Information, n.d. [1968?]) (document no. SPC/A10099/5,000/5/67–8).

31. Amnesty International, *Annual Report*, 1975–76. Mensah was released in 1978.

32. *Africa Contemporary Record*, vol.5 (1972–73), p. C188.

33. *West Africa*, July 2, 1979, p. 1151.

34. The Preventive Custody Law (2 March 1982: retroactive to 2 January 1982) lists 492 names; others were also interned. For releases, see Amnesty International, Telex Afr 28/WU 01/83 (12 January 1983); and *West Africa*, January 31, 1983, p. 295.

35. Amnesty International, *Annual Report* 1972–73, p. 31.

36. Skelton, "Standards of Procedural Due Process," p. 314.

37. Amnesty International, "Tanzania," *Annual Report* 1970–71, pp. 42–43; 1971–72, p. 28; 1972–73, p. 80; 1974–75, p. 56. Otini and Mattiya Kambona were detained almost continuously from 1967 to 1978.

38. Hank Chase, "The Zanzibar Treason Trial," *Review of African Political Economy* 6 (May–Aug. 1976): 14–33.

39. Ibid., p. 32. Babu was released on February 5, 1978. Amnesty International, "Tanzania," *Annual Report*, 1978.

40. Amnesty International, "Tanzania," *Annual Report*, 1977; and August 1979.

41. Personal communication from a Tanzanian Asian refugee.

42. Henry Kyemba, *A State of Blood: The Inside Story of Idi Amin* (New York: Ace Books, 1977), p. 27.

43. Colin Legum, "After the Amin Nightmare," *Africa Report*, Jan.–Feb. 1983, p. 18. But compare Amnesty International, "Memorandum to the Government of Uganda on an Amnesty International Mission to Uganda in January 1982 and Further Exchanges between the Government and Amnesty International" (April 1983) and "Uganda: Evidence of Torture" (June 18, 1985).

44. *Africa Contemporary Record*, vol. 9 (1976–77), p. B378; ibid., vol. 5 (1972–73), p. B276, and elsewhere.

45. Personal communication.

46. Yusef Lule, "Human Rights Violations in Uganda under Obote," *Munger Africana Library Notes* 67 (November 1982); Amnesty International, "Memorandum" (1983) and "Uganda: Evidence of Torture" (1985).

47. "Army Killing Thousands in Uganda, U.S. Says," *The Globe and Mail*, August 10, 1984.

48. Lule, "Human Rights Violations," p. 9.

49. Jeff Crisp, "National Security, Human Rights and Population Displacements: Luwero District, Uganda, January–December 1983," *Review of African Political Economy* 27/28 (1983): 164–74.

50. Ibid., p. 169.

51. Letter sent to the author by Hassan Ochen, Acting High Commissioner for Uganda in Canada, n.d. (1983). Ref. CONFD/INF/011. This letter was for general distribution within Canada.

52. Crisp, "National Security," pp. 164–65.

53. T. R. Lansner, "Can Obote Survive?," *Africa Report*, Jan.–Feb. 1982, p. 43.

54. Colin Legum, "Interview of Milton Obote, President of Uganda," *Africa Report*, Jan.–Feb. 1983, p. 20.

55. Lule, "Human Rights Violations," pp. 8–9.

56. Malawi Government, *His Excellency the Life President's Speeches (3–12 September 1971)* (Zomba: Government Printer, n.d.), n.p.

57. Tony Hodges, *Jehovah's Witnesses in Central Africa* (London: Minority Rights Group Report No. 29, June 1976), p. 2.

58. Republic of Zambia, "Report of the Commission of Inquiry into the Former Lumpa Church," (Lusaka: Government Printer, 1965), p. 11.

59. *The Times* (London), "Churches Pledge Support for Bishop of Accra: 'Terrible Risk' of Political Youth Movement," August 13, 1962.

60. *New York Times*, June 6, 1983, p. A6.

61. Anonymous, *In/Dependent Kenya* (London: Zed Press, 1982), p. 29.

62. Ibid., p. 30.

63. Government of Kenya, "Report of the Select Committee on the Disappearance and Murder of the Late Member for Nyandarua North, the Hon. J.M. Kariuki, M.P." (June 3, 1975).

64. Rajat Neogy, "Many Days in the Life of an African Detainee," *The Herald Tribune* (Paris), October 25, 1969.

65. Ngugi, *Detained*, p. 116.

66. "Inside Obote's Jail: A Personal Account," in Lule, "Human Rights Violations," pp. 16–24.

67. Kesse-Adu, *Politics of Political Detention*, p. 33.

68. Wole Soyinka, *The Man Died* (New York: Harper & Row, 1972), p. 101; Elechi Amadi, *Sunset in Biafra: A Civil War Diary* (London: Heinemann, 1973), p. 100.

69. Editor's note, *Index on Censorship* 7, no. 6 (Nov.–Dec. 1978): 78.

70. "Extracts from A Report of Acts of Intimidation and Victimization at Ikom Division of the South-Eastern State during the State Governor's Visit to the Division" (11 March 1971), Appendix B, in Soyinka, *The Man Died*, pp. 297–99.

71. Ebiasah, "Protecting Human Rights of Political Detainees," p. 270.

72. James Reid, "Kenyan Academics, Students Victims of Government Purge," CAUT (Canadian Association of University Teachers) *Bulletin*, May 1983, pp. 11–12.

73. Kesse-Adu, *Politics of Political Detention*, pp. 52–53.

74. The following two sections are an abridged version of Rhoda E. Howard, "Legitimacy and Class Rule in Commonwealth Africa: Constitutionalism and the Rule of Law," *Third World Quarterly* 7, no. 2 (April 1985): 323–47.

75. C.E.K. Kumado, *Constitutionalism, Civil Liberties and Development: A Case Study of Ghana since Independence* (Accra: Ghana Universities Press, 1980), p. 6.

76. Leo Baron (Deputy Chief Justice of Zambia), "Constitutional Aspects of the Rule of Law in a One-Party State," in International Commission of Jurists, *Human Rights in a One-Party State* (London: Search Press, 1978), p. 43.

77. Max Weber, *From Max Weber: Essays in Sociology,* ed. H.H. Gerth and C. Wright Mills (New York: Oxford University Press, 1958), pp. 296, 221.

78. A. Kodzo Paaku Kludze, "The Effect of Modernization on African Customary Law." Paper presented at the African Studies Association, Philadelphia, Pa., October 18, 1980, p. 6.

79. Sandra B. Burman and Barbara E. Harrell-Bond, "Introduction," in Burman and Harrell-Bond, eds., *The Imposition of Law* (New York: Academic Press, 1979) p. 7.

80. On the repugnancy clause, see Gerald M. Caplan, "The Making of 'Natural Justice' in British Africa: An Exercise in Comparative Law," *Journal of African Law* 13, no. 2 (1964): 120–34; H.B. Hooker, *Legal Pluralism: An Introduction to Colonial and Neo-Colonial Laws* (Oxford: Clarendon Press, 1975), 129–43; Kwamena Bentsi-Enchill, "The Colonial Heritage of Legal Pluralism," *Zambia Law Journal* 1, no. 2 (1969): 1–30; and Kludze, "The Effect of Modernization," pp. 21–34.

81. Steven B. Pfeiffer, "The Role of the Judiciary in the Constitutional Systems of East Africa," *Journal of Modern African Studies* 16, no. 1 (1978): 41.

82. Akinola Aguda and Oluwadare Aguda, "Judicial Protection of Some Fundamental Rights in Nigeria and in the Sudan before and during Military Rule," *Journal of African Law* 16 (1972): 133.

83. The above description is taken from James C.N. Paul, "Human Rights and Legal Development: Observations on Some African Experiences," in James C. Tuttle, ed., *International Human Rights Law and Practice* (New York: American Bar Association, 1978), pp. 23–37.

84. E.I. Nwogugu, "Abolition of Customary Courts—the Nigerian Experiment," *Journal of African Law* 20, no. 1 (1976): 11–12.

85. Pfeiffer, "The Role of the Judiciary," p. 39.

86. Ibid., p. 43. See also Robert Martin, *Personal Freedom and the Law in Tanzania* (Nairobi: Oxford University Press, 1974), p. 73.

87. Amos O. Odenyo, "Professionalization amidst Change: The Case of the Emerging Legal Profession in Kenya," *African Studies Review* 22, no. 3 (December 1979): 34–35.

88. "Zambia: Separation of Power," in International Commission of Jurists, *The Review* 4 (December 1969): 27. See also J.F. Scotton, "Judicial Independence and Political Expression in East Africa—Two Colonial Legacies," *East African Law Journal* 1 (1970): p. 1.

89. Kumado, *Constitutionalism, Civil Liberties and Development,* p. 14.

90. Y.P. Ghai, "Constitutions and the Political Order in East Africa," *International and Comparative Law Quarterly* 21 (1972): 425.

91. Pfeiffer, "The Role of the Judiciary," pp. 60–63.

92. Odenyo, "Professionalization amidst Change," p. 38. See also Kiraitu Murungi, "Constitutional Construction and Human Rights in Kenya" (Nairobi: n.d.), p. 35. Unpublished; available through Human Rights Internet, Washington, D.C.

93. Martin, *Personal Freedom and the Law in Tanzania,* p. 66.

94. "Freetown Lawyers Confer," *West Africa,* May 12, 1980, p. 832.

95. Kumado, *Constitutionalism, Civil Liberties and Development,* p. 21.

96. "Human Rights in the World: Ghana," International Commission of Jurists, *Review* 20 (June 1978): 4.

97. Ibid.

98. "Zambia Treason Trial: Another Delay," Amnesty International, *Bulletin* (Canada), January 1982; and "Kenya: Detentions Follow Call for an Opposition Party," Amnesty International, *Bulletin* (Canada), July 1982.

99. Paul Brietzke, "The Chilobwe Murders Trial," *African Studies Review* 17 (1974): 363.

100. Speech by Banda at Lilongwe (September 11, 1971), included in Malawi Government, *His Excellency the Life President's Speeches*, p. 44.

101. "Malawi—Criminal Jurisdiction," International Commission of Jurists, *The Review* 5 (March 1970): p. 6; "Malawi," ibid., no. 28 (June 1982): 14.

102. Dennis F. Olsen, "Protection of Individual Rights in Emergent African States: Luxury or Necessity?" Paper presented at the Seminar on Law and Human Rights in Development, Gaborone, Botswana, May 24–28, 1982, p. 5.

103. Amnesty International, *Bulletin* (Canada), June 1983 and October 1984.

104. The phrase quoted is from Saeed El Mahdi, "Criminal Justice Systems in Africa and Asia," International Commission of Jurists, *The Review* 15 (December 1975): 61.

105. S.B.O. Gutto, "Kenya's Petit-bourgeois State, the Public, and the Rule/ Misrule of Law," *International Journal of the Sociology of Law* 10 (1982): 351. On vagrancy laws, see also Murungi, "Constitutional Construction and Human Rights in Kenya," pp. 10–11, and Martin, *Personal Freedom and the Law in Tanzania*, p. 105.

106. "People's Court at Work," *West Africa*, October 18, 1982, p. 2706.

107. Government of Ghana, Law 24, Public Tribunals, 21 July 1982, article 9 (1).

108. "Bar's Boycott Bites," *West Africa*, October 25, 1982, pp. 2772–75.

109. Amnesty International, "Memorandum to the Government of the Republic of Ghana on Amnesty International's Concerns Relating to the Public Tribunals Established Pursuant to PNDC Law 24," in *The Public Tribunals in Ghana* (New York: Amnesty International U.S.A., July 1984), p. 8.

110. This is implied in Government of Ghana, Law 24, article 7, 6. See also ibid., "The Origins of Public Tribunals," p. 6.

111. "Justice and Violence at the AFRC's Courts," *West Africa*, January 7, 1980, pp. 10–12.

112. Amnesty International, *The Public Tribunals in Ghana*, p. 7.

113. Nii K. Bentsi-Enchill, "The Ghana Judges Affair," *West Africa*, July 12, 1982, pp. 1797–98.

114. "Ghana: Executions Take Place," *West Africa*, August 22, 1983, p. 1976. See also Amnesty International, *The Public Tribunals in Ghana*, p. 3.

115. "Ghana: Public Tribunals—2," *West Africa*, October 10, 1983, pp. 2341–43.

116. Government of Ghana, Law 2, National Investigations Committee, February 5, 1982, articles 3(e) and 11; ibid., Law 24, articles 3, 1, e, and 6, 1, b.

117. Onyema Ugochukwa, "Nigeria: Trials and Errors," *West Africa*, April 9, 1984, p. 768.

118. Details in this paragraph are from ibid.; Onyema Ugochukwa, "Nigeria: The Trials Begin," *West Africa*, May 21, 1984, pp. 1056–57; and Amnesty International, *Bulletin* (Canada), April 1985.

119. Martin, *Personal Freedom and the Law in Tanzania*, p. 70; and Pius Msekwa, "The Doctrine of the One-party State in Relation to Human Rights and

the Rule of Law," in International Commission of Jurists, *Human Rights in a One-Party State*, p. 34.

120. "Annual Report of the Permanent Commission of Enquiry, 1967–68," in Martin, *Personal Freedom and the Law in Tanzania*, p. 209.

121. Summary of J.B. Mwenda, "Procedures for Investigating Complaints in the Permanent Commission of Enquiry," in International Commission of Jurists, *Human Rights in a One-Party State*, p. 77.

122. Msekwa, "The Doctrine of the One-party State," p. 31.

123. For figures see Pfeiffer, "The Role of the Judiciary," p. 59.

124. R. Hayfron-Benjamin, "The Courts and the Protection and Enforcement of Human Rights in Africa," *CIJO* (Centre for the Independence of Judges and Lawyers) *Bulletin* 9 (April 1982): 37–40.

⑧ Women's Rights

Discussion of women's rights in underdeveloped countries is often linked with debate as to whether the concern with women's rights or women's liberation is merely a latter-day form of Western ideological imperialism. Women's rights are not merely a Western concern. While the provision of women's rights cannot be separated from the attempt to develop Commonwealth African countries, neither can women's rights be put aside until such utopian time as the governments of newly developed African countries see fit to grant them.

Macro-social global inequalities do not render inequalities between men and women within specific African societies irrelevant, nor are such gender inequalities merely the result of colonial ideological control. In indigenous social structures in Commonwealth Africa, women's rights and duties differed from men's, and in many cases rendered them unequal in family, lineage, and state affairs. Such differences have been elaborated during the colonial and post-colonial eras to create substantial legal, social, and material inequalities between the two sexes. In the post-colonial period, economic competition and social stratification have further widened the gap between the two sexes. Men have a material as well as an ideological interest in continuing women's subordination. Thus African women, as individuals and as a group, urgently require human rights. While many rights for women have been specifically codified in international and African human rights instruments, very few have actually been implemented in Commonwealth Africa.

The 1966 Covenants on Civil and Political (Article 2, 1), and Economic, Social and Cultural Rights (Article 2, 2) both contain explicit provisions against discrimination on the grounds of sex. In addition, a number of other conventions pertaining to women's rights have been adopted by the United Nations. The Supplementary Convention on the Abolition of Slavery, the Slave Trade and Practices similar to Slavery (1956) advocates abolition of any institution or practice whereby "A woman, without the right to refuse, is promised or given in marriage on payment of a consideration in money or kind . . . or . . . a woman on the death of her

---

This chapter is a revised and combined version of two previous articles: Rhoda Howard, "Human Rights and Personal Law: Women in Sub-Saharan Africa," *Issue: A Journal of Africanist Opinion* 12, nos. 1/2 (Spring/Summer 1982): 45–52; and idem, "Women's Rights in English-Speaking Sub-Saharan Africa," in Claude E. Welch, Jr., and Robert I. Meltzer, eds., *Human Rights and Development in Africa* (Albany: State University of New York Press, 1984), pp. 46–74.

husband is liable to be inherited by another person" (Article 1). The Convention on Consent to Marriage, Minimum Age for Marriage and Registration of Marriages (1962) declares that "certain customs, ancient laws and practices relating to marriage and the family [are] inconsistent with . . . the Universal Declaration of Human Rights," and that "all States [must ensure] complete freedom in the choice of a spouse, eliminating completely child marriages and the betrothal of young girls before the age of puberty" (Preamble). These conventions can be interpreted to prohibit bridewealth (the payment a prospective husband makes to his prospective wife's family) and widow inheritance (the marriage of a widow to her deceased husband's male relative), both practiced with some frequency in Commonwealth Africa, as well as prohibiting the companion customs of arranged marriages and child betrothal.

Two other conventions pertain to women's political rights. The Convention on the Political Rights of Women (1952) provides that women have equal rights with men to vote, to stand for and hold office, and to have access to the public service. The Convention on the Nationality of Married Women (1957) deals with problems consequent upon "the loss or acquisition of nationality by women as a result of marriage, of its dissolution or of the change of nationality by the husband during marriage" (Preamble).

All the above rights, and many more, are included in the omnibus Convention on the Elimination of All Forms of Discrimination against Women (1979). This convention resembles in part the 1967 "Declaration" on the Elimination of Discrimination against Women, which included all previously acknowledged rights, plus the right to equality of men and women in the family, the right to family planning, equal rights and duties regarding children, and equal rights regarding property and inheritance.[1] The 1979 convention also stresses the rights of women in development. In so doing it reflects the new influence of the underdeveloped countries in the United Nations, especially their concern for world economic reform, the provision of basic human needs, and the elimination of all forms of colonialism. The rest of this chapter will refer to the 1979 convention as the basic U.N. document on human rights for women.

The African Charter of Human and Peoples' Rights makes few references to women, other than in the anti-discrimination clause that prohibits distinction on the basis of sex (Article 2). Certain other articles, however, can also be taken to pertain to women, with somewhat contradictory consequences. Article 4, which specifies that "Human beings are inviolable. Every human being shall be entitled to respect for his [sic] life and the integrity of his person" could be used by African feminists as an argument for the abolition of the more physically harmful variants of female genital operations. So also could Article 16, guaranteeing every individual the right "to enjoy the best attainable state of physical and mental health."

Article 18 of the African Charter specifies both that "the family shall be the natural unit and basis of society" and that "the State shall ensure the elimination of every discrimination against women." While the rights of women are thus specifically protected, their inclusion with the protection of the family could result in ambiguities when the individual woman comes into conflict with family norms or with her husband's wishes. This potential ambiguity is also reflected in Article 17, 3: "The promotion and protection of morals and traditional values recognized by the community shall be the duty of the State." Some community values, such as child betrothal, bridewealth, and widow inheritance, are directly antithetical to individual women's rights as defined by United Nations conventions.

Political Rights of Women

In the formal, legal sense, women in Commonwealth Africa do not suffer extreme political disabilities as compared with men. Women still suffer some discrimination in the right to nationality. The 1979 Ghana Constitution, for example, specifies that a woman can attain Ghanaian nationality upon marriage to a Ghanaian male, but she would lose it should she divorce; whereas men can attain citizenship if the marriage is monogamous or has lasted five years, but they do not appear to lose it upon divorce.[2] Discrimination with regard to citizenship can adversely affect women, insofar as it affects a woman's right to become and remain a citizen of the country of which her husband is a citizen, or not to become such a citizen; and conversely either to retain or to give up her citizenship of birth upon marriage. From such a right flows the right to participate as a citizen in politics.

Once a woman is acknowledged to be a citizen of any of the nine countries, she enjoys equal political rights with men. In almost all these countries, women have enjoyed equal political rights since independence or before. Women were granted the right to vote in Gambia in 1961; in Ghana in 1950 (former Gold Coast Colony) and 1955 (former Togoland); in Kenya in 1963 at independence; in Malawi in 1964 at independence; in Nigeria in 1954 (former Eastern Region), 1958 (former Western Region) and 1979 (former Northern Region); in Sierra Leone in 1961 at independence; in Uganda in 1962 at independence; and in Zambia in 1964 at independence.[3] Women were also permitted to hold office and stand for election on the same basis as men. The single geographical area in which women have not always enjoyed equal political rights with men was in the former Northern Region of Nigeria: until the constitutional revision of 1979 women could neither vote nor stand for or hold office. Northern Nigeria is a predominantly Muslim area in which Muslim law had been entrenched during the colonial period, and the independent government

of Nigeria originally preferred not to disturb the indigenous legal structure.

Insofar as women's formal political rights are concerned, then, there is
now no discrimination. The problems faced by women are by and large
those also faced by men; namely, the irrelevance of formal political rights
in times of military or one-party rule. Formal political equality, moreover,
does not guarantee that there will be no cultural norms against women's
running for or holding office. In many African societies, the indigenous
custom was for men to hold formal political office as chiefs, while women
could be influential only in advisory capacities. The indigenous tendency
toward men's holding formal political office was reinforced by British legal
and cultural practice during the colonial period, with the result that few
politicians in contemporary Commonwealth Africa are women. Military
rule almost by definition precludes women's holding office.

The relative lack of importance of women in formal Commonwealth
African politics does not mean, however, that they are exempt from
political persecution, either as group members or as individuals. Women,
with their children, suffer in Africa as a result of civil wars, of class-biased
state agricultural policies that deprive them of their subsistence, and of
organized persecutions of religious groups, such as the Jehovah's Witnesses. Many courageous African women, as well as many courageous
men, risk their lives for matters of political principle and personal
integrity. In Uganda, Mrs. Teresa Nazire Mukasa-Bukenya, a lecturer at
Makerere University, was found beheaded on the roadside after she
refused to give Idi Amin false information about the sexual habits of a
Kenyan woman student, information which would have justified Amin in
claiming to the Kenyan government that the student, rather than having
been murdered, had merely run off with a group of Ugandan soldiers.[4] In
1982, Mrs. Cecilia Koranteng-Addow was one of three judges murdered in
Ghana.[5] The first Kenyan refugee in Tanzania, Chelegat Mutai, was a
woman. An outspoken backbench MP, she was imprisoned for two and a
half years in the mid-1970s and fled to Tanzania in 1982.[6]

Such political risks taken by women in contemporary Africa are part of
a long tradition of informal political leadership and protest. The granting
of formal political rights upon independence masks the adverse effects that
colonialism had on women's political rights in their indigenous societies.
In 1970, 10 of 146 district chiefs in Sierra Leone were women; this was not
a "modern" development, but a continuation of a traditional pattern.[7]
Oral histories in West Africa recount stories of women chiefs' forming
small states such as Mampong, Wenchi, and Juaben in Ghana and
receiving tribute (as did Queen Amina of Katsina, Nigeria in the early
15th century) from other chiefs.[8] Among the Igbo of midwestern Nigeria,
a "dual-sex" political system existed, in which "each sex managed its own
affairs, and women's interests [were] represented at all levels."[9] The best-

known example of female political action in the British colonies was the 1929 "Woman's War," in which tens of thousands of Igbo women attacked warrant chiefs (chiefs appointed by the British) and the so-called native courts. At least 50 women died after being fired upon by police and troops.[10] Although the immediate cause of the protest was the imposition of taxes on women, they were also protesting against abrogation of their own traditional power.

Thus, although women in post-colonial Commonwealth Africa have more formal political rights than they (or men) had under colonialism, their situation is not necessarily better than it would have been had there never been a colonial interlude. The effect of the introduction of Western ideology and the consolidation of nation-states along the Western model has been to deprive women of the political influence they seem to have had in many indigenous African societies. Formally legislated equality cannot compensate for the erosion of such influence.

Women and the Political Economy

Discussion of international human rights includes agreement that economic or subsistence rights are as important as civil and political rights. The omnibus 1979 convention on women's rights specifies what such economic rights should (in part) entail, particularly in Article 14. Special attention is paid to the rights of women to have access to health care, family-planning facilities, social security programs, education, and adequate living conditions. Moreover, the rights of rural women to take part in development programs and to have equal access to agricultural credit and equal participation in cooperatives or agrarian reform schemes are stressed. Were such economic and social rights granted in practice, African women would benefit substantially.

The delegates to the 1980 International Women's Year conference at Copenhagen placed responsibility for impoverishment of women in underdeveloped countries clearly on the West. "[T]his impoverishment is due mainly to the consequences of colonialism and neo-colonialism, inequitable international relations and the aftermath of uncontrolled industrialization and urbanization."[11] This perspective implies that economic underdevelopment is the key to understanding the position of women in poor countries, and that economic development is the solution to their problems. As discussed in Chapter 4, there is some truth to the above argument. Nevertheless, while economic development would certainly alleviate many of the problems women face, it is not a complete solution. The analysis of the status of women cannot be separated, even in the poorest of countries, from class analysis. Their continued subordination is as contingent upon social divisions into rich and poor as it is upon the effects of the world economic system. Furthermore, women as a group suffer more from poverty than men as a group, a direct result of their sexual status. Not only is the perpetuation of poverty in the material interests of the wealthy, but the perpetuation of inequitable access to productive resources, and inequitable work loads between males and females, is in the material interests of men.

Clearly, all rural Africans, male and female, suffer from economic underdevelopment. Clean water, for example, is necessary for the good health of both sexes. But what water there is, clean or unclean, is provided by women, who can spend "as much as one-third of their work day locating and transporting water for drinking, agriculture, food production and preparation, and family hygiene."[12] There is no particular reason linked to world political economy why women, not men, should perform such labor. Yet African women have a very heavy dual load of productive and domestic labor, while men have the single load of productive labor only. Aside from performing all the housework, childcare, and care of husbands and the elderly, African women perform about 70 percent of the labor in self-help projects, 50 percent of house repairs, and 30 percent of house construction. They are also responsible for the majority of all food production, supply, and distribution, and for locating water and fuel.[13]

A typical Zambian woman, for example, works for fifteen hours a day during the planting season;[14] moreover, during much of her adult life (typically ending at age 48) she is pregnant, lactating, and/or carrying a baby on her back. Malnutrition affects women and children more severely than men. With their extremely heavy workload, women may literally not have the time to prepare proper meals or feed them to their children.[15] Overworked poor women also tend to eat irregularly or skip meals. Taboos against eating certain foods exacerbate the problem, as does the cultural practice, in some ethnic groups, of allowing the male head of household to eat first and most, while the children and (pregnant and nursing) mothers eat what is left over.[16]

In this context, the provision of "appropriate technology" for women, such as small grinding mills for flour, clotheslines, and small power saws for fuel, could substantially reduce their workload. Another suggestion is that day-care centers be provided.[17] Yet attendance at day-care centers could deprive children of essential socialization and learning of agricultural skills, and it could also have the highly detrimental effect of discouraging breast-feeding. Day-care centers are more suited to urbanized societies with complex divisions of labor than to agricultural societies in which children work alongside their mothers. The real problem is one of mothers' overwork, not childcare.[18] When no husband is present, women are even more overworked. The incidence of female-headed households in rural areas in Commonwealth Africa is increasing as a result of male rural-urban migration in search of employment. In Kenya it was estimated that in 1975 a third of rural households were headed by women.[19]

The normal expectation in most indigenous African societies is that women will contribute substantially to their own and their children's support, through agricultural work, marketing, or wage labor. Sixty to 80 percent of agricultural labor in Africa is women's work.[20] Yet although women must perform the bulk of the subsistence agricultural labor, and although Article 14 of the covenant prohibiting discrimination against women provides for "equal treatment in land and agrarian reform as well as in land resettlement schemes," women's access to land in contemporary Africa is rapidly declining. In Kenya, although a quarter of the household heads are women, only 5 percent of women own land in their own name.[21] In large part, the loss of land by women has been a result of the integration of Africa into the world trade system, particularly as a consequence of the introduction of cash crops.

In Tsito, Ghana, for example, once men started to grow cocoa for cash they increased women's labor load by obliging their wives to "help" them—without pay—on their cocoa land while continuing to cultivate subsistence crops. Men also took over the better land for cocoa. As a result, the women of Tsito switched from cultivating yams to cultivating cassava, a food with far less nutritional value. Cassava can grow on poorer land and takes much less labor time to cultivate than yams.[22] Similarly in Kenya, infant malnutrition has been found to correlate with devotion of land to cash crops, especially tea and sugar. This suggests that women have neither decision-making power over whether to devote land to cash or subsistence crops, nor control over income from cash crops, with which they might purchase the food they can no longer cultivate themselves: "cash incomes tend to be at the disposal of husbands, whatever labor has been contributed by wives."[23] Dependence on world commodities markets undoubtedly contributes to the impoverishment of rural Africans, but the extra impoverishment of women is a consequence of indigenous cultural patterns regarding male control of land.

Women's use of land is contingent upon male permission. While men have the right to allocate land, women have only the declining right of access to land.[24] Since the beginning of the colonial period, Luo women in Kenya have had decreasing rights of access. As a result of the pressure upon land consequent upon the creation of the reserves system by the British, men began to usurp the customary use rights of women. In addition, the British introduced formal land registration in the names of individual, not lineage, title-holders and, because of their own cultural biases, registered land only in men's names. The independent Kenyan government chose to continue this practice, with the result that Luo women can now find themselves landless as their sons sell their land out from under them to finance their own migrations to the city.[25]

While Kenya, formerly dominated by settler farmers, presents perhaps the extreme case of removal of land from women's control, the pattern is similar throughout Commonwealth Africa. Even in Tanzania, which purports to base its economy on "African socialism" with roots in the indigenous organization of society, women are losing land rights. In some new ujamaa villages in formerly matrilineal areas, women settlers, who had had clearly defined land-use rights in their original communities, suddenly found themselves with no land-use rights in the new society. Widows, for example, were expected to quit the land they had helped their husbands to settle.[26] In 1975 Tanzanian law was revised to give women in ujamaa villages half the land rights of men.[27]

The problem of land access is also a problem of access to agricultural credit and extension services. In Kenya, women provide 80 percent of the "self-help" labor vital to such projects as construction of roads, schools, and village community centers.[28] But despite the evidence of combined male out-migration, female farming, and female "manual" labor on such projects, in the "education of farmers in the use of modern farming and stock raising methods . . . it seems to be assumed . . . that Kenyan farmers are men."[29] Kenyan extension officers are more likely to visit male farmers than female; since their services include assistance in filling out applications for farm credit, this differential actively hinders female success in farming.[30]

Whatever the original colonial impetus to disorganize African societies by depriving women of their lineage-based land rights, male African administrators have continued the practice in the independence period. It may perhaps be the case that African administrators, trained as they are in Eurocentric educational establishments, have adopted European ideological models of male-female relations, which they rather unthinkingly apply to their own land and development programs.[31] On the other hand, such European biases regarding women's role may merely reinforce indigenous cultural beliefs that women, whatever their productive role, should be under men's authority.

A male bias is also evident in the educational programs available to women in Commonwealth Africa. Article 10 of the 1979 convention on discrimination against women contains a number of provisions regarding women's education, most of which have to do with guaranteeing a similar type of education to both males and females, and similar access to education to both sexes. In particular, Article 10,f, proposes "the reduction of female student drop-out rates and the organization of programs for girls and women who have left school prematurely." But much remains to be done in Commonwealth Africa to translate these goals into reality.

With regard to access to education, Table 4.4 indicates that in 1981, between 30 percent (Sierra Leone) and 101 percent (Kenya) of girls of the relevant age group were enrolled in primary school. As for secondary school enrollments, figures for 1975 indicate that for girls aged 12–17, the percentage enrolled ranged from 14 (Nigeria) to 42 (Zambia). From 18 to 23 years (senior secondary and postsecondary level) only between 1 and 4 percent were enrolled in 1975. Extremely few women have access to the technical and scientific training so important to future economic development.[32] The vast majority of women over 15 are illiterate; moreover, more women than men are illiterate.

To compound the problem, educational policies based on the British model result in girls being offered education that is unsuitable to the economic realities of African women. In 1975, the Economic Commission for Africa estimated that more than 50 percent of mass education for girls consisted of so-called "domestic science."[33] Much of the education at one Ghana girls' secondary school in the late 1960s actually consisted of learning how to behave like Europeans; how to "cut out European style dresses with the use of patterns . . . [and] to produce fancy English cakes and biscuits."[34] In Kenya, women being trained as agricultural extension officers are encouraged to focus on home economics, while male trainees study agricultural engineering and soil conservation.[35]

Even such obsolete and irrelevant education, however, teaches basic literacy and numeracy, knowledge that is less easily obtained by females than by males. There are many reasons why African parents, with limited resources for school fees, would prefer to educate boys. Girls are required at home to assist their mothers in their numerous productive, household, and child-rearing chores, while boys are more easily spared.[36] Parents may lose bride price if their daughters fail to marry at an early age; in any case, when daughters marry into another lineage their parents' investment in their education is lost.[37] Girls may also be obliged to drop out of school should they become pregnant, a common problem in Zambia.[38] In short, the loss of a young girl's labor time is more costly to her parents than the loss of a boy's, while the returns to her education, from the parents' point of view, are lower.[39]

Uneducated girls become uneducated women; female adult illiterates find it more difficult to attend adult literacy classes than do male.[40] Nevertheless, the evidence suggests that women will attend adult literacy classes when given the chance. The variance in the female proportion of such classes (43 percent in Ghana, almost 75 percent in Malawi, and 65 percent in Tanzania in 1968, as against only 16 percent in Sierra Leone) suggests that government policies may also be a factor affecting women's education.[41]

The discussions above on women in development and on women's education have touched upon the division of women into social classes. Whatever the differential between men's and women's labor in rural Commonwealth Africa, the wife of a rich peasant will have more economic resources at her command than the wife of a landless or quasi-landless proletarian. Indeed, it appears that poor women may sometimes work as laborers on the land of richer women.[42] Similarly, rich peasants may be able to invest in education of their daughters, whereas poor peasants may not. In the urban environment, the educated, professional woman will have many more opportunities open to her than the illiterate petty market trader or wage-worker. In this connection, then, development issues and analyses of possibilities for the attainment of human rights cannot be separated from an analysis of social stratification. For the purposes of this discussion, women's occupations will be used as indicators of their class positions. As few adult women in Commonwealth Africa are completely dependent on a male, to categorize their class position according to their husbands' occupations or incomes would be highly misleading.

African women have comparatively good access to professions such as law or medicine but, as in the western world, they have very little access to administrative and managerial positions, either in the private or the government sector.[43] Yet it is the latter positions that are powerful, especially in economies dominated by a combination of multinational corporations and state monopolies. The picture for educated women, therefore, seems to be one of differential access to high-status positions. This violates Article 11, 1, b, of the 1979 convention, which specifies that women should have the same employment opportunities as men. Nevertheless, highly educated women have better access to the basic amenities of existence and more resources to fight for their rights, than the mass of women who work for wages or in trade in the cities.

Opportunities to work for salary are limited. Far fewer women are in the clerical or service occupations in Commonwealth Africa than in the West. Women constituted between 7 percent (Ghana) and 21 percent (Zambia) of such workers in 1968.[44] Clerical occupations, implying literacy and the status of being engaged in a nonmanual occupation, are dominated by men in Africa.[45] Formal domestic service also tends to be a male occupational category. The chief occupation for women in the urban areas, in West Africa in particular, is in trade.

There is, in the minds of many analysts of the West African urban scene, a pleasant fiction that the "market mammy" controlling vast fortunes in cloth, soap, or food is typical of the West African woman trader.[46] But most women traders are engaged in a very marginal, day-to-day existence, selling tiny quantities of one or two commodities, such as steel wool or cigarettes, or preparing food to sell to male workers on the streets.[47] Even the wealthier women traders have to contend with the problem that the more they make, the less money their husbands may give them as a contribution to family support.[48] Most women traders are more accurately called hawkers. While their economic activity is crucial to the circulation of goods in underdeveloped economies with limited large-scale wholesaling, retailing, and transportation establishments, their long-term survival, both as a group and as individuals, is precarious. As a group they are likely to be pushed out of trade as more (male-dominated) formal trading establishments are organized, either privately or by the state.[49] As individuals, their opportunities are blocked. Nevertheless, the attitude of "fear woman" results in an inaccurate picture of women traders as extremely powerful. In Ghana during the first Rawlings regime (1979), women traders were harassed, flogged, and in one case executed for allegedly hoarding goods, and thus, it was argued, contributing to that country's runaway inflation.[50]

Many urban women must thus turn to the sale of sexual services to make a living. It is commonplace in African cities for men to refer to all unattached women as prostitutes. In 1984, the government of Kano State (Nigeria) gave all unmarried women three month's notice to get married or risk being arrested for "loitering." The purpose of the law, allegedly to prevent "moral laxity," clearly shows the connection of women's unmarried status with prostitution.[51] This attitude in Africa suggests that there are large numbers of women whose only economic activity is streetwalking. In fact, however, "prostitution" often means that a woman establishes a series of nonmarital relationships with different men, all of whom are expected to provide her and her children with some material support. In other cases women must take up short-term prostitution to supplement their activities in trade, food preparation, and other marginal urban occupations. The most successful "prostitutes" invest in real estate or other businesses. Prostitution in Africa, as elsewhere, should not be analyzed as a moral issue, but rather as a reflection of women's extremely limited economic opportunities.

African women have very few opportunities in the steady wage sector, where the vast majority of jobs are held by men. Women are likely, if they are fortunate enough to be able to engage in wage labor in the first place, to be hired part time and at lower wages than males. In one Nigerian case study, it was found that a textile factory employed 1,300 men but only 62 women. Even these few women had been hired only because the state governments that owned the factory had made a rhetorical commitment to equality for women. The women were confined to unskilled "reserved" jobs with no opportunity for promotion within the factory.[52] In northern Nigeria, Hausa women working on a European-owned farm (growing vegetables for the European market) earned only about 15 percent of male workers' wage in the late 1970s.[53] Women farm-workers in Brong-Ahafo (Ghana) in 1973 were paid only half of men's wages and did not receive the same fringe benefits of meals, clothing, shelter, and medical care.[54] In Tanzania "there are no laws guaranteeing equal job opportunites and . . . sexual discrimination is rampant."[55]

The public role of women as active producers in rural agricultural societies, therefore, has not served to protect them against inequitable conditions in the modern sector. Rather, their pattern follows the European: from productive but subordinate rural worker, to subordinate and exploited female proletarian, to subordinate and economically dependent wife of the westernized ruling-class male. Robertson notes that "Central Accra women tend to equate financial dependence on a husband with high-status marriage."[56] Modernization for the ruling-class woman thus can have the contradictory effect of raising her material well-being while reinforcing her indigenous cultural subordination with the Western ideology of female economic dependence, privatization, and confinement to the home as a decorative symbol of her husband's prosperity. The elite African woman may prefer to brave the cultural stigma of being unmarried as an alternative to this stifling life.[57] To understand why African women are confronted with such limited choices, we must turn to an analysis of the cultural expectations regarding relationships between women and men.

Law and Custom: Women's Rights in the Personal Sphere

The rights of women in marriage and family matters are central to their rights as individuals. Insofar as women's lives are affected far more profoundly than are men's by their reproductive roles, lack of rights in this area can effectively mean that women cannot exercise any rights they may formally have in other areas. Nevertheless, the assurance of rights for women in this most personal of spheres is a complex matter, given that most societies value the preservation of the family as much as they purport to value individual freedom. If woman is the linchpin of the family, can her rights then be considered more important than those of the larger group? In Commonwealth Africa, where extended families predominate and marriages are usually a matter of lineage concern, this question is even more pressing than it is in areas where the nuclear family prevails. The customs of child betrothal, arranged marriage, bridewealth, and widow inheritance, all of which contravene United Nations provisions for human rights, are central to the organization of society. Marriages based on these principles are generally contracted in good faith, and the people who arrange the marriage are attempting to obtain a satisfactory outcome both for the individuals concerned and for the lineages that are allied by the particular marriage.[58]

The best position to take regarding this dilemma is one of "weak" cultural relativity.[59] That is to say, a sensitive understanding of the meaning and value of custom should temper any imposition of universal norms of human rights that, although philosophically valid, are not yet fully accepted by ordinary people (as opposed to the ruling class) in a society. Weak cultural relativism cannot be used to deny the existence of any right in principle. It can, however, be used to modify the implementation of a right so as not to offend the basic integrative norms of a society, as long as it is understood that those norms may well change, thus requiring the full implementation of a right under dispute at a later date. Advocacy of immediate implementation in Commonwealth Africa of laws that conform to U.N. provisions for women's rights in the sphere of marriage and the family could be interpreted as an imposition of a secularized, individualistic view of human relations upon Africa. On the other hand, there is almost universal evidence that marriage customs are hinged on the subordination of women as a group to men as a group. Customs are neither immutable in time nor neutral in their impact.

In Chapter 2 three principles were proposed regarding culture that can serve as a guide in understanding the difficulties in implementing women's rights in Commonwealth Africa. First, people value customs even when they seem to be irrational to an outsider; the symbolic value is a real personal value. Second, culture and customs can change endogenously, not merely as a result of colonialism or contact with Westernization or urbanization. Finally, just as those who attempt to modify or change customs may have personal interests in that change, so also do those who attempt to preserve customs. The preservation of custom can mask real conflicts over economic or political resources.

The discussion of cultural relativity is especially pertinent in Commonwealth Africa because of the continued existence, in all the countries under consideration except Tanzania, of more than one code of law. In most Commonwealth African countries there are customary and formal legal sectors, the latter being exemplified in the case of marriage law by the Marriage Ordinance. Codification of customary law is complicated by the fact that each ethnic group has its own customs, so that conflicts can occur, for example, when two people of different ethnic groups marry. In addition, some countries provide separate laws for Muslims, and Kenya also has a separate Hindu law for its Asian-origin citizens.

In this connection Tanzania's decision to adopt a unified marriage law, with new provisions, for instance that the rights of the child should be paramount in custody cases, is of particular interest. By abolishing legal pluralism, it puts all marriages on an equal footing. It also subordinates customs, including Islamic customs, to a secular, legal framework.[60] It is interesting that the Tanzanian law is based upon a proposed reform of Kenyan law that did not go through Parliament. The Kenyan Law Reform Commission had been instructed to frame a uniform law of marriage, paying "particular attention to the status of women." Two of the principles underlying the commission's report are of special interest: that "any such *uniform law must be founded in the African way of life*, always bearing in mind, however, that that way of life is rapidly changing," and that "the law must be based on a recognition of human dignity, regardless of sex."[61] Despite the stating of these principles, objections to the bill, from members of Parliament as well as others, included the idea that it was "un-African" and gave too many rights to women. It can by no means be taken for granted that the men in power in Commonwealth Africa will willingly grant women equal rights. In the culturally sacrosanct family, men retain a material, sexual, and moral dominance that many are unwilling to relinquish.

The custom of polygyny, which is permitted by both traditional and Islamic law in Commonwealth Africa (including Tanzania, where unification of the law has not prohibited polygyny), is often cited as an example of male dominance. There is no provision in any United Nations or Organization of African Unity convention, nor indeed in any International Women's Year recommendation, that polygyny should be abolished; nevertheless, its continuance is a matter of debate among Africans. The Economic Commission for Africa, for example, has advocated its abolition, although not by changes in the law.[62]

The case against polygyny seems to be that it is considered demeaning for one man to "own" several wives, and that it is impossible for the ideal of a companionate marriage based upon love, trust and mutual respect to be realized in a multiple-wife situation. From the wives' point of view, polygyny also means that they and their children must share their husband's material, emotional, and sexual resources; that they will be plagued by rivalry; and that senior wives will fear younger, prettier wives, while junior wives will live under the senior wives' authority.[63]

The case for polygyny, from the man's point of view, is that it allows him to accrue economic resources of female labor-power, and that it ensures him the status and long-term material security of large numbers of children.[64] From the woman's point of view, polygyny provides other women to share in child-rearing, husband care, and possible economic ventures such as marketing; it provides companionship; and it ensures her the right to postpartum celibacy so that she can space her children.[65]

The assumption among most women is that husbands are necessarily unfaithful; the Christian ideal of monogamy is seen as unrealistic. While men married under the Marriage Ordinance are not legally permitted to take customary wives as well, they often do so. This results in a situation in which the Ordinance wife has legal rights while the customary wives do not. The trend, therefore, in African legal reform circles is not to advocate that polygyny be abolished, but rather to advocate that marriages of all types (and wives of all types) be on an equal legal footing.[66]

Polygyny is in fact related to a complex of customs, prevalent in indigenous African societies, that violate U.N. norms: these include bridewealth (the payment made by a prospective husband to the bride's family), arranged marriages, child betrothal, and widow inheritance. To those who believe in the individual's right to choose her spouse, the ideas of child betrothal, arranged marriage in return for a monetary consideration, or the "inheritance" of a widow by her deceased male husband's relative, are certainly abhorrent. Yet these practices are far from abhorrent in a society that regards marriage as an alliance between lineages, that believes young people are incapable of making reasoned decisions regarding their future spouses, and that wishes to protect widows by providing them with a new male guardian on the death of their husbands.

Indications are contradictory, for example, whether bridewealth means that a daughter is subject to sale by her father. As late as 1980, Obbo argued that among the Nilotic groups of Uganda, "the amount of bridewealth determined the extent of the vested interest male lineage members . . . had in their women," whereas among the Buganda, bridewealth had declined to a mere token.[67] Writing in the early 1960s, Izzert noted that among the Yoruba, "acceptance [of bridewealth] indicates approval of the marriage and a willingness to render assistance if the bride's husband dies or turns out to be unreliable, the assistance being given to the bride and her children."[68] In the past, then, bridewealth served as a form of insurance. A man who divorced his wife without cause permanently forfeited his brideprice, which could then be used to support his wife and children. Similarly, a wife who left her husband without cause would know that her family would be obliged to return the brideprice. Nowadays, there are signs that "Fathers [are] tempted to hold up their daughters to the highest bidder";[69] yet among the more modernized population, "there is a growing tendency among educated parents . . . to refuse all money payments, saying their daughter is not for sale."[70]

Bridewealth is practiced extensively in Commonwealth Africa. An attempt to abolish it by legislation could well interfere with traditional means of protecting a woman from abuse by her husband. It seems that among the elite population the practice will die out in any case, as a new ideology of women's autonomy takes hold. The sensible legal course to take would probably be not to abolish the practice outright, but merely to ensure the right of any woman not to be subjected to the practice if she chooses otherwise.

The same principle should probably be applied to arranged marriages and child betrothal. No one should be forced against her or his will to enter a marriage. Registration of all marriages, and the enforcement of a rule that marriages can be finally formalized only after the age of majority has been reached, would ensure a mechanism to ascertain whether both spouses agreed to the marriage. Parental pressure would, however, still influence a young woman's decision.[71] Legislation cannot control how decisions to marry are made, but it can provide a means by which a young woman who wishes to escape from traditional family controls can do so. It can also embody a new ideology that can act as an impetus toward future relaxation of community norms.

A similar analysis can be applied to the custom of widow inheritance. Sagay discusses the case of a Yoruba *Oba* (chief) who inherited 50 "palace wives" on his succession.[72] The issue at hand was whether the Oba could actually marry these 50 women under customary law, since he had already married one woman under the monogamous Marriage Ordinance. One solution posited was that as long as the women were merely "institutional wives" and the marriages were not consummated, they would be legal. Such a solution suggests that widow inheritance is actually a form of protection for women; by being formally affiliated to a man from their husband's lineage, they maintain their residence rights and (limited) rights to support.[73] Sagay notes that "In modern times, an Oba's widow who does not wish to become the wife of her husband's successor may move out of the palace."[74] In practice, however, such a choice may not be tenable, since, in many parts of Africa, a woman who is not a wife is a woman without any rights to her children or property.[75]

The above statement brings up the necessity for women to have real, economic rights in marriage and at its dissolution by divorce or death. In this sense, inequitable access to divorce constitutes a discriminatory liability under which women suffer. Article 16, 1, c, of the 1979 convenant prohibiting discrimination against women guarantees women and men "the same rights and responsibilities during marriage and at its dissolution." But this right is not necessarily provided for all women in Commonwealth Africa. Muslim women are under the greatest legal disability. In Kenya and Sierra Leone, a Muslim husband can divorce his wife by repudiation, and even in Tanzania, a Muslim husband's repudiation can be taken as evidence of irreparable marriage breakdown.[76] Customary law seems to guarantee the most rights for women in divorce; marriage breakdowns are matters for negotiation between the two families. Nevertheless, matters to be negotiated can discriminate against women. For example, a husband can divorce a wife for barrenness or adultery, whereas she cannot leave him for the same reasons.

Moreover, a divorced wife may not have rights to maintenance for herself or her children, or even to retention of property acquired during marriage. Such a fact is not surprising. In indigenous societies, wives are expected to provide much of their and their children's own support through agricultural and marketing activities; the divorced wife presumably can return to her own lineage and acquire land-use rights there, so she is not in need of maintenance. Unfortunately, the contemporary urban or rural landless wife does not have the same resources at her command. The westernized wife married under the Ordinance, moreover, is subject to discriminatory provisions of British law, which assume that a wife's housework is not an economic contribution to the household, and which provide very weak sanctions against husbands who default on maintenance payments.

Article 16 1, h, of the 1979 convention against discrimination against women provides "the same rights for both spouses in respect of the ownership, acquisition, management, administration, enjoyment and disposition of property." This provision is acknowedged in some court decisions in Commonwealth Africa, so that educated urban women, who have the resources to avail themselves of the courts, have some recourse against ex-husbands who default or do not offer maintenance payments. In other cases even educated women have no such recourse: in 1969 Kenya repealed its Affiliation Act, which obliged fathers of children born out of wedlock to pay for their support.[77] In the customary sector the wife seems to be dependent upon family negotiations and the assumption of good-will between the two parties. For women living in "detribalized" urban settings, or married outside of their own ethnic groups, such provisions are of limited use.

The final area in which women suffer legal discrimination is in the matter of custody law. Article 16, 1, d, of the 1979 covenant specifies that women and men shall have "the same rights and responsibilities as parents . . . in matters relating to their children; in all cases the interests of the children shall be paramount." In Commonwealth Africa, however, the presumption seems to be that fathers' rights to custody are paramount, even in supposedly matrilineal societies. Although the interests of the child are supposedly paramount in Kenya, in practice "some judges insist on using the traditional concepts which considered the father as the 'owner' of the child."[78] Schuster reported that some of the mothers she interviewed in Lusaka (Zambia) did not want to accept badly needed maintenance payments from the fathers, as the father would then claim he had the right to custody of the children when they were older.[79] In many instances, as in Sierra Leone, the mother bears the full burden of raising the child until it is about seven; the child is then removed from her.[80] Aside from whatever emotional feelings a mother may have for a child she has raised for seven years, when she loses a child she loses a valuable economic resource, both for assistance in her day-to-day chores and as security for her old age.

Two themes run through the above discussion of women's rights in marriage. The first is that although many women may prefer to live under those customs with which they are most familiar, even though the customs deny them personal freedom, international human rights legislation, as well as some of the legislation of the countries concerned, requires that they be able to remove themselves from the control of these customs should they so desire. The second theme is that formal economic rights of women in marriage are becoming increasingly necessary as customary means for providing for women and children within the lineage break down.

A third comment which can be made regarding women's rights in the marriage and family sphere in Commonwealth Africa is that a number of the concerns of "western" feminists have been inadequately addressed in the United Nations and in individual African countries. These concerns are the sharing of domestic responsibilities, the issue of violence against women, and rights of women to control over their own reproductive systems.

To ignore these concerns under the pretense that they are indications of Western bias is to show disregard of the true nature of relationships between men and women in Africa. Regarding domestic labor, this chapter has clearly demonstrated that women do an inordinate share of productive and domestic labor. The provision of Article 16, 1, d, of the convenant prohibiting discrimination against women that both men and women share "the same rights and responsibilities as parents" may be interpreted to mean that men should share in day-to-day child-rearing chores. Yet there is no mention or discussion of this possibility in the literature on human rights.

Likewise, there is no specific mention of the problem of violence against women in the various United Nations covenants, although the 1980 International Women's Year conference did recommend that "Legislation should . . . be enacted and implemented in order to prevent domestic and sexual violence against women."[81] In Africa, violence against women usually takes the form of wife-beating, rather than of rape. (Although even here, the evidence is not clear; Schuster reports of her research sample in Lusaka that "Nearly everyone has submitted to sexual relations out of fear of the consequences of refusing.")[82] Izzert reported of her Yoruba sample that "married women often complain of physical cruelty—usually of frequent beatings without any justification."[83] In a large percentage of Nigerian divorce cases cruelty is cited as the reason for the divorce.[84] A number of cultures in East Africa give positive approval to wife-beating.[85] Among the Kaonde of Zambia, "It is accepted by both men and women that a man has the right to beat his wife."[86] Among the Teso of Uganda a man has a traditional right to beat his wife on the buttocks with a small stick but, according to one Teso woman, "that the stick grew in size and the area of the buttocks became the whole body is borne out by cases of severe wife-beating in Teso."[87]

Violence against women seems to be exacerbated by women's increasing tendency to step out of their presumptive roles, especially in urban areas. Mushanga explains wife-murder partly by the fact that many men believe that women should "remain subservient" to their husbands, and that they become enraged when their wives do not do so.[88] Men seem to use violence as a form of social control when communal norms break down and women assume freedom. The single woman of the city, who defies convention by living independent of a man, is especially likely to incite male hostility. Presumably the assumption that she is a "loose woman" can be used as a justification for attacking her, as sporadic assaults against women in miniskirts in Malawi, Tanzania, and Kenya, and periodic attempts to expel "prostitutes" (single women) from the city testify.[89] "Men are angry at women because they are no longer subservient";[90] but to defend oneself against violence from men by the assumption of a subservient role seems faint protection. This is an area in which cultural beliefs may require legislation, in conformity with the provision of the African Charter on Human and Peoples' Rights that "human beings are inviolable."

Finally, the provisions for women's rights to control their own reproductive powers are ambiguous. The 1979 covenant prohibiting discrimination against women reflects most U.N. documents in its provision (Article 16, 1, e) that women and men have "the same rights to decide freely and responsibly on the number and spacing of their children and to have access to the information, education, and means to enable them to exercise these rights." This statement ignores the reality that the burden of child-bearing falls only on women, and of child-rearing disproportionately on women. Moreover, there are differences between husbands and wives regarding desired numbers of children. For example, a study of nine rural Yoruba couples revealed that the husbands' ideal number of children was eleven, while the wives' was six.[91] The men in this small sample, as in many other cases, also preferred boys, so that wives can be compelled to bear children until they produce the requisite number of sons. Given the cultural domination of men in decision-making, combined with their physical capacity to impose sexual relations on their wives, the reality of the matter is that men usually have the last word on family size, as the Economic Commission for Africa has recognized.[92] Moreover, the "means to enable" the right to determine the number and spacing of children are denied to women insofar as abortion is denied by legislation, as in Kenya, Ghana, and probably other Commonwealth African countries.[93] Akingba found that "while Nigerian men still contend that all pregnancies are welcome, the incidence of unwanted pregnancies, and hence abortion, in both single and married women is a major problem."[94] In Accra, one of every four or five pregnancies is estimated to end in abortion.[95]

Female Genital Operations

The question of control by women over their own bodies includes, in Commonwealth Africa, the issue of female genital operations. This issue has received much attention in the Western press and among Western feminists since about 1979.[96] Much of the Western reaction has been couched in terms verging on the racist. Circumcision, both male and female, has been cited in Christian Europe for centuries as evidence not only that Africans, but also that Australian aborigines and, indeed,

European Jews are a lesser form of being.[97] A conference of African women meeting in Lusaka in 1979 referred specifically to the "moral and cultural prejudices of Judeo-Christian Western society" as influencing the "new [feminist] crusaders" against female genital operations, arguing that Western feminists are "totally unconscious of the latent racism which such a campaign [against female genital operations] evokes."[98] Hence, in contemporary debates about female genital operations, it is important to keep in mind the ideological context of previous discussions. To avoid discussion of the practice altogether, however, or to interpret it, as anthropological functionalists have done in the past, merely as an integrative indigenous custom,[99] is to avoid confrontation of its detrimental effects on women.

I use the term "female genital operations" rather than the term "female circumcision" because the latter term is inaccurate. Circumcision, the removal of the clitoris, is the mildest form of this operation, which also includes excision, or "the cutting of the clitoris and all or part of the labia minora" and infibulation, or "the cutting of the clitoris, labia minora and at least the anterior two-thirds and often the whole of the medial part of the labia majora."[100] "Several tens of millions of women" are estimated to have undergone these operations in Africa as a whole.[101] The operations are widespread in Ghana, Kenya, Nigeria, Sierra Leone, and northeast Tanzania. Infibulation appears to be practiced in northern Nigeria and northern Kenya, and excision in Kenya, northern Tanzania, Nigeria, Ghana, and Sierra Leone; some ethnic groups merely practice circumcision. Other ethnic groups, such as the Bemba in Zambia and the Luo in Kenya, do not practice any form of genital operation. While rejecting the term "female circumcision," this book does not adopt the currently fashionable term "female genital mutilation" in its place. The latter term implies a deliberate intent to mutilate (as in torture), which is not at the root of the practice, even though objectively, women are mutilated.

Overwhelming medical evidence proves that even the mildest form of this operation can, and often does, have very serious medical consequences. These consequences include

> shock, haemorrhage with often fatal results, infections complicated by tetanus, urinary retention, damage to urethra or anus, gynaecological complications resulting from ill-performed cuts, chronic pelvic infections, callous formation, infertility caused by damage to vital organs and infections, obstetric complications resulting in delayed labour or inability to deliver a baby normally [resulting in foetal death or brain damage].[102]

There is absolutely no evidence that female genital operations contribute to hygiene, as is sometimes claimed as their justification; on the contrary, retention of urine or menstrual flow as a result of excision or infibulation is extremely unhygienic.

The operations also have the consequence of interfering with basic physiological responses to sexual stimulation. This is fully acknowledged by the many Africans who cite (somewhat erroneously), as justification for the practice, that it will control promiscuity in young women. Some Western feminists therefore view female genital operations as a deliberate form of "sexual castration," an example of "contempt for the female of the species."[103] Sexuality, however, is a sociological and psychological as well as a physiological phenomenon, and it may be possible for African women to enjoy their sexual relationships even after having undergone these operations.

In any case, attribution of the origin of the practice to gross misogyny (woman-hatred) seems unwarranted. The origins are obscure. They may represent an attempt by males to control female reproductive powers or female sexuality. Some informants say that both male and female circumcision are intended to remove the "female" parts of males and the "male" parts of females; in this regard, the practice represents one among many attempts to impose order on an uncertain natural world. While some assume that female genital operations are required under Islam, this appears to be a misinterpretation of Islamic teachings.[104] Many women say that they perform genital operations on their daughters, or undergo them themselves, as otherwise they or their daughters would be unmarriageable. It would be useful to ascertain if women would still perform the operations on their daughters if they could be assured their daughters would be marriageable without them.

While, in general, it is educated African women who have publicly spoken out against the continuation of female genital operations, some adult, educated women have voluntarily undergone them. These cases serve as evidence for the proposition posed earlier that people value cultural practices even when they seem to be irrational or even harmful. Apparently many West African women regard female genital operations as sacrifices to ensure fertility.[105] A further rationale, in the eyes of those who practice female genital operations, is that they connect the individual to the ethnic group of which she is a part, as a mature, respected adult. Moreover, the practice may have a general symbolic meaning for the whole group, as male circumcision has for Jews. Jomo Kenyatta, defending female circumcision among the Kikuyu in the 1930s in response to British missionary efforts to suppress it,[106] argued that the practice was central to the entire symbolic and age-grading organization of society.[107] Writing of the Temne and Mende in Sierra Leone, a contemporary African scholar has suggested that "[female genital operations have] unquestionably become part and parcel of their existence. . . . by eradicating the practice, one is setting in motion a chain reaction that will have far-reaching social, cultural and psychological effects."[108]

Defenders of female genital operations seize upon such arguments to maintain that the custom is so culturally central that to abolish it would be to destroy the very fabric of society. In response, critics note that much of the ritual surrounding the custom has disappeared, and it is done at younger and younger ages, partly to avoid external censure and partly because girls run away to avoid "the razor." On the other hand, one could argue that if all that is left of an initiation ceremony is the operation itself, its symbolic importance may be even larger than it was before. Perhaps a better way to discuss the problem is to note that cultures change, and that people can learn to develop an identity through new ways, for example, as one female MP in Kenya suggested, "the expansion of girls' education as an alternative means of achieving self-identity."[109] Thus changes in one custom can be compensated for by adjustments in another; an ethnic group can identify itself by its language or its territory, rather than by its ritual.

What, then, ought to be done with regard to this practice? It is clearly detrimental to women's and children's health, and as such violates a number of United Nations and OAU principles regarding basic human rights, including Article 25, 2, of the Universal Declaration of Human Rights, which states that "Motherhood and childhood are entitled to special care and assistance"; and Articles 4 and 16 of the African Charter of Human and Peoples' Rights, regarding the inviolability of the human body, and the right to health. Female genital operations also violate provisions in the 1959 Declaration of the Rights of Children that children should be "protected from all forms of cruelty [and] have the possibility to develop physically in a healthy and normal way."[110]

In 1979, the Economic Commission for Africa condemned "infibulation and other female sexual mutilations" and called for an educational campaign and government assistance to attempt to eradicate these practices, while at the same time condemning international campaigns on the subject that "do not take into account the complexity of the African situation."[111] A year later the Organization of African Unity also condemned female genital operations.[112] It would seem that, for the moment at least, an educational campaign directed particularly at health professionals, school-girls, and patients in maternity clinics would be the most appropriate manner of beginning elimination of the custom. Legislation banning female genital operations might merely drive the operations underground, as it appears to have done in the Sudan.[113] Legislation that permits the operation only with the consent of the woman or girl involved might be considered, but such legislation would not solve the problem of genital operations on minor females. Clearly, operations upon adult females without their consent could be made illegal.

Since the overwhelming medical evidence is against female genital operations, and the practice is condemned by leading African women as well as by Western feminists, attempts to perpetuate it must be analyzed within the framework of the third proposition regarding culture presented in the previous section; namely, that those who attempt to retain a custom, as well as those who attempt to change it, may have personal interests in so doing. Men who oppose abolition of female genital operations may do so out of ignorance; it would be incumbent upon them, especially if they are academics, journalists, or political leaders, to avail themselves of the facts. Ogunmodende believes that in Nigeria most male political leaders support abolition.[114] If, with medical evidence in hand, men still oppose abolition on cultural grounds, then one must at least ask whether men as a group benefit from a system that restricts women's physiological capacity to enjoy sexual relations, and obliges them to undergo a painful operation that leaves many traumatized and passive.[115] It must be kept in mind, regardless of the specific issue, that the subordination of women to men in the cultural, economic, and political spheres, in Commonwealth Africa as elsewhere, is of direct benefit to men. It is neither a mere cultural hangover, a result of colonial ideological control, nor a consequence of world economic patterns.

Notes

1. Proclaimed by the General Assembly of the United Nations, 7 November 1967, resolution 2263 (XXII).

2. The Constitution of the Republic of Ghana, Chapter 5, 15, 3 and 4, in Albert P. Blaustein and Gisbert H. Flanz, eds., *Constitutions of the Countries of the World* (Dobbs Ferry, N.Y.: Oceana Publications, issued July 1980).

3. U.N. A/6647/Rev.1, Commission on the Status of Women: Report of the Secretary General, "Constitutions, Electoral Laws and Other Legal Instruments Relating to the Political Rights of Women" (New York: United Nations, 1968), table 4, pp. 121–35. This source does not mention Tanzania; however, I assume women were granted equal political rights to men in Tanzania at independence.

4. M. Louise Pirouet, "Religion in Uganda under Amin," *Journal of Religion in Africa* 11, no.1 (1980): 20. See also, *Africa Contemporary Record*, vol. 9 (1976–77), p. B385.

5. See Chapter 7 of this volume.

6. The *Sunday News* (Tanzania), January 31, 1982, p. 7.

7. Carol P. Hoffer, "Mende and Sherbro Women in High Office," *Canadian Journal of African Studies* 6, no. 2 (1972), special issue on women, ed. Audrey Wipper, p. 151.

8. Annie M. D. Lebeuf, "The Role of Women in the Political Organization of African Societies," in Denise Paulme, ed., *Women of Tropical Africa* (Berkeley: University of California Press, 1971), pp. 95–96.

9. Kamene Okonjo, "The Dual-Sex Political System in Operation: Igbo Women and Community Politics in Midwestern Nigeria," in Nancy J. Hafkin and Edna G. Bay, eds., *Women in Africa* (Stanford: Stanford University Press, 1976), p. 45.

10. Judith Van Allen, "Aba Riots or the Igbo Women's War?—Ideology, Stratification and the Invisibility of Women," *Ufahamu* 6, no. 1 (1975): 11–12.

11. U.N. A/CONF.94/35, "Report of the World Conference of the United Nations Decade for Women: Equality, Development and Peace" (Copenhagen, July 14–30, 1980), p. 90. Hereafter referred to as IWY 1980.

12. Ibid., pp. 87–88.

13. U.N. E/CONF.66/BP/8–8/Add.1, Economic Commission for Africa, "The Role of Women in African Development" (10 April 1975), prepared for the World Conference of the International Women's Year, Mexico City, p. 23. Hereafter referred to as ECA 1975.

14. Economic Commission for Africa, "Report on Five Workshops in Home Economics and Other Family-Oriented Fields" (1973), quoted in ECA 1975, p. 7.

15. Suellen Huntington, "Issues in Woman's Role in Economic Development: Critique and Alternatives," *Journal of Marriage and the Family* 37 (November 1975): 1007.

16. U.N. A/CONF. 94/17, "Report of the Regional Preparatory Meeting of the United Nations Economic Commission for Africa, Second Regional Conference for the Integration of Women in Development" (prepared for IWY 1980), p. 10. Hereafter referred to as ECA 1980.

17. ECA 1975, pp. 23–25.

18. These observations regarding day care were brought to my attention by Omega Bula, a former Master's student in sociology at McMaster University.

19. ECA 1975, p. 17.

20. Ibid., p. 5.

21. Rayah Feldman, "Women's Groups and Women's Subordination: An Analysis of Policies Towards Rural Women in Kenya," *Review of African Political Economy* 27/28 (1983): 71.

22. Jette Bukh, *The Village Woman in Ghana* (Uppsala: Scandinavian Institute of African Studies, 1979). See also Grace Akello, *Self Twice-Removed: Uganda Women* (London: Change International Reports, n.d. [1983]), p. 11.

23. Feldman, "Women's Groups," pp. 71, 73.

24. Ibid., p. 74.

25. Achola Pala Okeyo, "Daughters of the Lakes and Rivers: Colonization and the Land Rights of Luo Women," in Mona Etienne and Eleanor Leacock, eds., *Women and Colonization: Anthropological Perspectives* (New York: Praeger, 1980), p. 206.

26. James L. Brain, "Less than Second-Class: Women in Rural Settlement Schemes in Tanzania," in Hafkin and Bay, eds., *Women in Africa*, p. 278.

27. James L. Brain, personal communication.

28. ECA 1975, p. 9.

29. Susan Abbott, "Women's Importance for Kenyan Rural Development," *Community Development Journal* 10, no. 3 (1975): 179–80.

30. Kathleen A. Staudt, "Administrative Resources, Political Patrons and Redressing Sex Inequities: A Case from Western Kenya," *Journal of Developing Areas* 12 (July 1978): 407–8.

31. Abbott,"Women's Importance for Kenyan Rural Development," p. 180.

32. Figures for 1975 from IWY 1980, U.N. A/34/577/Add.1/Rev.1 (23 May 1980), Addendum to *Report of the Secretary-General*, "Status and Role of Women in Education and in the Economic and Social Fields," p. 3, "Principal indicators of women's condition and participation in development" (indicators 8–12).

33. ECA 1975, p. 19.

34. Vandra Masemann, "The 'Hidden Curriculum' of a West African Girls' Boarding School," *Canadian Journal of African Studies* 8, no. 3 (1974): 484.

35. Feldman, "Women's Groups," p. 76.

36. Claire C. Robertson, *Sharing the Same Bowl: A Socioeconomic History of Women and Class in Accra, Ghana* (Bloomington: Indiana University Press, 1984), p. 144. See also Akello, *Self Twice-Removed*, p. 10.

37. U.N. OPI/CESI/NOTE IWY/15 (December 1974), Center for Economic and Social Information, "The Situation and Status of Women Today: Some Essential Facts," p. 4.

38. Ilsa M. Glazer Schuster, *New Women of Lusaka* (Palo Alto, Calif.: Mayfield, 1979), p. 44.

39. ECA 1980, pp. 10, 12. See also Deborah Pellow, *Women in Accra: Options for Autonomy* (Algonac, Mich.: Reference Publications, 1977), pp. 112–21.

40. U.N. OPI/CESI/NOTE IWY/15, p. 4.

41. Elise Boulding, Shirley A. Nuss, Dorothy Lee Carson, and Michael E. Greenstein, *Handbook of International Data on Women* (New York: Sage, 1976), p. 139.

42. Feldman, "Women's Groups," p. 72.

43. ECA 1975, p. 16.

44. Boulding et al., *Handbook of International Data on Women*, p. 100.

45. Ester Boserup, *Woman's Role in Economic Development* (New York: St. Martin's Press, 1970), p. 133.

46. See, for example, Mudiaga Odje, "Human Rights of African Women." Paper presented to the African Bar Association, Fourth Conference, Nairobi, Kenya, 1981, p. 8.

47. On Ghanaian women, see Robertson, *Sharing the Same Bowl*, pp. 106–17; on Ugandan women, see Christine Obbo, *African Women: Their Struggle for Economic Independence* (London: Zed Press, 1980), pp. 134–37.

48. Claire Robertson, "Ga Women and Socioeconomic Change in Accra, Ghana," in Hafkin and Bay, eds., *Women in Africa*, p. 120.

49. Dorothy Remy, "Underdevelopment and the Experience of Women: A Nigerian Case Study," in Rayna R. Reiter, ed., *Toward an Anthropology of Women* (New York: Monthly Review Press, 1975), p. 370.

50. Anne Fraker and Barbara Harrell-Bond, "Feminine Influence," *West Africa*, November 26, 1979, p. 2182; and Nii K. Bentsi-Enchill, "Destruction of Accra's Makola Market," *West Africa*, August 27, 1979, p. 1539.

51. The *Democrat Weekly* (Nigeria), April 8, 1984, p. 1.

52. Carolyne Dennis, "Capitalist Development and Women's Work: A Nigerian Case Study," *Review of African Political Economy* 27/28 (1983): 109–19.

53. Sam Jackson, "Hausa Women on Strike," *Review of African Political Economy* 13 (May–Aug. 1978): 24.

54. Robertson, *Sharing the Same Bowl*, p. 77.

55. Deborah Fahy Bryceson, "The Proletarianization of Women in Tanzania," *Review of African Political Economy* 17 (Jan.–Apr. 1980): 20.

56. Robertson, "Ga Women . . . in Accra," p. 125.

57. Carmel Dinan, "Pragmatists or Feminists? The Professional 'Single' Women of Accra, Ghana," *Cahiers d'Etudes Africaines* 17, no. 1 (1977): 164.

58. Yaa Luckham, "Law and the Status of Women in Ghana," *Columbia Human Rights Law Review* 8, no.1 (Spring–Summer 1976): 69.

59. Jack Donnelly, "Cultural Relativism and Universal Human Rights," *Human Rights Quarterly* 6, no. 4 (1984): 400–419. See also the discussion in Chapter 2.

60. Roberta Ann Dunbar, "Legislative Reform and Muslim Family Law: Effects upon Women's Rights in Africa South of the Sahara." Paper presented at the African Studies Association, Philadelphia, October 1980, p. 28.

61. Notes and News, "The Rejection of the Marriage Bill in Kenya," *Journal of African Law* 23, no. 2 (1979): 111. Emphasis in original.

62. ECA 1980, p. 33.

63. Helen Ware, "Polygyny: Women's Views in a Transitional Society, Nigeria 1975," *Journal of Marriage and the Family* 41 (February 1979): 185–95.

64. Felix K. Ekechi, "African Polygamy and Western Christian Ethnocentrism," *Journal of African Studies* 3 (August 1976): 331.

65. Ware, "Polygyny"; Huntington, "Issues in Women's Role in Economic Development"; and A. Izzert, "Family Life among the Yoruba, in Lagos, Nigeria," in Aidan Southall, ed., *Social Change in Modern Africa* (London: Oxford University Press, 1961).

66. Notes and News, "Rejection of the Marriage Bill," p. 112; Luckham, "Law and . . . Women in Ghana," p. 93; and C.E. Donegan, "Marriage and Divorce Law in Sierra Leone: A Microcosm of African Legal Problems," *Cornell International Law Journal* 5, no. 1 (1972): 63.

67. Obbo, *African Women*, pp. 51–52.

68. Izzert, "Family Life among the Yoruba," p. 309.

69. Aidan Southall, "Problems of the New Morality," *Journal of African Studies* 1 (Winter 1974): 384.

70. Izzert, "Family Life among the Yoruba," p. 308.

71. Rose Maina, V.W. Muchai, and S.B.O. Gutto, "Law and the Status of Women in Kenya," *Columbia Human Rights Law Review* 8, no. 1 (Spring–Summer 1976): 189.

72. Itse Sagay, "Widow Inheritance Versus Monogamous Marriage: The Oba's Dilemma," *Journal of African Law* 18, no. 2 (August 1974).

73. Lakshman Marasinghe, "Traditional Conceptions of Human Rights in Africa," in Welch and Meltzer, eds., *Human Rights and Development in Africa*, p. 40, also interprets widow inheritance as a form of protection for women.

74. Sagay, "Widow Inheritance," p. 169, fn. 3.

75. A.N. Allott, "The Legal Status of Women in Africa," *Journal of African Law* (1961): 128.

76. Dunbar, "Legislative Reform and Muslim Family Law," p. 31.

77. S.B.O. Gutto, "The Status of Women in Kenya: A Study of Paternalism, Inequality and Underprivilege," Discussion Paper no. 235, Institute for Development Studies, University of Nairobi (April 1976), p. 30.

78. Maina et al., "Law and . . . Women in Kenya," p. 194.

79. Schuster, *New Women of Lusaka*, p. 137.

80. Donegan, "Marriage and Divorce Law in Sierra Leone," p. 73.

81. IWY 1980, p. 13.

82. Schuster, *New Women of Lusaka*, p. 93.

83. Izzert, "Family Life among the Yoruba," p. 315.

84. Delores E. Mack, "Husbands and Wives in Lagos: The Effects of Socioeconomic Status on the Pattern of Family Living," *Journal of Marriage and the Family* 40, no. 4 (November 1978): 815.

85. Tibamanya M. Mushanga, "Wife Victimization in East and Central Africa," *Victimology* 2, nos. 3–4 (1977–78).

86. Kate Crehan, "Women and Development in North Western Zambia: From Producer to Housewife," *Review of African Political Economy* 27/28 (1983): 60.

87. Akello, *Self Twice-Removed*, p. 6.

88. Mushanga, "Wife Victimization," p. 484.

89. Audrey Wipper, "African Women, Fashion and Scapegoating," *Canadian Journal of African Studies* 6, no. 2 (1972), special issue on African women, ed. Audrey Wipper; Obbo, *African Women*, pp. 26–27. On urban expulsions, see also Chapter 5 of this volume.

90. Southhall, "Problems of the New Morality," p. 371.

91. Mack, "Husbands and Wives in Lagos," p. 809.

92. ECA 1980, p. 29.

93. See Maina et al., "Law and . . . Women in Kenya," p. 200; Luckham, "Law and . . . Women in Ghana," p. 90.

94. J. B. Akingba, *The Problem of Unwanted Pregnancies in Nigeria Today* (Lagos: University of Lagos Press, 1971), quoted in Mack, "Husbands and Wives in Lagos," p. 808.

95. D.A. Ampofo, "Abortion in Accra: The Social, Demographic and Medical Perspectives," in N.O. Addo et al., eds., *Symposium on Implications of Population Trends for Policy Measures in West Africa* (Ghanaian Population Studies, no.3, 1971), cited in Robertson, *Sharing the Same Bowl*, p. 223, fn. 119.

96. Fran P. Hosken, *The Hosken Report: Genital and Sexual Mutilation of Females* (Lexington, Mass: Women's International Network News, 1979).

97. Harriet Lyons, "Anthropologists, Moralities and Relativities: The Problem of Genital Mutilations," *Canadian Review of Sociology and Anthropology* 18, no. 4 (November 1981): 499–518.

98. Resolution presented by the Association of African Women for Research and Development to the Lusaka Regional Conference on Women in Development, December 1979; quoted in Barbara Harrell-Bond, "Women's Attitudes to Circumcision Dispute," *West Africa*, September 22, 1980, p. 1846.

99. Lyons, "Anthropologists, Moralities and Relativities," p. 507.

100. Scilla McLean, ed., *Female Circumcision, Excision and Infibulation: The Facts and Proposals for Change* (London: Minority Rights Group, 1980), p. 3.

101. Ibid., p. 3.

102. Esther Ogunmodende, "Female Circumcision in Nigeria," quoted in Hosken, *The Hosken Report*, "Case History: Nigeria," p. 8.

103. Hosken, *The Hosken Report*, p. 1.

104. McLean, *Female Circumcision*, p. 7.

105. Harrell-Bond, "Women's Attitudes to Circumcision Dispute," p. 1845.

106. Jocelyn Murray, "The Church Missionary Society and the 'Female Circumcision' Issue in Kenya 1929–32," *Journal of Religion in Africa* 8, no. 2 (1976).

107. Jomo Kenyatta, *Facing Mount Kenya* (London: Heinemann, 1979; lst ed. 1938), pp. 131–35.

108. J. Sorie-Conteh, "Circumcision and Secret Societies," *West Africa*, August 18, 1980, p. 1541.

109. McLean, *Female Circumcision*, p. 17.

110. Ibid., p. 10.

111. ECA 1980, pp. 43–44.

112. Organization of African Unity, "On the Rights and Welfare of the African Child," *Africa Contemporary Record*, vol. 12 (1979–80), p. C25.

113. McLean, *Female Circumcision*, p. 19.

114. Ogunmodende, "Nigeria," in ibid., p. 18.

115. McLean, *Female Circumcision*, p. 6.

⑨ Summary and Assessment

In general, my prediction for the condition of human rights in Commonwealth Africa in the near future (50 years) is not an optimistic one. In the historical, comparative sense, the nine countries under discussion have performed relatively better than other places in other times (e.g., Europe during its period of nation-building). But if the nine nations' performance is measured according to an absolute standard of substantive human rights, such as the two 1966 United Nations covenants or even the somewhat weaker African Charter of Human and Peoples' Rights, the picture is far less encouraging. Africa's colonial heritage, her absolute poverty, the newness and fragility of her nation-states, and her rapidly consolidating class structure all conspire to deny human rights to most of her citizens. There is little likelihood that the nine countries will be able to break out of this syndrome in the foreseeable future.

This chapter will first summarize the evidence that has led to this rather unhappy conclusion. Then a set of propositions regarding human rights in Commonwealth Africa will be presented and applied to the various debates regarding international human rights. The chapter will conclude with a discussion of possible future human rights scenarios under socialist, capitalist, or underdeveloped fascist regimes.

Summary

Taking as a starting point the most basic civil security rights of physical inviolability and preservation of one's personal freedom, the performance in Commonwealth Africa varies by country. The most large-scale attacks on citizens' physical security occurred during the civil war in Nigeria and during Idi Amin's murderous reign in Uganda, followed by an apparently equally murderous five-year regime under Milton Obote. In other parts of Commonwealth Africa, select minority groups have been victims of state terrorism; that is, deliberate physical harassment by agents of the state or the ruling party. For example, Kenyan Somalis have suffered mass murders and internments.

The more general pattern in Commonwealth Africa, however, is not large-scale terrorism against any and all potential threats to class or party rule, but rather selective use of deprivation of liberty against political activists. In seven of the nine countries, selective preventive detention without charges, formal trial, or effective review procedure is a common occurrence. The exceptions are Gambia, where the rule of law has been preserved despite the attempted coup of 1981, and Nigeria, where preventive detention (at least until the December 31, 1983, coup) was seldom used, even in periods of military rule.

There is absolutely no human rights justification for the continued use of state terrorism in Commonwealth Africa. State terrorism by Idi Amin was universally denounced by international human rights activists early in his regime, yet the OAU permitted Amin to be its chairman for one year, and the United Nations did not condemn him until 1977.[1] Of the countries under discussion in this volume, only Zambia and Tanzania condemned Amin; Tanzania eventually led the forces that overthrew him, at great financial cost (sacrifice of subsistence rights) to her own people. Considering the enormous political (class-dominated) difficulties that stood in the way of condemning even Idi Amin, it is easy to understand why state terrorism of the sort practiced by Kamuzu Banda continues unabated. Banda's terrorization of all perceived opponents of his regime is supplemented by murder of political dissidents either through outright terrorist activities or by quasi-judicial executions ordered by the controlled Traditional Courts. Other Commonwealth African countries, for example Kenya, have also used state terrorism at various times. In no case is there a human rights justification for its use, which is solely for the purpose of preserving the regime or individual in power.

Nor is there any human rights justification for the continued use of preventive detention. Preventive detention is supposed to be used to prevent serious apprehended crimes. Its use, for instance, might be justifiable to prevent a South African agent from bombing a Zambian mine or factory. But in practice, it is used to detain political opponents of the incumbent regime, critical members of the press, student and academic activists, trade unionists, and sometimes even their lawyers. In Tanzania, it is used to punish the allegedly anti-socialist activities of large numbers of businessmen. Not only does preventive detention attack the most fundamental civil liberties of the detainees, but it also cuts off a major avenue of political participation. In largely illiterate or semiliterate societies, competition among factions of the ruling classes for political office is often the only existent form of political participation. Moreover, student, press, professional, or trade union opposition to a regime may be the only means of articulating widespread popular grievances.

Political rights, then, are as important as civil rights. In principle most Commonwealth Africans living under civilian rule are in full possession of political rights, if one keeps in mind that both the United Nations Covenant on Civil and Political Rights and the African Charter on Human and Peoples' Rights refer only to rights of political participation and nowhere specify that such participation should be implemented through competitive multiparty democracies. There are no ascriptive barriers (e.g., race, ethnicity, or sex) to political participation for citizens. Nevertheless, some people, especially the Lebanese in Sierra Leone, are denied citizenship rights because of discriminatory constitutional rules (or, in the case of some of East Africa's Asians, discriminatory practice) that prohibit people of non-Negro descent from becoming citizens.

Participation rights of voting are constitutionally guaranteed to African citizens in all civilian regimes, whether under multiparty or single-party rule. Single-party governments do, in Kenya, Zambia, and Tanzania (less regularly in Sierra Leone), hold elections. These elections are regarded as tests of popular support for the regime, as well as means either for the citizens, or for the government, to get rid of unpopular MPs. Multiparty systems appear to be less effective as regards political participation than single-party ones: nowhere in Commonwealth Africa (except in Sierra Leone, with the help of the military, in 1967) has a civilian government ever been voted out of office. In Ghana, Nigeria, and Uganda, the various civilian governments either have been removed by military coups or have deteriorated into armed conflict. On the whole, multiparty competitive political systems in Africa have been a failure.

If one is to make predictions for the future in Africa, it is more important to discuss the capacity for genuine political participation within one-party states than to pine for multiparty systems that seem destined for inevitable instability. In this connection, the models of Tanzania and Zambia are rather disappointing. Both provide for strict internal controls on party participation, especially through the vetting or vetoing of locally nominated candidates for office, and through procedures for expulsion of party members who criticize policy. The recent trend of the Chama Cha Mapinduzi in Tanzania toward political vanguardism bodes ill for internal party democracy. A more likely future in these now-stable one-party states is increasing entrenchment of a party-bureaucratic ruling class, at the expense of ordinary citizen's political and economic rights.

African societies increasingly resemble more developed societies in their subordination to a national ruling class based explicitly on property, as in Kenya or Nigeria; implicitly on access to office, especially party office, as in Tanzania; or on some combination of the two. Transitory populist regimes such as that of Rawlings in Ghana will either revert to capitalist rule or transform themselves into bureaucratized party systems. In either case, as national integration is consolidated and class rule is entrenched, violations of communal rights will become less important; "tribalism," especially, will become less salient.

To date in Commonwealth Africa, two types of so-called tribal (actually ethnic or national) conflict have occurred. In the first a formerly powerful political entity has had to accept subordination to a new central government. In Ghana, the Ashanti have so far been subdued, although Ashanti-based political parties or factions continue. In Uganda, the struggle between the central government and the Buganda continues, after the eight-year tragedy of Idi Amin's rule. The second type of conflict occurs when a particular ethnic group accrues more economic power and educational/bureaucratic advantage than others, who therefore resent it. In Kenya, the Kikuyu have dominated politics and economic life for some time. In Nigeria, the highly educated and entrepreneurial Igbo lost their bid for secession in the late 1960s and have been reintegrated into a federal Nigeria dominated largely by northerners (a regional and religious rather than a purely ethnic definition). Ethnic favoritism continues, of course, throughout Commonwealth Africa; but it is certainly not the only source of political conflict, nor can it be reasonably analyzed without understanding how ethnicity must coincide with economic factors to be a potent political force.

With the exception of ethnic conflicts, few severe human rights violations in Commonwealth Africa can be attributed to communal differences. Whereas other new nation-states have been forged through severe repression of linguistic and religious rights, such is not the case in Africa. Indeed, efforts are made to teach children and adults in their local tongue, English or Swahili being preserved or adopted as the national *lingua franca*, rather than a language specifically identified with one dominant ethnic group (e.g., Kikuyu in Kenya, Hausa in Nigeria). Nor has any large-scale conflict been caused by divisions between Christians and Muslims. Rather, the different religious groups have co-existed in a harmony that appears, to European eyes, quite surprising. The only severe cases of religious persecution have been of small sects, notably the Lumpas in Zambia and the Jehovah's Witnesses in Malawi and elsewhere, which have been perceived to be threats to the ruling regimes because of their refusals to swear loyalty to the government and to purchase Party cards.

Ordinary people in Commonwealth Africa, then, do not suffer the daily assaults on their personal lives that are endured, for example, by black people living under apartheid rule in South Africa. The nonpolitically active African citizen is normally "free" (subject to economic constraints) to live his day-to-day life as he pleases. He may be subject to periodic expulsions from the city to the countryside in Kenya or Tanzania, and in Tanzania he may already have been the victim of forced resettlement into ujamaa villages. Otherwise, if he minds his own business and is not overtly disloyal to the ruling regime, his only constraint is the economic one. But it is precisely the violation of economic rights, as defined and accepted both by the United Nations and the Organization of African Unity, which is to become the single most important rights abuse in the next 50 years.

The economic rights records of the post-colonial African states are mixed. Substantial progress has been made in the area of health and education. Life expectancy was on the average ten years longer in 1982 than 1960, and literacy rates were booming. Offsetting this long-term investment in human capital has been steadily decreasing food production per capita, and very high rates of population growth, which more than offset growth in productivity in the 1970s and '80s (although not in the 1960s). The population problem seems to be a typical cultural lag effect, with perceptions of probable child mortality not having caught up with the new reality. Perhaps, if cultural attitudes toward the role of women also change and children become less economically necessary, the awaited decline in population growth rates will take place within the next 50 years. The problem of food production may, however, be more dificult to solve.

In part the problem of food production has been a result of extremely misguided approaches to state planning, which have often favored export-oriented cash crops over food crops, have underpaid peasant farmers in order to subsidize food prices in urban areas, and/or relied on overcentralization of distribution despite extremely inadequate transportation, communication, and administrative resources. Some of these problems are being remedied in countries such as Tanzania and Zambia, partly as a result of pressure from the International Monetary Fund. But the problem is also one of developing class rule, likely to be entrenched, not ameliorated, in the predictable future.

In incompletely industrialized African economies, possession of adequate land to feed one's family is the basis of the ordinary person's security. But already more and more people in Commonwealth Africa are landless. The myth of the redistributive communal society in which everyone has access to land is precisely that, a myth. The privatization of land in the hands of wealthy members of the ruling class has combined with burgeoning populations to create societies in which millions must look to marginal existence in the cities for survival. Women, who are the culturally acknowledged providers for children, are particularly hard-hit by this phenomenon. Meanwhile, ruling-class Africans supplement their increasing hold on land with other mechanisms of wealth acquisition. Corruption—the use of state monies or government/bureaucratic office for private gain—is widespread. So is the inequitable advantage taken by the already-privileged of Africanization laws, which tend to benefit only those who can buy formerly European or Asian/Lebanese businesses. Radically inequitable income distributions are commonplace.

I suggest, following Henry Shue,[2] that two types of rights priorities are especially relevant to the underdeveloped world, the rights of security (of the person) and of subsistence. But both these rights are in their turn contingent upon some form of genuine popular participation in economic and political decision-making. Even the most benevolent of dictators, as Julius Nyerere might be characterized, grant only the substance of rights, not the rights themselves.[3] Thus, for example, health clinics may be provided to the rural poor by the state, but the right to demand better treatment when administrators become lax or self-serving may be denied. Benevolent dictators can easily be succeeded by dictators of a less benevolent frame of mind. Furthermore, as Nyerere's economic policy shows, arbitrary imprisonments of alleged economic criminals and idealistic but misguided agricultural policies have not provided even the substance of economic rights in Tanzania. Benevolence itself, on the part of a government, is an insufficient condition for the provision of either security or subsistence. While both security and subsistence are basic rights, neither can be guaranteed in a class society without popular political participation, which, therefore, must also be seen as a basic right.

Security, subsistence, and participation are interdependent and interactive rights. The human right of physical security must be protected in Commonwealth Africa not only for its own intrinsic value, but also because it is a condition for further popular participation in government, on which all other human rights are hinged. Similarly, minimal physical subsistence (economic rights) must be provided not only because economic rights are valued in and of themselves, but because a healthy population is more likely to be a thinking, politically active population. It is far more difficult for African governments to guarantee subsistence than security rights. In economic policy, the governments are genuinely constrained by their historical underdevelopment, by their extremely weak position in the contemporary world economy, and by the current burgeoning of population. Nevertheless, the economic rights of the African masses could be better implemented if governments regularly consulted their citizens and if the interests of the ruling classes were not, in a spurious ideology of development, accepted as the legitimate interests of the nation as a whole.

This summary of research findings regarding the empirical presence or absence of human rights in Commonwealth Africa has led to the conclusion that as the problems of nation-building (ethnic integration) are ameliorated, violations of human rights can be predicted to continue in both the civil/political and the economic spheres. In an underdeveloped economy, the costs to the ruling class of relinquishing political power are too great; money is made through office. Therefore, political rights of the press, of trade unions, and of real participation in party decision-making will continue to be severely curtailed. In ostensibly socialist economies such as Tanzania, it is even more important for members of the ruling class to hold onto political office than it is for independent capitalists. In the long run, neither capitalists nor party bureaucrats are likely to relinquish economic or political power without substantial pressure from below.

Is such pressure likely to occur, and if so, how? To answer such a question, one must first understand how large-scale social change occurs. Human rights violations vary with the structure of a society; as social structure changes, so will the human rights record.

The Human Rights Debates

In the general study of human rights in the international academic literature, insufficient attention is paid to the underlying causes of large-scale social change. Two aspects of social change frequently left unanalyzed are the relations between structure and culture, and the effects of social stratification on human rights. Yet without understanding these two aspects of social change, one can neither adequately understand human rights abuses, nor make predictions of future human rights remedies.

The following propositions summarize my view of how societies change, and how such change in its turn can affect human rights. Proposition (1a) is admittedly philosophical: it is a moral position that human rights ought to be universal, rather than a sociological position based on empirical evidence. The remaining propositions, however, derive from my thinking as a sociologist.

1. *Universality*

    a. Human rights must be universal; they inhere in human beings by virtue of their humanity alone.

    b. While the idea of "human rights" is Western in origin, it is not merely Western in applicability. Logically and in fact, ideas and knowledge are not limited in their applicability to those who originate them.

    c. While African societies may be unique insofar as they are African, they are also universal insofar as they are societies.

2. *The Individual versus the State*

    a. In all state societies, human rights are a matter between the individual and the state; they consist of claims by the individual on or against the state.

    b. Individuals exist in Africa; they are a product both of changing modes of production and of structural and psychological modernization.

    c. All African societies are now state societies; local communal groups are subordinate to the national state.

3. *Structure versus Culture*

    a. Structure dominates over culture; that is, structural economic, social, and political changes produce new cultural "needs" for and ideas of human rights.

b. Thus culture is neither static nor vulnerable only to exogenously generated changes.

c. Nevertheless, a cultural residue remains, as in "traditional" ideas of individual vs. community obligations, or of the proper role of women.

d. Such "traditional" ideas are not always neutral in their impact, however; rather, both their retention and their abolition can be advocated by self-interested groups.

e. Although ideas change with or after structural change, ideology is a partially independent variable; much government policy in Commonwealth Africa is in fact determined by leaders' ideologies (e.g., Nyerere's socialism, Kaunda's humanism).

4. *Structures of Production and Stratification*

a. The most important aspect of structure is the changing modes and relations of production (in Africa, the transition toward peripheral capitalism) and the consequent effects upon class relations, broadly defined.

b. Thus differentials in power, wealth, education, and access to office influence differential access to human rights.

c. Class divisions exist in both capitalist and socialist African societies.

5. *Abuse of Power*

a. Although redistribution of power (especially in the form of redistribution of property) would assist in the realization of human rights, it is unlikely to occur, as ruling classes do not willingly relinquish the resources they control, hence

b. Checks on abuses of power are necessary, namely
   i. constitutionalism and the rule of law and
   ii. popular participation in political decision-making and economic distribution.

c. All regimes, regardless of official ideology, tend to consolidate power and usurp property and other forms of privilege.

6. *Revolution*

a. Thus, even if popular revolution is possible in Commonwealth Africa, revolution in and of itself is never a complete answer to human rights abuses, unless it is accompanied by constitutionalism, the rule of law, and broad popular participation.

b. It follows that civil/political rights can never be "postponed" until economic rights are fulfilled, because
   i. the ruling class may (economically) "develop" a society, but will tend not to fulfil economic rights without pressure from below, and
   ii. civil/political rights, once relinquished, are very difficult to regain without a further revolution.

From this set of propositions, I derive my position on a number of debates current in the international human rights literature.

The first human rights debate has to do with the alleged uniqueness of African society and of its concept of human rights. While I accept that there is an African concept of human dignity, I do not find such a concept unique; rather, it is a view of a person's role in society that is typical of many pre-capitalist, nonindustrialized societies.[4] In any case, human dignity and human rights are not synonymous. The latter must inhere in a person solely because of his/her humanity, and for no other reason; thus, for example, aliens or strangers must, like citizens or in-groupers, be granted human rights. So must women. The allegation of uniqueness of Africa's concept of human rights may be offered in good faith, with reference to a nostalgic view of Africa's past. But it may also be used as a cover for indigenous, class-based violations of human rights.

Related to the problem of whether human rights are or ought to be universal is the assertion, enshrined in the new African Charter of Human and Peoples' Rights, that rights ought to be tied to duties. In part this is a truism, since even in the most classically liberal democracies, people who are convicted of crimes are deprived of a whole series of rights, most notably freedom of movement. In principle, however, such deprivations can be made only after the most scrupulous protection of a person's civil rights under the rule of law. The difficulty with the tying of rights to duties without the intermediate step of trial by an independent judiciary is the likelihood of wholesale cancellation of rights by the ruling class. In a non-state society, such as the idealized traditional Africa to which many advocates of the rights-duties twinning refer, the connection makes sense; privilege is conditional on performance. But in the new class societies of contemporary Africa, rights are largely either rights that individuals hold against the state, or claims they have on the state. In either case, if rights are tied to duties in a situation in which duties are defined by the ruling class, then they are likely to disappear.

The question of whether rights ought to inhere in individuals or in groups is also relevant to the issue of universality. The African Charter of Human and Peoples' Rights stresses the importance of group rights, allegedly as a means of retaining African communalism against the alienating individualism of the Western world. In practice, however, group rights in the African context mean national rights of political sovereignty and autonomy over material resources. They do not mean, in either the African or the United Nations context, minority national rights. Group rights are interpreted in this book as the communal rights of maintenance of religious, linguistic, and ethnic traditions, but these communal rights are not considered group rights in the international usage. Rather, they are viewed as individual civil/political rights.

In fact, the often fiercely defended notion of group rights has no real

SUMMARY AND ASSESSMENT   221

meaning. The assertion of group rights in Africa is, in my view, an ideological weapon for denying real individual claims on or against the state. The process of social change has detached many people, both physically through migration and psychologically through modernization, from the rural ethnic groups into which they or their forebears were originally born. Moreover, traditional group representatives—that is chiefs and elders—are not equipped to represent their people in modern conflicts with the state, for example, in wage disputes. In their multifarious modern roles, ordinary Africans need new individual rights. The universality of individual rights is thus a necessity in Africa, as in all modernized societies.

The second human rights debate has to do with whether Africans themselves are to blame, as it were, for human rights violations that have taken place in their countries since independence. Surely, many Africans argue, external factors have had more effect on human rights in Africa than internal ones. This argument contains two aspects. First, the historical dimension: Britain, it is argued, was itself a gross violator of human rights. Under colonialism, there were few if any civil and political rights and no attempts at economic development; in fact, colonial rule underdeveloped Africa. But whether Britain did underdevelop Africa is still a matter of much historical dispute. In any case, the extent to which historical constraints on human rights can be used to excuse gratuitous present-day violations is itself questionable.

Similarly, the second allegation, that contemporary human rights violations in the economic sphere are entirely the result of the influence of external economic forces on Africa, is highly questionable. It is true that economic progress has been constrained, sometimes tragically, by declining terms of trade for such resources as Zambian copper, by the rising price of oil since 1973, and by the inability of African governments successfully to control the activities of foreign-based transnational corporations on their soil. But such external factors, often defined as neo-colonialism, do not constitute the whole picture. In particular, they cannot be used to explain such wholesale policy disasters as forced villagization in Tanzania, or destructions of markets and nationalization of distribution in Rawlings' Ghana. Such economic decisions, whether taken as a result of benign or selfish motives, are undoubtedly indigenous in origin. As a group of nations, Commonwealth Africa is indeed in an extremely weak position vis-à-vis the world economy. Nevertheless, these nations have been politically independent for a quarter of a century, and their ruling classes now have an autonomous policy-making power they did not have during the colonial era.

A third debate on international human rights considers the issue of human rights priorities. Many Third World leaders have begun to stress economic rights as a priority over civil and political rights, especially in

debates over the New International Economic Order. I agree that economic rights are as necessary as civil/political rights. However, I do not
agree that civil/political rights can be postponed until economic rights are
realized. Even assuming (incorrectly) that ruling classes do not act for
their own selfish ends, civil and political rights of influence over the
decision-making process are necessary in order to implement reasonable
development policies and to ensure equitable economic distribution. To be
even more realistic, civil and political rights are necessary from the earliest
stages of independence because African societies, like all societies, are
class societies, and in situations of extreme scarcity ruling classes will
appropriate for themselves as much of the fruits of economic "development" as they can.

Civil and political rights are, then, necessary for the implementation of
economic rights. They are also necessary for the guarantee of communal
rights and to maintain the stable social order that is necessary for society
itself to exist. Uganda from 1971 to 1985 is one of the few examples in
modern history of a society in which all civil and political rights disappeared, even the most minimal physical protection. That such deprivations of rights do not normally occur in Africa does not imply that the
rights themselves are irrelevant. Moreover, even at the lowest levels of
economic development, people need and want individual freedom. Many
Africans, as the use of state terrorism and preventive detention makes
clear, have sacrificed both their physical security and minimal subsistence
in defense of their beliefs. One cannot argue away all necessities for
individual freedom on the spurious assumption that poor people have no
interest in any aspect of life beyond the immediately material.

A related aspect of the issue of priorities concerns women's rights. It is
sometimes argued that women's rights, like civil and political rights,
should "wait" until economic development has been achieved. My refuta-
tion of this position is threefold. First, from a philosophical point of view,
if human rights inhere in all people by virtue of their humanity, they must
inhere in women as well as in men. Second, from a purely practical point
of view, economic development is unlikely to occur in Africa unless the
needs and wants of women are considered. Agricultural development
projects that ignore the prominent role of women in agricultural production, antideforestation projects that fail to understand that the women
normally collect the firewood, and population control programs that fail to
consider the reproduction goals of women, as well as the differential power
of men and women in the home, will not succeed in their goals. Especially
in Africa, women are an integral part of the production and distribution of
food and other basic needs. Finally women, like men, are individuals who,
even at very low levels of development, have their own needs for political
participation. As African societies modernize, so women's attitudes to
their traditional roles change. If women are to be protected against
unwanted genital operations, against unwanted pregnancies, or against

unwanted marriages, they need the political clout to fight for changes in law and practice. The culturally approved view of women's roles is changing as social structures change.

These three debates—on universality vs. uniqueness of human rights, on internal vs. external causes of human rights abuses, and on the relative priorities of different kinds of rights—are all affected by the economic and class structures of a society. Yet it is precisely on the issues of class and power that the dominant literature of human rights is vaguest. Indeed, concerted attention does not appear to be given to the real constraints on human rights posed by differential access to material resources and political power. When such constraints are acknowledged, solutions such as "the eradication of poverty" and "political participation" are often posed in a sociological vacuum; ideal solutions are viewed as practical ones.[5] Yet class power is the ultimate (though not the only) reality constraining realization of human rights in Commonwealth Africa, as everywhere else.

This statement raises the problem of tone. How can one criticize the human rights policies of seemingly sincere, honorable men such as Julius Nyerere or Kenneth Kaunda, given the constraints of poverty and under-development, Africa's colonial heritage, and problems connected with the formation of stable nation-states? If the structural approach is adopted, should it not be acknowledged that the structural problems of colonialism and neo-colonialism outweigh any possibility for realization of the full range of human rights in Africa? Surely, comparison with the history of Europe during its own period of nation-building and economic development will point to the successes, not the failures, of Africa in this regard?

This book has indeed argued for a structural approach, supplemented by both an historical and a comparative sense.[6] Nevertheless, I also maintain that individuals are ultimately responsible for their own moral activities. Explanations of structural constraints on human rights protection do not constitute excuses for human rights abuses, especially for political actors who command far more economic and political resources than the average citizen. "Power morality," to quote the Nigerian writer Wole Soyinka,[7] is undoubtedly the most enduring enemy of human rights. Thus we must now turn to an investigation of whether social arrangements can be structured, and citizens empowered, to defend human rights against the encroachments of the ruling class.

The Future

Because of the seemingly unending lists of human rights abuses even in relatively stable Commonwealth African countries such as Zambia, some commentators, especially students imbued with the study of Marxism (in its theoretical, not its practical, form) call for socialist revolution as the only solution to the problem. While revolution is sometimes the only possible solution (for example, in contemporary South Africa) to the problem of an entrenched ruling class that systematically violates the human rights of the masses, it is not a solution to the human rights problems of contemporary Commonwealth Africa. This is the case because, first, the conditions are not right for revolution, and second, at the present level of underdevelopment any revolutionary cadre group that took power would at best repeat, and in all likelihood exacerbate, the human rights abuses that already exist.

In peasant societies broadly analagous to those of Commonwealth Africa, revolutions have normally taken place only when a middle-class cadre group led a guerilla war against an externally identifiable enemy, in situations in which an indigenous ruling class was either nonexistent, or too closely allied with the external enemy to be credible.[8] Thus in China, which is often cited as a model for Africa, Mao led a peasant-based guerilla war not only against the Chinese landlords and bourgeoisie, but also against the Japanese occupiers. In sub-Saharan Africa, socialist regimes have been established through revolutionary struggle only in the former Portuguese colonies, where the political leadership fought long guerilla wars against Portugal. Elsewhere the peasantry is too ethnically divided, isolated from national politics by illiteracy and inadequate communications systems, and lacking in leadership to be revolutionary. Classical proletarian revolution is also irrelevant to Commonwealth Africa at present. The proletariat is both underdeveloped and too fragmented and subject to state control to be a revolutionary force: its representative trade unions are usually either repressed or incorporated into the state framework. Thus revolution seems not to be a realistic political option in present-day Commonwealth Africa.

Even if a revolution were to take place, would it be likely to solve the two overriding human rights problems of Commonwealth Africa—the need for physical security and protection of one's freedom against the state, and the need for economic subsistence? Many revolutionaries ignore the pertinence of the first set of civil rights, arguing that they are a form of "bourgeois" rights which are a luxury for starving people. I have argued throughout that poverty does not preclude the need for civil and political rights. Even leaving that issue aside, it is still questionable whether, at Africa's present level of underdevelopment, socialism would be the best provider of economic rights. African students of revolution frequently point to China as a model for Africa to follow. But state planning and collectivized agriculture have not been the best economic option for China; post–Cultural Revolution evidence suggests that in the late 1970s, her rate of agricultural production was no higher, or at best only marginally higher, than it had been in 1949.[9] In the 1980s, China has turned to profit incentives as a model for economic development.

The revolutionary model assumes that no class rule exists under socialism.[10] But all societies produce ruling classes, regardless of official ideology. Power, in itself, is an independent variable: those who have power never willingly relinquish it. If, therefore, one takes physical security and political participation as real goals for human rights policies in Commonwealth Africa, along with economic subsistence, then socialist revolution is not the answer. Ruling classes whose power is based on coercion and control of state office are likely to be as brutal as, if not more brutal than, ruling classes whose power is based on direct control of the economy. In general, "socialist" revolutionaries in Commonwealth Africa turn out to be populists such as Kwame Nkrumah or Jerry Rawlings. Their genuine concern about the poverty-stricken lives of their fellows, and their genuine outrage at the corruption of the indigenous bourgeoisie, cannot be translated into achievable goals of economic development, for they simply do not have the planning and infrastructural capacity to generate or implement such goals. Furthermore, once the evangelical fervor is abated and the economic goods fail to be delivered, populist leaders require a great deal of state coercion to stay in power. Nkrumah consolidated his rule through widespread use of preventive detention, spying, and state terrorism.

Socialism and populism are not, then, realistic means for the entrenchment of human rights in Commonwealth Africa in the near future. There are two other possible scenarios of political development in Africa in the next few decades. One is that a reasonably complete transition to capitalist social structure will begin, with the possible development of bourgeois democracy. The other is that peripheral capitalism will continue to stagnate or regress, resulting in various forms of military takeover, populist *putsches*, and pseudo-socialist attempts at solving an essentially unsolvable economic, political, and social crisis.

If a complete transformation of Commonwealth African societies into more stable capitalist societies should take place, there would be more room for human rights. Bourgeoisies firmly established with economic power would find it less necessary, in the face of demands from below, to maintain complete control over the political superstructure. At the same time more literate, educated, and organized proletariats would be in a better position to fight for both political and economic rights. That is what appears to have happened in capitalist Europe. Despite differences of culture and history, it might also occur in Africa.

It appears, with hindsight, that premature attempts at state control of the economy have been responsible for many of Africa's economic woes in the past fifteen years. Commentators from a variety of political perspectives are now convinced that the encouragement of small-scale local capitalism and initiative, and the de-controlling of the economy, are key measures for economic progress in Commonwealth Africa. Such measures might (although not necessarily) increase income disparities, but they would also encourage overall economic growth. If ordinary people were consequently better off than they had been before, they might well consider that the increasing inequality was worth the price.

An economic policy recommendation that encourages individual initiative and personal acquisition of wealth would undoubtedly be welcomed by many members of Commonwealth Africa's indigenous, proto-capitalist ruling classes, as well as by those party and bureaucratic officials who are chafing at the economic bit in the so-called socialist regimes of Tanzania, Zambia, and allegedly revolutionary Ghana (since 1981). The difficulty is to increase the incentive for economic growth and innovation while at the same time controlling the economic exploitation that might well be its corollary. One means suggested to check such exploitation is to attempt to implement the equitable distribution of land to small-scale, peasant landholders.

Unfortunately, however, the privatization of land in the hands of small-scale landholders is an unlikely outcome in Commonwealth Africa, where there is already plenty of evidence that the creation of a market in land is followed by its acquisition by rich peasants and by various members of the urban ruling classes. It appears inevitable that the full development of capitalism entails the alienation of land from peasant producers. But precisely such alienation might, in the very long run, produce a fully proletarianized working class that would demand subsistence, security, and participation rights from the bourgeoisie. Capitalism is not an automatic formula either for economic development or for the attainment of human rights. It is, however, a social system whose particular productive and stratificatory arrangements open the possibility for citizens to make claims for human rights on or against the state.[11]

The establishment of a bourgeoisie whose power is independent of that of the state might allow for the development of a genuine rule of law. The rule of law developed in Europe partly as a result of the struggle of the bourgeoisie for protection against the arbitrary interference of the state in its affairs. Furthermore, it is likely that a developed, independent bourgeoisie might well become factionalized, both by economic interest (e.g., industry vs. agriculture) and by other loyalties (e.g., region). Such a bourgeoisie would demand the entrenchment of real rights of political representation and participation in order to have an influence over the ruling class faction that controls the offices of the state. It would also start to use mediating voluntary organizations as pressure groups in defense of its own interests.

This view of the development of an African bourgeoisie, with its concomitant demands for human civil/political rights, assumes a relatively prosperous economy over the long haul. Maintaining that assumption for the time being, one can predict that a politically active proletariat will also arise. Already the substantial human capital investments made by all African governments in education and health presuppose a more productive, politically aware populace in the next generations. Insofar as this populace is also increasingly urbanized and concentrated, it is likely to become more capable of organizing in its own interests. The most important variable in discussing future proletarian political activity is the transformation of Africa's still disease-plagued, partially illiterate, and isolated peasant masses into a healthy, literate, and organized urban proletariat.

The above model of complete transition to capitalism in a prosperous world economy is based on a view of human rights as obtained by political action (class struggle) initiated from below. No ruling class, whether based on economic or political power, is benign. The bourgeoisie in Africa, as elsewhere, may be able to promote economic growth; but it will not distribute economic rights unless either such rights are in its own interests (e.g., it might wish to have a healthier labor force), or unless the organized proletariat demands such rights and threatens both the bourgeoisie and the state. What the transition to capitalism can do is increase the absolute amount of economic wealth in poor African countries, and provide the structural conditions for the creation of a politically organized social class (the proletariat) that, in very broad terms, would represent the interests of the masses (workers, peasants, urban underemployed) against the (state and/or capitalist) ruling class.

But why should one assume that Commonwealth Africa is likely to develop in such a classically capitalist direction in the next 50 years? Surely a more realistic assessment is that the nine countries under discussion will remain in their present underdeveloped, peripheral capitalist state, with parasitic ruling classes using physical force and economic exploitation to control the masses of peasants and economically marginal urban inhabitants? I do not suggest that such stagnation will necessarily be broken. There are, however, some possible roads to a higher level of development. The world economic recession of the 1970s and '80s will not necessarily be permanent. Economic recovery in the Western world could be followed by economic recovery in Africa. Moreover, the underdevelopment thesis that suggests that it is in the interests of the developed capitalist countries to keep Africa poor may well be incorrect. Whatever the historical origins of underdevelopment, in the late 20th century developed economies look for prosperous markets; it is not necessarily in their interests to keep the poor poor.

On the other hand, the stagnant, peripheral capitalist structure of Commonwealth Africa may continue unchanged, or indeed sink into an even worse state. The cost of oil, and the gap between the world prices of Africa's raw materials and the manufactured goods she must import, may continue to grow. Africa's debt burden may become even more unmanageable than at present. If such is the case, there will be incomplete class formation. The ruling classes, without an independent profitable economic base, will continue to feed off the state. Without new industries to provide jobs, the urban masses will become increasingly discontented and willing to support authoritarian populist regimes.

The future for Commonwealth Africa, then, may well be a political system best described as underdeveloped fascism. The Nigerian political scientist Claude Ake suggests that fascism is the political future of Africa.

> The present state of economic stagnation will continue, deepening class contradictions and causing governmental instability but not necessarily sparking off revolution. . . . the politics of anxiety will become institutionalised; increasingly, the ruling class will display signs of paranoia while the subordinate classes become frustrated, demoralised and available for induction into extremist . . . movements. . . . the ruling class will increasingly appeal to loyalty, patriotism, discipline and dislike for outsiders. Enemies of society will be found all too ubiquitously and will be dealt with summarily. Fascism—that is the reality staring us in the face in most of Africa.[12]

Fascism in Africa will display many of the characteristics of fascism elsewhere. State coercion will intensify. There will be more preventive detention, more political murder, more spurious treason trials. Political scapegoatism will also become a standard mechanism to deflect popular hostility from the capitalist or party-bureaucratic ruling classes. In the absence of any viable economic options for growth, non-Negro or non-citizen minorities, especially those who are visibly active in retail trade, will become increasingly vulnerable to attack, both by the state and by the enraged poor. Misogynistic propaganda against women traders ("hoarders") will intensify. Romantic reactionary ideologies of homogeneous consensual communities will be used to justify the stifling of dissent and the persecution of political and economic deviants.

Yet even so, African fascism will be underdeveloped, and thus unable to use all the resources that were available to its European counterparts. As the size of the national bowl of stew continues to shrink, there will be fewer payoffs to offer competing (regional or ethnic) ruling-class factions or recalcitrant union leaders. Corporatism will not be an effective strategy in situations in which identifiable corporate groups are incompletely formed, and resources to buy them off are lacking. Finally, the resources needed to satisfy demands by the military for high pay, comfortable accommodations, and internationally competitive armaments will be lacking. Commonwealth Africa lacks the basic physical infrastructure of totalitarian fascism: the repressive apparatus of transportation, communication and, most important, control of the military simply does not exist. The result may be that even the most stable one-party states will succumb to military rule, and that Commonweath Africa is in for a long period of coups and countercoups.

In all this, the peasantry will continue to be exploited by allegedly anti-capitalist measures, and prevented from selling either its cash crops or its food crops for their true market value. More and more land will be alienated to urban-based "strangers"—capitalists, bureaucrats, military men, and party officials—either in return for patronage or cash or as a consequence of outright coercive theft. Those peasants who do not give up and migrate to the cities will then retreat, if they still have access to land, to low-level rural subsistence. Such a withdrawal occurred in Uganda during the reign of Idi Amin, when subsistence producers (including many women) were able to hold their families together by providing low-level basic needs, which they often had to transport to their urban relatives as well.[13] There are signs that a similar withdrawal into subsistence is also occurring in contemporary Ghana.[14] Return to village-level subsistence may become a generalized phenomenon in the face of severe economic crisis and the irresponsibility and incompetence of ruling classes. But with burgeoning populations, increasing scarcity of land, deforestation, and the desire for more material wealth than can possibly be provided even to the poorest at the present economic-political juncture, such a rural withdrawal will not be a return to an idyllic, mythical, pre-capitalist past. A return to a truncated subsistence economy will signal the complete breakdown of hopes for economic growth and development.

The only possible political option for the ruling classes in such a situation of economic regression will be increased parasitism, of either the capitalist or the socialist variety. Where capitalism remains the dominant form, as in Nigeria or Kenya, corruption will become more blatant and class theft more frequent. Under populistic fascism, privileges will be acquired through control of office rather than of private property. As regimes change, allegedly revolutionary cadres will merely reorganize these bases for primitive accumulation of wealth. None of these scenarios will allow the promotion of human rights.

These are long-term speculations, the accuracy of which can be tested only by time. The central point here, to repeat, is that remedies for current human rights abuses will arise only out of the real structural changes that occur in Commonwealth Africa. Idealist interpretations that seek to guarantee human rights in laws and constitutions, disregarding underdevelopment and class structure, will not change African society. Neither will premature (assuming that there may be a future point at which socialism is relevant) imposition, again for idealist reasons, of centralized state planning without the relevant resources of human capital and physical infrastructure.

In the last analysis, consolidated class structures will constitute the most immovable barriers to human rights in Commonwealth Africa, as elsewhere. This is not a happy analysis of human rights in Africa. But it is, I believe, a realistic one.

Notes

1. A. Glenn Mower, "Human Rights in Black Africa: A Double Standard?" *Human Rights Journal* 9, no. 1 (1976): 39–70.

2. Henry Shue, *Basic Rights: Subsistence, Affluence and U.S. Foreign Policy* (Stanford: Stanford University Press, 1980).

3. Ibid., p. 76.

4. Rhoda Howard, "Evaluating Human Rights in Africa: Some Problems of Implicit Comparisons," *Human Rights Quarterly* 6, no. 2 (May 1984): 176.

5. See, e.g., Philip Alston, "Human Rights and Basic Needs: A Critical Assessment," *Human Rights Journal* 12, no. 1 (1979), who calls for "techniques" to satisfy basic non-material needs "without provoking government hostility," p. 49.

6. Howard, "Evaluating Human Rights in Africa."

7. Wole Soyinka, *The Man Died* (New York: Harper & Row, 1972), p. 90.

8. Eric Wolf, *Peasant Wars of the Twentieth Century* (New York: Harper & Row, 1969).

9. Nick Eberstadt, "Has China Failed?" *New York Review of Books* 26, no. 5 (April 5, 1979): 38–39.

10. Rhoda E. Howard, "Third World Trade Unions as Agencies of Human Rights: The Case of Commonwealth Africa," forthcoming in Roger Southall, ed., *Trade Unions and the Industrialization of the Third World* (London: Zed Press, 1986).

11. Rhoda E. Howard and Jack Donnelly, "Human Dignity, Human Rights and Political Regimes" (forthcoming in *American Political Science Review*, September 1986).

12. Claude Ake, *A Political Economy of Africa* (Harlow, Essex: Longman, 1981), p. 189.

13. Grace Akello, *Self Twice-Removed: Ugandan Women* (London: Change International Reports, n.d. [1982 or 1983]), p. 15.

14. Merrick Posnansky, "How Ghana's Crisis Affects a Village," *West Africa*, December 1, 1980, pp. 2418–20; and G.J.S. Dei, "Food in the Domestic Economy of a Ghanaian Forest Community." Paper presented at the Canadian Association of African Studies, Antigonish, Canada, May 10, 1984, p. 5.

 Bibliography

Frequently Used Sources

Amnesty International. *Annual Reports, Bulletins,* etc. London and Canada.

Blaustein, Albert P., and Gisbert H. Flanz, eds. 1971–. *Constitutions of the Countries of the World.* Dobbs Ferry, N.Y., Oceana.

The Globe and Mail. Toronto.

Index on Censorship. London.

International Commission of Jurists. *Journal* and *Review.* Geneva.

International Press Institute. *Reports.* London.

Legum, Colin, ed. 1968–84. *Africa Contemporary Record.* New York, Africana Publishing Co. Vols. 1–15.

New York Times. New York.

Weekly Review. Nairobi.

West Africa. London.

Official Documents

African Charter on Human and Peoples' Rights. In Welch and Meltzer, eds., *Human Rights and Development in Africa.* Appendix 1.

Commonwealth Observer Group. 1980. *Uganda Elections, December 1980: Report.* London, Commonwealth Secretariat.

Economic Commission for Africa. 1975. "The Role of Women in African Development." Prepared for the World Conference of the International Women's Year, Mexico City. United Nations Document E/CONF.66/BP/8–81, Add.1.

———. 1977. "Code of Conduct for Transnational Corporations: (ECA African Regional Meeting's Report, Addis Ababa, 31 January–4 February 1977)." Reprinted in *Africa Contemporary Record* (1977–78), vol. 10, pp. C157–59.

Federal Republic of Nigeria. 1977. *Report of the Tribunal of Inquiry into the Activities of the Trade Unions.* Lagos: Federal Ministry of Information.

Government of Kenya. 1975. "Report of the Select Committee on the Disappearance and Murder of the Late Member for Nyandarua North, the Hon. J.M. Kariuki, M.P." June 3.

Government of Kenya, Central Bureau of Statistics, Ministry of Finance and Planning. 1977. "The Rural Kenyan Nutrition Survey, Feb.–March 1977." *Social Perspectives* (Nairobi) 2, no. 4.

Government of Malawi. 1971. *His Excellency the Life President's Speeches, Malawi Congress Party Convention, Lilongwe, 3–12 September 1971.* Zomba: Government Printer.

Kaunda, Kenneth D. 1967. "Humanism in Zambia and a Guide to Its Implementation." Lusaka: Government Printer.

"No Genocide: Final Report of Observer Team to Nigeria from 1. Organization of African Unity 2. Britain, Canada, Poland, Sweden." n.d. [1968?]. Apapa, Nigeria: Federal Ministry of Information, document no. NNPG/279/68.

Obote, Milton. 1970. "The Common Man's Charter." Entebbe, Uganda: Government Printer.

Organization of African Unity. *Charter*. In Ian Brownlie, ed., *Basic Documents in International Law*. 2nd. ed. Oxford, at the Clarendon Press. 1972.

————. 1981. "Lagos Plan of Action for the Economic Development of Africa: 1980–2000." Geneva: International Institute for Labour Studies.

Republic of Ghana. 1958. The Preventive Detention Act 1958. In United Nations, *Yearbook of Human Rights*.

————. n.d [1968?] *Dr. J. B. Danquah: Detention and Death in Nsawam Prison: Extracts from Evidence of Witnesses at the Commission of Enquiry into Ghana Prisons*. Accra-Tema: Ministry of Information, Document No. SPC/A10099/5,000/67–8.

————. n.d. [probably 1975] "Ghana Today 10: 0peration Feed Yourself." Accra: Government Information Services.

Republic of Kenya. 1965. *African Socialism and Its Application to Planning in Kenya*. G.P.K. 3938–5m-12/65.

————. 1966. The Public Security (Detained and Restricted Persons) Regulations 1966. In United Nations, *Yearbook of Human Rights*.

Republic of Nigeria. 1969. "Ibos in a United Nigeria." Pamphlet.

Republic of Sierra Leone. 1971. The Public Emergency (No.2) Regulations, 1971. In United Nations, *Yearbook of Human Rights*.

Republic of Zambia. 1965. "Report of the Commission of Inquiry into the Former Lumpa Church." Lusaka: Government Printer.

————. 1971. "Report of the Commission of Inquiry into the Allegations Made by Mr. Justin Chimba and Mr. John Chisata." Lusaka: Government Printer. May.

————. 1972, "A Nation of Equals—the Kabwe Declaration." Addresses to the National Council of UNIP, Hindu Hall, Kabwe, December 1–3.

————. 1972. "Report of the National Commission on the Establishment of a One-Party Participatory Democracy in Zambia." Lusaka: Government Printer.

————. 1976. "Invocation of the Full Powers of the State of Emergency by H.E. the President Dr. K. D. Kaunda: Text of his address to the nation on ZBS Radio/TV." January 28.

————. 1980 "Household Budget Survey 1974/75: Preliminary Report." Lusaka: Central Statistical Service. February.

United Nations A/6647/Rev.1. 1968. Commission on the Status of Women: Report of the Secretary General, "Constitutions, Electoral Laws and Other Legal Instruments Relating to the Political Rights of Women." New York: United Nations.

United Nations A/34/577/Add.1/Rev.1. 1980. Addendum to Report of the Secretary-General: "Status and Role of Women in Education and in the Economic and Social Fields." May 23.

United Nations A/CONF.94/17.1980. "Report of the Regional Preparatory Meeting of the United Nations Economic Commission for Africa, Second Regional Conference for the Integration of Women in Development."

United Nations A/CONF.94/35. 1980. "Report of the World Conference of the

United Nations Decade for Women: Equality, Development and Peace."
Copenhagen, July 14–30.
United Nations OPI/CESI/NOTE IWY/15. 1974. Center for Economic and Social
Information. "The Situation and Status of Women Today: Some Essential
Facts." December.
United Nations General Assembly. 1974. Resolution 3201 (S-VI) (1 May). "Decla-
ration on the Establishment of a New International Economic Order." In
United Nations, *Resolutions* (1972–74), vol. 14, pp. 527–29.
————. 1974. "Charter of Economic Rights and Duties of States." *Official
Records: Twenty-Ninth Session.* Supp. no. 31, res. 3281 (XXIX).
————. 1977. Resolution 32/130. "Alternative approaches and ways and means
within the United Nations system for improving the effective enjoyment of
human rights and fundamental freedoms." 32nd Session, Resolutions and
Decisions. (20 Sept-21 Dec. 1977). Supp. 45 (A/32/45).
United Republic of Tanzania. 1964. "Report of the Presidential Commission on
the Establishment of a Democratic One-Party State." Dar es Salaam: Government Printer.
————. 1967. Government Paper no. 2, "Proposals of the Tanzanian Government
on the Recommendations of the Presidential Commission of Inquiry into the
National Union of Tanganyika Workers." Dar es Salaam: Government Printer.
————. 1967. "Report of the Presidential Commission on the National Union of
Tanganyika Workers." Dar es Salaam: Government Printer.
————. 1980. "Tanzania: Who Is Dreaming? A Statement by the Government of
the United Republic of Tanzania." Dar es Salaam: Tanzanian Information
Services.

Selected Secondary Sources

The sources listed below do not constitute a complete list of secondary works used
in the text.

BOOKS

Ake, Claude. 1981. *A Political Economy of Africa.* Harlow, Essex: Longman.
Akello, Grace. n.d. [1983] *Self Twice-Removed: Ugandan Women.* London: Change
International Reports on Women and Society.
Amadi, Elechi. 1973. *Sunset in Biafra: A Civil War Diary.* London: Heinemann.
Anonymous. 1982. *In/Dependent Kenya.* London: Zed Press.
Ananaba, Wogu. 1979. *The Trade Union Movement in Africa.* London: C. Hurst
and Co.
Boserup, Ester. 1970. *Women's Role in Economic Development.* New York: St.
Martin's Press.
Brown, David N. 1985. "The Transformation of Agrarian Structure: A Ghanaian
Case Study." Ph.D. dissertation, McMaster University, Hamilton, Canada.
Bukh, Jette. 1979. *The Village Woman in Ghana.* Uppsala: Scandinavian Institute
of African Studies.
Donnelly, Jack. 1985. *The Concept of Human Rights.* London: Croom Helm.
Elias, T.O. 1956. *The Nature of African Customary Law.* Manchester: University of
Manchester Press.

Hafkin, Nancy J., and Edna G. Bay, eds. 1976. *Women in Africa*. Stanford: Stanford University Press.

Hodges, Tony. 1976. "Jehovah's Witnesses in Central Africa." Report no. 29. London: Minority Rights Group. June.

Hosken, Fran P. 1979. *The Hosken Report: Genital and Sexual Mutilation of Females*. Lexington, Mass.: Women's International Network News.

Howard, Rhoda. 1978. *Colonialism and Underdevelopment in Ghana*. London: Croom Helm.

Hyden, Goran. 1980. *Beyond Ujamaa in Tanzania: Underdevelopment and an Uncaptured Peasantry*. Berkeley: University of California Press.

———. 1983. *No Shortcut to Progress: African Development Management in Perspective*. Berkeley: University of California Press.

International Commission of Jurists. 1977. *Uganda and Human Rights: Reports to the U.N. Commission on Human Rights*. Geneva: International Commission of Jurists.

———. 1978. *Human Rights in a One-Party State*. London: Search Press.

Jackson, Robert H., and Carl G. Rosberg. 1982. *Personal Rule in Black Africa: Prince, Autocrat, Prophet, Tyrant*. Berkeley: University of California Press.

Kaunda, Kenneth D. 1966. *A Humanist in Africa*. London: Longmans.

Kesse-Adu, Kwame. 1971. *The Politics of Political Detention*. Accra-Tema: Ghana Publishing Corporation.

Kenyatta, Jomo. 1979. *Facing Mount Kenya*. London: Heinemann (1st. ed. 1938).

Kyemba, Henry. 1977. *A State of Blood: The Inside Story of Idi Amin*. New York: Ace Books.

Laqueur, Walter, and Barry Rubin, eds. 1979. *The Human Rights Reader*. New York and Scarborough, Ont.: The New American Library.

Lovejoy, Paul, ed. 1981. *The Ideology of Slavery in Africa*. Beverly Hills: Sage.

Markovitz, Irving Leonard. 1977. *Power and Class in Africa*. Englewood Cliffs, N.J.: Prentice-Hall.

Martin, Robert. 1974. *Personal Freedom and the Law in Tanzania*. Nairobi: Oxford University Press.

McLean, Scilla, ed. 1980. "Female Circumcision, Excision and Infibulation: The Facts and Proposals for Change." Report No. 47. London: Minority Rights Group.

Meebelo, Henry S. 1973. *Main Currents of Zambian Humanist Thought*. Lusaka: Oxford University Press.

Ngugi wa Thiong'o. 1981. *Detained: A Writer's Prison Diary*. London: Heinemann.

Nyerere, Julius K. 1968. *Ujamaa: Essays on Socialism*. London: Oxford University Press.

Obbo, Christine. 1980. *African Women: Their Struggle for Economic Independence*. London: Zed Press.

Odetola, Olatunde T. 1982. *Military Regimes and Development: A Comparative Analysis in African Societies*. London: George Allen and Unwin.

Odinga, Oginga. 1967. *Not Yet Uhuru: An Autobiography*. London: Heinemann.

Peil, Margaret. 1977. *Consensus and Conflict in African Societies*. London: Longman.

Pollis, Adamantia, and Peter Schwab, eds. 1979. *Human Rights: Cultural and Ideological Perspectives*. New York: Praeger.

Robertson, Claire C. 1984. *Sharing the Same Bowl; A Socioeconomic History of Women and Class in Accra, Ghana*. Bloomington: Indiana University Press.

Rodney, Walter. 1972. *How Europe Underdeveloped Africa*. London: Bogle L'Ouverture Press.

Sandbrook, Richard. 1982. *The Politics of Basic Needs: Urban Aspects of Assaulting Poverty in Africa*. Toronto: University of Toronto Press.

Shivji, Issa G. 1976. *Class Struggles in Tanzania*. London: Heinemann.

Shue, Henry. 1980. *Basic Rights: Subsistence, Affluence and U.S. Foreign Policy*. Princeton: Princeton University Press.

Soyinka, Wole. 1972. *The Man Died*. New York: Harper & Row.

Tandon, Yash, and Arnold Raphael. 1973. "The New Position of East Africa's Asians: Problems of a Displaced Minority." Report No. 16. London: Minority Rights Group. Revised 1978.

Welch, Claude E., Jr., and Robert I. Meltzer, eds. 1984. *Human Rights and Development in Africa*. Albany: State University of New York Press.

World Bank. 1981. *Accelerated Development in Sub-Saharan Africa*. Washington, D.C.: The World Bank.

————. 1984. *World Development Report*. New York: Oxford University Press.

ARTICLES

Aguda, Akinola, and Oluwadare Aguda. 1972. "Judicial Protection of Some Fundamental Rights in Nigeria and in the Sudan before and during Military Rule." *Journal of African Law* 16: 130–44.

Ake, Claude. 1976. "The Congruence of Political Economies and Ideologies in Africa." In Peter C. W. Gutkind and Immanuel Wallerstein, eds., *The Political Economy of Contemporary Africa*. Beverly Hills: Sage. Pp. 198–211.

All Africa Council of Churches. 1976. "Factors Responsible for the Violation of Human Rights in Africa." *Issue: A Journal of Africanist Opinion* 6, no. 4: 44–46.

Aluko, Olajide. 1981. "The Organisation of African Unity and Human Rights." *The Round Table* 283: 234–42.

Assimeng, J.M. 1970. "Sectarian Allegiance and Political Authority: The Watch Tower Society in Zambia, 1907–1935." *Journal of Modern African Studies* 8, no. 1: 97–112.

Ayoade, John A.A. 1980. "Electoral Laws and National Unity in Nigeria." *African Studies Review* 13, no. 2: 39–50.

Bentsi-Enchill, Kwamina. 1969. "The Colonial Heritage of Legal Pluralism." *Zambia Law Journal* 1, no. 2: 1–30.

Brown, David. 1982. "Who Are the Tribalists? Social Pluralism and Political Ideology in Ghana." *African Affairs* 81, no. 322: 37–69.

Bryceson, Deborah Fahy. 1980. "The Proletarianization of Women in Tanzania." *Review of African Political Economy* 17: 4–27.

Chase, Hank. 1976. "The Zanzibar Treason Trial." *Review of African Political Economy* 6: 14–33.

Chongwe, R.M.A. 1982. "An Address to the African Seminar on Human Rights and Development." Gaborone, Botswana, May 24–29.

Conboy, Kevin. 1978. "Detention without Trial in Kenya." *Georgia Journal of International and Comparative Law* 8, no. 2: 441–61.

Cox, Robert W. 1979. "Ideologies and the New International Economic Order:

Reflections on Some Recent Literature." *International Organization* 33, no. 2: 257–302.

Crisp, Jeff. 1983. "National Security, Human Rights and Population Displacements: Luwero District, Uganda, January–December 1983." *Review of African Political Economy* 27/28: 164–74.

Dei, G.J.S. 1984. "Food in the Domestic Economy of a Ghanaian Forest Community." Paper presented at the Canadian Association of African Studies, Antigonish, N.S., May 10.

Donnelly, Jack. 1982. "Human Rights and Human Dignity: An Analytical Critique of Non-Western Human Rights Conceptions." *American Political Science Review* 76, no. 2: 303–16.

———. 1984. "Cultural Relativism and Human Rights." *Human Rights Quarterly* 6, no. 4: 400–19.

Ebiasah, John K. 1979. "Protecting the Human Rights of Political Detainees: The Contradictions and Paradoxes of the African Experience." *Howard Law Journal* 22, no. 3: 249–81.

Eicher, Carl K. 1982. "Facing Up to Africa's Food Crisis." *Foreign Affairs* 61, no. 1: 151–74.

Ekechi, Felix K. 1976. "African Polygamy and Western Christian Ethnocentrism." *Journal of African Studies* 3: 329–49.

Ekwelie, Sylvanus A. 1976. "Ghana: Legal Control of the Nationalist Press, 1880–1950." *Transafrica Journal of History* 5, no. 2: 148–60.

Eze, Osita. 1981. "Ecowas and Freedom of Movement: What Prospects for Nigeria?" *Nigeria Forum* (March): 22–28.

Feldman, Rayah. 1983. "Women's Groups and Women's Subordination: An Analysis of Policies Towards Rural Women in Kenya." *Review of African Political Economy* 27/28: 67–85.

Ghai, Y.P. 1972. "Constitutions and the Political Order in East Africa." *International and Comparative Law Quarterly* 21: 403–34.

Gutto, S.B.O. 1976. "The Status of Women in Kenya: A Study of Paternalism, Inequality and Underprivilege." Discussion Paper no. 235. Nairobi: University of Nairobi, Institute for Development Studies.

———. 1982. "Kenya's Petit-Bourgeois State, the Public, and the Rule/Misrule of Law." *International Journal of the Sociology of Law* 10: 341–63.

Hansen, Emmanuel. 1981. "Public Policy and the Food Question in Ghana." *Afrique et Developpement* 6, no. 3: 99–115.

Hayfron-Benjamin, R. 1982. "The Courts and the Protection and Enforcement of Human Rights in Africa." *CIJO* (Center for the Independence of Judges and Lawyers) *Bulletin* 9: 33–48.

Howard, Rhoda. 1980. "Formation and Stratification of the Peasantry in Colonial Ghana." *Journal of Peasant Studies* 8, no. 1: 61–80.

———. 1982. "Human Rights and Personal Law: Women in Sub-Saharan Africa." *Issue: A Journal of Africanist Opinion* 12, nos.1/2: 45–52.

———. 1983. "The Full-Belly Thesis: Should Economic Rights Take Priority over Civil and Political Rights? Evidence from Sub-Saharan Africa." *Human Rights Quarterly* 5, no. 4: 467–90.

———. 1984. "Evaluating Human Rights in Africa: Some Problems of Implicit Comparisons." *Human Rights Quarterly* 6, no. 2: 160–79.

———. 1984. "Women's Rights in English-Speaking Sub-Saharan Africa." In

Claude E. Welch, Jr., and Robert I. Meltzer, eds., *Human Rights and Development in Africa*. Albany: State University of New York Press. Pp. 46–74.

————. 1985. "Legitimacy and Class Rule in Commonwealth Africa: Constitutionalism and the Rule of Law." *Third World Quarterly* 7, no. 2: 323–47.

Howard, Rhoda E. 1986 (forthcoming). "Third World Trade Unions as Agencies of Human Rights: The Case of Commonwealth Africa." In Roger Southall, ed., *Trade Unions and the Industrialization of the Third World*. London: Zed Press.

Howard, Rhoda E., and Jack Donnelly. 1986 (forthcoming). "Human Dignity, Human Rights and Political Regimes." *American Political Science Review*, September.

Ihonvbere, Julius O., and Timothy M. Shaw. 1984. "Petroleum Proletariat: Nigerian Oil Workers in Contextual and Comparative Perspective." Paper presented at a conference on "Third World Trade Unionism: Equity and Democratization in the Changing International Division of Labour." Ottawa, Canada, October 25–27.

Kannyo, Edward. 1980. *Defending Civil and Political Rights in Africa: The Case of Ghana, 1976–1979*. New York: The Jacob Blaustein Institute for the Advancement of Human Rights.

————. 1980. "Human Rights in Africa: Problems and Prospects." New York: International League for Human Rights.

Kludze, A. Kodzo Paaku. 1980. "The Effect of Modernization on African Customary Law." Paper presented at the African Studies Association, Philadelphia, Pa., October 18.

Kraus, Jon. 1976. "African Trade Unions: Progress or Poverty?" *African Studies Review* 19, no. 3: 95–108.

Kumado, C.E.K. 1980. *Constitutionalism, Civil Liberties and Development: A Case Study of Ghana since Independence*. Accra: Ghana Universities Press.

Legesse, Asmarom. 1980. "Human Rights in African Political Culture." In Kenneth W. Thompson, ed., *The Moral Imperatives of Human Rights: A World Survey*. Washington, D.C.: University Press of America. Pp. 123–36.

Lofchie, Michael F. 1978. "Agrarian Crisis and Economic Liberalisation in Tanzania." *Journal of Modern African Studies* 16, no. 3: 451–75.

Luckham, Yaa. 1976. "Law and the Status of Women in Ghana." *Columbia Human Rights Law Review* 8, no. 1: 69–94.

Lule, Yusef. 1982. "Human Rights Violations in Uganda under Obote." *Munger Africana Library Notes*, no. 67. November.

Lyons, Harriet. 1981. "Anthropologists, Moralities and Relativities: The Problem of Genital Mutilations." *Canadian Review of Sociology and Anthropology* 18, no. 4: 499–518.

Mafeje, Archie. 1971. "The Ideology of 'Tribalism.' " *Journal of Modern African Studies* 9, no. 2: 253–61.

Maina, Rose, V.W. Muchai, and S.B.O. Gutto. 1976. "Law and the Status of Women in Kenya." *Columbia Human Rights Law Review* 8, no. 1: 185–206.

McChesney, Allan. 1980. "The Promotion of Economic and Political Rights: Two African Approaches." *Journal of African Law* 24, no. 87: 163–205.

Menkiti, Ifeanyi A. 1979. "Person and Community in African Traditional Thought." In Richard A. Wright, ed., *African Philosophy: An Introduction*. 2nd. ed. Washington, D.C.: University Press of America. Pp. 157–68.

Mihyo, Paschal. 1975. "The Struggle for Worker's Control in Tanzania." *Review of African Political Economy* 4: 62–84.

Mijere, Nsolo N. 1984. "Zambian Decentralization and Integration Policy: The Case of the Mineworkers' Union." Paper presented at a conference on Third World Trade Unionism, Ottawa, Canada, October 25–27.

Mojekwu, Chris C. 1980. "International Human Rights: The African Perspective." In Jack L. Nelson, and Vera M. Green, eds., *International Human Rights: Contemporary Issues.* Stanfordville, N.Y.: Human Rights Publishing Group. Pp. 85–95.

Mower, A. Glenn. 1976. "Human Rights in Black Africa: A Double Standard?" *Human Rights Journal* 9, no. 1: 39–70.

Mubako, Simbi V. 1973. "Zambia's Single-Party Constitution—A Search for Unity and Development." *Zambia Law Journal* 5: 67–85.

Mukandala, Rwekaza. 1983. "Trends in Civil Service Size and Income in Tanzania, 1967–1982." *Canadian Journal of African Studies* 17, no. 2: 253–63.

Murungi, Kiraitu. 1982. "Legal Aspects of Detention without Trial in Kenya." (unpublished)

———. n.d. "Constitutional Construction and Human Rights in Kenya." (unpublished)

Mushanga, Tibamanya M. 1977–78. "Wife Victimization in East and Central Africa." *Victimology* 2, nos. 3–4: 479–85.

Nwogugu, E.I. 1976. "Abolition of Customary Courts—the Nigeria Experiment." *Journal of African Law* 20, no. 1: 1–19.

Odenyo, Amos O. 1979. "Professionalization amidst Change: The Case of the Emerging Legal Profession in Kenya." *African Studies Review* 22, no. 3: 33–44.

Odje, Mudiaga. 1981. "Human Rights of African Women." Paper presented to the African Bar Association, Fourth Conference, Nairobi.

Okeyo, Achola Pala. 1980. "Daughters of the Lakes and Rivers: Colonization and the Land Rights of Luo Women." In Mona Etienne and Eleanor Leacock, eds., *Women and Colonization: Anthropological Perspectives.* New York: Praeger. Pp. 186–213.

Perham, Margery. 1968–69. "Nigeria's Civil War." *Africa Contemporary Record* 1: 1–12.

Pfeiffer, Steven B. 1978. "The Role of the Judiciary in the Constitutional Systems of East Africa." *Journal of Modern African Studies* 16, no. 1: 33–66.

Pirouet, M. Louise. 1980. "Religion in Uganda under Amin." *Journal of Religion in Africa* 11, no. 1: 13–29.

Pratt, Cranford. 1978. "Democracy and Socialism in Tanzania: A Reply to John Saul." *Canadian Journal of African Studies* 12, no. 3: 407–28.

———. 1981. "Tanzania's Transition to Socialism: Reflections of a Democratic Socialist." In Bismarck U. Mwansasu and Cranford Pratt, eds., *Towards Socialism in Tanzania.* Toronto: University of Toronto Press. Pp. 193–236.

Sagay, Itse. 1974. "Widow Inheritance Versus Monogamous Marriage: The Oba's Dilemma." *Journal of African Law* 18, no. 2: 168–72.

Saul, John. 1977. "Tanzania's Transition to Socialism." *Canadian Journal of African Studies* 11, no. 2: 313–39.

Schatz, Sayre P. 1984. "Pirate Capitalism and the Inert Economy of Nigeria." *Journal of Modern African Studies* 22, no. 1: 45–57.

Shepherd, Andrew. 1981. "Agrarian Change in Northern Ghana: Public Investment, Capitalist Farming and Famine." In Judith Heyer, Pepe Roberts, and

Gavin Williams, eds., *Rural Development in Tropical Africa*. London: Macmillan. Pp. 168–92.

Skelton, James W., Jr. 1980. "Standards of Procedural Due Process under International Law vs. Preventive Detention in Selected African States." *Houston Journal of International Law* 2, no. 2: 307–31.

Sklar, Richard L. 1979. "The Nature of Class Domination in Africa." *Journal of Modern African Studies* 17, no. 4: 531–52.

————. 1983. "Democracy in Africa." *African Studies Review* 26, no. 3/4: 11–24.

Tall, Mamadou. (pseudonym). 1982. "Notes on the Civil and Political Strife in Uganda." *Issue: A Journal of Africanist Opinion* 12, no. 1/2: 41–44.

Wambui wa Karanja, 1981. "Women and Work: A Study of Female and Male Attitudes in the Modern Sector of an African Metropolis (Lagos)." In Helen Ware, ed., *Women, Education and Modernization of the Family in West Africa*. Canberra: Australian National University Press. Pp. 42–66.

Weinstein, Warren. 1976. "Africa's Approach to Human Rights at the United Nations." *Issue: A Journal of Africanist Opinion* 6, no. 4: 14–21.

Welch, Claude E., Jr. 1978. "The Right of Association in Ghana and Tanzania." *Journal of Modern African Studies* 16, no. 4:. 639–56.

Westerlund, David. 1982. "Freedom of Religion under Socialist Rule in Tanzania, 1961–77." *Journal of Church and State* 24, no. 1: 87–103.

Wiredu, J. E. 1979. "How Not to Compare African Thought with Western Thought." In Richard A. Wright, ed., *African Philosophy: An introduction*. 2nd. ed. Washington, D.C.: University Press of America. Pp. 133–47.

Wiseberg, Laurie S. 1974. "Humanitarian Intervention: Lessons from the Nigerian Civil War." *Human Rights Journal* 7, no. 1: 61–98.

————. 1976. "Human Rights in Africa: Toward a Definition of the Problem of a Double Standard." *Issue: A Journal of Africanist Opinion* 6, no. 4: 3–13.

World Bank. 1983. "Sub-Saharan Africa: Progress Report on Development Prospects and Programs." Washington, D.C.: The World Bank.

Zvobgo, Eddison Jonas Mudadirwa. 1976. "The Abuse of Executive Prerogative: A Purposive Difference between Detention in Black Africa and Detention in White Racist Africa." *Issue: A Journal of Africanist Opinion* 6, no. 4: 38–43.

Index

Abban, Justice K., 171
Acheampong regime, 71, 96, 126, 156, 171
Action Group (Nigeria), 136
African Charter of Human and Peoples' Rights, 4–8, 16, 31, 68, 90, 91–92, 99, 107, 119, 133, 143, 151–52, 185–86, 202, 205, 212, 213, 220
African concept of human rights. *See* Culture, uniqueness of African
African National Congress, 109
African People's Congress (Sierra Leone), 138
African Socialism and Its Application to Planning in Kenya (Republic of Kenya, 1965), 68
Africanization laws, 102, 134, 216; *see also* Indigenization policies
Afro-Shirazi party (Zanzibar), 97, 141
Agha Khan, 122
Agyepong, K. A., 174
Aid, foreign. *See* Foreign aid
Ake, Claude, 26, 228
Akello, Grace, 19
Akingba, J. B., 202
Aliens, 99–107; citizenship rights denied to, 99–107, 112–13, 134, 214, 200, 228; conflicts with, 13, 91, 101, 112–13; discrimination against, 6, 48, 78, 84, 111, 220, 228; expulsions of, 9, 99–107, 111, 112–13; *see also* Asians; Lebanese
All People's Congress (Sierra Leone), 155
Alternative approaches and ways and means within the United Nations system for improving the effective enjoyment of human rights and fundamental freedoms (UN resolution, 1977), 80
Amadi, Elechi, 95
Amin, Idi, 5, 51, 52, 53, 65, 72, 74, 82, 93, 102–4, 106, 107, 123, 124, 135, 158, 159, 160, 172, 187, 212–13, 215, 229
Amnesty International, 153, 158, 159
Anyona, George, 154
Apartheid, 5, 215
Arabs, in Africa, 39, 68, 97
Arusha Declaration, 12, 51, 70, 130
Ashanti Pioneer (Ghana), 122, 163
Ashanti state. *See* Ghana
Asians: discrimination against, 48, 101–4, 168, 214, 216, 228; Great Britain and, 100–101, 103; in judicial system, 168; Tanzanian suppression of, 51, 71, 102–3, 158; Ugandan expulsions of, 5, 51, 100–104, 106, 112
Azikewe, Nnmadi, 97

Babu, Abdul Rahman, 158
Banda, H. Kamuzu, 51, 55, 98, 110, 138, 157, 160–61, 170, 172, 213
Banjul Charter. *See* African Charter of Human and Peoples' Rights
Barclay's Bank, 77
Basic Rights (Shue), 13
Bemba (Zambia), 98, 108, 141, 203
Biafra, 5, 54, 94–95, 162
Botswana, 1
Bourgeoisie, African: Asians in, 101–4; "comprador," 49; development of, 42–43, 48–51, 60, 83–84, 104, 225–27; and European, 42–43, 48, 225–26; "peasant bourgeoisie" in, 40; ruling class and, 46, 48, 225
Brain drain, 105
Brandt Commission on North-South relations, 81
Brazil, 38, 41, 82
Bridewealth, 156, 185, 186, 195, 197–98
British Colonial period. *See* Colonialism
Buganda, 21, 54, 93, 98, 104, 112, 124, 135, 158, 159, 170, 198, 215

Buhari, Muhamadu, 137, 154, 175
Busia, Dr. Kofi, 93, 135, 156

Cameroon, 104, 111
Canada, 55, 73, 110, 124
Capitalism, 4, 8, 16, 20, 21, 22–23, 38–39, 41, 43, 44–45, 48, 50, 53, 72, 77, 103, 173, 212, 214, 217, 219, 225–29; see also Peripheral capitalist economy
Carter, Jimmy, 138
Cash crops, 28, 39–41, 44, 74, 190, 216, 229
Castes, 18, 21, 22
Censorship. See Freedom of the press
Central Organization of Trade Unions (Kenya), 130
Chama Cha Mapinduzi (CCM) (Tanzania), 141–44, 214
Charter of Economic Rights and Duties of States (UN, 1974), 79–80
Chiefs, 9, 33, 40, 46, 49, 50, 165–66, 221; traditional role of, 18, 20, 22, 165–66, 168, 187
China, peasant revolt in, 43, 224
Chirwa, Orton and Vera, 172
Christianity, 10, 24, 27, 30, 32, 55, 94, 107–8, 109, 143, 197, 202–3, 215; see also Jehovah's Witnesses; Lumpa sect
Cinemas, influence of, 28–29, 30
Citizenship rights, 13, 99–107, 112–13, 134, 185–86, 214
Civil and political rights, 2–5, 11, 13–14, 52–53, 79, 90, 132, 151–77, 213–14, 219–29; bias toward, in International Bill of Rights, 3–4, 7; and class theory, 42–43, 48, 217, 219, 222, 224–29; under colonial rule, 9, 221; defined, 2–3, 151; as important as economic rights, 13–14, 80, 84–85, 119, 219, 222, 224; lack of, in contemporary African states, 3–5, 11, 53–54, 57, 90, 113, 117; politically motivated abuses of, 5, 113, 151–75, 228; ruling classes and, 52–54, 80, 85, 177, 219–20
Civil service, 37, 44, 46, 51, 55, 94, 101, 134, 164
Class structure, 8, 11–14, 17, 24–25, 32–34, 37–38, 40, 83, 85, 92, 93, 212, 216, 218, 219, 222, 223–29; of contemporary Africa, 11–13, 17, 22–23, 33–34, 37, 119, 165, 173, 184,

219–29; human rights and, 12, 56–57, 85, 104, 106, 212, 214, 216, 219–29; evolution of, 11, 17, 22–23, 42–43, 52; women in, 184, 192–93, 195; see also Bourgeoisie, African; Proletariat; Ruling class
Coffee, 9, 38, 71, 73, 74, 82
Common Man's Charter (Obote), 21
Colonialism, 1, 6, 9–11, 13–14, 23, 25, 38, 40, 95, 128, 185, 196, 212, 213, 223; British law and native law, 1, 164–69, 172–73, 176; citizenship under, 100, 112–13; effects on African economy of, 10, 11, 23, 60, 73, 78, 101, 221; freedom of press under, 121; human rights abuses and, 8–11, 152, 165, 221; ideological imperialism and, 10, 24, 25–26, 184, 188, 195, 196; underdevelopment and, 13, 73, 78, 80, 101, 221; women's rights and, 184, 185, 187–88, 190–92, 199, 206
Communal society, 6, 7, 8, 11, 12–13, 16–27, 31, 34, 84, 91, 113, 124, 133, 163, 169, 173, 216, 218, 220, 228; see also Traditional society
Conference on Local Courts and Customary Law (Dar es Salaam, 1963), 167
Constitutionalism, 2, 4, 6, 100, 106, 120–21, 134, 136–37, 138, 151–53, 164–73, 176–77, 186, 214, 219, 229; freedom of expression and, 120–21; lack of popular legitimacy for, 164–72; original independence constitutions and, 121, 134, 136, 152–53, 166, 169–71; states of emergency and, 121, 152–53
Convention on the Elimination of All Forms of Discrimination against Women (UN, 1979), 185, 188, 193, 199, 200, 201–2
Convention on Consent to Marriage, Minimum Age for Marriage and Registration of Marriages (UN, 1962), 185
Convention on the Nationality of Married Women (UN, 1957), 185
Convention People's Party (Ghana), 93, 130, 134–35, 156, 160, 161, 170
Convention on the Political Rights of Women (UN, 1952), 185
Copper, Zambian. See Zambia
Corruption, 26, 49–53, 73, 77–78, 80,

90, 97, 113, 128–29, 173, 216, 225, 229; *see also* Ruling class

Corruption, in trade unions. *See* Trade Unions

Creoles, 97, 98, 134

Culture: dynamic nature of, 23–25, 28; relativism and, 11, 12, 16, 23, 34, 38, 195–96; versus structure, 24, 218–19; uniqueness of African, myth of, 12, 13, 16–23, 25–26, 218, 220, 223

Danquah, Dr. J. B., 156

Daily Nation (Kenya), 122, 126

Debt burden, 74–76, 79, 81, 84, 227–28

Declaration of the Rights of Children (UN, 1959), 205

Democracy, 1, 26, 33, 42, 45, 48, 56, 119, 136, 138, 140–44, 164, 213, 220, 225

Democratic Party (Buganda), 93, 104, 135, 159–60

Dependency thesis. *See* Economic dependency

Detention. *See* Preventive detention

Development, right to, 6, 7–8, 67–73, 78–85, 119, 127, 131–32, 188, 217, 222, 225

Donnelly, Jack, 17

East African Common Market, 82

East African Community, 72

Economic Commission for Africa, 65, 80, 192, 197, 202, 205

Economic Commission of West African States (ECOWAS), 82

Economic dependency, theory of, 72–79, 83

Economic rights, 2–4, 7, 13–14, 42–43, 52–53, 60–85, 90, 152, 215–17, 219; African and UN emphasis on, 3, 4, 7, 61, 78–85, 215–16, 221–22; Universal Declaration and, 3, 78–79; women's rights and, 188–202

Economy, 11–13, 38–39, 42, 60–85, 144, 216, 221, 223–28; NIEO and, 79–83, 127, 222; policies for, 13, 37, 60, 70–72, 76–85, 128, 216–17, 221, 225–26; underdevelopment and, 11, 13, 27, 43, 50, 53, 67–85, 99, 101, 128, 164, 184–85, 188–89, 216–17, 221, 223–24, 227, 229; world economy and, 11–13, 27, 38–39, 72, 78,

85, 217, 221; *see also* Peripheral capitalist economy; Trade

Education, 3, 28–30, 33, 55, 60–61, 67–69, 94, 112, 188, 191–93, 215–16, 219, 227

Elections, right to, 3, 8, 20, 119, 133–44, 214

Ethnic conflicts, 10, 11, 12, 13, 90–97, 112-13, 126, 170, 214–15; in Ghana, 92–93, 96–97, 113, 214; in Kenya, 95–96, 98, 215; in Nigeria, 94–95, 97, 98, 99, 137, 170, 215; in Uganda, 10, 93–94, 97, 98, 99, 214–15; in Zanzibar, 97; in other Commonwealth African countries, 97–98

Ethnic groups in African society, 10, 24–26, 31–33, 45, 55, 90–97, 112–13, 214, 220–22; *see also* specific groups

Exports. *See* Trade

Ewe (Ghana), 93, 96, 97, 98, 99, 112, 113, 156

Expulsions. *See* Aliens; Asians

Eze, Osita, 106

Factories, assembly, 42, 45

Family, 7, 28, 31, 91, 185–86, 195–97, 200

Fascism, 212, 228–29

Food: African crisis in, 61–63, 67, 70–72, 73–74, 216; monoculturalism and, 73; policies for, 70–72, 216; privileged access to, 52, 61, 71; statistics for, 61–63; *see also* Subsistence, right to

Foreign aid, African dependence on, 75–76, 79–81, 84, 126

Freedom of association, right to, 3, 13, 84–85, 119–20, 124–25, 128–33

Freedom of expression, 3, 13, 84–85, 98, 119–28, 133, 213; *see also* individual countries

Freedom of movement, 90, 99–107, 112–13, 220

Freedom of the press, 13, 84–85, 119–28, 213, 217; *see also* individual countries

Freedom of religion. *See* Religions

Gambia, 1, 29, 107, 186; Creole conflict in, 97, 98, 134; economy of, 61–62, 64–66, 69, 73, 74–76, 82, 134; freedom of press in, 122, 123; multiparty system in, 134, 153; 1981 coup

attempt, 56, 134, 153, 213; preventive detention in, 153, 213
Genital operations, 185, 202–6, 222
Ghana, 1, 9, 20, 25, 28–29, 31, 47, 50, 52, 56, 97, 104, 105, 107, 161, 170, 171–72, 186, 187, 190, 192, 202, 214, 229; aliens in, discrimination against, 99–101, 104; Ashanti state in, 19, 20, 21, 56, 71, 92–93, 122, 135, 156, 214; economy of, 50–51, 61–67, 69, 70–71, 75, 77, 82, 174, 186, 192, 193–94, 221, 229; Ewe secessionism and, 93, 96, 97, 98, 99, 112, 113, 156; freedom of expression in, 120, 122, 124–25, 126; freedom of press in, 122; gold mining in, 42; land conflicts in, 51, 63, 229; legal activism in, 171–72, 174–75; one-party state in, 133–36, 170, 214; "People's Courts" in, 172–75, 176; preventive detention in, 98, 153, 156–57, 163–64, 225; Rawlings' coups in, 52, 53, 93, 157, 172–74, 194, 214, 221; socialism in, 53, 156, 158, 226; state terrorism in, 160–61, 162, 225; trade unions in, 130; transnationals in, 77
Ghana Bar Association, 171, 174
Ghana Professional Bodies' Association, 125
Gifford, Lord, 174
Gold Coast People, 121
Gowon, Yakubu, 53, 94, 95
Group rights, 6, 16, 31, 90–113, 220–21
Gutto, S.B.O., 173

Hausa-Fulani (Nigeria), 21, 32, 94, 98, 194, 215
Hayfron-Benjamin, R., 177
Health, 28, 60–61, 63–65, 68, 188, 215–16, 227
Helleiner, G. K., 72
Humanism, African (Zambia), 18, 26, 68, 70, 144, 219
Hyden, Goran, 47, 76, 78

Igbo (Nigeria), 20, 21, 53, 94–95, 97, 98, 108, 162, 187, 215
Imports. See Trade
Income, 61–63, 67, 73, 80, 84, 131, 216, 226
Independence, 1, 5, 11, 113, 166–70

Indigenization policies, 50–51, 95; see also Africanization laws
Individualism, 6, 8, 11, 18, 19, 23, 24, 27–34, 48–49, 218, 220
Industrial production, 41–42, 43, 44–45, 72, 74, 76–77, 83, 128, 228
Informal sector, 28, 44–45, 49, 71, 76, 84, 131, 225
Intellectuals, African, 125, 126, 128, 132; communalism and, 6, 21–23, 25–27, 28; important to development, 67, 125, 126; Marxism and, 43; see also Professionals
International Bill of Rights, 2–4, 6, 7, 8, 91
International Commission of Jurists, 156
International Covenant on Civil and Political Rights (1966), 2, 3, 4, 8, 20, 79, 91, 99, 103, 105, 107, 119, 133, 151–52, 184, 212, 213; Optional Protocol, 2
International Covenant on Economic, Social and Cultural Rights (1966), 2, 4, 79, 91, 105, 107, 119, 184, 212
International Monetary Fund, 216
Infant mortality. See Health
International Women's Year Conference (Copenhagen, 1980), 188, 197, 201
Investment, 41, 50, 76–77, 81, 84
Ironsi, General Aguiyi-Johnson, 53, 94
Islam, 27, 32, 94, 107–8, 111–12, 176, 215; genital operations and, 204; marriage laws and, 196–97, 199; Shari'a courts (Nigeria), 55
Izzert, A. 198, 201

Jawara, Sir Dawda, 134
Jehovah's Witnesses, 109–10, 111, 113, 160, 187, 215
Journal of Church and State, 107
Journalists, harassment of. See Freedom of the press
Judicial system, evolution of in Africa, 1, 9, 164–72; see also Law, rule of

Kabaka, of Buganda, 93, 124, 135, 158, 170
Kaiser Aluminum Company, 77
Kambona, Oscar, 157
Kapwepwe, Simon, 141, 156
Kariuki, J.M., 139, 161

Karume, Sheik Abeid, 157
Kaunda, Kenneth, 18, 19, 26, 33, 68, 70, 103, 109, 126, 132, 141, 143–44, 155–56, 219, 223
Kawadwa, Byron, 124
Kenya, 1, 7, 9, 10, 29, 45, 47, 50, 107, 154–55, 163, 168, 170–71, 172, 187, 189, 190, 229; "African socialism" of, 68; air force coup attempt (1982), 53, 125, 139, 154–55; Asians in, 101-3, 196; economy of, 50, 62–69, 73–75, 77, 82, 191; freedom of expression in, 123–25; freedom of press in, 120, 122, 123, 126, 127–28; Kikuyu in, 98–99, 123, 139, 204, 215; land conflicts in, 1, 9, 39, 63, 98–99, 100, 105–6, 190–91, 215; Luo in, 98, 139, 154, 161, 190, 203; one-party government in, 47, 133, 138–40, 154, 214; preventive detention in, 96, 98, 123–24, 139, 153, 154–55; religions in, 109–10, 199; ruling class in, 48, 78, 139, 173, 214; socialism in, 53, 68, 98, 154; Somali secessionism in, 56, 95–96, 98, 112, 154, 212; state terrorism in, 161, 212, 213; trade unions in, 129–30, 161; transnationals in, 77–78; women in, 186, 190, 192–92, 196–97, 199, 202
Kenya African National Union (KANU), 139–40, 154, 171
Kenya Gazette, 154
Kenya People's Union (KPU), 98, 105–6, 139, 154
Kenyan Law Reform Commission, 196–97
Kenyatta, Jomo, 7, 10, 98, 139, 154, 155, 161, 204
Kesse-Adu, Kwame, 163
Kibaki, Mwai, 127
Kikuyu (Kenya), 98–99, 123, 204, 215
Kirk-Greene, Anthony H. M., 32
Kopytoff, Igor, 19, 21, 26
Koranteng-Addow, Cecilia, 174, 187

Labor, 11, 12, 32, 40–42, 44, 68, 76, 84, 192–94
Lagos Plan of Action (1980), 73, 80
Land, 1, 22, 31, 39–40, 51, 63, 100; alienation of, 84, 226, 229; equitable distribution of, as right, 60, 128, 216, 226; increasing scarcity of, 28, 40, 44, 100, 216, 226, 229; privatization of, 100, 101, 216, 226; women's

rights to, 190–93, 216, see also individual countries; Peasants
Languages, indigenous, 10, 55, 90–91, 112, 215
Law, rule of, 1, 5, 13, 55, 131, 151, 164–77, 219, 220, 226, 229; in colonial era, 1, 9, 164–69, 175; people's courts (Ghana) and, 172, 173–75, 176; traditional and modern systems of, conflict between, 55, 165–70, 175–76, 196–97, 200; traditional courts (Malawi) and, 166, 172–73, 176, 213
Lawyers, 33, 168, 171–72, 174, 177, 213
Lebanese, 48, 100–101, 104, 214, 216
Legesse, Asmaron, 22
Legislative Councils, 9
Legon Observer (Ghana), 122
Lenshina, Alice, 108–9, 113
Lesotho, 1
Life expectancy. See Health
Limann, Dr. Hilla, 135
Literacy. See Education
Local Courts (Amendment) Act (Malawi, 1970), 172
Lonrho Corporation, 77, 122
Lovejoy, Paul, 21
Lubeck, Paul, 129
Lule, Yusef, 159, 160
Lumpa sect (Zambia), 108–9, 111, 113, 155, 161, 215
Luo (Kenya), 98, 139, 154, 161, 190, 203
Lusaka Conference of African Women (1979), 203
Luwum, Archbishop, 108, 124

Magoti, James, 158
Makerere University, 124, 187
Malawi, 1, 6, 29, 51, 55, 56, 96, 100, 107, 138, 170, 186; economy of, 61–62, 64–66, 69, 73–75, 82, 130, 192; ethnic favoritism in, 97–98; freedom of expression in, 120, 125, 126, 128; freedom of the press in, 122; Jehovah's Witnesses in, 110, 113, 160, 215; one-party state in, 133–34, 138; preventive detention in, 153, 156, 157; religions in, 107, 110; state terrorism in, 160–61, 213; trade unions in, 130; traditional courts in, 166, 172–73, 176, 213

Malawi Congress Party, 110, 130, 138, 160
Malawi Youth Congress (League), 110, 160
Malnutrition, 63, 68, 95, 190
Mamdani, Mahmood, 102
The Man Died (Soyinka), 95
Mao Zedong, 224
Marketing boards. *See* Monopolies
Marriage laws and practices, 17, 184–86, 195–201
Marriage Ordinance, 196–97, 199
Marwa, Alhaji Muhammadu, 111
Marx, Karl, 41
Marxism, 4, 27, 41, 42–43, 47, 125, 159, 223
Masai, 21
"Mau Mau," 9, 98
Mayanga, Abu, 123
Mboya, Tom, 161
Media, 28–31, 55, 112, 122–23, 126, 127
Menkiti, Ifeanyi A., 18
Mensah, J. B., 156
Miers, Suzanne, 19, 21
Military, 6, 37, 44, 45, 46, 47–48, 52–53, 54, 55, 56, 95, 121, 163, 164, 177, 187, 228–29
Mineral extraction, 42, 45, 84
Moi, Daniel arap, 50, 125, 139, 155, 163
Mojekwu, Chris C., 20
Monopolies, 40, 41, 44, 48–49, 70, 77–78, 193
Movement for Justice in Africa (MOJA), 153
Mpakati, Dr. Ahaki, 138
Mukasa-Bukenya, Teresa Nazire, 187
Multinationals. *See* Transnationals
Multi-party system, 8, 47, 56–57, 119, 133–37, 140–41, 169, 213–14; in Gambia, 134, 153; in Ghana, 47, 134–36; in Nigeria, 47, 94, 136–37; in Tanzania, 140–41; in Uganda, 47, 135–36
Murders, mass. *See* State terrorism
Muruka, slaughter in, 9
Mushanga, Tibamanya, 201
Muslim states. *See* Nigeria, Islam in
Mutai, Chelegat, 187

National Commision on the Establishment of One-Party Participatory Democracy (Zambia), 141

National Liberational Movement (Ghana), 93, 156
National Party of Nigeria and the Cameroons, 136–37
National Redemption Council (Ghana), 71,125
National Resistance Army (Uganda), 159
National Union of Tanganyika Workers (NUTA), 130–32
Nationhood, 54–56, 90–91, 95, 98–99, 106, 136
Neo-colonialism, 73, 78, 126, 188, 221, 223
Neogy, Rajat, 102, 123, 161
New International Economic Order (NIEO), 79–83, 127, 222
New international information order (UNESCO), 127
Ngugi wa Thiong'o, 98, 123–24, 154, 161
Nigeria, 1, 20, 21, 26, 28–29, 30, 31, 42, 45, 47, 106, 134, 162, 171, 175, 186, 187, 194, 201, 202, 212, 229; civil war in, 5, 54, 94–95, 98, 108, 137, 153, 162, 170, 212; corruption in, 49, 52, 94, 122, 137, 154, 175; coups in, 49, 52–53, 94, 137, 153, 175, 214; economy of, 50, 61–62, 64–69, 73–76, 82, 137, 154, 175, 192; ethnic conflicts in, 94–95, 97, 98, 99, 137, 170, 215; expulsions of aliens from, 100–101, 104–6, 111; freedom of expression in, 120–21, 124; freedom of press in, 121–23, 125, 128; Igbo in, 20, 21, 53, 94–95, 97, 98, 108, 162, 187, 215; Islam in, 20, 55, 94, 104, 111-12, 134, 186-87; multi-party politics in, 47, 94, 136–38, 214; oil industry in, 38, 42, 45, 49, 53, 73, 74, 82, 137; preventive detention in, 153–54, 213; religions in, 107–8, 111–12; ruling class dominance in, 47, 48, 137, 214; Special Tribunals in, 172, 175; trade unions in, 129–30
Nigerian Bar Association, 175
Njonjo, Charles, 155, 162
Nkrumah, Kwame, 77, 93, 121, 130, 133, 135–36, 156, 160, 163, 170, 225
Nkumbula, Harry, 109
Northern People's Convention (Nigeria), 136
Numeiri, General Gaafar Al-, 126

Nupe, slavery among, 21
Nyerere, Julius, 12, 18, 26, 70, 97, 103, 122, 127, 140–41, 143–44, 157–58, 216–17, 219, 223

Obbo, Christine, 19, 198
Obote, Milton, 21, 52, 54, 93, 102, 104, 123, 133, 135–36, 158, 159–60, 162, 170, 212
Odinga, Oginga, 98, 139
Ogunmodende, Esther, 206
Oil, 71–72, 74, 82, 221, 227; Nigerian, 38, 42, 45, 49, 53, 73, 74, 82, 137
Ojukwu, Emeka, 94, 97
One-party states, 8, 22, 26, 45, 47–48, 52, 55, 107, 112, 130–31, 132–36, 138–44, 177, 214, 228; see also individual countries
OPEC (Organization of Petroleum Exporting Countries), 82
Organization of African Unity (OAU), 4–5, 6, 54, 92, 95, 197, 205, 213, 215

Parastatal corporations, 46, 47, 51, 95, 174
Peasants, 28, 39–41, 43–44, 46, 48–49, 60, 70, 72, 78, 84, 85, 131, 143, 216, 224, 226–27, 229; land and, 1, 9, 39–40, 44, 51, 63, 70–71, 97, 98–99, 100, 105–6, 143, 190, 215, 226, 229
People's courts. See under Law
People's National Party (Ghana), 135
People's National Party (Nigeria), 97
Peripheral capitalist economy, 12, 13, 38–39, 44–45, 53, 219, 225, 227–28; see also Capitalism; Economy
Political participation, 3, 8, 9, 13, 26, 56–57, 60, 84–85, 119, 128–44, 152, 185–88, 213–14, 216–17, 219, 223, 225–26; see also Democracy; Elections; Multi-party system
Polygyny, 24, 27, 197–98
Population, increases in, 65–67, 216, 217, 229
Poverty, 13, 38, 67, 212, 223
Pre-colonial African societies. See Traditional society
Press. See Freedom of the press
Press Bills, 121, 122
Preventive detention, 3, 9, 13, 47, 57, 98, 124, 131, 144, 151–59, 163–64, 165, 166, 169, 172, 212–13, 222, 228; in Gambia, 153, 213; in Ghana, 98, 153, 156–57, 163–64, 225; in

Kenya, 96, 98, 123–24, 139, 153–55; in Malawi, 153, 156, 157; in Nigeria, 153–54, 213; in Sierra Leone, 153, 155; in Tanzania, 132, 140, 142, 153, 156–58, 176, 217; in Uganda, 98, 123, 153, 156, 158, 160; in Zambia, 141, 153, 155–56
Professionals, 33, 55, 65, 67, 68, 105, 124–25, 132, 213; see also Intellectuals
Proletariat, 42–43, 48, 224–27
Propaganda, 30, 54–55, 161
Prostitution, 194
Public Emergency Regulation (Sierra Leone, 1971), 155
Public Security Act (Kenya, 1966), 154

Rawlings, Jerry, 52, 53, 93, 96, 157, 172–74, 194, 214, 221, 225
Recovery of Public Property (Special Military Tribunals) Decree (Nigeria), 175
Redistributive economy, 12, 18, 22, 23, 25, 26, 84, 216
Religions, 3, 10, 13, 24, 45, 55, 90–91, 107–13, 187, 215; Jehovah's Witnesses, 109–11, 113, 160, 187, 215; Lumpa sect, 108–9, 111, 113, 155, 161, 215; Yen Izala sect, 111–12
Revolution, 4, 43, 219, 223–25
Reynolds Metals, 77
Rhodesia. See Zimbabwe
Robertson, Claire, 195
Roles, social: breakdown of traditional, 10, 19, 28, 31–33, 191, 200–202, 216, 222–23; in traditional society, 10, 18–19, 219
Rule of law. See Law, rule of
Ruling class, 4, 7, 8, 11, 12, 13, 16–17, 22, 25, 33–34, 37–38, 42–44, 45–57, 60, 77–78, 80, 83–85, 104, 106, 119, 127, 133, 136, 144, 154, 163, 164, 168–69, 173, 177, 214, 217, 220–21, 223–24, 225–29; corruption in, 46–47, 49–53, 77–78, 173, 216; defined, 37–38, 46–47; land bought up by, 51, 63, 216, 226; political office important to, 12–13, 37, 48–53, 56–57, 85, 119, 136, 144, 164–65, 177, 213, 214, 217, 219, 225; and transnationals, 47, 49, 77–78
Rumors Decrees, 126
Ruwuma Development Association (Tanzania), 143

Rwandans, expelled from Uganda, 104

Sagay, Itse, 199
Sandbrook, Richard, 129
Sarkodee, F. P., 174
Schuster, Ilsa M. Glazer, 200, 201
Seccessionist and irredentist movements. *See* Ethnic conflicts
Security, basic right of, 2, 3, 13, 43, 98, 151, 212, 216–17, 222, 224–26; *see also* Civil and political rights
Self-determination, of African states. *See* Development, right to
Senegal, 56, 97, 134
Seroney, John-Marie, 154
Shagari, Shehu, 49, 97, 111, 121, 125, 137, 171
Shikuku, Martin, 154
Shue, Henry, 3, 13, 216
Sierra Leone, 19, 28–29, 107, 155, 171, 186, 187, 200, 204; diamond mines in, 42, 82; discrimination against aliens in, 101, 104, 214; economy in, 61, 62, 63–65, 69, 74–75, 82, 191–92; ethnic conflicts in, 97, 98; freedom of expression in, 120–21, 125, 128; freedom of the press in, 121, 122, 127; one-party regime in, 97, 133–34, 138, 155, 214; preventive detention in, 153, 155; religions in, 199
Sierra Leone Broadcasting Company, 127
Sierra Leone People's Party, 138, 155
Slaves: African domestic, 10, 18–19, 20–21, 24, 162; trade in, 21, 39
Social classes. *See* Class structure
Social statification. *See* Class structure
Socialism, African, 18, 26, 45, 50, 53, 68, 98, 154, 156, 158, 173, 191, 212, 219, 224–26, 229
Socialism, in Tanzania. *See* Tanzania
Socialist League of Malawi, 138
Solarin, Dr. Tai, 154
Somali seccessionism (Kenya), 56, 95–96, 98, 112, 154, 212
South Africa, 1, 5, 41, 76, 100, 215, 224; and Malawi, 126; and Zambia, 124, 126, 155
Sovereignty, 5, 6, 54, 56, 79, 80, 83, 92, 106, 220
Soyinka, Wole, 95, 223
The Standard (Tanzania), 126

Standard Bank, 77
State, as key to power and wealth, 7, 11–12, 37, 45–54, 56–57, 83, 85, 119
State Security (Detention of Persons) Decree (Nigeria), 154
State terrorism, 13, 57, 95–96, 97, 151, 159–64, 172, 212–13, 222; in Malawi, 160–61, 213; in Uganda, 52, 59–60, 93, 102, 135, 159–60; *see also* Preventive detention
Students, 124–26, 128, 155, 213
Subsistence, right to, 13, 37, 39, 60–61, 63, 67, 79, 85, 90, 128, 216–17, 222, 224–26
Supplementary Convention on the Abolition of Slavery, the Slave Trade and Practices Similar to Slavery (UN, 1956), 184
Swaziland, 1

The Tablet (Sierra Leone), 121
Tanzania, 1, 9, 12, 15, 18, 50–51, 107, 175–76, 187, 213; Asians in, 51, 71, 102–3, 158; economy of, 28–30, 50, 61–69, 70–76, 81, 82, 131–32, 176, 216–17; ethnic conflicts in, 97, 158; freedom of expression in, 120–21, 127; freedom of press in, 122–23, 126, 128; Jehovah's Witnesses in, 110; land conflicts in, 70–71, 97, 100, 105–6, 143, 215; legal system in, 55, 172, 176–77, 196–97, 199; one-party system in, 47, 50–51, 133–34, 140–44, 173, 214, 217; preventive detention in, 132, 140, 142, 153, 156, 157–58, 176, 217; socialism in, 12, 26, 45, 61, 70–71, 123, 127, 131–32, 140, 143, 173, 176, 191, 213, 217, 219, 226; trade unions in, 130–32, 144; "villagization" policy in, 70–71, 143, 191, 215, 221; women in, 191, 192, 196, 199, 202
Tanzania African National Union (TANU), 140–42
Terrorism. *See* State terrorism
Theater, censorship of, 123–24
Third World, 1, 2, 7, 11, 30, 73, 78, 81–83, 127, 221
Times of Zambia, 122
Tinto, Pio, 161
Togo, 96
Torture, 2, 95, 96, 97, 110, 123, 128, 135, 151, 158–63, 172, 173–74

Trade, 38–41, 73–76, 79, 81–82, 190, 221, 227–28
Trade Licencing Act of 1967 (Kenya), 102
Trade unions, 3, 9, 13, 33, 45, 55, 84, 119, 128–33, 213, 217, 224, 228; in Kenya, 129–30; in Malawi, 130; in Nigeria, 129–30; in Uganda, 120
Trades Union Congress (Ghana), 130
Traditional courts. *See* Law
Traditional society, 8, 10, 12, 16–23, 27, 31–33, 38, 39, 50, 55, 92, 219, 220–21; justice system in, 165–68, 172, 176; women in, 18, 19, 20, 33, 184, 186–88, 191, 196–200, 219, 222–23; *see also* Communal society
Transition (Uganda), 123, 161
Transnationals, 42, 47, 49, 73, 76–78, 80–81, 129, 193, 221
Transportation, 42, 47, 49, 56, 70–71, 83, 90, 113, 216, 228
"Tribalism," 11, 13, 91–99, 112, 113, 214; *see also* Ethnic conflicts; Traditional society
Tribunal of Inquiry into Trade Unions in Nigeria (1977), 129
Tsikata, Cptn. Kojo, 174
Tumbo, Charles, 140

Uganda, 1, 9, 10, 21, 29, 47, 52–53, 54, 112, 170–72, 186, 187, 198, 214, 222, 229; Asian expulsions in, 5, 51, 100–104, 106; economy of, 61–69, 73–76, 82, 229; ethnic conflicts in, 93–94, 97, 98, 99, 112, 170, 214–15; freedom of expression in, 120, 123, 124, 128; freedom of press in, 123, 128; multi-party elections in, 47, 135, 214; one-party state in, 93, 133, 135–36, 158; preventive detention in, 98, 123, 153, 156, 158, 160; religions in, 107–8; state terrorism in, 52, 59–60, 93, 102, 135, 159–60, 162, 212–13, 222; trade unions in, 120
Uganda Freedom Movement, 159–60
"Ujamaa" socialism. *See* Tanzania
Underdevelopment. *See* Economy, underdeveloped
Unemployment, 3, 7, 44, 100
United Africa Company, 77
United Church of Zambia, 108
United National Independence Party (UNIP) (Zambia), 109, 113, 122, 141, 143–44, 156, 161
United National Recovery Force (Uganda), 159
United Nations, 2–4, 5, 6, 9, 13, 24, 78–83, 92, 99, 107, 133, 143, 185, 195, 196, 197, 201, 205, 212–13, 215, 220; African conduct in fora of, 5, 213; and African emphasis on economic rights, 3, 4, 5–7, 61, 78–85, 215; conventions on women's rights adopted by, 184–86, 196, 197, 201–2
United Nations Covenants. *See under* International Covenants
U.N. Educational, Scientific and Cultural Organization (UNESCO), 127
United People's Convention (UPC), (Uganda), 93
United Progressive Party (UPP) (Zambia), 156
United States, 2, 27, 110, 163
Universal Declaration of Human Rights (1948), 2, 3, 4, 5, 9, 78–79, 120, 185, 205
Universities, 55, 68, 105, 124–27, 155
University of Nairobi, 125
Upper Volta, 104
Urbanization, 24, 25, 28–29, 31–33, 44, 55, 188, 196, 227
USSR, 2, 4, 27, 52, 163

Villagization policy. *See* Tanzania
Vote, right to, 3, 84, 133–34, 186, 214

Wai, Dunstan M., 20
Water, 63–65, 189
Weber, Max, 165
Weekly Review (Kenya), 122
Widow inheritance, 185, 186, 195, 197–99
Wilson, Bryan R., 110
Wiredu, J. E., 25–26
Woman's War (1929), in Nigeria, 188
Women, 8, 11, 12, 13, 14, 28, 40, 44, 45, 184–206, 216, 220, 222–23; in agriculture, 188–91, 192, 194–95, 222; education of, 67, 188, 191–93; genital operations and, 185, 202–6, 222; land and, 190–91, 216; occupations of, 44, 189–90, 193–94; politics and, 185–88, 222; poverty and, 189, 190, 194; reproduction and, 195, 201–2, 222–23; violence against,

201–2; see also Marriage laws; Traditional society

Women traders, 48, 71, 78, 84, 193–94, 228

World Bank, 67, 70, 72, 76

Yen Izala sect (Nigeria), 111–12

Yoruba (Nigeria), 21, 94, 108, 198, 199, 201, 202

Young Pioneers Movement (Ghana), 160–61

Zambia, 1, 18, 28–29, 33, 45, 50, 51, 70, 97–98, 100, 103, 107, 108–9, 110, 124, 126, 168, 172, 186, 189, 200, 213, 223, 226; copper in, 38–39, 42, 73, 74, 82, 100, 132, 221; economy of, 61–69, 73–75, 82, 132, 192, 193, 216; freedom of expression in, 124, 126, 128; freedom of press in, 122, 126, 127–28; indigenization policies in, 50–51; land conflicts in, 51, 100; Lumpa sect in, 108–9, 111, 113, 155, 161, 215; one-party system in, 47, 131, 132, 133–34, 140–43, 214, 226; preventive detention in, 141, 153, 155–56; trade unions in, 98, 131, 132, 156

Zambia Daily Mail, 122

Zambian Youth Service, 168

Zanzibar, 21, 97, 102, 141, 157–58

Zanzibar Nationalist Party, 97

Zimbabwe, 1, 5, 155

DATE DUE

NOV 2 7 1989			
FEB 2 1 1994			
FEB 2 0 1995			
DEC 0 8 1995			
FEB 0 5 1997			